THE ASSUMPTION OF MOSES

STUDIA
IN VETERIS TESTAMENTI
PSEUDEPIGRAPHA

EDIDERUNT

A.-M. DENIS ᴇᴛ M. DE JONGE

VOLUMEN DECIMUM

J. TROMP

THE ASSUMPTION OF MOSES

THE ASSUMPTION OF MOSES

A CRITICAL EDITION WITH COMMENTARY

BY

JOHANNES TROMP

E.J. BRILL
LEIDEN · NEW YORK · KÖLN
1993

The paper in this book meets the guidelines for permanence and durability of the Committee on Production Guidelines for Book Longevity of the Council on Library Resources.

ISSN 0169-8125
ISBN 90 04 09779 1

TABLE OF CONTENTS

ACKNOWLEDGMENTS

The present work was submitted as a doctoral thesis at Leiden University in December 1992, and is published here in unaltered form.

I wish to thank my supervisor, Prof. Dr. M. de Jonge, and his successor on the New Testament chair at Leiden, Prof. Dr. H.J. de Jonge, for their indefatigable help and advice. I am also grateful to Prof. Dr. J. Hoftijzer whose linguistic expertise has been of great assistance in describing the Latinity of the Assumption of Moses. The preparation of the dissertation has taken me over four years. During this period, Dr. J.W. van Henten, Dr. R. Oost, as well as my colleagues J. Holleman, M.A., and L.J. Lietaert Peerbolte, M.A., have continually been prepared to read and criticize my drafts. Also, I owe a good deal to the inspiring conversations I was privileged to have with Dr. H.W. Hollander. Dr. M.C. de Boer and Mrs. P. Pumplin, M.S., graciously helped me by correcting the English text of this book.

Finally, I am grateful to Father A.-M. Denis and Prof. Dr. M. de Jonge for accepting this commentary for publication in the *SVTP*-series, as well as to Mr. J. van der Meij, M.A., and Mr. W.P.J. Rietbroek of Brill's publishing house for their assistance in its technical production.

Joh. Tromp

PART ONE

A CRITICAL EDITION OF THE TEXT OF THE ASSUMPTION OF MOSES

The edition presented in the following pages is an emended text of the Assumption of Moses. It is primarily based on the *editio princeps* of the manuscript's text by A.M. Ceriani of 1861. I have compared this edition to the edition by C. Clemen of 1904, which occasionally differs from Ceriani's edition, and to photographs of the manuscript which were available to me[1]. Four readings proposed by F.C. Burkitt, presumably based on fresh examination of the manuscript, are also taken into account[2].

The photographs were taken in the early 1960's, and their quality is rather poor. They have, nevertheless, been very useful in establishing in several places the abbreviations, contractions and *nomina sacra* used in the manuscript. Also, some of the readings recorded by Ceriani and Clemen could be corrected with the help of the photographs. It was possible to compare the photographs to the printed editions in the following passages: p. 112b (1:7-13)[3]; p. 111 (1:13-2:2); p. 110 (2:2-3:2); p. 109 (3:2-11); p. 86 (4:5-5:4); p. 78 (5:4-6:3); fragments of p. 77 (6:8-9; 7:4); p. 67 (8:1-9:3); p. 91 (9:3-10:4); fragments of p. 92 (10:5-8, 10:9-11, 14); p. 100 (10:14-11:10); p. 99 (11:10-16); p. 98 (11:16-12:4). For the remaining passages, the photographs were available but of no value, because of their inferior quality. It should furthermore be noted that, apart from p. 91, the photographs could not be deciphered without the help of Ceriani's and Clemen's editions; my readings of the photographs do not therefore represent an entirely independent collation[4].

In the present edition, the following symbols have been used:

---

[1] I am grateful to R. Oost for lending me these photographs.

[2] For bibliographical references, see the Introduction, and the list of consulted literature.

[3] The page numbers given are those of the manuscript (*scriptio superior*), the chapter and verse numbers are the modern ones, introduced by Hilgenfeld and Fritzsche (see the Introduction, section I, b).

[4] Unfortunately, I was unable to examine the manuscript *meis oculis* at the Ambrosian Library (C 73 inf.) where, because of construction work, the collections are temporarily inaccessible.

[ ]   Square brackets include letters or words that must be deleted from the text offered by the manuscript.

{ }   Braces are used (once) to indicate an editorial transposition of part of the manuscript's text.

< >   Pointed brackets include letters or words that must be added to the manuscript's text; alternatively, they indicate that the manuscript is partly illegible, and that the letters or words included in these brackets are the proposed supplements; these instances are consistently recorded in the apparatus.

<...> Three dots, included in pointed brackets, designate that a word or words are obviously lacking from the manuscript's text, but that no satisfactory restoration could be proposed.

. . . Dots indicate an illegible section in the manuscript, each dot representing approximately one letter.

vọx   A dot under a letter indicates that it is uncertain.

vox Italics designate an editorial emendation of the manuscript's text; the manuscript's text is recorded in the apparatus.

† †   Daggers indicate that the manuscript's text is corrupt or illegible, and that no satisfactory emendation could be proposed.

Punctuation marks and orthographic particularities occurring in the manuscript, such as superscribed dots, capitalization and paragraph indentations, have been ignored in the edition. Abbreviations, contractions and *nomina sacra* have been resolved.

The apparatus contains the following data:

(1) a line number, printed in bold-face, referring to the corresponding line of the present edition;

(2) the word or words of the main text on which a text-critical observation is made;

(3) if appropriate, the *auctor* of the conjectural emendation is mentioned, followed by "cj." (*conjecit*); alternatively, "conjeci" is used to indicate that the emendation in question is proposed by the present editor. The main text, alone or together with conjectural emendations, is separated from further text-critical information by a square bracket:]. After this,

(4) the manuscript's reading is recorded, followed by one of the following abbreviations:

MS (the manuscript's reading according to all editions and photographs [when available]); Ceriani (the manuscript's reading according to the *editio princeps* by A.M. Ceriani);

Peyron (the manuscript's reading according to the fragment published by A. Peyron); Clemen (the manuscript's reading according to the edition by C. Clemen); MSph (the manuscript's reading according to the photographs);

(5) in the MS text quoted in the apparatus, abbreviations and contractions (resolved in the main text) are recorded if they could be discerned in the photographs. The following symbols are used to indicate the different kinds of abbreviation occurring in the manuscript:

— In the apparatus, a stroke over a letter represents a stroke (sometimes slightly curved) over this letter in the manuscript. It should be observed that in the manuscript, especially at the end of a line, the stroke may be placed to the right of the last letter. The stroke may indicate an abbreviation, contraction, or a *nomen sacrum*. For example: "dn̄s", which stands for "Dominus", is written in the manuscript as ƆN̄S , but also as ƆN̂S .

— A half square ⌐ represents a horizontal stroke, usually with serifs, under which a comma is drawn. In the manuscript it stands to the right of the last letter of a word or of a line, or above it. It indicates an abbreviation, usually of a final M or N; occasionally it indicates a contraction or a *nomen sacrum*. For example: "aute⌐", which stands for "autem", is written in the manuscript as aUTeᵔᵗ.

— The sign ~ is used to represent an abbreviation marker occurring in the manuscript after B or Q to indicate -BUS (not only in case endings) or -QUE (in USQUE). Sometimes the manuscript uses to the same end a superscribed point ·. For example: "trib~", which stands for "tribus", is written in the manuscript as TRIB ꝛ ; "usq·", which stands for "usque", is written in the manuscript as USq·.

— Occasionally, an apparent abbreviation is not marked at all. These cases are recorded in the apparatus unmarked as well.

— If a word is written on two lines in the manuscript, the place at which a new line begins is indicated by two slashes // in the apparatus. This is noted only when the manuscript's text has had to be quoted for other reasons.

(6) if necessary, further comment is given.

The *auctores* of conjectural emendations are indicated with shorthand references, which are explained as follows.

Previous editions of the text are referred to by the editors' names only; their conjectures are to be found in their text editions, in each instance in the passage concerned.

The various editions made by A. Hilgenfeld are distinguished by the years of their publication. "Hilgenfeld 1866" refers to his edition of the Latin text in *Novum testamentum extra canonem receptum*; "Hilgenfeld 1868" refers to his retranslation into Greek in his "Die Psalmen Salomo's", *ZWT* 11 (1868). No proposals by Hilgenfeld from other editions have been adopted in the present edition.

The suggestions made by Hilgenfeld's early collaborators are recorded by Hilgenfeld himself. In the present edition, their names are followed by "in Hilgenfeld 1866".

To the four readings of the manuscript registered by F.C. Burkitt reference is made by his last name only. He published these readings in "Moses, Assumption of", in *Hastings' Dictionary of the Bible* (1909), p. 449a.

A number of conjectures adopted in this edition were suggested to me *viva voce* by H.J. de Jonge; they are referred to with his name only.

Some emendations have been adopted from books and articles, other than critical editions. Each of these is referred to with the author's name, short title and page number. Full biographical references may be found in the list of consulted literature.

1 ₁ . . .

₂ qui est bis millesimus et quingentesimus annus a creatura orbis terrae, ₃ —nam secus qui in oriente sunt numerus . . . mus et . . mus—, et . . . . mus profectionis Fynicis ₄ cum exivit plebs; post profectionem quae

5   fiebat per Mo[s]ysen usque Amman trans Jordanem;

₅ profetiae quae facta est a Moysen in libro Deuteronomio, ₆ qui vocavit ad se Jesum filium Nave—hominem probatum Domino, ₇ ut sit successor plebi et scene testimonii cum omnibus sanctis illius, ₈ ut et inducat plebem in terram datam *pa*tribus eorum, ₉ ut detur illis per tes-

10   tamentum et per jusjurandum—; quod locutus est in scenae dare de Jesum, dicendo ad Jesum:

"<Custodi> verbum hoc, ₁₀ et promitte secus industriam tuam omnia quae mandata sunt, ut facias quemadmodum sine quaerellam est. ₁₁ Ideo haec dicit Dominus orbis terrarum. ₁₂ —Creavit enim orbem ter-

15   rarum propter plebem suam, ₁₃ et non coepit eam in*te*ntionem creaturae et ab initio orbis terrarum palam facere, ut in eam gentes arguantur et humiliter inter se disputationibus arguant se. ₁₄ Itaque excogitavit et invenit me qui ab initio orbis terrarum praeparatus sum ut sim arbiter testamenti illius. ₁₅ Et *n*unc palam facio tibi, quia consummatum est

20   tempus annorum vitae meae et transio in dormitionem patrum meorum, et palam omnem plebem . . .

₁₆ <Tu> autem, percipe scribturam hanc ad recognoscendam tutatio-

---

1 ...] In MS the first three lines (originally written in red ink) are illegible; see further the commentary on 1:1. | **5** Mo[s]ysen Hilgenfeld 1866 cj.] Cf. Volkmar, *Mose Prophetie*, p. 19: "Der Schreiber wollte erst Mos-en schreiben, setzte dann noch das -ysen hinzu". | usque] usq~ MS^{ph} | **6-7** qui vocavit ad se Jesum filium Nave] προσκαλεσάμενος Ἰησοῦν υἱὸν Ναυῆ Gelasius Cyzicenus, *Comm. Act. Conc. Nic.* II, 18; see Denis, *Fragmenta*, p. 66. | **9** plebem] plebē MS^{ph} | *pa*tribus Schmidt-Merx cj.] extribus MS. Cf. e.g. Josh. 1:6 πατράσιν; in capitals, P̦ and E, and A and X may be easily confused. Schmidt and Merx assumed that "ex" stems from a now lost line, which ended with the "pa" of "patribus". | **9-10** testamentum] testame̅//tum MS^{ph} | **10-11** Jesum] ihm̅ MS^{ph} | **11** Jesum] ihm⌐ MS^{ph} | **12** <Custodi> conjeci] Cf. 10:11; the combination of "custodire" (φυλάσσεσθαι, φυλάσσειν) with "verba (legis)", "mandata" and "ut facias" occurs frequently in Deuteronomy and Joshua, e.g. Josh. 1:7. | **14** Dominus] d̅n̅s MS^{ph} | **15** in*te*ntionem H.J. de Jonge cj.] inceptionem MS. In uncials, C and T are easily confused; possibly, the scribe was influenced by the nearby "coepit". | **17** disputationibus] disputationib~ MS^{ph} | **17-19** Itaque - illius] καὶ προεθεάσατό με ὁ θεὸς πρὸ καταβολῆς κόσμου εἶναί με τῆς διαθήκης αὐτοῦ μεσίτην Gelasius, ibid. (see note to lines 6-7). | **17** Itaque] itaq~ MS^{ph} | **18** sum] su MS^{ph} | **19** *n*unc Hilgenfeld 1866 cj.] tunc MS | **20** dormitionem] dormitio̅ne MS^{ph} | **21-22** . . . <Tu> Hilgenfeld 1866 cj.] Clemen indicates with dots a lacuna which may have contained five or six letters. Ceriani, not giving dots, but a blank space, seems to indicate that the manuscript is not illegible, but that the scribe has deliberately left some space open, perhaps planning to fill it in later. "Tu" is an obvious supplement; see further the commentary on 1:15. | **22** autem] aute⌐ MS^{ph} | scribturam] scribtura⌐ MS^{ph} | **22-23** tutationem] tutatio̅ne MS^{ph}

TRANSLATION

1 1 ...

2 which is the two thousand fivehundredth year since the creation of the earth 3 —but according to those who live in the East the number is the ... and ...th—, and the ...th since the departure from Phoenicia, 4 when the people left; after the departure that took place through Moses, until Amman over the Jordan;

5 (*sc.* the book) of the prophecy, which was given by Moses according to the book of Deuteronomy, 6 when he called unto him Joshua, the son of Nun, a man deemed worthy by the Lord 7 to be the (*sc.* Moses') successor for the people and for the tabernacle of the testimony with all its holy objects, 8 and to lead the people into the land that was given to their fathers, 9 so that it would be given to them on account of the covenant, and on account of the oath—the things he (*sc.* Moses) said in the tabernacle, namely that he (*sc.* God) would give it (*sc.* the land) through Joshua; saying to Joshua:

"Keep this word, 10 and promise to do impeccably everything that is commanded, according to your zeal. 11 Therefore, thus says the Lord of the world. 12 —For he created the world on behalf of his people, 13 but he did not also reveal this purpose of the creation from the beginning of the world, so that the nations would be put to disgrace on their account, and, through their deliberations among themselves, to their own humiliation disgrace themselves. 14 Therefore, he has devised and invented me, I who have been prepared from the beginning of the world to be the mediator of his covenant. 15 But now, I will reveal it (*sc.* the purpose of God's creation) to you, because the time of the years of my life is fulfilled, and I will go to the resting-place of my fathers, and before the entire people ...

16 You, however, receive this writing, which serves to acknowledge the trustworthiness

nem librorum quos tibi tradam, ₁₇ quos ordinabis et chedriabis et reponis in vasis fictilibus in loco quem fecit ab initio orbis terrarum, ₁₈ ut
25　invocetur nomen illius, usque in diem paenitentiae, in respectu quo respicit illos Dominus in consummatione exitus dierum.

2 ₁ . . . . intrabunt per te in terram quam decrevit et promisit
dare patribus eorum, ₂ in qua tu benedicis, et dabis unicuique et stabilibis eis sortem in *eam*, et constabilibis eis regnum, et magisteria loco-
30　rum dimittes illis secus quod placebit Domino eorum in judicio et justitia.

₃ . . . . autem, postquam intrabunt in terram suam anno s . . . . . . et
postea dominabitur a principibus et tyrannis per annos XVIII, et
XVIIII anno s<e> abrumpen*t* t<r>ibus X. Nam descendent tribus duae
35　et transferunt scenae testimonium. ₄ Tunc Deus caelestis fi*get* pal*u*m
scenae suae et *turrim* sanctuarii sui, et ponentur duae tribus sanctitatis ₅
(nam X tribus stabilient sibi secus ordinationes suas regna).

₆ Et adferent victimas per annos XX, ₇ et VII circumvallabunt mu-
ros. Et circumi*to* VIIII et adcedent ad testamentum Domini, et fi*dem*
40　polluent, quem fecit Dominus cum eis. ₈ Et immolabunt natos suos diis

---

23 quos² MS] The MS reading is probably not correct, but it is not possible to achieve a true read-
ing with any certainty; see commentary on 1:17. | 24 fictilibus] fictilib~ MSᵖʰ | 25 usque] usq~
MSᵖʰ | 26 Dominus] dns MSᵖʰ | 27 . . . . Clemen] The blank space indicated by Ceriani
(see note to lines 21-22) may be an indentation to designate a new paragraph. On the other hand, a
new section begins here, and one would expect some introductory formula; see further the commen-
tary on 2:1. | 28 patribus] patrib MSᵖʰ | unicuique] unicuiq~ MSᵖʰ | 29 *eam* Hilgenfeld 1866 cj.
(but he wrote "ea")] me MS. Rönsch, "Weitere Illustrationen", pp. 222-223, defended the manuscript's reading by citing 2 Sam. 20:1, which shows that it is possible to say that someone "has part
in someone". In 2 Sam. 20:1, however, a stock phrase is used (that passed into English and other
languages), which is always negated: "to have neither part nor share in something", more loosely
used: "in someone" (οὐ μερὶς οὐδὲ κληρονομία [κλῆρος] = "pars nec sors"); Rönsch withdrew
his suggestion in "Xeniola theologica", p. 558. | 30 Domino] dno MSᵖʰ | terram] terra⟩ MSᵖʰ | anno s . . . . .] The s in "annos" must probably be understood as the
first letter of an ordinal number. Rönsch, "Xeniola theologica", p. 547 conjectured "s<exto>", but
s<eptimo> (Schmidt and Merx, p. 128 cj.) or s<ecundo> fit better into the lacuna. | 33 principibus]
principib~ MSᵖʰ | 33-34 XVIII, et XVIIII] Ceriani transcribes "xuiii" and "xuiiii", but MSᵖʰ actu-
ally uses V, not U, for the numeral 5. | 34 anno s<e> abrumpen*t* t<r>ibus Rönsch, "Xeniola
theologica", p. 547 cj.] annosabrumpenstib· MSᵖʰ; Clemen reads "abrumpent tib", MSᵖʰ confirms
Ceriani's reading "abrumpens tib". | tribus²] tri//b MSᵖʰ | 35 Deus] ds⟩ MSᵖʰ | fi*get* pal*u*m Rönsch,
"Sprachliche Parallelen", pp. 86-87 cj.] fecit palam MS. Both in form and pronunciation, C and G are
similar; in a verbal ending, I and E are phonetically exchangeable (see grammatical note nr. 2); the
frequent occurrence in the preceding sections of the expression "palam facere" may have contributed to
the misreading. | 36 *turrim* Charles cj. (but he wrote "turrem")] ferrum MS. | 36-37 tribus (twice)]
trib~ MSᵖʰ | 38 VII] See note to "XVIII, et XVIIII", lines 33-34. | 39 circumi*to* H.J. de Jonge cj.]
circumibo MS | et²] Following "et", which is the last word of a line in MS, Clemen found room for
the numeral "IV". This conjecture, however, is unnecessary. | Domini] dni MSᵖʰ | fidem Schmidt-
Merx cj.] fine⟩ MSᵖʰ. According to Charles, "finem" goes back to Gr. ὅρον, which would be corrupt
for ὅρκον. But the corruption can also have taken place in the Latin textual tradition: fidem > finem.
| 40 Dominus] dns MSᵖʰ

of the books which I will hand to you, 17 and you must order them, embalm them, and put them in earthenware jars in a place which he made from the beginning of the creation of the world, 18 so that his name be invoked; until the day of repentance, in the visitation with which the Lord will visit them in the fulfilment of the end of days.

2 1 But now, they will enter through you into the land which he decided and promised to give to their fathers. 2 And in it (*sc.* the land) you must give blessings, and you must give to each of them their share in it, and you must found for them a kingdom and arrange for them local rule according to their Lord's wish in justice and righteousness.

3 ..., however, after they will have entered into their land in the ...th year, and afterwards, they will be ruled by princes and kings for eighteen years, but in the nineteenth the ten tribes will break themselves loose. And the two tribes will separate themselves and transfer the tabernacle of the testimony. 4 Then the heavenly God will fasten the pole of his tabernacle and the tower of his sanctuary, and the two (*sc.* tribes) will be appointed as holy tribes. 5 The ten tribes, however, will establish for themselves kingdoms according to their own ordinances.

6 And they will offer sacrifices for twenty years. 7 And in the seventh they will surround themselves with walls, and as the ninth will have elapsed they will also abandon the covenant of the Lord, and defile the alliance the Lord made with them. 8 And they will sacrifice their children to foreign

alienis, et ponent idola scenae servientes illis, ₉ et in domo Domini faciunt
cient sceleste, et sculpent omn*iu*m animalium idola multa.

3 ₁ Illis temporibus veniet illis ab oriente rex, et teget equitatus terram
eorum et ₂ incendet colonia<m> eorum igne cum aede sancta Domini,
45 et sancta vasa omnia tollet; ₃ et omnem plebem eiciet et ducet 'illos in
terram patriae suae et duas tribus ducit secum.

₄ Tunc invocabunt duae tribus X tribus et ducent se ut liena in
campis, pulverati, esurientes et sitientes. ₅ Et clamabunt: 'Justus et
sanctus Dominus. Quia enim vos peccastis et nos pariter adducti sumus
50 vobis[cum] {cum infantibus nostris}.' ₆ Tunc plorabunt X tribus audientes
entes inproperia verborum tribum duarum, ₇ et dicent: 'Quid faciemus
vobis, fratres? Nonne in omnem domum Istrahel advenit *t*libsis haec?' ₈
Et omnes tribus plorabunt clamantes in caelum et dicentes: ₉ 'Deus
Abraham, et Deus Isaac, et Deus Jacob, reminiscere testamentum tuum
55 quod factasti cum eis, et jusjurandum quod jurasti eis per te, ne
umquam deficiat semen eorum a terra quam dedisti illis.'

₁₀ Tunc reminiscentur me die illo, dicentes tribus ad tribum, et
homo de proximo suo: ₁₁ 'Nonne hoc est quod testabatur nobis *t*um
Moyses in profetis, qui multa passus est in Aegypto et in Mari Rubro et
60 in heremo annis XL? ₁₂ Testatus et invocabat nobis testes caelum et terram,
ram, ne praeteriremus mandata illius in quibus arbiter fuit nobis; ₁₃
quae advenerunt nobis de isto secus verba ipsius et secus adfirmationem
ipsius, quomodo testatus est nobis temporibus illis, et quae convenerunt
usque nos duci captivos in partem orientis'; ₁₄ qui et servient circa annos
65 nos LXXVII.

4 ₁ Tunc intravit unus qui supra eos est et expandit manus et ponit
genua sua et oravit pro eis dicens: ₂ 'Domine, omnis rex in alta sede,
qui dominaris saeculo, qui voluisti plebem hanc esse tibi plebem [hanc]

---

41 Domini] d̄ni MS^ph I **42** omn*iu*m Hilgenfeld 1866 cj.] omnem MS I **43** Illis] Preceding this word
MS has a blank space with room for two or three letters; it probably indicates the beginning of a new
paragraph. I temporibus] temporib~ MS^ph I **44** colonia<m> Hilgenfeld 1866 cj. I **46** tribus] trib~
MS^ph I **47** duae tribus X tribus] duae trib~ x· trib~ MS^ph I **48** clamabunt] In MS^ph, the second
stroke of the U is at the same time the first stroke of the N, whereas the second upright stroke of the
N is provided with a horizontal stroke, functioning in this way as the T, as well. I **50** vobis[cum]
{cum infantibus nostris} Schmidt-Merx cj.] The manuscript has "cum infantib· nostris" after
"esurientes et sitientes" (line 48); the transposition of this phrase assumed here explains the tautological
ical "-cum" with "vobis" as a relic of the phrase's earlier, correct position. I tribus] trib~ MS^ph I **52**
omnem] omne⌐ MS^ph I *t*libsis Hilgenfeld 1866 cj. (but he wrote "thlibsis")] clibsis MS. Cf. note on
"in*t*entionem" in line 15. I **53** tribus] trib~ MS^ph I **53-54** Deus (three times)] ds MS^ph I **56** umquam]
quam] umquam Ceriani, u⌐//quam MS^ph I semen] seme⌐ MS^ph I quam] qua⌐ MS^ph I **57** tribus] trib~
MS^ph I **58** *t*um Schmidt-Merx cj.] c̣um MS. Cf. note on "in*t*entionem" in line 15. I **64** servient Ceriani,
riani, MS^ph] serviet Clemen. I **68** [hanc] Volkmar cj.

gods, and erect idols in the tabernacle and serve them, 9 and they will act disgraciously in the house of the Lord, and sculpt many idols of all kinds of animals.

3 1 In those days a king from the East will come to them, and his cavalry will cover their land, and 2 he will burn their city with fire, including the holy house of the Lord, and he will carry off all holy objects; 3 and he will expel the entire people and lead them to his fatherland, and he will lead the two tribes with him.

4 Then the two tribes will call upon the ten tribes, and they will retire into the fields like a lioness, covered with dust, starving and thirsting. 5 And they will cry: 'Righteous and holy is the Lord! Truly, because you have sinned, we and our children have been carried off just like you.' 6 Then the ten tribes will weep, hearing the reproaches of the two tribes, and they will say: 7 'What can we say to you, brethren? Has not this distress come over the entire house of Israel?' 8 And all tribes will weep, crying unto heaven, and saying: 9 'God of Abraham, and God of Isaac, and God of Jacob, remember your covenant, which you made with them, and the oath, which you swore by yourself, that their seed would never be absent from the land that you gave to them!'

10 Then, on that day, they will remember me, each tribe saying to the other, and each man to his neighbour: 11 'Is it not this, the things which Moses formerly testified to us in his prophecies? Moses, who suffered many things in Egypt, and in the Red Sea, and in the desert, during forty years. 12 And having testified, he also called on heaven and earth to be witnesses, lest we should transgress his commandments, which he had mediated to us. 13 But since then, these things have come over us, in accordance with his words and his solemn confirmation, which he testified to us in those days, and which have come true up to our expulsion into the land of the East.' 14 And they will be slaves there for seventy-seven years.

4 1 Then someone will enter who is above them, and he will spread his arms and bend his knees, and pray for them, saying: 2 'Lord, King of All in the throne on high, who rulest the world, who wanted this people

exceptam. Tunc voluisti invocari eorum Deus secus testamentum quod
70 fecisti cum patribus eorum. ₃ Et ierunt captivi in terram alienam cum
uxoribus et natis suis et circa ostium allofilorum et ubi est ma[j]est*itia*
magna. ₄ Respice, et miserere eorum, Domine caelestis!'

₅ Tunc reminiscitur Deus eorum, propter testamentum quod fecit
cum patribus illorum, et palam faciet misericordiam suam et tempori-
75 bus illis. ₆ Et mittit in animam regis ut misereator eorum, et dimittit
illos in terram eorum et regionem.

₇ Tunc ascendent aliquae partes tribuum et venient in locum consti-
tutum suum et circumvallabunt locum renovantes. ₈ Duae autem tribus
permanebunt in praeposita fide sua, tristes et gementes, quia non po-
80 terint referre immolationes Domino patruum suorum. ₉ Et X tribus
crescent et devenient apud nat<i>o<ne>s in tempore tribu<lationu>m.
5 ₁ Et cum adpropiabunt tempora arguendi, et vindicta surgit de reges
participes scelerum ₂ et punientes eos. Et ipsi dividentur ad veritatem;
propter quod factum fuit: ₃ 'Devitabunt justitiam et accedent ad iniqui-
85 tatem', et 'contaminabunt in*qui*nationibus domum servitutis suae'; et
quia: 'Fornicabunt post deos alienos.'

₄ Non enim sequentur veritatem Dei, sed quidam altarium inquinabunt de muneribus quae inponent Domino; qui non sunt sacerdotes, sed
servi de servis nati. ₅ Qui enim magistri sunt doctores eorum illis tem-
90 poribus, erunt mirantes personas cupiditatum et acceptiones munerum,
et pervendent justitias accipiendo poenas. ₆ Et ideo implebitur colonia
et *fines habitationis sceleribus et iniquitatibus a Deo, ut qui faciunt
erunt impii judices: inerunt in campo* judicare quomodo quisquae volet.

---

71 ma[j]est*itia* Merx in Hilgenfeld 1866 cj.] majestas MS | 74 patribus] patrib~ MS^ph | 74-75
temporibus] temporib~ MS^ph | 75 misereator MS] Peyron read "misereatur", but this probably is an
unconscious correction. | eorum] eor~ MS^ph | 78 suum] suuꟷ MS^ph | tribus] trib~ MS^ph | 79 sua
MS] Peyron omits "sua". | 80 Domino] dno Peyron, MS^ph | 81 nat<i>o<ne>s Hilgenfeld 1868 cj. |
tribu<lationu>m conjeci] Hilgenfeld 1866 conjectured "tribulationis", but the M of the manuscript's
"tribum" makes the plural more probable. | 85 in*qui*nationibus Hilgenfeld 1866 cj.] ingenationib~
MS^ph | domum] domu MS^ph | 87 Dei] d̄ī MS^ph | 88 muneribus] m̊unerib· MS^ph. Preceding "mu-
neribus", at the beginning of a line (the first one of a new column), Ceriani indicated a blank space
which may have contained two or three letters, but, to judge from MS^ph, it is not at all certain that
anything had been written there; if it had, it is likely to have been erased as a slip of the pen. Clemen
found some room after "de" at the end of the previous line, as well. However, in MS^ph the E of "de"
has the curled middle horizontal stroke which is used to fill out a line; therefore MS will not have
read anything following "de" on this line. | Domino] dno MS^ph | 89-90 temporibus] t̄e//porib·
MS^ph | 92-93 *fines habitationis* ... *quisquae volet* conjeci] MS has a large dittography here:
et ideo implebitur colonia et finis habitationes eorum sceleribus et iniquitatibus (MS^ph:
scelerib~ et iniquitatib~) a deo ut qui facit erunt impii judices erunt in eam post fines habitationis
sceleribus et iniquitatibus a domino (MS^ph: d̄no), qui faciunt erunt impii judices inerunt in
campo judicare quomodo quisquae volet,
which becomes clear by a presentation of the text in parallel columns:

to be your elect people. Then you wanted to be called their God, according to the covenant which you made with their fathers. ₃ But (now) they have gone as captives into a foreign land, with their wives and children, and to the gate

of the gentiles, where there is great sadness. ₄ Behold, and have mercy on them, heavenly Lord!'

₅ Then God will remember them, on account of the covenant which he had made with their fathers, and he will manifest his mercy in these days, too. ₆ And he will give it into the heart of the king to have mercy on them, and to let them return to their land and region.

₇ Then some parts of the tribes will go up, and they will come in the place that was appointed to be theirs, and they will rampart the place anew. ₈ But the two tribes will hold on to the allegiance that was ordained for them, mourning and weeping, because they will not be able to bring offerings to the Lord of their fathers. ₉ And the ten tribes will be more and more absorbed among the nations in a time of tribulations.

5 ₁ And when the times of judgment will approach, revenge will come through kings who participate in crime and who will punish them. ₂ And they themselves will move away from the truth; ₃ wherefore it has been said: 'They will avoid justice and turn to iniquity,' and: 'they will will defile the house of their worship with pollutions,' and that 'they will go whoring after foreign gods'.

₄ For they will not follow the truth of God, but some people will defile the altar with the offerings they will bring to the Lord, (*sc.* people) who are not priests, but slaves born of slaves. ₅ For the scholars who will be their teachers in those times will favour the persons that please them, and accept gifts; and they will sell legal settlements, accepting fees. ₆ And so their city and dwelling-place will be filled with crimes and injustice against God, since those who will do them will be impious judges: they will continually judge according to their own liking.

6 ₁ Tunc exurgent illis reges imperantes et in sacerdotes summi Dei
95 vocabuntur. Facient facientes impietatem ab sancto sanctitatis.

₂ Et succedit illis rex petulans qui non erit de genere sacerdotum,
homo temerarius et improbus; et judicabit illis quomodo digni erunt, ₃
qui elidit principales eorum gladio, et locis ignotis se*pe*liet corpora illorum ut nemo sciat ubi sint corpora illorum. ₄ Occidit majores natu et
100 juvenes et non parcet. ₅ Tunc timor erit illius acervus in eis in terram
eorum. ₆ Et faciet in eis judicia quomodo fecerunt in illis Aegypti per
XXX et IIII annos et puni*vi*t eos. ₇ Et <p>roducit natos <su>*cc*edentes
sibi; breviora tempora do<mi>na*bu*nt.

et ideo implebitur colonia et	
finis	fines
habitationes	habitationis
eorum	-
sceleribus	sceleribus
et	et
iniquitatibus	iniquitatibus
a	a
deo	domino
ut	-
qui	qui
facit	faciunt
erunt	erunt
impii	impii
judices	judices
erunt	inerunt
in	in
eam	cam
post	po
	judicare quomodo quisquae volet.

From these two columns, the likeliest words and forms have been adopted in the main text. "Fines habitationis" is chosen because of its correct spelling; "eorum" is left out because the use of the possessive pronoun is more natural, and therefore more easily added than omitted; "a deo" and "a domino" ("dno"?) are of equal merit, but the following "ut" is problematic (and therefore *lectio difficilior*), so that the choice is made in favour of "a deo ut" instead of "a domino"; "in eam post" makes no sense, "in campo" is problematic, but not impossible, and therefore to be preferred. One clause, "qui … impii judices" is not entirely satisfactory either, but again it is not impossible; for "faciunt", lacking an object, "ea" may be supplemented, and a sentence like "qui faciunt ea (sc. iniquitates) erunt impii judices" can well be translated, although it is of little substance. For an alternative solution, see the commentary to 2:6. | **94** summi Dei] su²//mi d͞i MS^ph | **95** sancto sanctitatis] s͞co//sis· MS^ph | **97** improbus] improb~ MS^ph | **98** eorum] eoru MS^ph | sepeliet Hilgenfeld 1866 cj.] singuliet MS | **102** puni*vi*t Hilgenfeld 1866 cj. (but he wrote "punibit")] puniunt MS. Here, the vulgar form "-vit" is preferred, because of its graphical similarity to "-unt" (see Clemen, *APAT* II, p. 329). | <p>roducit Hilgenfeld 1866 cj. (but he wrote "producet")] puniunt MS was not sure what was to be read; in his *Monumenta* he printed "rodincit", leaving space for one or two preceding letters, but later he wrote to Volkmar, that "producit" was quite possible, although the manuscript did not confirm the suggested reading (Ceriani in Volkmar, p. 155). | <su>*cc*edentes Hilgenfeld 1866 cj.] MS reads "ecedentes" preceded by a space for two or three letters. | **103** do<mi>na*bu*nt conjeci] donarent MS. In capitals and uncials, R and B are similar.

6 ₁ Then, kings will arise for them to assume government, and they will proclaim themselves priests of the Most High God. They will act most impiously against the Holy of Holies.

₂ And a petulant king will succeed them, who will not be of priestly stock, a wicked and cruel man. And he will rule over them as they deserve. ₃ He will kill their men of distinction, and he will bury their corpses at unknown places, so that no one knows where their corpses are. ₄ He will kill old and young, and he will not spare. ₅ Then there will be bitter fear of him in their land. ₆ And he will judge them like the Egyptians for 34 years, and he will punish them. ₇ And he will bring forth children who will succeed him. They will rule for shorter periods.

$_8$ In par<t>es eorum *chortis* venient et occidentes rex potens qui[a]
105 expugnabit eos $_9$ et duce[n]t captivos, et partem aedis ipsorum igni incendit, aliquos crucifigit circa coloniam eorum.

7 $_1$ Ex quo facto finientur tempora momento † . . . . etur cursus a . . .
. horae IIII veniant $_2$ coguntur secun . . . . . . ae . . . . pos . . . . . . initiis tribus ad exitus VIIII propter initium tres septimae secunda tria in
110 tertia duae h . . ra . . tae†

$_3$ Et regnabunt de his homines pestilentiosi et impii docentes se esse
justos, $_4$ et hi suscitabunt iram animorum suorum, qui erunt homines
dolosi, sibi placentes, ficti in omnibus suis, et omni hora diei amantes
convivia, devoratores, gulae, $_5$ †s . . . n . . . ca . . . . nusdiis . . .
115 . . . . omnis . . . . u . . . . o . . . . rae . . . .
† <d>elentes $_6$ . . . . . rum bonorum comestores, dicentes se haec facere
propter misericordiam †qu . . . $_7$ seet† exterminatores, quaeru<losi>,
fallaces, celantes se, ne possent cognosci impii, in scelere pleni et
iniquitate ab oriente usque ad occidentem, $_8$ dicentes: 'Habebimus dis-
120 cubitiones et luxuriam, edentes et bibentes. Et putavimus nos tamquam
principes erimus.' $_9$ Et manus eorum et mentes inmunda tractantes et os
eorum loquetur ingentia et super dicent: $_{10}$'Noli <ne me> tange, ne inquines me loco in quo †. . . s . . . . . . isd . . . . su . . . . . us . . . .
. in . . . . re . . . . ravi . . . . in plebem quae s . . a . . illis†
125 **8** $_1$ Et <ci>ta <ad>veniet in eos ultio et ira quae talis non fuit in illis a
saeculo usque ad illum tempus in quo suscitavit illis regem regum terrae et potestatem a potentia magna, qui confitentes circumcisionem in
cruce suspendit. $_2$ Nam necantes torquebit, et tradi[di]t duci vinctos in
custodiam, $_3$ et uxores eorum di[i]sdonabuntur gentibus. Et filii eorum
130 pueri secabuntur a medicis [pueri] inducere acrobis<ti>am illis. $_4$ Nam
illi in eis punientur in tormentis et igne et ferro, et cogentur palam bajulare idola eorum, inquinata quomodo sunt pariter contin<g>entibus

---

104 par<t>es von Gutschmid in Hilgenfeld 1866 cj. I *chortis* Schmidt in Hilgenfeld 1866 cj. (but he wrote "cortes")] *mortis* MS. In uncials, the combination CH is quite similar to M. I qui[a] Hilgenfeld 1866 cj. I **105** duce[n]t Hilgenfeld 1866 cj. I **111** regnabunt Hilgenfeld 1866 cj.] regnarunt MS. Cf. note on "dominabunt", line 103. I **116** <d>elentes Volkmar cj. I **117** quaeru<losi> Charles cj.] MS is illegible. I **122** <ne me> Clemen cj.] MS is illegible; Ceriani indicates room for about four letters. I **125** <ci>ta <ad>veniet Hilgenfeld 1866 cj.] MS is illegible; the supplements fit into the room indicated by Ceriani. I **128** tradi[di]t Hilgenfeld cj. (but he wrote "tradet"). I **129** di[i]sdonabun-tur Haupt in Hilgenfeld 1868 cj.] diisdonabu//tur MS[ph] I **130** secabuntur Hilgenfeld 1866 cj.] se-cabantur MS I [pueri] Schmidt-Merx cj. I acrobis<ti>am Hilgenfeld 1866 (but he wrote "acrobys-tiam")] According to Ceriani and Clemen, MS reads "acrosisam"; Burkitt, however, found MS reading "acrobisam"; MS[ph] is illegible. I **132** contin<g>entibus H.J. de Jonge cj.] continentib~ MS[ph]

8 Cohorts will come into their territory, and a mighty king from the West, who will defeat them, 9 and lead them off in chains. And he will burn part of their temple with fire, some he will crucify near their city.

7 1-2 . . .

3 And pestilent and impious men will rule over them, who proclaim themselves to be righteous. 4 And they will excite their wrathful souls; they will be deceitful men, self-complacent, hypocrites in all their dealings, and who love to debauch each hour of the day, devourers, gluttons, 5 . . . . . . 6 who eat the possessions of . . . , saying they do this out of compassion . . . 7 murderers, complainers, liars, hiding themselves lest they be recognized as impious, full of crime and iniquity, from sunrise to sunset 8 saying: 'Let us have extravagant banquets, let us eat and drink. And let us act as if we are princes'. 9 And their hands and minds will deal with impurities, and their mouth will speak enormities, saying in addition to all this: 10 'Keep off, do not touch me, lest you pollute me...'

8 1 And suddenly revenge and wrath will come over them, such as there will never have been over them since eternity until that time, in which he will raise for them the king of the kings of the earth, and a power with great might, who will hang on the cross those who confess circumcision, 2 but who will torture those who deny it. And he will lead them chained into captivity, 3 and their wives will be divided among the gentiles, and their sons will be operated on as children by physicians in order to put on them a foreskin. 4 But they will be punished by torments, and with fire and sword, and they will be forced to carry publicly their idols, that are defiled, just like those who touch

ea. ₅ Et a torquentibus illos pariter cogentur intrare in abditum locum eorum, et cogentur stimulis blasfemare verbum contumeliose. Novis-
135 sime post haec et leges quod habe*bu*nt supra altarium suum.

9 ₁ Tunc illo di*e e*rit homo de tribu Levvi cujus nomen erit Taxo, qui habens VII filios dice*t* ad eos rogans: ₂ 'Videte, filii, ecce ultio facta est in plebe altera crudelis, inmunda, et traductio sine misericordia et emi-nen*s* principatum. ₃ Quae enim gens, aut quae regio, aut quis populus
140 impiorum in Dominum qui multa scelesta fecerunt, tanta mala passi sunt quanta nobis contegerunt?

₄ Nunc ergo, filii, audite me! Videte enim, et scite quia numquam temptan<te>s Deum nec parentes nec proavi eorum, ut praetereant mandata illius. ₅ Scitis enim, quia haec sunt vires nobis. Et hoc facie-
145 mus: ₆ jejunemus triduo, et quarto die intremus in spelunca quae in agro est, et moriamur potius quam praetereamus mandata Domini dominorum, Dei parentum nostrorum. ₇ Hoc enim si faciemus et moriemur, sanguis noster vindicavitur coram Domino.'

10 ₁ Et tunc parebit regnum illius in omni creatura illius. Et tunc
150 zabulus finem habebit, et tristitia[m] cum eo adducetur. ₂ Tunc imple-buntur manus nuntii qui est in summo constitutus, qui protinus vindi-cavit illos ab inimicis eorum.

₃ <Exur>get enim Caelestis a sede regni sui et exiet de habitatione sancta sua cum indignationem et iram propter filios suos. ₄ Et tremebit
155 terra, usque ad fines suas concutietur, et alti montes humiliabuntur et concutientur et convalles cadent. ₅ Sol non dabit lumen et in tenebris convertent se cornua lunae et confringentur, et tota convertit se in san-guine; et orbis stellarum conturvavitur. ₆ Et mare usque ad abyssum decedit, ad fontes aquarum deficient et flumina expavescent. ₇ Quia ex-

---

133 torquentibus] torquentib~ MS^ph I **135** habe*bu*nt conjeci] haberent MS. Cf. note on "domina-bunt", line 103. I suum] suū MS^ph I **136** di*e e*rit Schmidt-Merx cj.] dicente MS. For the tautological indication of time, see line 57 "Tunc reminiscentur me die illo", and cf. Joel 3(4):1. I **137** dice*t* Hilgenfeld 1866 cj.] dicens MS. In As. Mos., there are three instances in which a T appears to be an error for S, or *vice versa,* cf. "eminens" lines 138-139; "dicent" line 199. I **138-139** eminen*s* Rönsch, "Sprachliche Parallelen", p. 100 cj.] eminent MS. Cf. note on "dicet" line 137. I **140** impiorum] ...oru⌐ MS^ph I Dominum] domum MS. The reading "Dominum" is not a conjectural emendation, but the resolution of the (unmarked) abbreviation "domum", cf. lines 146-147 "dn̄i domum", i.e. "Domini dominorum". I **142** numquam] numqua MS^ph I **143** temptan<te>s Volkmar cj. I Deum] dm MS^ph I **146** mandata] mā//data MS^ph I **146-147** Domini dominorum Dei] dn̄i domumdī MS^ph I **148** Domino] dn̄o MS^ph I **150** finem] fine⌐ MS^ph I tristitia[m] Hilgenfeld 1866 cj.] tristitia⌐ MS^ph. The manuscript's text is probably due to misreading the phrase as "zabulus finem habebit et tristitiam", see grammatical note nr. 34. I **153** <Exur>get Ceriani cj.] Traces of the supplemented letters were seen by Ceriani (*Monumenta* I, p. 64b); but even without such traces, the restoration is virtually certain. I **154** sancta] sca MS^ph them. ₅ And they will also be forced by those who torture them to enter into their hidden place, and they will be forced with goads to disgracefully blaspheme the word. Finally, after these things (*sc.* they will be forced to blaspheme) also the laws through the things they will have upon their altar.

9 ₁ Then, on that day, there will be a man from the tribe of Levi, whose name will be Taxo, who, having seven sons, will speak to them, saying: ₂ 'See, my sons, behold, a second, cruel and unclean retribution is made against the people, and a punishment without mercy, and it surpasses the first one. ₃ For what nation, or what land, or what people rebellious against the Lord, having committed many crimes, has suffered woes as great as have come over us?

₄ Now then, my sons, hear me! See, then, and know that neither our parents, nor their ancestors have tempted God by transgressing his commandments. ₅ Surely you know that here lies our strength. And this we shall do: ₆ Let us fast for three days, and on the fourth day let us enter into the cave which is in the field, and let us die rather than transgress the commandments of the Lord of lords, the God of our fathers. ₇ For as we shall do this and die, our blood will be avenged before the Lord.'

10 ₁ And then his kingdom will appear in his entire creation. And then the devil will come to an end, and sadness will be carried away together with him. ₂ Then, the hands of the messenger, when he will be in heaven, will be filled, and he will then avenge them against their enemies.

₃ For the Heavenly One will rise from his royal throne, and he will go out from his holy habitation with anger and wrath on account of his sons. ₄ And the earth will tremble until its extremes it will be shaken, and the high mountains will be made low, and they will be shaken, and the valleys will sink. ₅ The sun will not give its light, and the horns of the moon will turn into darkness, and they will be broken; and (*sc.* the moon) will entirely be turned into blood, and the orbit of the stars will be upset. ₆ And the sea will fall back into the abyss, and the fountains of the waters will defect and the rivers will recoil. ₇ For the

160   urgit summus Deus aeternus solus, et palam veniet ut vindicet gentes et
perdet omnia idola eorum.

     8 Tunc felix eris, tu Istrahel, et ascendes supra cervices et alas
aquilae, et inplebuntur. 9 Et altavit te Deus, et faciet te herere caelo
stellarum, loco habitationis *ejus*. 10 Et conspiges a summo, et vides

165   inimicos tuos in terram et cognosces illos et gaudebis et agis gratias et
confiteberis creatori tuo.

     11 Nam tu, Jesu Nave, custodi verba haec et hunc librum. 12 Erunt
enim a morte, receptione m<ea> usque ad adventum illius tempora
CCL quae fiunt. 13 Et hic cursus <erit> horum, que[m] conveniunt,

170   donec consummentur. 14 Ego autem ad dormitionem patrum meorum
e[r]am. 15 Itaque tu, Jesu Nave, firma <te>. Te elegit Deus esse mihi
successorem ejusdem testamenti."

    11 1 Et cum audisset Jesus verba Moysi tam scripta in sua scriptura,
omnia quae praedixerant, scidit sibi vestimenta et procidit ad pedes

175   M*onsi*. 2 Et hortatus est *e*um Monse et ploravit cum eo. 3 Et respondit
illi et dixit Jesus: 4 "Quid me *te*rres, domine Monse, et quo genere celabor de qua locutus es[t] voce acerva, que exivit de ore tuo, quae est
plena lacrimis et gemitibus, quia tu discedis de plebe ist<a> . . . . .?

     5 Quis locus recipit te, 6 aut quod erit monumentum sepulturae, 7 aut

180   quis audevit corpus tuum transferre, *sic*ut homo, de loco in locum? 8
Omnibus enim morientibus secus aetatem sepulturae suae sunt in terris;
nam tua sepultura ab oriente sole usque ad occidentem, et ab austro
usque ad fines aquilonis. Omnis orbis terrarum sepulcrum est tuum.

---

164 *ejus* conjeci] eorum MS. I inimicos Clemen, MS^ph] **165** immicos Ceriani I **166** confiteberis]
co//fiteberis MS^ph I **167** Jesu] ihu MS^ph I librum] libru⁻ MS^ph I **168** receptione m<ea> Volkmar
cj.] receptionem MS I **169** <erit> Volkmar cj.] MS is illegible; Ceriani indicated room for about
three letters; MS^ph suggests that "erit" is quite possible. I que[m] conjeci I **171** e[r]am Hilgenfeld
1866 cj. I firma <te> von Gutschmid in Hilgenfeld 1866 cj.] forma MS. "Te" may have been omitted
as a result of haplography. I Deus] d̄s MS^ph I **172** ejusdem] eiusdē MS^ph I **173** Jesus] īhs MS^ph I
tam Ceriani, Clemen] jam MS according to Burkitt; according to MS^ph, both readings are possible. I
174 praedixerant Ceriani, MS^ph] praedixerat Clemen I **175** M*onsi* Hilgenfeld 1866 cj. (but he wrote
"M*oysis*")] meos MS. The form "Monsi" ("M̄osi"?) seems preferable, because it is closer to the
manuscript's "meos"; see further grammatical note nr. 83. I *e*um Rönsch, "Sprachliche Parallelen",
pp. 201-202 cj.] cum Ceriani, but eum MS according to Burkitt; according to MS^ph, "cum" seems
slightly preferable, but "eum" is possible. I **176** Jesus] īhs MS^ph I *te*rres H.J. de Jonge cj.] celares
MS. See note on "in*te*ntionem" line 15. I domine] dne MS^ph I **177** es[t] Hilgenfeld 1866 cj. I **178**
gemitibus] gemitib~ MS^ph I ist<a> . . . . .] MS is illegible here and has space for about 6 letters.
The supplementation of the A is virtually certain; for "plebs ista" cf. 11:9, 19. I **179** recipit MS]
Ceriani seems to indicate space for about 4 letters following "recipit", although, for reasons which
remain obscure, he uses a kind of dots which he does not normally employ. MS^ph is hardly legible;
it seems, however, that the T of "recipit" already exceeds the right hand margin (which in this
particular column is very irregular). I **180** *sic*ut Burkitt cj.] ineut Ceriani, MS^ph, incut MS according
to Burkitt. I **181** morientibus] morientib~ MS^ph I **182-183** usque (twice)] usq· MS^ph

Highest God, the sole Eternal One, will rise, and he will manifest himself in order to punish the nations, and to destroy all their idols.

₈ Then you will be happy, Israel, and you will mount on the neck and the wings of an eagle, and they will be filled, ₉ and God will exalt you, and make you live in the heaven of the stars, the place of his habitation. ₁₀ And you will look down from above, and you will see your enemies on the earth, and you will recognize them. And you will rejoice, and you will thank and praise your Creator.

₁₁ But you, Joshua son of Nun, keep these words and this book. ₁₂ For from my death, my being taken away, until his (*sc.* God's) advent, there will be 250 times that will happen. ₁₃ And this is the course of events that will come to pass, until they will be completed. ₁₄ But I shall go to the resting-place of my fathers. ₁₅ Therefore you, Joshua son of Nun, be strong. It is you, whom God has chosen to be my successor to his covenant."

11   ₁ And when Joshua had heard Moses' words as they were written in his writing, everything they foretold, he rent his clothes and fell at Moses' feet. ₂ And Moses comforted him and wept with him. ₃ And Joshua answered him and said: ₄ "Why do you terrify me, lord Moses, and how will I hide myself from what you have said with the bitter voice that came from your mouth, and which is full of tears and sighs, because you will presently go away from this people?

₅ What place will receive you, ₆ or what will be the monument on your grave, ₇ or who, being human, will dare to carry your body from one place to another? ₈ For all who die when their time has come have a grave in the earth. But your grave extends from the East to the West, and from the North to the extreme South. The entire world is your grave.

₉ Domine, abhis. Et quis nutrit plebem istam, ₁₀ aut quis est qui mi-
185   serebitur illis, et quis eis dux erit in via, ₁₁ aut quis orabit pro eis, nec
patiens ne uno quidem die[m] ut inducam illos in terram Amorreorum?
      ₁₂ Quomodo ergo potero <...> plebem hanc tamquam pater unicum
filium, aut tamquam filiam domina[m], virginem quae paratur t<r>adi
viro, quae timebat, corpus custodiens ejus a sole et ne scalciati pedes
190   ejus ad currendum supra terram? ₁₃ <Aut un>de voluntatem eorum
praestabo illis ciborum et potui secus voluntatem voluntatis eorum? ₁₄ .
. . . . enim illorum erant C milia. Nam isti in tantum qui creverunt in
tuis orationibus, domine Monse. ₁₅ Et quae est mihi sapientia aut intellectus in Domini verbis aut judicare aut respondere?
195   ₁₆ Sed et reges Amorreorum, cum audierint, expugnare nos credentes, jam non esse sanctum et sacrum spiritum dignum Domino
multiplicem et inconpraehensibilem dominum verbi, fidelem in omnia,
divinum per orbem terrarum profetem, consummatum in saeculo doctorem, jam non esse in eis, dicent: 'Eamus ad eos. ₁₇ Si inimici impie
200   fecerunt semel adhuc in Dominum suum, non est defensor illis, qui
ferat pro eis praeces Domino, quomodo Monse erat magnus nuntius,
qui singulis horis, diebus et noctibus habebat genua sua infixa in terra,
orans, et intuens Omnipotentem orbem terrarum cum misericordia et
justitia, reminiscens testamentum parentum, et jurejurando placando

---

186 quidem] quidē MSᵖʰ | die[m] Hilgenfeld 1866 cj. | Amorreorum Ewald, *Geschichte Christus*, p.
81 cj.] araborum MS | **187-190** The style and grammar of these lines is clumsier than usual, per-
haps due to more corruptions than can be detected. | **187** <...> Fritzsche cj. (but he filled in "du-
cere")] The verb "potero" needs a complement infinitive, see further commentary on 11:12. This in-
finitive need not have immediately followed "potero". | plebem] plebē MSᵖʰ | **188** domina[m]
Fritzsche cj. | virginem] virginē MSᵖʰ | t<r>adi Rönsch, "Sprachliche Parallelen", pp. 105 f. cj.] tali
MS | **190** <Aut un>de conjeci] MS is illegible and has a space of about 5 letters; for "unde" see e.g.
πόθεν Matt. 15:33; Mark 8:4; John 6:5. | **192** illorum] illorū MSᵖʰ | **193** orationibus] orationib~
MSᵖʰ | domine Monse] dnemō//se MSᵖʰ | **193-194** intellectus MSᵖʰ] Ceriani and Clemen read
"intellelectus" and naturally suggested to read "intellectus"; but MSᵖʰ clearly has "intellectus". | Do-
mini conjeci] domo MS. After "domo", Ceriani and Clemen recorded enough space for a following
"dni", that is, "domini"; however, MSᵖʰ seems to offer space for only one, possily two letters, and
certainly not for large letters like D and N; to judge from MSᵖʰ, it even seems likely that MS has
never had letters or words between "domo" and "verbis". The proposed emendation of "domo" into
"domini" assumes the omission of an abbreviation marker and a change to the ablative because of
"in"; the original reading would have been "domī", cf. the abbreviation "domum" = "dominorum" in
lines 146-147, and "domum" = "Dominum" in line 140; see further the commentary. | **196** sanctum
et conjeci (but cf. Hilgenfeld 1868] semet MS. The conjecture assumes a misreading of an
abbreviation "s̄cm", cf. the abbreviation "sco//sis·" = "sancto sanctitatis" MSᵖʰ line 95; "habita//tio-
ne sca sua" MSᵖʰ line 154. | spiritum] s̄pm MSᵖʰ | Domino] dn̄o MSᵖʰ | **197** inconpraehensibilem]
in//conpraehensibile⌐ MSᵖʰ | dominum] dn̄m MSᵖʰ | **198** consummatum] cō//summatum MSᵖʰ |
199 jam] ī MSᵖʰ | **199** dicent Hilgenfeld 1866 cj.] dicens MS. Cf. note to "dicet" line 137. | **202**
diebus et noctibus] dieb~ et noctib~ MSᵖʰ | **203** Omnipotentem Hilgenfeld 1866 cj.]
hominipotentem MS

₉ Lord, you are leaving. And who will feed this people, ₁₀ or who will be there to take mercy on them, and who will be their leader on the way, ₁₁ or who will pray for them, not omitting one single day, so that I can lead them into the land of the Amorites?

₁₂ How will I be able to <guard> this people, like a father his only son, or like a woman her daughter—a virgin who is being prepared to be given to a man—, and who is anxious to protect her (*sc.* daughter's) body from the sun and her feet from going unshod over the ground? ₁₃ And whence will I procure for them the food and drink they urgently need? ₁₄ For their <number> was a hundred thousand, but now they have grown into this multitude here, only because of your prayers, lord Moses. ₁₅ And what wisdom or understanding have I to administer justice or pronounce a verdict in accordance with the words of the Lord?

₁₆ Furthermore, the kings of the Amorites, after they have heard—whilst believing that they can defeat us—, that the holy and sacred spirit, the worthy one before the Lord, the versatile and inscrutable lord of the word, the trusted one in everything, the divine prophet for this world, the perfect teacher for this earth, is no longer with them, will say: 'Let us go at them. ₁₇ If the enemies will sin against their Lord once more, there is no longer an advocate for them, who will supplicate to the Lord for them, as Moses was, the great messenger, who bent his knees on earth every hour of the day and of the night, praying; and who could look at him who rules the entire world with mercy and justice, reminding him of the covenant with the fathers, and placating the Lord

205 Dominum'; ₁₈ dicent enim: 'Non est ille cum eis. Eamus itaque, et confundamus eos a faciae terrae.' ₁₉ Quod ergo fiet plebi isti, domine Monse?"

12 ₁ Et postquam finivit verba Jesus, iterum procidit ad pedes Monsi. ₂ Et Monse prendit manum ipsius et erexit illum in cathedra ante se. Et

210 respondit et dixit illi: ₃ "Jesus, *te* ne contemnas, sed praebe te securum, et adtende verbis meis.

₄ Omnes gentes quae sunt in or<b>e terrarum Deus creavit, et nos praevidit, illos et nos, ab initio creaturae orbis terrarum u*sque* ad exitum saeculi. Et nihil est ab eo neglectum, usque ad pusillum, sed omnia

215 praevidit et pro*n*ovit. Cum *fecit*, ₅ Dominus omnia quae futura essent in hoc orbe terrarum providit.

Et ecce aufertur . . . . ₆ . . . . s me constituit pro eis et pro peccatis eorum <ut orarem> et in<pr>e̦care<r> pro eis. ₇ Non enim propter meam virtutem aut in firmitatem, sed temperantius mi

220 sericordiae ipsius et patientia contegerunt mihi. ₈ Dico enim tibi, Jesu, non propter pietatem plebis hujus exterminabis gentes. ₉ Omnia caeli firmamenta <et fundamenta> orbis facta ut provata a Deo et sub <a>nullo dexterae illius sunt.

₁₀ Facientes itaque et consummantes mandata Dei crescunt et bonam

225 viam exigunt. ₁₁ Nam peccantibus et neglegentibus mandata <...> carere bona[m] quae praedicta sunt, et punientur a gentibus multis tormentis. ₁₂ Nam in totum exterminet et relinquat eos fieri non potest. ₁₃ Exivit enim Deus qui praevidit omnia in saecula, et stabilitum est testamentum illius. Et jurejurando quod

RELIQVA DESVNT.

---

205 Dominum] d̄m MS^ph | itaque] itaq~ MS^ph | **208** Jesus] īhs MS^ph | **210** Jesus] īhs· MS^ph | *te* Hilgenfeld 1866 cj.] et MS | **212** or<b>e Hilgenfeld 1866 cj. | Deus] d̄s MS^ph | **213** u*sque* Rönsch in Hilgenfeld 1866 cj.] ut MS | **213-214** exitum] exitū MS^ph | **215** pro*n*ovit Volkmar cj.] provovit MS | *fecit* H.J. de Jonge cj.] Ceriani and Clemen could discern "eis", followed by an illegible space of 2 letters. | Dominus] dns MS | **217** aufertur ...-...s MS] Ceriani indicates an illegible space of about 9 letters, Clemen one of 16! For possible reconstructions, see commentary on 12:5-6. | **218** <ut orarem> et in<pr>e̦care<r> Volkmar cj.] These words fill out the illegible parts of MS. The first E of "inprecarer" is a conjectural correction of the manuscript's (uncertain) C. | **222** <et fundamenta> Fritzsche cj.] Perhaps this supplement is superfluous, see the commentary on 12:9. | **223** <a>nullo von Gutschmid and Weiss in Hilgenfeld 1866 cj. (but they wrote "annulo"). | **225** <...> conjeci] For possible reconstructions, see commentary on 12:11. | **226** bona[m] Hilgenfeld 1866 cj.

with his oath'; 18 surely they will say: 'He is no longer with them. Let us go, then, and let us wipe them from the face of the earth.' 19 What then will happen to this people, lord Moses?"

12 1 And after Joshua finished speaking, he again fell at Moses' feet. 2 But Moses took his hand and raised him up into the seat before him. And he answered and said to him: 3 "Joshua, do not think too lightly of yourself, but show yourself free from care. And give heed to my words."

4 God has created all nations on earth, and he foresaw us, them as well as us, from the beginning of the creation of the earth until the end of the world. And nothing has been overlooked by him, not even the smallest detail, but he has seen and known everything beforehand. When he made them, 5 the Lord saw beforehand all things that were to happen in this world.

And behold, ... will be taken away. 6 The Lord has appointed me for them and for their sins, that I should pray and supplicate for them; 7 yet not on account of my virtue or strength, but out of long-suffering his mercy and his patience have befallen me. 8 Therefore, I say to you, Joshua, not on account of the piety of this people will you defeat the nations. 9 All the firmaments of heaven and fundaments of the earth are made as approved of by God, and they are under the ring of his right hand.

10 If they therefore do the commandments of God perfectly, they will grow and prosper. 11 But the sinners and those who neglect the commandments <must> miss the goods that have been foretold, and they will be punished by the nations with many torments. 12 But it cannot happen that he will exterminate and leave them entirely. 13 For God, who sees everything beforehand in eternity, will go out, and his covenant stands firm. And through the oath which ...

PART TWO

THE LATIN OF THE ASSUMPTION OF MOSES

The following grammatical notes intend to give a systematic account of the Latin that is preserved in As. Mos. The main purpose is to describe the peculiarities of the language of As. Mos. for the benefit of the non-specialist. Moreover, the study of the language and grammar of As. Mos. often helps to establish its text with greater certainty, sometimes with the aid of an emendation, more often without an emendation. This linguistic description takes the manuscript's text as its lead; emended words or phrases are as a rule only adduced as comparative material, consistently marked by the abbreviation "l. em." (*lectio emendata*).

Two earlier attempts have been made to survey the Latin of As. Mos., the first by H. Rönsch, in his article "Die Leptogenesis" of 1871. There, on pp. 89-91, he lists orthographic vulgarisms, Vulgar Latin words and some syntactical "anomalies". He does so, however, in order to compare these peculiarities with similar ones in Jubilees (this comparison is not repeated in his *Das Buch der Jubiläen* of 1877). The list is a bare enumeration of linguistic phenomena, without explanatory notes, and it is far from complete, especially where syntax is concerned. R.H. Charles's list in his *The Assumption of Moses*, pp. xxx-xxxiv is even less complete, and poorly organized. For instance, Charles makes no distinction between scribal errors such as "c for e in cum" (11:2) and vulgarisms such as "ae for e in quaerella" (6:1).

Many separate grammatical observations on the Latin of As. Mos. have been made, especially again by Rönsch. These are scattered throughout his numerous articles in Hilgenfeld's *Zeitschrift für wissenschaftliche Theologie*, but most of them are collected in his grammar *Itala und Vulgata* or in his *Semasiologische Beiträge*.

My treatment of the Latin of As. Mos. will mainly follow the pattern of H. Väänänen's *Introduction au latin vulgaire*, a general, yet comprehensive and clear survey. Besides this book, much use has been made of H. Rönsch, *Itala und Vulgata*, a work dealing specifically with the Latinity of the Vetus Latina and Vulgate of the Bible. In addition, several volumes in the series "Aus der Geschichte der Lateinischen Bibel" (Freiburg, vols. 1-21, 1957-1992) supplied useful information. In the syntactical part, my model has been *Syntaxe latine* by A. Ernout and F. Thomas, in the stylistic part Szantyr's "Stilistik" (in Volume II of the Latin Grammar by Hofmann-Szantyr).

In the following pages the term "Vulgar Latin" will be frequently used[1]. I use this term to refer to that form of written Latin that is influenced to a certain extent by the rules of colloquial Latin; these influences may concern the domains of phonetics, morphology, the lexicon, syntax and style. It must be distinguished from other written forms of Latin such as late and Christian Latin, although these forms of Latin often underwent similar influences. My use of the terms "classical", "classical Latin", etc., refers to the regular usage of Latin prose writers of the first centuries B.C.E. and C.E. such as Cicero, Caesar, Sallust, Livy and Curtius Rufus.

---

[1] I am well aware that this term is ambiguous, but see Väänänen, pp. 3-6.

I. PHONOLOGY AND ORTHOGRAPHY

a. *Vowels*

1. In the course of their history, the vowels of Latin have undergone great changes. These were caused by a process whereby the opposition between vowels, originally based on duration, changed to an opposition based on timbre.

    Thus, the opposition /ī/::/ĭ/[1] became /i/::/ę̣/ (compare Latin *vivo*, *bibo* with Italian *vivo*, *bevo*), and /ē/::/ĕ/ became /ę̣/::/ę̧/. An important consequence of this is that the opposition /ĭ/::/ē/ disappeared altogether: both became /ę̣/.

    Similarly, the timbre-based opposition distinguishing former /ŏ/ and /ō/ as /ǫ/ and /o/, and that of former /ŭ/ and /ū/ as /o/ and /u/ made the opposition /ō/::/ŭ/ disappear, both becoming /o/ (Väänänen §§ 42-45).

    Of course, not all these changes took place at the same time or pace in the whole Latin speaking world, or at the same level of society. Furthermore, Latin literature (apart from epigraphical documents) resisted the influence of spoken Latin for a very long time.

2. The most common confusion of vowels in As. Mos. is that between w e a k *e* a n d *i*, especially in present and future tense verb-endings (third and fourth conjugations), forms which were in general subject to confusion (cf. Väänänen § 55, and see nr. 94).

    In As. Mos. there are four instances of the second person singular future tense endings written as *-is* instead of the classical *-es*: *agis* 10:10; *benedicis* 2:2; *discedis* 11:4; *reponis* 1:17. Three

---

[1] The classification of the vowels used here is rather rough and serves to indicate only the pertinent opposition (opposition is denoted by "::"). The slashes indicate that the letters included indicate sounds, not characters. A point under a phoneme denotes its "closed" pronunciation (e.g., Eng. /mǫnk/), opposed to an "open" pronunciation, indicated by the comma-like sign under a vowel (e.g., Eng. /mǫst/; "open" and "closed" refer, in a crude way, to the relative aperture of the mouth).

times,the classical spelling -*es* is used: *ascendes* 10:8; *cognosces* 10:10; *dimittes* 2:2.

There are fifteen to seventeen instances of the third person singular future tense endings written as -*it* instead of -*et*: *convertit* 10:5; *crucifigit* 6:9; *decedit* 10:6; *dimittit* 4:6; *ducit* 3:3; *elidit* 6:3; *expandit* 4:1; *exurgit* 10:7; *incendit* 6:9; *mittit* 4:6; *occidit* 6:4; *ponit* 4:1; *succedit* 6:2; *surgit* 5:1; *suspendit* 8:1; cf. *producit* 6:7 l. em.; *tradit* 8:2 l. em. Fifteen to nineteen times, the classical spelling -*et* is used: *adveniet* 8:1; *ducet* 4:3; *eiciet* 3:3; *faciet* 4:5; 6:6; 10:9; *fiet* 11:18; *incendet* 3:2; *parcet* 6:4; *perdet* 10:7; *teget* 3:1; *tollet* 3:2; *veniet* 3:1; 10:7; *volet* 5:6; cf. *dicet* 9:1 l. em.; *exurget* 10:3 l. em.; *figet* 2:4 l. em.; *sepeliet* 6:3 l. em.

There are no instances in As. Mos. of the inverse phenomenon in verb-endings[1]. For *conspiges* 10:10 instead of *conspicis* or *conspicies*, see nr. 10.

3.   The phenomenon occurs not only in verb-endings, but also in the following instances:

—*e* instead of *i*, protonic: twice *contegerunt* instead of *contigerunt* 9:3; 12:7[2]. Possibly, *descendent* stands for *discedent* in 2:3; *discendere*, *descendere* and *discedere* are frequently confused in all sorts of Latin manuscripts (including those containing classical texts)[3]. In As. Mos. 2:3, it is not certain which word is meant: both *descendere* and *discedere* are difficult to fit into the context; see further the commentary on 2:3;

—*e* instead of *i*, posttonic: *occidentes* 6:8, a singular genitive (instead of *occidentis*);

---

[1] This suggests that the substitution of *i* for *e* reflects a "genuine phonetic change"; see Adams, *The Vulgar Latin*, pp. 18-19.

[2] Cf. *ThLL* V,1, col. 712:58-60.

[3] *ThLL* V,1, col. 641:58-60 quotes the grammarian Caper (late 2nd c.A.D.): "*discendit dicimus, non descendit*", and adds: "sed admodum frequenter in libris permutatur et cum hoc verbo et cum *discedere*"; cf. Haussleiter, "Die lateinische Apokalypse", p.60: "Anspruch auf Beachtung erhebt das ungemein häufige discendere für descendere", and Rönsch, *Itala und Vulgata*, pp. 458-459, 463-464; see further the manuscript variants *discedere*//*descendere* of the Vulgate in Gen. 26:17; 1 Sam. 15:6. The extent of the confusion can be explained by the fact that in many cases the two words are near-synonyms. *Discedere* is confused with other words as well, which also have related meanings, e.g. Matt. 14:13 (cod. *k*) *disecessit* (from *descindere*); see *ThLL* V,1, col. 1275:59.

—*i* instead of *e*, posttonic[1]: perhaps the plural nominative *chortis* 6:8 1. em.; perhaps also the genitive *Fynicis* 1:4, if this is not the singular genitive of the adjective *Fynix* (see further nrs. 111 and 196).

4.   In hiatus, *e* and *i* are weakened, both sounding as the consonant /y/ (Väänänen § 76). This sound is occasionally represented by an *i* instead of the classical *e* (and not the other way around; cf. nr. 2): *liena* 3:4 (for *leaena*; see further nr. 8), *transio* (for *-eo*) 1:15 and *scalciati* 11:12 (for *-eati* [2]).

5.   Because of regressive assimilation (Leumann I, p. 101) the *o* in *diabolus* has become *u* in *zabulus* 10:1 (for the *z* in *zabulus*, see nr. 15)[3].

6.   Weak posttonic *u* is written *o* in *misereator* 4:6[4].

7.   The grapheme *y* normally occurs in Greek loanwords (*abyssus* 10:6; *Aegyptius* 6:6; *Aegyptus* 3:11; *Moyses* 1:4, 5; 3:11; 11:1; *tyrannus* 2:3). In *Fynicis* 1:3, the *y* is probably a transcription of a Greek υ as well; in Greek, the confusion of οι and υ occurs regularly[5]. The *y* is written as *i* in *allofilorum* 4:3 only (cf. *acrobistiam* 8:3 1. em. rendering -βυστια-).

8.   At an early stage, /ae/ was m o n o p h t h o n g i z e d   as /ę/ (Väänänen § 59), which development is exceptionally represented in As. Mos. in the spelling of classical *ae* as *e*: *Amorreorum* 11:16

---

[1] In the case of the ablative of *ignis*, the uncertainty between *-e* and *-i* has existed since classical Latin. In later Latin, the form tends progressively to be *igne* instead of earlier *igni* (conforming to the consonant paradigm); cf. *ThLL* VII, col. 288:55-73: the Vulgate uses 76 times *igne* and 82 times *igni*; in As. Mos. we find twice *igne* (3:2; 8:4) and once *igni* (6:9).

[2] Cf. codex *k* Matt. 10:10 *calciamento* (Hoogterp §10,8).

[3] Cf. Leumann I, pp. 85-86, on the weakening of *-ol* - before a vowel to *-ul-*.

[4] Haussleiter, "Die lateinische Apokalypse", p. 61: "Die Übergang von *u* in *o* tritt sehr häufig in der kurzen paenultima mehrsilbiger Wörter ein"; however, he also quotes an example of this phenomenon in the last syllable: *proeliator* ("er kämpft"). Schuchardt, *Der Vokalismus* II, pp. 167-168 mentions 18 examples of the 3rd person singular passive ending written as *-tor*, one of which, in a 7th century codex, is *missereator*.

[5] See Schuchardt, *Der Vokalismus* II, pp. 278-287, "Die Schreibung OE=Υ u.s.w.", p. 283: "Griech. οι hat sich in υ verwandelt (...) in Inschriften und Handschriften sehr häufig Υ = OI: εὔμυρος, κάρυνον, ῥυκός, σχῦνος, φυνίσσα"; cf. Volkmar, *Mose Prophetie*, p. 17. Rönsch, "Die Leptogenesis", p. 89, quotes from Numb 28:5 in the Vetus Latina ms 100 (siglum according to Fischer, *Vetus Latina* 2: Genesis, pp. 5*-7*) *yfi* = οἰφί.

(cf. 11:11 l. em.); *herere* (instead of *haerere*) 10:9; *liena* 3:4; *que* 11:4 (cf. *que* 10:13 l. em.); *scene* (instead of *scenae*) 1:7[1].

9.   The same process is illustrated by some over-correct spellings *faciae* 11:18; *inconpraehensibilis*[2] 11:16; *praeces* 11:17; *quaerella*[3] 1:10; *quisquae* 5:6.

10. In hiatus, vowels of the same timbre (*-ii-, -ie-, -uu-, -uo-*) are c o n t r a c t e d (Väänänen § 74).

In As. Mos. this is graphically represented in the verb-endings of *nutrit* 11:9; *recipit* 11:5; *respicit* 1:18 (classical: *-iet*). The alternative way to express the contracted sound in hiatus (with *e* instead of *i*) is found in *conspiges* (instead of *-cies*) 10:10, unless this form represents the classical present tense *conspicis* (on *g* instead of *c* see nr. 22).

11. This contraction is found also in the declinational endings *Aegypti* 6:6 (instead of *-ii*), *profetis* 3:11 (instead of *-iis*) and *tribum* 3:6 (instead of *-uum*).

12. An over-correct form is *patruum* 4:8 (classical: *patrum*).

13. When in classical Latin two vowels of the same timbre are separated by *h* (which then serves as an indicator of diaeresis, not of aspiration; see further nrs. 17-18), they are in hiatus as well, and therefore contracted, as may be seen in *prendit* 12:2 (contraction of *prehendit*), but cf. *inconpraehensibilis* 11:16, retaining *h*). Cf. *chortis* 6:8 l. em., for *cohortes*[4]. *Mihi* 10:15; 11:15; 12:7 and *nihil* 12:4 retain the *h*.

14. The development of prothetic *i-* before a word beginning with *s* + consonant (e.g., *spiritus* becoming *ispiritus*) has led inversely to the a p h a e r e s i s of /ek/ before *s* in initial position (Väänänen §§ 82-83): *scalciati* 11:12 (instead of *excalceati*; see further nr. 4);

---

[1] In the case of *scene*, one could argue that *ae* is twice represented as *e* (classical: *scaenae*). The classical *scaena* ("scene") is a loanword with a secondary *ae* (see Leumann I, p. 68). But in As. Mos., the Gr. σκηνή, usually translated as *tabernaculum*, is probably transliterated anew, independently of the earlier, classical transliteration.

[2] In this word, *-prae-* could also be an etymological spelling (Leumann I, pp. 106, 119).

[3] *Quaerella* is written with *ae* as well in the bilingual codex Boernerianus (Greek: ms G[P]; Latin: ms *g*) 1 Thess 2:10 (Rönsch, "Die Doppelübersetzungen", *ZWT* 26, p. 313).

[4] *Cors* or *chors* is a frequently occurring variant of *cohors*; see *ThLL* III, col. 1549:79-1550:32.

sculpent 2:9 (instead of *exculpent*)[1]. Rönsch suggested[2] that in 6:3, the manuscript's *singuli et* should be restored to *stinguet*, that is: *extinguet*; see further commentary on 6:3.

b. *Consonants*

15. The process in colloquial Latin and Roman of p a l a t a l i z a -
t i o n - a s s i b i l a t i o n (which caused the development of for
instance /ki/ to /tʃi/ in Italian and /si/ in French, Väänänen § 95) is
graphically realized in As. Mos. in *zabulus* 10:1[3]. In Greek, a
parallel development δια– > ζα– occurred[4]. Therefore, the possibility cannot be ruled out that *zabulus* reflects a Greek form.

16.   The assibilation of *c* preceding *e* or *i* is a late development[5].
Therefore *ch* in *chedriare* 1:17 probably is a hyperurban spelling
or popular etymology (Leumann I, p. 161; cf. Väänänen § 103),
and is not intended to indicate the pronunciation /k/ of *c* before *e*,
as it does in Italian.

17. The letter *h* served primarily in Latin to mark d i a e r e s i s
(Väänänen § 101), as in *Istrahel* 3:7; 10:8, possibly also *Abraham*
3:9[6].

18.   Possibly, the *h* is over-correct in *abhis* 11:9. The translator or
copyists of As. Mos. must have had great difficulty with the verb
ire and its compounds (see nr. 96). One may compare Haussleiter,
"Die lateinische Apokalypse", p. 68, who quotes *habiit* and *habii*
for *abiit* and *abii*; also, there are many examples of *hii* instead of
ii in Jubilees[7], which shows that the use of very short words

---

[1] In the manuscript, the *s* of *sculpent* is written at the end of a line, and *culpent* is written on the following line. Because of this, Rönsch, "Sprachliche Parallelen", p. 88, suggested that this *s* was long, long enough to be treated as a syllable.

[2] "Sprachliche Parallelen", pp. 88-89.

[3] In Jubilees, as well, it is restricted to one instance: *Lydia* instead of *Luza*, 32:5 (Rönsch, "Die Leptogenesis", p. 75). *Zabulus* or *zabolus* (see nr. 5) instead of *dia-* occurs very often indeed (*ThLL* V,1, col. 940:65-80).

[4] Schwyzer, *Griechische Grammatik* I, p. 330.

[5] The earliest datable witnesses are from the fifth century C.E. (Leumann I, p. 152).

[6] Fischer, "Limitations", p. 372, leaves open whether the *h* in *Johannes* is an instance of diaeresis, or "whether a remembrance of Jewish origins in the Hebrew comes into play here".

[7] Rönsch, "Die Leptogenesis", p. 75, quotes four examples, which Denis-Janssens, *Concordance latine du liber Jubilaeorum*, list under *hic*, interpreting the form *hii* as a hyperurban gemination, instead of *hi*, which is equally possible. Cf., however, Hofmann-Szantyr II, p.

(cont.)

extinct in colloquial Latin has caused similar difficulties in other
texts. On the other hand it is possible that the *h* is used here to
mark the correct separation of the two syllables (*ab-is*, not *a-bis*).

19.   The *h* marks a s p i r a t i o n in the Greek loanword *heremus*
3:11 (which aspiration is without ground in Greek and' may be
seen as hyperurban, Väänänen § 103). It is absent in the transliteration *tlibsis* (θλίψις) 3:7 l. em., but does occur in *cathedra* 12:2.

        The urban spelling of -ρρ- as -*rrh*- (Leumann I, p. 140) is not
used in *Amorreus* 11:16; cf. 11:11 l. em.

20.   *Ph* is consistently written as *f* (Väänänen § 102).

21.   I n t e r v o c a l i c *b* becomes fricative (Väänänen § 107) and is
written *v* in *provatus* 12:9 (contrast *probatus* 1:6), but mainly in
future tense verb-endings (cf. nr. 2): *altavit* 10:9; *audevit* 11:7;
conturvavitur 10:5; *intravit* 4:1; *oravit* 4:1; *putavimus* 7:8; *suscitavit* 8:1; *vindicavit* 10:2; *vindicavitur* 9:7; cf. *punivit* 6:6 l. em.
To this phenomenon must be added intervocalic *rb* becoming *rv* in
acervus[1] 6:5; 11:4 and *conturvavitur* 10:5. The classical spellings
with *b*, however, are far in the majority.

        The inverse phenomenon (*b* written instead of *v*, for instance
in perfect tense endings) does not occur in As. Mos.

22.   Intervocalic *c* is voiced to /g/ (Väänänen § 104; Hoogterp,
Etude § 29,2); confusion of *c* and *g* occurs rarely: *conspiges* 10:10
(see further nr. 10); *necantes* 6:2. It should be noted, however,
that the uncial letters *c* and *g* are nearly identical.

23.   The g e m i n a t i o n of *l* in *quaerella* 1:10 (classical: *querela*; cf.
nr. 9) is perhaps dialectical, but the spelling -*ll*- is problematic in
general (Väänänen § 110); cf. also *anullo* 12:9 l. em. Gemination
occurs frequently in Jubilees (Rönsch, *Jubiläen*, p. 445), e.g.: *se-*

186, and Haussleiter, "Die lateinische Apokalypse", p. 63, who gives from the African MSS
of Revelation the following examples: *his* (= *is*) *qui* (4:3; 7:15; 22:11); *hii* (=*ii*) (7:13; 17:13;
22:6, 11); and even: *hiis qui* = *his qui* = *eis qui* (2:9 in various MSS). Haussleiter (by the way
considering the aspiration to be phonetically real) concludes "dass hiis und hii nicht von hic,
sondern von is abzuleiten sind".

    [1] Haussleiter, "Die lateinische Apokalypse", p. 63, cites two African MSS of Rev. 6:13, in
which *acervos* is written for *acerbos*. See also the Greek transcription of *cervical* in Hermas
and elsewhere as κερβικάριον (Hilhorst, *Sémitismes*, pp. 165-168; p. 166: "Il est courant, à
cette époque, de rendre *v* ... par β"). See also Boyce, *The Language of the Freedmen*, p. 44.
Priest's attempt, "Testament of Moses", p. 930, to translate *acervus* in 6:5 as "to be heaped"
is rather curious. In 11:4, he simply (and correctly) translates *acervus* with "bitter".

pellire 19:4; *cottidie* 32:8; *nurrus* 41:5; *Sarra* 16:10; *Charran* 27:15.

24.   The gemination of *v* in *Levvi* 9:1 (cf. Jub. *passim* and *Evveus* Jub. 30:2) is not necessarily a direct, orthographic Hebraism (לוּוִי ?), since the spelling Λευυί is not unusual in Septuagint manuscripts either (where, in its turn, it may of course be a Hebraism).

25.   As often in later Latin texts, the a s s i m i l a t i o n   of prefixes tends to be graphically undone (Väänänen § 113: "notation inverse ou étymologique"). But the "recomposite" forms, having no ground in the colloquial language, only occur with words that are recognized as composites. Recomposition occurs in *adferre* 2:6; *adfirmatio* 3:13; *adpropiare* 5:1; *adtendere* 12:3; *inconpraehensibilis* 11:16; *inmundus* 7:9; 9:2; *inponere* 5:4; *improperium* 3:6; cf. *disdonare* 8:3 l. em.; *inprecari* 12:6 l. em.

        Not recomposed are *acceptio* and *accipere* 5:5; *exurgere* (classical: *exsurgere*) 6:1; 10:7 (cf. *exurget* 10:3 l. em.); *immolare* 2:8; *immolatio* 4:8; *imperare* 6:1, 7; *impietas* 6:1; *impius* 5:6; 7:3, 7; 9:3; 11:17; *improbus* 6:2; *improperium* 3:6; *occidere* 6:4, 8; 7:7; *succedere* 6:2; *successor* 10:15.

        Partial assimilation in *auferre* 12:5 is not recomposed.

26.   Two words appear with a recomposite form and with the classical form (*adcedent* 2:7 vs. *accedent* 5:3; the difference in meaning is probably coincidental; *implere* 5:6; 10:2 vs. *inplebuntur* 10:8).

27.   In *plebs* 1:4 the etymological spelling with *b* occurs (as it does in classical texts, but many Vulgar Latin texts have *pleps*). The etymological spelling with *b* in *scribtura* 1:16[1] (but cf. *verba ... scripta in sua scriptura* 11:1) is vulgar. Even a Greek loan word, θλίψις (from θλίβειν), has a *b* in the Latin transliteration *tlibsis* 3:7 l. em.

28.   The forms *adducti sumus* 3:5 and *adducetur* 10:1 reflect the apparent assimilation of the prefix *ab-* to *ducere*; in these instances, *adducere* must mean "to lead off" (cf. Ernout-Thomas §

---

[1] Cf. Jub. 30:21 *scribsi*, 49:17 *scribtum* (Rönsch, "Die Leptogenesis", p. 74; Haussleiter, "Die lateinische Apokalypse", p. 62: "In der Verbalbildung widerstrebt die Gruppe *bt* der Assimilation"; his examples are *scribtura, scribtum* and *scribsi*.

90)[1]. In the Vulgate New Testament, ἀπάγειν is three times translated by *adducere* (Matt. 27:2; Mark 14:53; John 18:13)[2], whereas this translation is found in several manuscripts of the Vetus Latina six times out of fourteen in the Gospels alone (Matt. 27:2; Mark 14:44, 53; Luke 22:66; John 18:13; 19:16).

29. Because of n a z a l i s a t i o n , the *n* in *-ns-* preceded by a vowel was lost in pronunciation at a very early stage[3], but it was restored (in writing, possibly in speech, as well) by the urbane in the classical period[4]. In Vulgar Latin texts this has given rise to a flood of over-correct forms (Väänänen § 121). In As. Mos. we find from 11:2 on *Moyses* consistently written as *Monses*, as in Jubilees (Rönsch, *Jubiläen*, p. 445).

30.   The insertion of an *n* occurs most often before *s*, but it also occurs before non-assibilized *t* and *ct* (Rönsch, *Itala und Vulgata*, pp. 458 f.; Väänänen § 119); cf. *ducent* 6:9 instead of *ducet* l. em. In 2:3, *-end-* in *descendent* is written instead of *-ed-* of the normally expected *discedent*[5].

31. The cluster *sr* is impossible in Latin (disregarding recomposite spellings, *dis-* in compounds lost its *s* before *r*[6]). Therefore, the e p e n t h e s i s of *d* in *Isdrahel* is very common (Rönsch, *Itala und Vulgata*, pp. 459-460). The epenthesis of *t* in *Istrahel* 3:7; 10:8 is less common and considerably older than the spelling with *d* (Rönsch, "Worauf beruht die Italaform").

32.   The *p* in the spelling of *temptare* (9:4) must be considered the result of epenthesis as compared to the classical spelling *tentare*. In fact, this classical form *tentare* is an over-correct spelling of a historically correct *temptare* (Leumann I, p. 215; cf. pp. 221-222). In other words, the vulgar way of spelling returns to the original word form.

---

[1] Cf. the revealing remark in Niermeyer, *Lexicon*, p.1a: "**ab-** in compositis, v. etiam ad-".

[2] Twice, it is translated by *abducere*, in the remaining thirteen instances by other verbs, mostly other compounds of *ducere*.

[3] Cf. the transcription Κλήμης for Clemens in Hermas (see Hilhorst, *Sémitismes*, pp. 165-168).

[4] This *n* is absent both in ancient Latin and in Vulgar Latin texts; see Leumann I, p. 145.

[5] On the frequent confusion of *discedere* and *descendere*, see note to nr. 3.

[6] Leumann I, p. 204.

33. One could consider the possibility that the manuscript's reading *clibsis* 3:7 (*tlibsis* l. em.) is due to phonetics, and not to textual corruption: as a rule, original *tl* became *cl*, in Greek loan-words as well as in proper Latin words (where the group *tl* arose mainly from syncope of *-tul-*, Leumann I, pp. 153-154). However, this development is known only from intervocalic instances, and there seem to be no analogies for *tl* > *cl* in initial position. Furthermore, the scribal confusion of *c* and *t* is a common phenomenon (also in As. Mos.; see the apparatus to *intentionem* l. em. line 15), and the word *tlibsis* may have become unknown to later scribes, so that a textual corruption is more likely.

34. Although f i n a l *- m* a n d *- s* are not pronounced in spoken Latin (Väänänen §§ 127-128), they are retained in literary Latin. Sometimes in As. Mos., especially in case-endings, a final *-m* or *-s* is missing, or, inversely, mistakenly added[1]. This is rare, however, and may in most instances be ascribed to the textual transmission, e.g., to the omission or accidental addition of an abbreviation marker; so *colonia* 3:2. The cause of corruption is still clearer in *qui̲d̲e̲m̲ d̲i̲e̲m̲* 11:11; *tamqua̲m̲ fili̲a̲m̲ domin̲a̲m̲ virgin̲e̲m̲* 11:12; *zabulus finem habebit et tristitiam* 10:1. Finally, we find in a corrupt context *bonam* 12:11. All these instances have been emended in my edition.

35. From a very early stage on, f i n a l *- t* a n d *- d* are confused, especially in the words *apud/aput* and *ad/at* (Väänänen § 131). In As. Mos. we find *ad* (second instance) for *at* in 10:6[2].

---

[1] This kind of mistake is not due to the confusion of accusative and ablative after a preposition; see nr. 80.

[2] Many examples in *ThLL* II, col. 992:46-59; Stone, *The Language*, p. 20: *ad* is "almost universally used" for *at* in the Codex Bezae. On the causes of this confusion, see Adams, *The Vulgar Latin*, pp. 27-28.

II. WORDS

a. *Vulgar and Late Latin Idiom*

36. The use of typical Vulgar Latin words caused by "p s y c h o -
l o g i c a l factors", i.e., a preference for longer and more powerful words (often compounds; Väänänen §§ 140-163), is limited
in As. Mos. Words like *ire, edere, scire, magnus* are often used,
while words as *fabulare, sapere, caballus* and the like, as well as
diminutives are avoided[1]. A few words, however, definitely belong to this category: *bajulare* 8:4 (instead of *ferre*); *currere*
11:12 (instead of *ire* or *gradiri*); *se ducere* 3:4 (instead of *abire*,
but cf. *abhis* 11:9[2]); *factare* 3:9 (instead of *facere*)[3]; *plorare* 3:6, 8;
11:2 (instead of *flere*); cf. *donare* in the compound *disdonare* 8:3
l. em.

37. The following words are vulgar neologisms, used virtually exclusively by Christians, without having a specifically Christian
meaning[4]: *adpropiare* 5:1, *fornicari* 5:3.

38. From an early stage, Latin adopted Greek l o a n w o r d s. A
number of Greek loan words found in As. Mos. were already cur-
rent in classical Latin: *cathedra* 12:2; *idolum* 2:8, 9; 8:4; 10:7;
tyrannus 2:3. However, *idolum* has a meaning influenced by Hellenistic Jewish and Christian usage: "idol".

39.   In late and Vulgar Latin, the number of Greek loan words
greatly increased (Väänänen § 167). *Propheta*, or *profetes* as in
As. Mos. 11:16, is a post-classical loan word. Jewish and Christian
authors naturally adopted more Greek words. Apart from names
derived from Greek, such as *Moyses* and *Deuteronomium*, a considerable number of such Greek loan words is found in As. Mos.:

---

[1] On *ire*, see nr. 96.

[2] *ThLL* V,1, col. 2146:20-45 mentions As. Mos. 3:4 as the sole instance in which *se du-cere* would mean *se gerere*, "to behave", "to conduct oneself". However, the ordinary vulgar use of *se ducere* for "to go" makes excellent sense in this instance, too.

[3] *ThLL* VI,1, col. 140:9-16 mentions five instances of *factare*, including As. Mos. 3:9.

[4] Mohrmann, *Etudes* III, pp. 38, 105.

abyssus 10:6[1]; *allofilus*[2] 4:3; *blasfemare*[3] 8:5; *heremus*[4] 3:11; *profetia* 1:5; 3:11; *zabulus* 10:1; perhaps also *tlibsis* 3:11[5].

40.   This must be compared to Latin words with a meaning borrowed from Greek influenced by the Hebrew scriptures: *confiteri* + dative "to praise" 10:10 (contrast *confiteri* + accusative "to confess" 8:1); probably *saeculum* "world"[6] 4:2; 11:16.

b. *Word-formation*

41.   In chapter 7, the author of As. Mos. describes men of low moral standards. His description is hateful without reserves. It is not surprising, therefore, that in the Latin version of As. Mos. 7 a concentration of vulgarisms is found (cf. the footnote to *gula* 7:4 in nr. 50). The translator has chosen word-formations in this chapter that reflect colloquial usage. Thus, the derivation of *nomina agentis* using the suffix *-tor* was common in all stages of the Latin language (Väänänen § 174), but the following words in As. Mos. belong to the more recent, vulgar ones: *comestor* 7:6; *devorator* 7:4; *exterminator* 7:5.

Also, adjectives in *-osus* are known from classical literature (so *contumeliosus* 8:5), but enjoyed great popularity in Vulgar Latin (Väänänen § 186: "indique surtout l'abondance d'une substance ou d'une caractéristique"). This suffix is relatively often used in As. Mos. 7, where wicked men are described as "full of" all kinds of vices: *dolosus* 7:4; *pestilentiosus* 7:3; cf. *quaerulosus* 7:7 l. em.; perhaps also *questuosus* 7:6 l. em. (see the commentary).

---

[1] Mohrmann, *Etudes* III, p. 206: "C'est un de ces mots qui, de par leur caractère biblique, ont obtenu de bonne heure une nuance solennelle et presque sacrée. Aussi *abyssus* se rencontre hors de la bible surtout dans la poésie chrétienne".

[2] *ThLL* I, col. 1692:18-19.

[3] *ThLL* II, col. 2045:24-25: "in scripturis sacris, hinc passim ap. Eccl. inde a Tert.".

[4] Rönsch, *Itala und Vulgata*, p. 242; Hoogterp, *Etude*, pp. 227-228; Mohrmann, *Etudes* III, p. 61.

[5] *Tlibsis* or *thlipsis* does not occur very often; yet it seems that it was generally understood, especially in the earlier days of Latin Christendom, before it was ousted by *tribulatio* (cf. As. Mos. 4:9). It is used by Lucifer († 317); *thlibomeni* is known from the Cyprianic correspondance (8, 3, 1); see Mohrmann, *Etudes* III, p. 123.

[6] For *saeculum* meaning "world" in Christian Latin literature, see Orbán, *Les dénominations du monde*, pp. 174-192.

42.   A late Latin formation, based on the Greek of the scriptures, occurring in As. Mos. is *creatura*[1] 1:2, 13; 10:1; 12:4.

The older formation *tribulatio* 4:9, attested in Cato, was very popular among Christians as an equivalent of θλίψις, until it was eliminated as a vulgarism in the fourth century[2].

43.   The following words are rare v e r b a l   d e r i v a t i o n s of nouns, formed by affixing verbal endings *-are* or *-iare* (Väänänen § 191): *adpropiare* 5:1[3]; *altare* 10:9[4]; *chedriare* 1:17, from κέ–δρος, the only instance of the verb in the *Thesaurus* (*ThLL* III, col. 735:38-39); possibly also *factare* 3:9, derived from *factum* (according to Lewis and Short, p. 781c, *factare* is a frequentative formation).

44.   C o m p o u n d s are used with the meaning of the simplex words (Väänänen § 204) in the following instances: *constabilire* 2:2 (used for variation, standing in the immediate vicinity of *stabilire*; see nr. 167); *invocare* 4:2 ("to call", i.e., "give a name"; cf. Heb. 11:16); *pervendere* 5:5 (Rönsch, *Itala*, pp. 205-206); *referre* 4:8 ("to bring").

45.   In As. Mos. 10:4-5, in a passage which describes the disruption of the natural order as a result of the appearance of God, many verbs are compounded with the prefix *con-*, apparently to express the all-embracing character of the changes described: *usque ad fines suas [terra] concutietur* 10:4; *alti montes ... concutientur* 10:4; *in tenebris convertent se cornua lunae et confringentur, et tota convertit se in sanguine; et orbis stellarum conturvavitur* 10:5. Possibly, the word for "valley" in 10:5, *convallis*, was compounded for the same reason[5].

---

[1] *ThLL* IV, cols. 1115:84-1117:51.

[2] Mohrmann, *Etudes* III, pp. 206-207.

[3] Rönsch, *Itala und Vulgata*, pp. 181-182.

[4] *ThLL* I, col. 1770:8-23; in Christian literature, the compound *exaltare* is much more common than this simplex; see Mohrmann, *Etudes* II, p. 121. Cf. the use of the simplex *parere* instead of *apparere* 10:1.

[5] In the old Latin versions of the Bible, *convallis* is often used in places where the Vulgate has *vallis*; see *ThLL* IV, col. 813:39-42, 71-74. Ancient grammarians assumed a difference in meaning between the two, but the sources using the words appear not to sustain that assumption; see *ibid.*, 18-19.

46.   In compounds, the prefixes *prae-* and *pro-* are frequently confused (Hofmann-Szantyr II, p. 269). In As. Mos. we find *praeposita fides* 4:8 instead of *proposita fides sua*, "the belief laid before them" (according to classical use, *praeposita fides* would mean something like "the belief in charge", or "the preferred belief"; see further commentary on 4:8); the reverse in *providere* 12:5 instead of *praevidere*[1], "to see beforehand" (cf. *praevidere* 12:4bis). Cf. *pronovit* 12:4 l. em.; *pronoscere* does not exist in Latin, but *praenoscere* has the meaning required in 12:4.

47.   In Latin influenced by the scriptures, the expression *bene dicere* + dative was used as a single, compound word (*benedicere* + accusative 2:2), meaning "to bless"[2].

48.   *Altaria*, "altar", was a p l u r a l e   t a n t u m   in earlier Latin, but the singular form *altarium* is frequently used in the old Latin versions of the Bible and by Christian writers[3]; in As. Mos. twice, 5:4 and 8:5.

       Cervices originally was a *plurale tantum*[4]. It was also used in the singular form (*cervix*), but in *ascendes supra cervices ... aquilae* 10:8 the original plural is used. That passage can simply be translated and explained as "you will mount on the eagle's neck".

       Either the singular *pars* 3:13 or the plural *partes* 6:8 may be used for "country"[5].

49.   In Christian Latin, it was customary to use the plural *caeli* to indicate "Heaven". However, in As. Mos. 3:8, 12; 10:9; 12:9, the classical singular is used.

c. *Change of Meaning*

50.   In late Latin, a number of words received a s p e c i a l i z e d meaning (Väänänen § 207). From As. Mos. the following may be

---

[1] So also in the Vulgate of Acts 2:31; Gal. 3:8.

[2] Mohrmann, *Etudes* III, p. 53, referring to Wölfflin, *Rheinisches Museum* 37, pp. 117 ff.

[3] *ThLL* I, col. 1725:17-19, 24-25: "apud auctores antiquiores non traditur nisi pluralis tam pro singulis quam pro compluribus altaribus ... *altarium, -i* in Itala et ap. christianos frequens."

[4] Löfstedt, *Syntactica* I, p. 31: "von Haus aus ... ein Plural". Cf. already Hilgenfeld, "Die Himmelfahrt des Moses", p. 617.

[5] Löfstedt, *Philologischer Kommentar*, p. 245; *Syntactica* II, pp. 440-442.

quoted: *colonia* 3:2; 5:6; 6:9 ("city")[1]; *confundere* 11:18 ("to destroy"[2]); *elidere* 6:3 ("to kill"); *exterminare* 12:8, 12; *exterminator* 7:7 ("to destroy", "destroyer"[3]); *gula* 7:4 ("glutton"[4]); *pars* and *partes* 3:13; 6:8 ("country"[5]).

The following words in As. Mos. are used with the special meaning they have in texts influenced by the Bible: *inponere* 5:4 ("to offer"[6]); *judicare* 6:2 ("to rule"[7]; in 11:15, *judicare* simply means "to administer justice"); *oratio* 11:14 ("prayer"[8]); *testamentum* passim ("covenant"[9]); *traductio* 9:2 ("rebuke"[10]).

51.   A g e n e r a l i z e d meaning (Väänänen § 208) is to be found in *fictus* 7:4 ("hypocrite"[11]); *ostium* 4:3 ("gate"[12]).

52.   *Facere* functioned as an "Universalverbum", that is, a verb which, according to the context, can be used with practically any meaning. Thus, we find: *testamentum facere* 4:2, 5; *impietatem facere* 6:1; *facere judicia* 6:6 (twice); *scelesta facere* 9:3.

With adverbs, it is used instead of *agere: facere sceleste* 2:9; *impie facere* 11:17.

In 5:2, *facere* possibly means "to say", as Löfstedt suggested[13]. In 3:7, *facere* also occurs: *Quid faciemus vobis, fratres?* Here, too, the meaning "to say" would suit the context very well: "What shall we say to you, brethren?".

---

[1] Cf. Friedländer, *Petronii Cena Trimalchionis*, p. 259: "Die Ausdrücke urbs und oppidum braucht keiner der Teilnehmer der Cena, sondern ausschließlich colonia (44, 55, 76) oder patria (76 u. 45), das sich schon hier abschwächt zu dem Begriff 'meine (unsre) Stadt'".

[2] *ThLL* IV, col. 263:55; Niermeyer, *Lexicon*, p. 245b.

[3] Niermeyer, *Lexicon*, p. 400b.

[4] The word is used with this meaning by Cicero, but clearly as an abusive term, which makes it likely that it is a colloquialism in this instance. See further *ThLL* VI, 2, col. 2357:12-19.

[5] Löfstedt, *Philologischer Kommentar*, p. 245.

[6] Rönsch, *Semasiologische Beiträge*, III, p. 46.

[7] *ThLL* VII, 2, 618:59-77.

[8] Rönsch, *Itala und Vulgata*, p. 319.

[9] Mohrmann, *Etudes* III, p. 113.

[10] So e.g. in the Vulgate of Wisd. 2:14 for ἐλεγμός; see further Rönsch, *Itala und Vulgata*, pp. 326-327, 383; *Semasiologische Beiträge*, I, p. 72; III, pp. 82-83.

[11] Rönsch, *Itala und Vulgata*, p. 338.

[12] *Ostium* meaning "gate" instead of "door" occurs several times in the Itala translations (both for πύλη and θύρα, *ThLL* IX,2, col. 1154:33-45), but is purged from the Vulgate, which uses *porta* for "gate". For *circa ostium* 4:3 meaning "at the gate" cf. Gen. 19:1 ולום סדם ישב בשער *Loth ... juxta ostium* Itala; for *circa = juxta*; cf. Deut. 31:14 *state circa* (παρά) *januas tabernaculi testimonii* Itala (Vulgate [with MT] *in tabernaculo*).

[13] *Philologischer Kommentar*, pp. 162-168.

Ponere in 2:4 is used in a similar universal way as *facere*, here meaning "to make" (cf. Greek τιθέναι, "much the same as ποιεῖν", Liddell and Scott, p. 1791b).

53. With f i g u r a t i v e meaning (Väänänen § 210): *circumcisio* 8:1 ("being Jewish"; see commentary on 8:1); *discubitio* 7:8; *dormitio* 1:15; 10:14 (a very usual euphemism for "death", Rönsch, "Sprachliche Parallelen", p. 82; *Itala und Vulgata*, p. 312). In Latin texts influenced by biblical idiom, the abstract *iniquitas* is often used for concrete "crimes", as in 5:3, 6; 7:7[1]. *Sepultura* ("burial") is used concretely as a synonym for *sepulcrum* ("grave") 11:6, 8[2].

d. *The Use and Meaning of the Pronouns*

54. Nominative forms of the p e r s o n a l p r o n o u n s are not generally used to express the subject, as they are in colloquial Latin (Väänänen § 281). In accordance with the classical usage, they are found only when the subject is emphasized: *ego autem* 10:14; *nam tu* 10:11; cf. *tu autem* 1:16 l. em. So also the contrast in 3:5 *Quia enim vos peccastis et* (=*etiam*; see nr. 140) *nos adducti sumus vobiscum*. This suggests that *tu* in 2:2; 11:4 should be understood emphatically as well.

55. For the third personal pronoun, *is* and *ille* are used (see further nr. 84).

56. *Is* is almost exclusively used as a personal pronoun. It is anaphoric only in *eam intentionem* 1:13 l. em. *Ille* has its classical demonstrative meaning in six instances (seven in the emended text); see further below, nr. 59.

57. With regard to p o s s e s s i v e p r o n o u n s, the distinction between *suus* and *ejus/eorum* is as a rule maintained. Twenty-three times, *suus* is used in reference to the formal subject of the clause in which it occurs.

In one instance, *cum audisset Jesus verba Moysi tam scripta in sua scriptura* 11:1, *sua* does not refer to the subject of the clause in which it occurs (cf. Väänänen § 284).

---

[1] Mohrmann, *Etudes* III, p. 213.
[2] Niermeyer, *Lexicon*, p. 960a.

Two instances, both in 8:5, are uncertain: (1) *et a torquentibus illos ... cogentur intrare in abditum locum eorum*; (2) *novissime post haec et leges quod habebunt* (1. em.) *supra altarium suum.* Exegesis requires that the *abditus locus* and the *altarium* are parts of the same sanctuary. However, although the subject is the same in both clauses, the pronouns referring to the subject are *eorum* and *suum* respectively.

In *omnibus enim morientibus ... sepulturae suae sunt in terris* 11:8, *suae* is redundant. The construction may be described as an anacoluthon ("For all those who die ... their graves are in the earth"), and *suae* as referring to the subject of the implicit clause ("Those who die, they have their graves in the earth").

58. *Hic* is used as a regular d e m o n s t r a t i v e p r o n o u n, adjectively or absolutely. In 7:4, *hi* comes close to being used as a personal pronoun (perhaps also *de his* 7:3).

59.   In adjuncts of time, *ille* is also used as a demonstrative pronoun: *illis temporibus* 3:1; 5:5; *temporibus illis* 3:13; 4:5; *usque ad illum tempus* 8:1; *die illo* 3:10; cf. *illo die* 9:1 l. em. Eight or nine times *illius* is used without antecedent, clearly referring, however, to God (1:14, 18; 3:12; 9:4; 10:1bis, 12; 12:13; perhaps also in 1:7). This pregnant use of *illius* is expressive of respect (as opposed to the unmarked *ejus*)[1]. The same is expressed by *ejusdem* in 10:15, and by *ipsius* in 12:7.

60.   *Ipse* is once, in the genitive, pregnantly used for God (12:7; cf. nr. 59), once (12:2) instead of *is*, but for the rest it still retains its contrasting function (four times).

61.   *Iste* is rare, but retains, apart perhaps from 11:14, its demonstrative meaning (without any negative connotation). In four out of five instances it is used in the speech of Joshua, in chap. 11, each time referring to Israel (though *hic* is used there as well). *De isto* 3:13 may mean "by him, sc. God" (so Clemen, *APAT* II, p. 322), but more probably means "since then" (see nr. 188).

62. In 5:6, the i n d e f i n i t e pronoun *quisquae* (classical: "everyone"; on orthography see nr. 9) possibly means "anyone whosoever" (see further the commentary). In that case, *quisque*

---

[1] For a comparable expressive use of a personal pronoun, cf. Ernout-Thomas § 215: "Chez les Comiques, dans le langage des esclaves, *ipse* désigne couramment le maître."

has been confused with *quisquis* (Ernout-Thomas § 219-220). In 2:2, *unusquisque* is used in accordance with classical rules.

63.　　*Quidam* 5:4 indicates, in the usual way, people whom the author knows, but whose identity he does not want to state more precisely ("certain people") (Ernout-Thomas § 219b).

e. *The Prepositions*

64. The preposition *a, ab* is frequently used in its classical meaning, denoting
    —the point of departure in space: 3:1, 9; 10:3, 10; 11:8bis;
    —the point of departure in time: 1:2; 7:7; 8:1 (first instance); 10:12; 12:4 (first instance); *ab initio* in 1:13, 14, 17 is best translated with "in" the beginning, so also in 2 Ki. 19:25; Judith 9:11; Wisd. 9:8; 14:13; Sir. 15:14; 24:14 and in many other instances.
    —with passive verbs the agent 1:5; 2:3; 8:3, 5; 12:4 (second instance), 9, 11.

65.　　Furthermore, *a, ab* is used:
    —to denote the person or matter injured by an action: *iniquitas a Deo* 5:6 and *impietas ab sancto sanctitatis* 6:11[1];
    —with verbs of defending or protecting against: *custodire a sole* 11:12; *vindicare ab inimicis* 10:2. In the Vulgate, *vindicare* in this meaning ("to take revenge on someone") is constructed with various prepositions, most often with *de*, e.g. Isa. 1:24 (*de inimicis*). Cf. however Lewis and Short, p. 4a *ulcisci se ab aliquo*.

66.　　In *potestas a potentia magna* 8:1, *a* + ablative has the function of the genitive of quality (Hofmann-Szantyr II, p. 71).

67. *Ad* is used in accordance with the classical standards to denote direction or aim.
    In compounds, the prefix *ad-* is confused with *ab-* (see nr. 28). Apparently, the final *b* of *ab* was sufficiently weak to cause confusions of the prepositions *ab* and *ad* as well. Instead of *abscedere ab*, we find *adcendere ad* 2:7[2]. Probably, *ad* has this meaning, too,

---

[1] *Iniquitas* and *impietas* are usually constructed with *in* (*ThLL* VII,1, col. 2092:21-26; see also *impie facere in Dominum* 11:17), sometimes with *adversus, contra* or *de*.

[2] In 5:3, which appears to be a quotation, *accedere ad* has the meaning one would expect it to have.

in *dividentur ad veritatem* 5:2 ("they will move away from the truth"; so *ThLL* IV, cols. 1604:15-17; 831:39-43 and 823:7-12; it is possible that the phrase means "they will be divided with regard to the truth"; see the commentary; cf. also Hoogterp, *Etude* § 438; Jub. 33:19 *adtendere ab*). In the textually difficult passage 11:12 *ad currendum* may have to be taken as *a currendo*; see the commentary.

68. The preposition *de* competes with the partitive genitive and with the prepositions *ex* and *ab* (Väänänen § 250).
—Its classical meaning, denoting provenance, is found in 6:2; 9:1 and 11:7.
—It has an instrumental meaning, like the classical *ab*, in *inquinare de muneribus* 5:4.
—It denotes a mediating agent in *ut detur illis de Jesum* 1:9[1]; *vindicta surgit de reges* 5:1.
—It is used with a verb of defending or protecting against (see nr. 65) in *celari de* 11:4.
—It is used to indicate separation, instead of *ex*, in *exire de* 10:3; 11:4; instead of *ab* or *ex* in *discedere de* 11:4[2]. As a preposition, *ex* occurs only once, *ex quo facto* 7:1.

69.   Rönsch, "Sprachliche Parallelen", pp. 93-96, explained the use of *de* in *dicentes tribus ad tribum, et homo de proximo suo* 3:10 as a mechanical translation of a Greek dative (τῷ πλησίον) that was mistaken for an instrumental dative. It must in any case be regarded as an instance of variation (see nr. 167).

70. The preposition *in* is normally used to denote position or direction (both locally, temporally and in analogy to the local and temporal uses). The cases are no longer used to differentiate between these two main meanings (see nr. 79).
    In denotes:
—the agent (= *ab*): *nam illi in eis punientur* 8:4;

---

[1] Clemen, *APAT* II, p. 319, noted the translation in cod. Corbeiensis (*ff*²) of Luke 11:24 διέρχεται δι' ἀνύδρων τόπων: *peraumbulat de loca quae non habent aquam.*
[2] *Discedere* with *de* does occur elsewhere, but is rare (Lewis-Short, p. 585c).

—the instrument used in an action: *punientur in tormentis* 8:4[1]; cf. *in Domini verbis judicare* 11:15 l. em.;

—the aim of an action (= *ad*, Väänänen § 359): *in sacerdotes summi Dei vocabuntur* 6:1;

—the result of an action or event: *magisteria locorum dimittes illis ... in judicio et justitia* 2:2; *in tenebris convertent se cornua lunae ... et tota convertit se in sanguine* 10:5;

—the person or matter injured by an action: *in omnem domum Istrahel advenit tlibsis* 3:7 l. em.; *adveniet in eos ultio* 8:1 l. em.; *judicia ... fecerunt in illis Aegypti* 6:6; *ultio facta est in plebe* 9:2; *populus impiorum in Dominum* 9:3; *impie facere ... in Dominum suum* 11:17;

—the cause or ground of a condition (= *propter*): *isti ... creverunt in tuis orationibus* 11:14; *non enim propter meam virtutem aut in firmitatem* 12:7.

71. It forms part of the adverbial expressions *in tantum* "so much" 11:14, and *in totum* (εἰς τέλος), "completely" 12:12.

72. To the construction of *plenus* with this preposition in *in scelere pleni et iniquitate* 7:7 compare ἐν τούτοις πλήρης 2 Clem. 16:4; πλήρης ἐν τῇ πίστει Hermas, *Mand.* V 2, 1; XII 5, 4.

73. *Per* denotes
—a mediating agent: *fieri per Moysen* 1:4; *intrare per te* 2:1;
—a lapse of time during which something takes place: *per annos* 2:3, 6; 6:6;
—the extension in space: *per orbem terrarum profetem* 11:16;
—the basis on which something is done: *per testamentum et per jusjurandum* 1:9;
—the one "by" whom one swears: *jurasti per te* 3:9.

74. *Circa* in *circa ostium allofilorum* 4:3 is used in its broad sense ("near, at"[2] or "towards", even "in"; cf. *ThLL* III, cols. 1084:68-1086:49; 1087:46-1088:6, 59-66; see further footnote to *ostium*, nr. 51; in 4:3, *circa* is used instead of *in* for the sake of variation; see nr. 167).

---

[1] This use of *in* emerged in late Latin from influence of the (Greek) biblical language; see Löfstedt, *Syntactica* II, pp. 452-454.

[2] Cf. Rönsch, *Jubiläen*, p. 449, who quotes Jub. 18:15 *harena quae est circa litora maris*; Vulgate of Mark 4:4 *et dum seminat, aliud cecidit circa viam*.

Possibly, but not necessarily, *circa* means "around" in *circa coloniam eorum* 6:9.

In *circa annos LXVII* 3:14, *circa* probably has its classical meaning "about 77 years", even if the combination of an exact figure with an adverb meaning "approximately" seems somewhat unnatural. Possibly, "77" is rather used as a perfect number than as an exact number of years (see further the commentary).

75. The preposition *coram*, "before", is obsolete in colloquial Latin. It is used in Christian Latin instead of *apud* especially with God. In translation literature it is often used as a translation of ἐνώπιον. In Biblical literature, *coram*/ἐνώπιον is occasionally used in a way which invites us to render it with "by". To the two instances quoted by Bauer, *Griechisch-deutsches Wörterbuch*, col. 547 (Proto-Gospel of James 20:3; Ps. Sol. 1:2), some may be added: Isa. 17:13; Jer. 18:17; Dan. 5:23 (Vulgate and Septuagint); Ps. Sol. 2:37 εὐλογητὸς κύριος εἰς τὸν αἰῶνα ἐνώπιον δούλων αὐτοῦ; cf. *a facie* Gen. 6:13; Isa. 7:2; Micah 1:4. A similar use of *coram* is probably found in As. Mos. 9:7 *sanguis noster vindicavitur coram Domino*, which must be understood as: "our blood will be avenged by God".

76. *Cum* is used in accordance with classical norms. In *incendet coloniam eorum igne cum aede sancta Domini* 3:2, *cum* means "including". *Cum* occurs enclitically in *secum* 3:3. *Inter*, in *ut ... inter se disputationibus arguant se* 1:13 is used to specify tautologically a reciprocal aspect. *Secus* is consistently used as a preposition (= *secundum*). *Usque* is with preference used in combination with *ad* (nine times), once with *in* (1:18). On its own, it occurs twice (1:4; 3:13).

77.   With regard to the other prepositions occurring in As. Mos. (*ante, apud, post, pro, sine, sub, supra*) no peculiarities are to be noted.

78. *Palam* 1:13, 15 (first instance); 8:4; 10:7 and *super* 7:9 are used adverbially. *Palam* 1:15 (second instance) may be a preposition, but the text is uncertain[1].

---

[1] Rönsch, *Itala und Vulgata*, p. 399.

III. FORMS

a. *Nouns*

79. In Vulgar Latin c a s e s were in the process of disappearing, mainly because of changes in the phonetic system. The weakness of the final consonants and the loss of opposition of most final vowels made it difficult to maintain the opposition of most declensional endings. For instance, the singular nominative, dative, accusative and ablative of the second declension were all phonetically similar or identical (e.g. /annu/ or /anno/). In order to maintain the functional distinctions, the case system was gradually replaced by a prepositional system, which was eventually to oust the genitive as well. At the beginning of the Romance period (around 600[1]), the case system was reduced to a diptote paradigm, consisting of the nominative and the accusative with prepositions (Väänänen §§ 242-243; a detailed account of this process is found in Grandgent-Moll, *Introducción* §§ 354-376).

80. As a result of the replacement of the case system by the prepositional system in spoken Latin, the cases after prepositions are regularly confused in written Latin.

   In As. Mos. the prepositions *ab, cum, de* and *sine* are followed by an accusative in: *a Moysen* 1:5; *cum indignationem et iram* 10:3; *de Jesum* 1:9; *de reges* 5:1[2]; *sine quaerellam* 1:10. The classical ablative is used with *ab* 26 times, with *cum* 15 times, and with *de* 11 times. *Sine* is attested with the ablative once (9:2).

   The preposition *in*, which can classically be constructed with either the accusative or the ablative, is constructed with both disrespecting the original difference in meaning. Two examples may suffice[3]: *ut in eam gentes arguantur* 1:13; *in tenebris convertent se cornua lunae* 10:5.

   The prepositions that are constructed with the accusative only are not attested in As. Mos. with the ablative. This confirms that

---

[1] Grandgent-Moll, *Introducción* § 3.

[2] The preposition *de* is in these instances used to denote the mediating agent (see nr. 68); perhaps the use of the accusative is influenced by the accusative with *per*.

[3] Many examples are given by Rönsch, *Itala und Vulgate*, pp. 406-412.

the direction of the uniformization of the oblique cases is towards the accusative.

81   The fourth and fifth declensions have visibly survived in *consummatio exitus* 1:18; *major natu* 6:4; *in respectu* 1:18; *omni hora diei* 7:4; *de tribu* 9:1; cf. *ad exitus VIIII* 7:2. The form *potui* in *potui et ciborum* 11:13 must be a genitive (classical: *potus*)[1].

82.   The noun *scenae* seems to be undeclined throughout. It occurs in one form only (a mere orthographic variant is *scene* 1:7; see nr. 8), even where syntax requires an accusative or ablative. *Scen(a)e* in 1:7 and 2:4 appear as a normal dative and genitive respectively; *ponent idola scenae* 2:8 could just be explained as a Grecism[2] (though in Greek, too, the omission of a preposition is strange); so could *in scenae* 1:8 (= ἐν σκηνῇ?). In *transferunt scenae testimonium* 2:4, which should logically have been *scenam* or *scenen testimonii*, the translator seems to have considered the two words as a stock phrase, and applied the accusative form to its second half, *scenae* simply remaining indeclined. Rönsch[3] wanted to translate literally "the testimony of the tabernacle" and adduced two parallels[4]: six codices of the Vulgate read *testimonium tabernaculi* in Ex. 30:20, and thirty-three manuscripts *coram testimonio tabernaculi* in Ex. 30:26. However, apart from the word-order, which differs from that in As. Mos., the instances quoted by Rönsch are equivalents of εἰς τὴν σκηνὴν τοῦ μαρτυρίου and ἐν τῇ σκηνῇ τοῦ μαρτυρίου respectively. This shows that, in the course of the transmission in Latin, mistakes with these two words were made more than once. In As. Mos. a further instance of this type of error may be *finis habitationes* in the large dittography 5:6, which has the correct forms *fines habitationis*, as well. However, this may also be a phonological confusion (cf. nr. 3). In Jub. 19:5, the place of Sarah's grave is called *agrum spelei duplicem* (cf. 19:6 *in speleo duplici*).

---

[1] *ThLL* X,2, col. 366:47-49 mentions three examples of this form, among which As. Mos. 11:13. Of the two remaining forms, one is uncertain.

[2] So Hilgenfeld, "Die Psalmen Salomo's", p. 281: τῇ σκηνῇ.

[3] "Xeniola theologica", p. 548-549

[4] "Xeniola theologica (Fortsetzung)", p. 443.

83. The p r o p e r   n a m e s *Abraham, Isaac* and *Jacob* (3:9), are not declined. *Nave*, the name of Joshua's father, occurs only in a genitive function, so that nothing can be said about its declination.

The name *Jesus* occurs in the nominative, accusative and vocative cases: *Jesus* 11:1, 3; 12:1, *Jesum* 1:6, 9bis, and *Jesu* 10:11, 15; 12:8 respectively. Once, the vocative form is *Jesus* 12:3[1].

The proper name Moses seems to switch between Greek and Latin declensions: whereas the accusative is *Moysen* 1:5; cf. 1:4 l. em., the genitive is *Moysi* (first instance); or *Monsi* 12:1; cf. *Monsi* 11:1 (second instance) l. em. The form of the nominative is *Moyses* in 3:11, but *Monse* in 11:2, 17; 12:2. The vocative form is *Monse* as well in 11:4, 14, 19.

b. *Pronouns*

84. In Vulgar Latin, the pronouns *is* and *ille*, and in some texts also *ipse*, progressively lost their demonstrative meanings, and were both mainly used as personal pronouns. The loss of opposition made their indiscriminate use possible with a resulting tendency to merge into a single pronominal paradigm in which forms of *ille* replaced the monosyllabic forms of *is* (*is, ei, ii, id* etc.; Väänänen § 274).

In As. Mos., *is* and *ille* are, as far as meaning is concerned, interchangeable as personal pronouns (for the surviving demonstrative use of *ille* in As. Mos., see nr. 59). *Is* is still the most frequent pronoun, but, apart from *eis*, the monosyllabic forms *is, ei, ii, id* are avoided.

85.   In the following table, the occurrences of *is* and *ille* in As. Mos. are listed. The numbers mentioned are based on the emended text; instances in which *is* and *ille* are anaphorically or demonstratively used are left out, as well as those instances in which *illius* has a pregnant meaning (see nr. 59). The occurrences of the feminine and neutre gender are too few to be fruitfully compared. In the following tables, a slash / separates the numbers for the singular and plural forms.

---

[1] So also in the Vetus Latina of Luke 18:38.

	is	*ille*
nom.	0/0[1]	1/1
gen.	3/29	2[2]/4
dat.	0/4	2/13
acc.	1/9	1/8[3]
abl.	3/12	0/2

86. These proportions resemble those in the urbane speeches in Petronius[4] and those in codex *k* of the Gospels[5], especially with regard to the differentiation between the dative and ablative as *illi, illis* and *eo, eis* respectively[6]. If the proportions in these three texts are systematized, the following schema can be made of the forms of the third personal pronoun that are favoured. The reader should note that this paradigm does not reflect an actual situation, but is the imaginary outcome of an uncompleted development.

	sing.	plur.
nom.	*ille*	*illi*
gen.	*ejus*	*eorum*
dat.	*illi*	*illis*
acc.	*eum* or *illum*	*eos* or *illos*
abl.	*eo*	*eis*

---

[1] Cf. however *hi* 7:4; see nrs. 18 and 58.

[2] Perhaps only one is to be counted, if *illius* in 1:7 refers to the Lord, rather than to the tabernacle; see nr. 59.

[3] Perhaps the number should be reduced, if *illos* in *illos et nos* 12:4 is used as a demonstrative pronoun.

[4] Boyce, *The Language of the Freedmen*, pp. 67-68. Boyce adds up the oblique forms of *is, ea* and *ille, illa* used in Petronius, and concludes that the forms of *ille* are preferred overall, even in urbane speech (p. 68). In drawing this conclusion, he disregards the clear preference for *ejus* (22 times) instead of *illius* (not used), and, with less impressive numbers, that for the ablative *eo, ea* (4 against 0) and the accusative *eos, eas* (4 times against once *illos*).

[5] Hoogterp, *Etude*, §§ 234 and 262, provides tables of the numbers of occurrences in this codex, from which I derive the following numbers: *ille* 32:: *is* 2; *illius* 3:: *ejus* 74; *illi* (dat.) 80:: *ei* 15; *illum* 67:: *eum* 105; *illo* 9:: *eo* 23; *illi* (nom.) 21:: *ii* 0; *illorum* 3:: *eorum* 19; *illis* (dat.) 73:: *eis* (dat.) 9; *illos* 20:: *eos* 25; *illis* (abl.) 8:: *eis* (abl.) 11. Note that these numbers include the demonstrative use of both words.

[6] *Illis* is used four times in As. Mos. as an ablative, but in those instances it is used as a demonstrative pronoun, not as a personal pronoun; see nr. 59.

This reconstruction gives the impression that the ousting of *is* by
ille in written Latin[1] was a gradual process which started with the
replacement of the monosyllabic forms of *is*.

87. In Jubilees, contained in the same codex as As. Mos., the situation
     is different, because of the additional competition of *ipse*
     (Väänänen § 272)[2]. The free use of *ipse* in Jubilees shows that
     Jubilees and As. Mos. were not translated by the same person.

	is	*ille*	*ipse*	*ille+ipse*
nom.	0/0	6/1	8/8	14/9
gen.	134/14	11/0	24/50	35/50
dat.	19/6	54/25	1/0	55/25
acc.	76/42	19/12	4/4	23/16
abl.	20/7	16/5	20/16	36/21

88. Because of the acceptance of *ipse* as a personal pronoun, it was
     apparently no longer necessary to use the monosyllabic *eis* in Ju-
     bilees. The place of the differentiation between *illis* and *eis* (dative
     and ablative) is now taken by the differentiation between *illis* and
     ipsis.
          However, if one assumes an opposition between *is* and not-*is*
     (that is, in this case, *ille* or *ipse*), the polysyllabic forms of *is* ap-
     pear almost as tenacious as in As. Mos.[3] The only form of *is*
     which has clearly yielded to not-*is*, is *eorum*. For Jubilees, the
     following schema can be made of the forms of the third personal
     pronoun that are favoured:

---

[1] In purely Vulgar Latin, as used in the letters of Claudius Terentianus, *is* and its inflections
hardly occur at all (Adams, *The Vulgar Latin*, p. 44); on the other hand, the Vulgate restores
many monosyllabic forms of *is* where the old Latin versions use forms of *ille* (Hoogterp, §§
245-248). The survival of *is* must be understood as a survival in written Latin only.

[2] The numbers in this table are based on Denis-Janssens, *Concordance latine du liber Jubilaeorum*.

[3] A quick check with the aid of the *Enumerationes formarum* by Cetedoc of the works by
Augustine and Jerome confirms this conclusion, although the situation in their works is somewhat complicated through the emergence of *ipse*. Some notable numbers may be mentioned
here: *is* 125 in Aug., 69 in Jer.; *ille* 10,046 in Aug., 1,255 in Jer. (*ipse* 11,578 and 2,341 respectively); *ejus* 17,171 in Aug., 7,136 in Jer.; *illius* 2,448 in Aug., 1,137 in Jer. (*ipsius*
2,655 and 293 respectively); *eorum* 6,894 in Aug., 3,273 in Jer.; *illorum* 1,025 in Aug., 109
in Jer. (*ipsorum* 756 and 68 respectively); *eos* 6,864 in Aug., 3,316 in Jer.; *illos* 2,270 in
Aug., 374 in Jer. (*ipsos* 1,398 and 118 respectively).

nom.	*ille* or *ipse*	*ipsi*
gen.	*ejus*	*ipsorum*
dat.	*illi*	*illis*
acc.	*eum*	*eos*
abl.	*eo* or *illo* or *ipso*	*ipsis*

89. The neutre form of the d e m o n s t r a t i v e p r o n o u n *ille* is *illum* instead of classical *illud* in *usque ad illum tempus* 8:1 (cf. *ThLL* VII, col. 340:59-71).

90. The r e l a t i v e and i n t e r r o g a t i v e p r o n o u n s, which resemble each other in form, were eventually to merge (Väänänen § 285). In As. Mos. *quod* and *quid* are confused. Though *quid* is used in 3:7 and 11:4, *quod* is used as an interrogative in *quod erit monumentum* 11:6 and *quod ergo fiet plebi isti* 11:19. *Quem* instead of *quam* occurs very early (Väänänen § 285) and may be supposed in 2:7 *fidem* (l. em.) ... *quem*. *Quem* confused with *quae* of the neutre gender seems to be of late date and regionally restricted, so that it may not be wise to assume it to be original in 10:13.

c. *Verbs*

91. The treatment of d e p o n e n t s as actives occurs at an early stage in Vulgar Latin (Väänänen § 294). In As. Mos. we find *fornicare* 5:3; *dominari* with passive meaning in 2:3 (as a deponent in 4:2); cf. *dominabunt* 6:7 l. em. Regularly used as deponents are *confiteri, hortari, mori, reminisci* (for occurrences, see word-list).

92. *Dominabitur* in *dominabitur a principibus et tyrannis* 2:3 is to be taken as a passive, as is shown by the complement of the agent introduced by·*a* + ablative (Ernout-Thomas § 228). The singular form, on a par with the preceding plural *intrabunt*, must be explained by assuming a suppressed singular collective subject, such as *plebs* or *Istrahel* (less likely *terra*).

93. In spoken Latin, the classical p e r f e c t and f u t u r e t e n s e forms were gradually replaced by periphrastic constructions

(Väänänen §§ 299-305). As. Mos. avoids these periphrastic constructions with the exception of *coepit ... palam facere* 1:13[1].

Habebat genua sua infixa 11:17 is probably not a periphrastic pluperfect (Väänänen § 302). It is more likely that in this particular case, *habere* is used to express the durative aspect of the action.

In *omnia quae futura essent* 12:5, *futura essent* is not a periphrastic substitute of a future tense form, but a conscious use of the determinative meaning of this construction in classical Latin: "all things that were bound to happen" (cf. Ernout-Thomas § 290).

94. Nevertheless, As. Mos. clearly shows the causes of the ruin of the classical system, particularly in the future tense.

First, there is the differentiation of grammatical morphemes into four conjugations, whereas these paradigms have identical functions (for instance, depending on the conjugation, the second person of the active indicative future tense is marked by the morpheme *-bis* or *-es*). Second, the individual grammatical morphemes can have different functions in the various paradigms (for instance, the morpheme *-es* marks not only the second person of the active indicative present tense of the second conjugation, but also the second person of the active indicative future tense of the third and fourth conjugations) (Väänänen § 303).

This was aggravated by phonetic-phonological developments, as a result of which most present and future tense forms of the third conjugation sounded identical (see nr. 2), as did most perfect and future tense forms of the first conjugation (see nr. 21)[2]. Also, the present tenses of the second and fourth conjugations were phonetically identical, and, finally, the third person singular and the first person plural of the future tense of the fourth conjugation in *-ies, -iet* etc. sounded very similar to the corresponding forms of the perfect tense of the fourth conjugation, in *-ivi = -ii* (see nr. 10); contraction of *-ii-* and *-ie-* complicated matters further.

---

[1] The constructions with ἄρχεσθαι and *coepisse* emerged independently in Greek and Latin; see Löfstedt, *Syntactica* II, pp. 450-452; Hilhorst, *Sémitismes*, pp. 66-70.

[2] The confusion is explicit in codex *g* of the Pauline epistles, which gives two possible translations for τηρήσει 2 Thess. 3:3: *confirmavit vel confirmabit*, and also for ἄξει 1 Thess 4:14: *adducet vel adducit* (Rönsch, "Die Doppelübersetzungen", *ZWT* 26, p. 93).

95.   This loss of opposition between and within the conjugations gives rise to new forms as *tremebit* 10:4, *stabilibis* and *constabilibis* 2:2 (contrast *stabilient* 2:5).

96.   In As. Mos., few forms of the verb *i r e* and its compounds are correct according to classical standards; indeed, it is a very short verb, and in some personal forms very similar to the forms of *esse*. In spoken Latin, the verb was impracticable, and it was replaced by *ambulare, vadere* and *se ducere* (Väänänen § 141). It seems that the translator or copyists of As. Mos. did know that the word *ire* belonged to the elevated literary style, but that they had great difficulty in conjugating it. The adhortatives *eamus* 11:16, 18, the subjunctive imperfect *praeteriremus* 3:12 and the perfect *ierunt* 4:3 are correct. But one finds *transio* 1:15 for *transeo* (both /-yo/; see nr. 4), *abhis* 11:9 for *abis*, *exivit* 1:15 for *exiit* and *exiet* 10:3 for *exibit*[1]. Cf. *eam*[2] 10:14 l. em.

97.   Finally, *poterint* 4:8 must stand for *poterunt*[3], and *possent* 7:7 for *possint*. *Fecerunt* in *si inimici impie fecerunt semel adhuc* 11:17 must be translated as an exact future tense ("if the enemies will have sinned once again"); perhaps confusion with *fecerint* plays a role here.

---

[1] These perfect and future tense forms often occur in the Vetus Latina; see Rönsch, *Itala und Vulgata*, pp. 289-293 (cf. his comment in "Sprachliche Parallelen", p. 101: "Bei Hinweisungen, die mit einer gewissen Feierlichkeit ausgesprochen werden, ist in der altlateinischen Bibelsprache e x i e t die stets wiederkehrende Futuralform von exire"); also in Jubilees; see Rönsch, *Jubiläen*, pp. 447, 453, and cod. *k*; cf. Hoogterp, *Etude* §§ 72-73.

[2] *Eam* occurs often instead of *ibo* (*ThLL* V, col. 626:37-40; cf. Väänänen § 303).

[3] Often and almost consistently so in Vetus Latina ms 100 (Rönsch, "Die Leptogenesis", p. 90).

IV. (MORPHO-)SYNTAX

a. *Agreement and Word-Order*

98. Agreement of gender and number is usually respected in As. Mos.; there are, however, a few exceptions.

The masculine *pulverati* in *(tribus) ducent se ut liena in campis pulverati* 3:4 refers *ad sensum* to the members of the tribes. In 3:9, *illis* refers *ad sensum* to *semen*.

The plural *terris* in *omnibus ... sepulturae suae sunt in terris* 11:8 is an instance of attraction of number.

99. In As. Mos., the w o r d - o r d e r in the simple sentence is usually (subject)-verb-object, in accordance with the usage in Vulgar Latin (Väänänen §§ 354-355). A number of exceptions may be mentioned: *sancta vasa omnia tollet* 3:2; *partem aedis ipsorum incendit, aliquos crucifigit* 6:9; *qui confitentes circumcisionem in cruce suspendit, nam necantes torquebit* 8:1-2; *omnes gentes ... Deus creavit* 12:4; *omnia praevidit* 12:4; *omnia ... firmamenta ... facta ... sunt* 12:9; cf. *fidem polluent* 2:7 l. em.

The precedence of the object reflects a specific emphasis in all these instances. In some cases, the object is placed at the beginning of a clause, receiving even stronger emphasis: *Ideo, haec dicit Dominus* 1:11; *Hoc enim si faciemus* 9:7; *Te elegit Deus* 11:15; cf. *Te ne contemnas* 12:3 l. em.

100. The unmarked word-order in a noun phrase is noun-adjective. Sometimes an a d j e c t i v e precedes the noun it modifies: *abditum locum* 8:5; *unicum filium* 11:12; *sacrum spiritum ... divinum profetem ... consummatum doctorem* 11:16; cf. the position of the personal pronoun *ejusdem testamenti* 10:15 (see also nr. 102).

101. Emphatic adjectives of size or quantity (*omnis, multus, brevis*) usually precede the noun they modify[1].

---

[1] So also in the Latin letters of Terentianus; see Adams, *The Vulgar Latin*, p. 71.

—*Omnis*, if adjectively used, precedes the noun it modifies ten times. Only once, in *sancta vasa omnia* 3:2, the order is reversed, probably because of the importance attached to the word *sanctus*.

—*Multus* precedes the noun it modifies twice (9:3; 12:11): Once, in *omnium* (l. em.) *animalium idola multa* 2:9, the order is reversed because *omnium animalium* had to precede *idola* in order to express the author's dismay.

—*Brevis* occupies the first position in *breviora tempora* 11:17.

—*Magnus*, however, occupies the second position twice: *maestitia* (l. em.) *magna* 4:3; *potentia magna* 8:1; obviously, in unmarked word-order. Once, in *magnus nuntius*, the adjective is emphatic.

102.   In a group of determinants (genitives, adjectives and personal pronouns), the personal pronoun indicating possession tends to occupy the final position[1]. In *corpus custodiens ejus a sole* 11:12, the peculiar word-order *corpus custodiens ejus* may have been caused by the tendency of the present tense participle in Vulgar Latin to be used as an adjective, *custodiens* being taken as an adjective belonging to *corpus* instead of to *quae* and *domina*. It should be noted, however, that *eorum* appears elsewhere in rather unexpected positions: *voluisti invocari eorum Deus* 4:2 (cf. Ps. Sol. 18:10 μέγας ἡμῶν ὁ θεός)[2]. *In terram eorum et regionem* 4:6 must be considered as a hyperbaton; see nr. 166.

b. *Cases*

103. The n o m i n a t i v e and v o c a t i v e cases are used in accordance with classical usage. There are no instances of absolute nominative constructions.

104. The a c c u s a t i v e is used to denote the object, or the subject of an accusative with infinitive construction (see nr. 128)[3].

---

[1] Not so in *idola eorum inquinata* 8:4, but here the adjective belongs to the following clause as well: *inquinata quomodo sunt* &c. (see further nr. 171 for the resulting ἀπὸ κοινοῦ construction).

[2] In the LXX translation of Job, the Greek translator had a certain preference for the position of the possessive personal pronoun (e.g., Job 6:4 μου τὸ αἷμα), a practice followed slavishly in some Spanish glosses; see Ziegler, *Randnoten*, pp. 31-32.

[3] For the use of the accusative with prepositions, see section II, e.

105.   There are a few instances of accusatives of the internal object
        (Ernout-Thomas § 33): *circumvallabunt muros* 2:7; *jusjurandum
        quod jurasti* 3:9.
106.   The complement of *reminisci* has the accusative form in 3:9,
        10 and 11:18, whereas a genitive is used in 4:5 (both constructions
        are possible in classical Latin, Ernout-Thomas § 65).
        Confiteri meaning "to confess (a crime)" is constructed with an
        accusative in *confitentes circumcisionem* 8:1 (on the substantivised
        participle with an accusative, see nr. 107), in accordance with
        classical standards. In Latin influenced by the biblical language,
        confiteri meaning "to praise (God)" (see nr. 40) can be con-
        structed with the dative. This construction is found in *confiteberis
        creatori tuo* 10:10.
        Though *carere* is sometimes constructed with an accusative in
        classical texts, this construction is much more prominent in Vul-
        gar and late Latin texts[1], as in 12:11 *carere bona* l. em.
107.   In Vulgar Latin, as in Greek, a substantivised participle may
        be complemented by an accusative instead of an objective genitive
        (Ernout-Thomas § 287). In As. Mos., the only complement used is
        the accusative; there are no instances of substantivised participles
        with an objective genitive: *confitentes circumcisionem* 8:1; *a
        torquentibus illos* 8:5; *neglegentibus mandata* 12:11; cf. *omnipo-
        tentem orbem terrarum* 11:17 l. em.

108.   The a b l a t i v e is used locatively (e.g. *locis ignotis* 6:3) and
        temporally (e.g. *illis temporibus* 3:1). Also, it is used:
        —instrumentally: *disputationibus arguant se* 1:13; *in respectu quo
        respiciet* 1:18; *incendere igni* or *igne* (see note to nr. 3) 3:2; 6:9;
        elidere gladio 6:3; *cogi stimulis* 8:5; *jurejurando placare* 11:17;
        —as an ablative of respect: *major natu* 6:4;
        —duratively: *annis XL* 3:11; *triduo* 9:6; *singulis horis, diebus et
        noctibus* 11:17;
        —as a partitive ablative: *implere sceleribus* 5:6 l. em. The adjec-
        tive *plenus* is constructed with partitive ablatives in *plena lacrimis
        et gemitibus* 11:4; contrast *in scelere pleni* 7:7. According to the
        classical rules, *plenus* is constructed with a genitive (Ernout-
        Thomas §§ 65, 115);

---

[1] *ThLL* III, 454:67-455:11; Ernout-Thomas § 26.

—as an ablative of price: *dignus Domino* 11:16.

109.   For a possible instance of an absolute ablative construction, see nr. 135.

110. The g e n i t i v e is in steady decline in Vulgar Latin, and it was eventually replaced by prepositional constructions (Väänänen §§ 250-251). In As. Mos., the genitive is still frequently used.

It is used to denote possession and "belonging to" *passim*. In these functions, the genitive is not substituted by prepositional constructions in As. Mos. Furthermore, the genitive is used in As. Mos. as the genitive of definition (e.g. *tempus annorum* 1:15; possibly also *terra patriae suae* 3:3); as the genitive of quality (e.g. *dies paenitentiae* 1:18); as the objective genitive (e.g. *acceptio munerum* 5:5; *voluntas ... ciborum et potui* 11:13); as the genitive of relation (*successor ejusdem testamenti* 10:12).

111.   Some notable surviving uses of the genitive are:
—the genitive denoting the point of departure in time[1]: ...*mus (annus) profectionis* "the ...th year since the departure" 1:3;
—the genitive denoting the point of departure in space (Hofmann-Szantyr II, p. 67): *profectio Fynicis* "the departure from Phoenicia" 1:3[2];
—the genitive of the rubric[3]: *improperia verborum* "the reproaches of the words" = "the reproachful words" 3:6.

112.   In late Latin, the partitive genitive was to a great extent replaced by prepositional phrases (Ernout-Thomas § 60; see also nr. 68). In As. Mos. it is only found as the complement of words that themselves express the notion of division or partition: *pars* 4:7; 6:8; also *particeps scelerum* 5:1 (Ernout-Thomas § 61).

113.   A substantive determined by the genitive of the same substantive serves to denote uniqueness. This usage must in many cases be

---

[1] See Löfstedt, *Philologischer Kommentar*, pp. 149-151, commenting on Peregrinatio Aetheriae 5:9 *completo anno profectionis filiorum Israhel de terra Aegypti*: "Der Genetiv *profectionis* gibt nach einer im Spätlatein nicht ungewöhnlichen Konstruktionsweise den Ausgangspunkt der Zeitbestimmung an" (pp. 149-150). See also Ernout-Thomas, § 55; Hofmann-Szantyr II, p. 64. This use of the genitive does not seem to be a Graecism, although the commonness of the construction in Greek may have furthered its use in Latin. Schalit, p. 26, adds eight examples from the Vulgate and Septuagint.

[2] *Fynicis* is the genitive either of the noun *Phoenice*, or of the adjective *Phoenix*; see nr. 196.

[3] Woodcock, *A New Latin Syntax*, p. 53.

regarded as a biblical style-figure, but the following instances are also perfectly conceivable in pagan Latin (Ernout-Thomas § 64; Hofmann-Szantyr, p. 55): *rex regum terrae* 8:1; *Dominus dominorum* 9:6 (see further nr. 191).

114.   With verbs, the genitive form is used for the complement of *misereri* 4:4, 6 and *reminisci* 4:5. However, *misereri* is constructed with a dative *commodi* in 11:10 (Ernout-Thomas § 73, quoting the Vetus Latina of Matt. 9:27 *miserere nobis*, Vulgate *nostri*). The object of *reminisci* is set in the accusative in 3:9, 10 (Hofmann-Szantyr II, p. 81[1]).

115.   In *potestas a potentia magna* 8:1, the genitive of quality is replaced by a prepositional phrase for the sake of variation (see nr. 66). The complement of a substantivised participle is an accusative; in As. Mos. the alternative possibility of the objective genitive is not used (see nr. 107). The complement of *implere* and *plenus* is classically set in the genitive, but in late Latin the genitive is replaced by (*ab* +) the ablative, in As. Mos. by *in* + ablative (for the possibility of a Greek ἐν underlying this *in*, see nr. 72).

116. The d a t i v e is used to denote persons or matters to whose advantage or disadvantage actions take place, e.g. *dare, immolare*. This dative (*commodi* or *incommodi*) is sometimes replaced by a prepositional phrase: *dicere ad* + acc. 1:10; 3:10; 9:1 (Väänänen § 249; the phenomenon appears already in classical texts, but becomes prominent only in late Latin; see also Löfstedt, *Syntactica* I, pp. 187-193; Hoogterp , *Etude* § 102). For *dicere de* 3:10 see nrs. 69, 167 and 185. *Dicere* has a dative in 12:2, 8.

Related to this usage is the use of the dative for the complement of such intransitive verbs as *confiteri* meaning "to praise" 10:10 (see nr. 40), and *misereri* (see nr. 117), and the complement of intransitive verbs that express an event happening to someone, *advenire, contingere, fieri*; furthermore the dative in *te elegit Deus esse mihi successorem* 10:15[2].

The dative is further used to denote

---

[1] The difference which Ernout-Thomas § 56 (following Löfstedt, *Syntactica* II, p. 27) see between the use of genetive or accusative with *reminisci* is absent in these instances.

[2] In *ut sit successor plebi* 1:7, however, *plebi* is a dative *commodi*.

—the complement of the impersonal form *placet* 2:2; in 12:11, the datives *peccantibus et neglegentibus* probably depend on an omitted *necesse est* or *propositum est*, or something similar;

—the complement of an adjective: *homo probatus Domino* 1:6 (but contrast *omnia ... facta ut provata a Deo* 12:9);

—possession, *haec sunt vires nobis* 9:5; *omnibus ... morientibus ... sepulturae sunt* 11:8; *quae est mihi sapientia* 11:15; *non est defensor illis* 11:17.

117.   The dative replaces the genitive in *miserebitur illis* 10:10 (see further nr. 114). In 6:2, *judicare* is constructed with the dative *illis*. In Biblical and Christian Latin, this construction is not unusual (*ThLL* VII,2, cols. 620:73-621:4). In most instances, the dative accompanying *judicare* denotes the one in whose favour justice is spoken. In 6:2, however, the dative in *judicabit illis* must be interpreted as a dative *incommodi*.

In 8:4, the adverb *pariter* rules a dative: *bajulare idola eorum inquinata quomodo sunt pariter contingentibus* (l. em.) *ea*, "to carry their idols that are defiled just as those who touch them" (on the ἀπὸ κοινοῦ construction *inquinata ... contingentibus* see nr. 171); cf. *pariter... vobis* 3:5 l. em. (Ernout-Thomas § 82, quoting Livy 38, 16, 11: [*gentes*] *pariter ultimae propinquis*[1]).

The dative is used instead of the accusative after *dominari* in *dominaris saeculo* 4:2 (Ernout-Thomas § 85; contrast the passive use of *dominabitur* 2:3).

c. *Tenses*

118. The p r e s e n t tense, denoting events or situations that are viewed as true at the moment of speaking, is used in discourse: *haec dicit Dominus* 1:11; *palam facio tibi* 1:15; *hoc est quod testabatur ... Moyses* 3:11; *scitis enim quia haec sunt vires nobis* 9:5; *non est ille cum eis* 11:18; *dico enim tibi* 12:8.

119.   Occasionally, the present tense is used instead of the future tense, undoubtedly because of the general problems connected with the future tense in Vulgar Latin (Hofmann-Szantyr II, p. 308; see nrs. 94-95): *transferunt* 2:4; *vides* 10:10; *conveniunt* 10:13; no

---

[1] Cf. *ThLL* X,1, col. 279:29-34.

doubt, some of the confusions *-et/-it* (see nr. 2) belong under this heading.

120.　　　In *transio* 1:15; *domine, abhis* 11:9; *non est defensor illis* 11:17; *et ecce aufertur* 12:5, the present tense is used to indicate an event which is expected in the immediate future.

　　　In 12:10, the present tenses *crescunt et bonam viam exigunt* convey the idea that the fulfillment of this promise is certain if the condition (*facientes ... et consummantes mandata*) is met.

121.　　　On the present tense in relative clauses, see further nr. 163.

122. In As. Mos., the historic p e r f e c t tense is mostly used to narrate events that have taken place in the past and that are recorded by the narrator without any additional subjective nuance. The i m p e r f e c t tense[1] is used seven times: *fiebat* 1:4; *testabatur* 3:11; *invocabat* 3:12; *timebat* 11:12; *erant* 11:14; *erat* 11:17; *habebat* 11:17. Apart from *fiebat* all these instances are found in direct speech, but in direct speech the perfect tense is used as well. In contradistinction to the perfect, which functions as the normal narrative tense, the imperfect serves to describe background (*erat* 11:17), to phrase additional (more or less parenthetical) information (1:4; 11:14), or to express the durative aspect of a situation or action (11:12, 17). In 3:11, 12 the imperfect is possibly used to indicate the enduring consequences of the event referred to.

123. The f u t u r e tense is practically only used to indicate events that are to happen. In 2:1-2, the future tense forms have an imperative aspect. The future tense is used instead of the adhortative subjunctive in *habebimus discubitiones ... et putavimus ... (et) erimus* 7:8 (on the contamination of direct and indirect speech in this sentence, see nr. 155). The future tense replaces the subjunctive of doubt in *quid faciemus vobis, fratres?* 3:7; *<un>de voluntatem eorum praestabo?* 11:13 (Ernout-Thomas § 267).

124. In main clauses, the p l u p e r f e c t and e x a c t f u t u r e tenses are not used.

---

[1] Cf. Ernout-Thomas § 242.

d. *Moods*

125. The s u b j u n c t i v e in main clauses is adhortative (Ernout-Thomas § 251): *jejunemus, intremus, moriamur* 9:6; *eamus* 11:16, 18; *confundamus* 11:18; or prohibitive (negated imperative; Ernout-Thomas § 251B): *ne contemnas* 12:3. The other functions of the subjunctive in main clauses are taken over by the future tense (see nr. 123). For the subjunctive in subordinate clause, see nrs. 156-162.

126. The i m p e r a t i v e is used in accordance with classical standards. *Noli ne me tange* in 7:10 l. em. is a contamination of *noli me tangere* and *ne me tange* (for *ne* with imperative, see Ernout-Thomas § 251B).

127. The i n f i n i t i v e occurs often in its normal function as complement of another verb (e.g. *cogentur palam bajulare* 8:4; for accusative with infinitive constructions, see nr. 128). Furthermore, it occurs with a final or consecutive meaning (as in Greek, Ernout-Thomas §§ 275, 297; see further nr. 184): *locutus est ... dare* "he has said that he would give" 1:9; *tradit* (l. em.) *duci vinctos* "he will hand them over to be led off as captives" 8:2; *sapientia ... judicare* "such wisdom as to give (proper) judgement" 11:15; *inerunt ... judicare* "they will be there in order to give judgement" 5:6 l. em.; *secabuntur ... acrobistiam inducere* "they will be operated on in order to induce a foreskin" 8:3 l. em. In classical Latin several other constructions would be used in such cases.

128.   A c c u s a t i v e with i n f i n i t i v e constructions occur quite often[1]: *voluisti plebem hanc esse tibi plebem exceptam* 4:2; *docentes se esse justos* 7:3; *dicentes se haec facere* 7:6; *te elegit Deus esse mihi successorem* 10:15. An accumulation of the use of this construction is found in 11:16: *cum audierint expugnare nos, credentes jam non esse ... doctorem, jam non esse in eis*. An alternative punctuation, however, puts the phrase *expugnare nos cre-*

---

[1] In the letters of Terentianus, the accusative with infinitive construction is used "with considerable freedom ... the construction was at home in the spoken register of the author" (Adams, *The Vulgar Latin*, pp. 61-62).

dentes in parenthesis: *cum audierint (expugnare nos credentes) jam non esse &c.*; see further the commentary.

129.   The g e r u n d is twice used as in classical Latin: *tempora arguendi* 5:1; *ad currendum supra terram* 11:12 (see, however, the commentary). In Vulgar Latin the gerund in the ablative case replaces the participle (Väänänen § 328). This occurs three times in As. Mos.: *(vocavit) dicendo ad Jesum* 1:9; *pervendent justitias accipiendo poenas* 5:5; *reminiscens testamentum parentum et jurejurando placando* 11:17. The gerundive construction is once used, in *scribtura ... ad recognoscendam tutationem* 1:16. The supine is not used in As. Mos.

130. The present p a r t i c i p l e is mostly used to indicate an action that accompanies the action of the finite verb in the clause in which it stands, but also very often as a (substantivised) adjective, the only function that it was eventually to retain in Vulgar Latin (Väänänen § 327).

131. In late Latin, the participle *constitutus* often functions as the present participle of *esse*. In the phrase *qui est in summo constitutus* 10:2 its meaning is not entirely clear. The clause may mean: (a) "who is in heaven"; (b) "who has been appointed in heaven"; or, in the event it renders a participial clause, (c) "when he will have been appointed in heaven."

(a) The perfect passive participle of *consitutere* indicates both the action and the result; *constitutus* means "having been made", and therefore: "being"[1]. Translators from Greek to Latin often used a construction with *constitutus (esse)* in order to render Greek constructions that were impossible in Latin, especially constructions in which the article or the participle ὤν was involved, but no equivalent of the verb *constituere*, e.g. Exod. 29:30 *qui pontifex pro eo fuerit constitutus*, Septuagint: ὁ ἱερεὺς ὁ ἀντ' αὐτοῦ; 1 Sam. 22:2 *omnes qui erant in angustia constituti*, Septuagint: πᾶς ἐν ἀνάγκῃ; John 5:13 *Jesus enim declinavit turba constituta in loco*, translated from ὁ γὰρ Ἰησοῦς ἐξένευσεν ὄχλου ὄντος ἐν τῷ τόπῳ; cf. Sir. 46:8(10) *ipsi duo constituti a periculo liberati sunt* corresponding to αὐτοὶ δύο ὄντες διεσώθησαν.

---

[1] Ernout-Thomas § 237.

Functioning as the participle of *esse, constitutus (est)* gained great popularity in later Latin, whether translated or not, especially among Christian authors[1].

From this point of view, the Greek text of As. Mos. 10:2 may have contained a phrase such as (χεῖρες τοῦ ἀγγέλου) τοῦ ἐν ὑψηλοῖς, or similar words with the meaning "the messenger in heaven".

132.   (b) However, most examples of *constitutus* in the Vulgate do reflect a Greek passive participle of some verb meaning "to order" or "to appoint". In these and other instances, both the Greek and the Latin participles usually indicate the result of *constituere* rather than the action[2], e.g. Jer. 20:1 *et audivit Phassur... sacerdos qui constitutus erat princeps in domo Domini*, Septuagint: καὶ ἤκουσεν Πασχώρ ... ὁ ἱερεύς, καὶ οὗτος ἦν καθεσταμένος ἡγούμενος οἴκου κυρίου ("And Passhur ... the priest, who was the leader in the house of the Lord, heard..."; cf. 2 Macc. 3:4); 2 Macc. 3:31 *ei qui in supremo spiritu erat constitutus*, Septuagint: τῷ παντελῶς ἐν ἐσχάτῃ πνοῇ κειμένῳ (in this instance, the Greek participle is rendered by a relative clause; see nr. 183).

133.   On the other hand, there are examples in which the same constructions do not simply describe a present situation, but have a past tense meaning[3], such as 1 Macc. 16:11 *et Ptolemeus ... constitutus erat dux*, LXX: Καὶ Πτολεμαῖος ... ἦν καθεσταμένος στρατηγός, "And Ptolemy was appointed general"; or 2 Macc. 5:22 *(Philippum) moribus crudeliorem eo ipso a quo constitutus est*, "who was even more barbaric than he by whom he had been appointed", LXX: (Φίλιππον) τὸν δὲ τρόπον βαρβαρώτερον ἔχοντα τοῦ καταστήσαντος, "who was even more barbaric than he who had appointed him". A particularly instructive example is Ps. 2:6 LXX; on grounds of inner consistency, the Septuagint version has changed the Hebrew active voice (ואני נסכתי מלכי על ציון הר קדשי, "I have appointed my king over Zion, my holy mountain") into a passive voice: Ἐγὼ δὲ κατεστάθην βασιλεὺς

---

[1] *ThLL* IV, cols. 523:45-524:21; see also Blaise-Chirat, *Dictionnaire*, p. 209b, who quote Minucius Felix 32, 7: *Deus in caelo constitutus*.

[2] Compare Luke 7:8 *ego homo sum sub potestate constitutus*, translated from ἐγὼ ἄνθρωπός εἰμι ὑπὸ ἐξουσίαν τασσόμενος with the parallel in Matt. 8:9, which leaves out the participle in both the Greek and Latin texts.

[3] Ernout-Thomas § 249.

ὑπ' αὐτοῦ ἐπὶ Σιὼν ὄρος τὸ ἅγιον αὐτοῦ, so also the Vulgate *juxta LXX: ego autem constitutus sum rex ab eo super Sion montem sanctum ejus*, "I have been appointed king over Zion, his holy mountain". From Sus. 5, too, it appears that *constitutus esse* may be used as a passive perfect: *et constituti sunt de populo duo senes judices*, Θ: καὶ ἀπεδείχθησαν δύο πρεσβύτεροι ἐκ τοῦ λαοῦ κριταί; cf. finally Acts 10:42 *testificari quia ipse est qui constitutus est a Deo judex*, a translation of διαμαρτύρασθαι ὅτι οὗτός ἐστιν ὁ ὡρισμένος ὑπὸ τοῦ θεοῦ κριτής.

Therefore, As. Mos. 10:2 can be interpreted as "the messenger who has been appointed in heaven".

134.   (c) Finally, a relative clause can be used as a translation of a Greek participle (see nr. 183). The Greek text of As. Mos. 10:2 may then have contained something like ... τοῦ ἀγγέλου (τοῦ) ἐν ὑψηλοῖς καθεσταμένου[1]. This could be interpreted temporally: "when he will be in heaven", or, if the stronger meaning of *constituere* is preferred, "after he will have been appointed in heaven".

135. Absolute ablative constructions are rare in Vulgar Latin (Väänänen § 382). There are no certain instances of the absolute ablative construction in As. Mos., but cf. *circumito VIIII* (= *nono*, sc. *anno*) 2:7 l. em.

136.   As. Mos. contains two instances of the participle functioning as a verbal substantive (the *ab Urbe condita*-construction, Ernout-Thomas § 292A): *ex quo facto* "after the coming about of this event" = "after this will have happened" 7:1; *ab oriente sole usque ad occidentem* 11:8 "from the rising sun unto the setting" = "from where the sun rises (the East) unto where it sets (the West)"; cf. the same phrase, without explicitly mentioning the sun, and temporally used, in 7:7.

137.   In late Latin, the participle, esp. the present participle, can occasionally be used instead of a finite verb (that is, as a predicate without a form of *esse*, Hofmann-Szantyr II, pp. 389-390). In 7:9 *et manus eorum et mentes inmunda tractantes* (paratactically connected with *et os eorum loquetur ingentia et superdicent*), this use

---

[1] Or even τοῦ ἀγγέλου ὑψωθέντος; cf. 2 Macc. 3:21 *in agone constitutus* = ἀγωνιῶν. Cf. Hilgenfeld's retranslation ("Die Psalmen Salomo's", p. 292): τοῦ ἀγγέλου τοῦ ἐπάνω κατασταθέντος.

of the participle is probably due to the many participles and adjectives which describe a group of persons in 7:3-8 (Hofmann-Szantyr II, p. 420[1]).

Negative clauses with exclamatory character often have the predicate in the form of a participle (Hofmann-Szantyr II, p. 421[2]). An example of this usage is *numquam temptantes* (sc. *erant* or *fuerunt*) *Deum nec parentes, nec proavi eorum, ut praetereant mandata illius* 9:4 l. em.

For another case of a predicate in the form of a participle, see nr. 173.

138.   The future participle occurs once in As. Mos.: *omnia quae futura essent* 12:5; see further nr. 93.

e. *Coordination*

139. Coordination is usually expressed by *et* (212 occurences in the emended text[3]), or, when appropriate, by *nec* (three times); once by *at* 10:6 (written as *ad*; see nr. 35), but never by *-que*.

Twice, *et* is placed in second position in a sentence instead of the first: *ut et* 1:8; *testatus et invocabat* 3:12; this may indicate the influence of *etiam* in second position, and even from *-que*, which also came to be used in first position, as in *fratresque sorores* (Löfstedt, *Philologischer Kommentar*, pp. 312-318; for *qui et* 3:14 see nr. 148).

140.   *Et* must have the same meaning as *etiam* (Ernout-Thomas § 424) in 1:13 (second instance); 8:5 (third instance) and 11:16 (first instance; see further nr. 144), probably also in 4:5 (second instance).

141. D i s j u n c t i v e coordination is consistently expressed in As. Mos. by *aut*, as in other Vulgar Latin and Romance texts (Väänänen § 370). *Aut* is also used to link successive questions in 11:6-7, 10-15; cf. 11:13 l. em. *An, seu, sive* and *vel* do not occur.

---

[1] "Oft gehäuft, ... später sehr oft z.B. bei Amm. in Beschreibungen der menschlichen Charaktere".

[2] "Vielfach mit Ausrufscharakter".

[3] This number includes both the phrase- and clause-copulatives.

142. The variety of adversative, explicative and conclusive particles in classical Latin gradually disappeared after their increasing loss of opposition[1] (Väänänen § 370; esp. Löfstedt, *Philologischer Kommentar* pp. 27-85). However, many of them still exist in As. Mos.[2], though not all in their classical meaning.

143. *Autem* is used four times as an emphasized a d v e r s a t i v e: *transio in dormitionem patrum meorum ... <tu> autem* 1:15-16; *aliquae partes tribuum ... duae autem tribus* 4:7-8; *hic <erit> cursus horum que[m] conveniunt ... ego autem ad dormitionem ... eam* 10:13-14.

144. A similar function is fulfilled by *sed*, which occurs five out of six times after a negative clause (cf. German "sondern"), e.g. *non enim sequentur veritatem Dei, sed quidam altarium inquinabunt de ipsis muneribus quae inponent Domino, qui non sunt sacerdotes, sed servi de servis nati* 5:4. The combination *sed et* 11:16 announces a climax (Lewis and Short, p. 1658b).

145. *Enim* is used perfectly in accordance with classical usage. Its demonstrative corroborative function ("indeed", "for") can also be performed by the particle *nam*. In this function, *enim* differs from *nam* only in its position in a sentence. *Nam* stands in first position, *enim* in second position (Ernout-Thomas § 432).

146. However, *nam* is also used adversatively (8:2; 10:11; 11:8, 14; 12:11, 12)[3]. In three cases, *nam* is used to introduce a parenthesis (Hofmann-Szantyr II, p. 472): 1:3; 2:3, 5.

147. No particulars are to be recorded with regard to the meaning and use of *ideo* (twice) and *itaque* (four times).

148. Coordination by a r e l a t i v e p r o n o u n is uncommon in Vulgar Latin (Ernout-Thomas § 423), but is found in As. Mos. in *in qua tu benedicis* (= *et in ea terra tu benedicis* 2:2); *quae advene-*

---

[1] *Autem, vero, nam* and *enim* are all used to translate δέ in the old Latin translations of the Johannine letters (Thiele, *Wortschatz*, p. 15b).

[2] The most important of these copulatives that do not occur in As. Mos. are *vero, immo, quin* and *tamen*.

[3] On the early date of this adversative use, see Rönsch, "Itala-Studien", pp. 202-204. Many examples, esp. from LAB and 4 Ezra, in Schalit, pp. 18-20.

runt nobis (= *et haec advenerunt nobis*) 3:13; pleonastically in *qui et servient* 3:14.[1]

f. *Direct Speech. Indirect Statements and their Complement-Clauses*

149. In As. Mos., direct speech is always introduced by a verb of saying, usually *dicere*.

Four times, the introduction is simply (*et*) *dicet/dicent*: 3:7; 7:9; 11:16, 18. In 3:5 *et clamabunt* is used. Twice, the formula *respondit illi et dixit*[2] is used: 11:3; 12:2.

150.   In Hebrew direct speech can be introduced by לֵאמֹר. This word is reflected in the Septuagint as λέγων, λέγοντες[3]. The construction occurs also in pagan Greek, but is especially widespread in Jewish and Christian Greek[4] (and hence in later Latin[5]). In As. Mos. *dicens, dicentes* occurs four times: 3:8, 10; 4:1; 7:8. In 1:9, *dicendo* is used (for the ablative gerund instead of the participle, see nr. 129).

151.   In 9:1, direct speech is introduced by the phrase *dicet* (l. em.) *ad eos rogans*, while *rogabit dicens ad eos* is what one would expect.

152.   Probably, *propter quod factum fuit* 5:2 introduces a scriptural quotation. In 5:3, an additional quotation is introduced by *quia*, a reflection of the Greek ὅτι *recitativum*[6].

153. Indirect speech occurs less often. After *verba dicendi* or *sentiendi*, the indirect speech is constructed as an accusative with infinitive: *docentes se esse justos* 7:3; *dicentes se haec facere* 7:6. In 3:9, the contents of an oath are given in a subordinate clause: *jusjurandum ... ne umquam deficiat*. So also the contents of a prohibition in 3:12 *invocabat nobis testes ... ne praeteriremus mandata illius*.

---

[1] Charles, *The Assumption*, pp. xxxiii, 56, also regards *qui vocavit* 1:6 as an instance of coordination by a relative pronoun (= וַהוּא), but this obviously is a translation of a Greek participle, as the quotation in Gelasius shows: προσκαλεσάμενος.

[2] Blaß-Debrunner § 420.

[3] Soisalon-Soininen, *Die Infinitive*, pp. 68-75.

[4] Blaß-Debrunner § 420; Hilhorst, *Sémitismes*, pp. 78-81.

[5] Mohrmann, *Etudes* I, pp. 415-416; Hofmann-Szantyr II, pp. 389-390.

[6] In Greek, this ὅτι *recitativum* is good classical usage; see Blaß-Debrunner § 470,1. In Latin, the equivalent *quia* probably emerged under Greek (biblical) influence; see Hofmann-Szantyr II, pp. 578-579.

154.   In 9:4, 5, the complement-clause of the verb *scire* is introduced by *quia* instead of *quod*[1]. In *nunc* (l. em.) *palam facio tibi, quia consummatum est tempus annorum vitae meae* 1:15, *quia* may stand for *quod* ("Now I reveal to you that etc."), but it is more likely that it has here its normal causal meaning ("Now I reveal [*sc.* it, the intention of the creation] to you, because etc."). In 6:3, the complement-clause is introduced by *ubi*: *ut nemo sciat ubi sint corpora illorum.*

155.   In 7:8, direct and indirect speech are contaminated: *et putavimus nos tamquam principes erimus*, from (1) *et putavimus nos principes (esse)*, and (2) *et tamquam principes erimus.*

g. *Other Subordinate Clauses*

156. S u b o r d i n a t e clauses with a f i n a l meaning are introduced by *ut* with a present tense subjunctive: 1:7, 8, 9, 10, 13, 14, 18; 10:7; perhaps 6:3 (see nr. 157).

Negative final (prohibitive) clauses are introduced by *ne* with a present tense subjunctive: 3:9; 7:7 (cf. nr. 97); 7:10; 12:3. In 3:12, the imperfect tense subjunctive (*ne praeteriremus*) is used because the main clause is in the imperfect tense as well.

157.   *Ut* with present tense subjunctive has a c o n s e c u t i v e meaning in 4:6; 9:4; 11:11; perhaps 6:3 (see nr. 156). In 5:6, *ut* introduces a consecutive subordinate clause in which the verb-form is indicative. In the sentence *in totum exterminet et relinquat eos fieri non potest* 12:12 the subordinate clause, which precedes the main clause (*fieri non potest*), is not introduced by *ut* ("konjunktionslose Hypotaxe", Hofmann-Szantyr II, p. 531).

158.   T e m p o r a l subordinate clauses are introduced by *cum* with the indicative: 1:4; 5:1; 11:16; 12:4 l. em.; cf. *postquam* with indicative 2:3; 12:1.

In contrast to the classical rules[2], *postquam* 2:3 is followed by a future tense form, *intrabunt*, to denote the exact future tense. In

---

[1] Cf. Väänänen, § 374.

[2] Woodcock, pp. 172-173: "*postquam* is never used with either the future or the future perfect". Hofmann-Szantyr II, p. 598 mention only *postquam* with imperfect, perfect, pluperfect and present tenses.

11:16, the exact future tense is denoted in the classical way: *cum audierint.*

Vulgar Latin increasingly uses the pluperfect subjunctive form in temporal subordinate clauses in past tense introduced by *cum* (Ernout-Thomas, §§ 358, 362); in As. Mos. this occurs once: *cum audisset* 11:1.

Donec 10:13 is followed by a future indicative.

159.   C a u s a l subordinate clauses are introduced by *quia* and the verb is normally in the indicative mood: 3:5; 4:8; 10:7; 11:4; probably also 1:15. On *quia* instead of *quod* introducing indirect statements, see nr. 152.

160.   *Si* introduces an open c o n d i t i o n a l subordinate clause, the verb being indicative, in 9:7 and 11:17. In 11:17, *si ... fecerunt* the perfect has the function of an exact future tense (see nr. 97).

161.   *Quemadmodum* 1:10 introduces a c o m p a r a t i v e subordinate clause, indicating similarity, and therefore having the indicative mood. Likewise, the conjunctions *quantus* (correlated with *tantus*, 9:3) and *quomodo* always have the indicative.

Potius quam in *moriamur potius quam praetereamus* 9:6 is used to denote a possibility which the speaker rejects (Ernout-Thomas § 354), and therefore is followed by the subjunctive.

Tamquam introduces an unreal comparison ("as if"), and the subordinate clause requires a subjunctive according to classical standards. In 7:8, however, it is followed by an indicative form, *erimus*, probably due to the contamination of direct and indirect speech in that sentence (see nr. 155).

162. Practically all r e l a t i v e subordinate clauses are attributive and therefore have a verb in the indicative mood. In *non est defensor illis, qui ferat pro eis praeces Domino* 11:17, *ferat* is a subjunctive in a relative subordinate clause with consecutive meaning.

163.   In a number of relative clauses, the *consecutio temporum* is not observed: whereas the main clause is set in the future tense, the *qui*-clause is in these cases constructed with a present (or passive perfect) tense: *intravit unus qui supra eos est* 4:1; *quidam altarium inquinabunt ... qui non sunt sacerdotes* 5:4; *qui enim magistri sunt ... erunt mirantes personas* 5:5; *implebuntur manus nuntii qui est in summo constitutus* 10:2; *erunt ... tempora CCL quae fiunt* 10:12; cf. *qui faciunt erunt impii judices* 5:6 l. em.;

cursus erit horum que conveniunt 10:13. Possibly, some of these cases are renderings of Greek participles (see nr. 183).

164.   In 2:2 the personal pronoun *eam* (l. em.) is used to indicate again the object of the relative clause: *in qua* (sc. *terra*) *tu ... stabilibis eis sortem in eam*[1]. This use, well known from Hebrew, occurs occasionally in classical Greek, but is greatly expanded in Jewish and Christian Greek[2] and Latin[3].

---

[1] Thus Rönsch, "Xeniola ... Chronologisches und Kritisches", p. 558.

[2] Blaß-Debrunner § 297.

[3] Hofmann-Szantyr II, pp. 556-557.

V. STYLE-FIGURES

165. For the biblical style-figures in As. Mos., see nrs. 189-192.

166. The separation of syntactically connected parts of a sentence (h y p e r b a t o n, Hofmann-Szantyr II, p. 689) is widespread in all kinds of Latin. In As. Mos. it occurs in its least extreme form (Hofmann-Szantyr II, p. 693: "Typus: *justus vir ac bonus*"): *in terram eorum et regionem* 4:6; *in scelere pleni et iniquitate* 7:7; *manus eorum et mentes* 7:9.

167. There are several instances of v a r i a t i o n in As. Mos.
—Variation of prepositions in parallel clauses (Hofmann-Szantyr II, p. 818: especially in Late Latin): *tribus ad tribum, et homo de proximo suo* 3:10; *in terram alienam ... et circa ostium allofilorum, et ubi est maestitia magna* 4:3; *Exurget enim Caelestis a sede regni sui et exiet de habitatione sancta sua* 10:3; *Non enim propter meam virtutem aut in firmitatem* 12:7.
—Variation of simplex and compound verbs (Hofmann-Szantyr II, p. 818: a mechanical device for variation in Late Latin): *stabilibis eis sortem in eam* (sc. *terram*), *et constabilibis eis regnum* 2:2; compare the variation of various prefixes in 12:4-5 *praevidit ... praevidit et pronovit* (l. em.) *... providit*.
—Variation of construction: *rex regum terrae et potestas a potentia magna* (instead of *potentiae magnae*; see nr. 66) 8:1.

168. A notable instance of c h i a s m is found in 11:12:

> *tamquam pater unicum filium, aut*
>   X
> *tamquam filiam domina* (l. em.).

169. In 11:11, a tendency towards v e r b o s i t y is found: *nec patiens ne uno quidem die*, literally "and indeed not leaving out not one single day". *Nec* can have the same function as *ne ... quidem*. *Ne ... quidem* was a literary expression, quite unfamiliar to colloquial

Latin (Hofmann-Szantyr II, p. 448[1]). Here *ne ... quidem* is added to *nec* to highlight Moses' unremitting assiduity in his daily prayers for the people.

170. The author of As. Mos. displays a certain preference for the pairing of near-synonyms, aiming at solemnity, e.g. *decrevit et promisit* 2:1; *principes et tyranni* 3:1; *terra et regio* 4:6; cf. *sanctus et sacer* 11:16 l. em.; *praevidit et pronovit* 12:4 l. em. A number of these word-pairs may be attributable to the translator, who may have used two words to render one, as in *excogitavit et invenit me* 1:14, which corresponds to the Greek προεθεάσατό με in Gelasius' quotation (assuming that the Greek text used by the translator of As. Mos. was identical to the text quoted by Gelasius; see further nr. 180).

171. In *et ponentur duae tribus sanctitatis* 2:4, the subject must be supplemented from the predicate: *et ponentur duae* (sc. *tribus*) *tribus sanctitatis* (the figure ἀπὸ κοινοῦ).

In *bajulare idola eorum inquinata quomodo sunt pariter contingentibus* (l. em.) *ea* 8:4, the adjective *inquinata* ("defiled") is constructed ἀπὸ κοινοῦ with both *idola* and the subject of *sunt*. The subject of *sunt* is set in the dative or ablative (*contingentibus*) due to the adverb *pariter* (see nr. 117). The clause must be understood as *bajulare idola eorum inquinata quomodo sunt pariter inquinati contingentes ea*.

In 2:2, the figure ἀπὸ κοινοῦ occurs twice. The sentence reads: *in qua tu benedicis, et dabis unicuique, et stabilibis eis sortem in eam*. The objects of *benedicere* in the first clause and of *dare* in the second must both be supplemented from the third clause: *in qua tu benedicis* (sc. *eos*[2]), *et dabis unicuique* (sc. *sortem*), *et stabilibis eis sortem in eam*.

172. A related form of conciseness is z e u g m a . In 2:4 l. em., a verb is used with two objects, but suits only one[3]: *figet palum ...*

---

[1] Especially in late Latin, the contamination *nec ... quidem* was often used; see Hofmann-Szantyr II, pp. 449-450.

[2] Corresponding to *eis* in the third clause ("zeugma rectionis" or syllepsis, Hofmann-Szantyr II, pp. 831-832). For the construction of *benedicere* with an accusative in Latin influenced by the biblical literature, see nr. 47.

[3] Blaß-Debrunner § 479; Hofmann-Szantyr II, pp. 831-832.

et turrim 2:4. In the sentence *omnia caeli firmamenta ... facta, ut provata a Deo et sub anullo* (l. em.) *dexterae illius sunt* 12:9, the verb *sunt* functions both as an auxiliary (*provata* sc. *sunt*) and as a substantive verb (*sub anullo sunt*).

173.   In *corpus custodiens ejus a sole et ne scalciati pedes ejus ad currendum supra terram* 11:12, *custodiens* introduces a zeugma in which two different constructions (*a* + ablative and *ne*) are used, each of which corresponds to a different meaning of *custodire*. There may be influence from Greek[1]: "to protect from" (*custodiens a sole*, φυλάσσειν ἀπό), and "to take care lest" (*custodiens ne scalciati pedes ejus* sc. *sint*, φυλάσσειν ἀπό [τοῦ] + infinitive). For the predicate *scalciati* without *sint* (or the like), see nr. 137.

174. Although the omission of the antecedent of a relative pronoun oc-curs in classical texts (Väänänen § 371; Ernout-Thomas § 331), it especially agrees with the Vulgar Latin tendency to syntactical conciseness (Hofmann-Szantyr II, p. 824)[2]. In As. Mos. we find: *nam secus* (sc. *eos*) *qui in oriente sunt* 1:3; *secus* (sc. *id*) *quod placebit* 2:2; *propter* (sc. *id*) *quod factum fuit* 5:4; cf. *et (cogentur blasfemare) leges quod habebunt supra altarium suum* 8:5 l. em. (instead of *[blasfemare] eo quod*)[3].

175.   The complement of *parcere* (usually denoted by the dative) is often omitted, especially in clauses of the type *occidit (interfecit, destruxit) et non parcet*[4]; see e.g. 2 Sam. 12:6; Job 27:22; Lam. 2:17; 3:43; so also in *occidit majores natu et juvenes et non parcet* 6:4.

176.   The tendency towards brevity to the detriment of clarity is also reflected in *(liber) profetiae quae facta est a Moysen in libro Deuteronomio* 1:5. Literally translated this would be "(the book) of the prophecy that was given by Moses in the book of Deutero-nomy". However, the intention is clearly to say that the present

---

[1] Though "to take care lest" can be expressed in Greek as φυλάσσειν μή, as well.

[2] Stone, *The Language*, p. 61: "Very commonly throughout the MS. (*sc.* codex Bezae) the antecedent of a relative pronoun is omitted". Stone cites 15 instances from codex Bezae.

[3] Cf. Rönsch, *Jubiläen*, pp. 450, 456, who quotes Jub. 17:3 *et (Abraham) benedixit toto ore suo* (sc. *eum*) *qui creavit universa*; Acts 16:10 (cod. *d*) *evangelizare* (sc. *eis*) *qui in Mace-donia sunt*; further examples from old Latin translations of Luke in Rönsch, "Sprachliche Parallelen", pp. 79-80.

[4] Cf. καὶ οὐκ ἐφείσαντο/ἐφείσατο in Ps. Sol. 2:23; 17:12.

book, namely As. Mos., contains a prophecy referred to in the book of Deuteronomy (sc. in Deut. 31:14-23; see the commentary). One may compare to this LAB 20:6 *ego et pater vester missi sumus per Moysen in heremo, et ascendimus cum ceteris decem viris*, where *in heremo* must be taken to mean *cum in heremo fuimus*.

177. In 1:8 it is said that the land was given to the people's forefathers (*terra data patribus eorum* l. em.), whereas elsewhere it is more accurately stated that it had been promised to the patriarchs that the land would be given to their posterity (As. Mos. 2:1; cf. Num. 14:23; Deut. 1:8 and many other instances); this may be called an instance of p r o l e p s i s ; *terra data* is meant as *terra quam Deus promisit dare* (cf. e.g. Gen. 12:1; 15:7)[1]. In 1:9, the sentence is continued, as if the full expression had been used: *terra (sc. per promissionem) data patribus, ut detur (sc. terra promissa) illis &c.*[2]

178. On the participles as predicates, see nr. 137.

179. In *(ut) humiliter inter se disputationibus arguant se* 1:13, *humiliter* is best understood as an "Adverb des Urteils", that is, not belonging to *arguant*, but as an evaluative comment by the author on the things he describes in the sentence concerned (Hofmann-Szantyr II, p. 827[3]). A possible translation then is: "to their own humiliation they will convict themselves".

---

[1] Even if the expression is used in its full form, the equivocality remains. In *terra quam ... promisit dare patribus* 2:1, the dative *patribus* can be connected with *dare*; in *jusjurandum ... ne umquam deficiat semen eorum a terra quam dedisti illis* 3:9, *illis* refers to *semen*, but can also be connected with the patriarchs mentioned before.

[2] In Kings, Chronicles, Jeremiah and Ezekiel reference is often made to the land "given to their/your fathers", but it is not certain whether the patriarchs are meant, or the first generation of Israel to have entered into the land; contrast Neh. 9:23 with 9:36.

[3] From this grammar, one gets the impression that this drastic brachylogy occurs only or mainly with *bene* and *male*. But Madvig, who first described the phenomenon (in *Adversaria critica*, II, p. 507) also gives instances with *turpiter, honestius, superbius, satis, insanius*.

VI. THE ORIGINAL LANGUAGE OF AS. MOS.

a. *The Extant Latin text of As. Mos. as a Translation from Greek*

180. The Latin text of As. Mos. is certainly a translation from Greek. This conclusion is based on the following grounds. (1) A prior version of the narrative is alluded to by relatively early, Greek speaking, Christian authors, including Ps.-Jude and Origen. As. Mos. must have been available to them in Greek. (2) In any event, the quotations in Gelasius of Cyzicus (fifth century) prove that As. Mos. existed in Greek. (3) The Latin text contains several phrases that reflect Greek grammar and idiom; see nrs. 181-185, 188. Although it must be admitted that not all Grecisms are proof that the text in which they occur has been translated from Greek, some Grecisms in As. Mos. seem to be best explained as renderings of the idiom of a Greek text.

As. Mos. 1:6, 14 are of special importance, because these passages exist partly both in Latin and in Greek: the Greek version is quoted by the fifth-century ecclesiastical historian Gelasius of Cyzicus, whose quotations are usually accurate. Gelasius' quotations are good, natural Greek, whereas the Latin text is less smooth, and can easily be explained as a translation of Gelasius' or a similar Greek text:

προσκαλεσάμενος Ἰησοῦν υἱὸν Ναυῆ ...
qui vocavit ad se Jesum filium Nave ...
καὶ προεθεάσατό με ὁ θεὸς πρὸ καταβολῆς κοσμοῦ εἶναί με τῆς διαθηκῆς αὐτοῦ μεσίτην
Itaque excogitavit et invenit me qui ab initio orbis terrarum praeparatus sum ut sim arbiter testamenti illius.

In accordance with Latin translation practice, the participle προσκαλεσάμενος is rendered by a *qui*-clause (see further nr. 183), and the final infinitive εἶναι is rendered by an *ut*-clause (see further nr. 184). In Greek the sentence means to say that God, before he created the world, took care that Moses would become the mediator of his (God's) covenant. This meaning is reasonably well expressed by the Latin translator, although his rendering of πρὸ καταβολῆς κοσμοῦ is slightly impractical and awkward. In any case the Latin text can more easily be explained as a translation of the Greek than the other way around.

181. That the Latin text of As. Mos. is based on a Greek text is evident above all from the Grecisms in the Latin text. True, not every Grecism is proof of a Greek original. Many Greek words and constructions have penetrated the Latin language in its various stages, especially Christian Latin (see nrs. 38-40). Three words, however, are unattested in other Latin texts: *chedriare* 1:17; *scen(a)e* meaning "tabernacle" 1:7, 9; 2:3, 4, 8; *acrobistia* 8:3 l. em. These may be used as evidence of an underlying Greek text. *Chedriare* may have been formed by the translator himself (see nr. 43); *scen(a)e* meaning "tabernacle" is a secondary borrowing from Greek (see footnote to nr. 8); *acrobistia* is a simple transliteration of ἀκροβυστία.

182.   It is difficult to demonstrate convincingly that certain Latin words are mistranslations from Greek, since attempts to point out mistranslations are always liable to the suspicion of being biased. A few may nevertheless be mentioned here.

—*disputatio* 1:13 means "dispute", but exegetically, the meaning "consideration" is to be preferred. The Greek διαλογισμός can convey both meanings;

—*pati* 11:11 means "to allow"; the required meaning, however, is "to allow to pass" (of time). Several Greek words, including παριέναι[1], convey both meanings;

—*rogare* 9:1, meaning "to ask" probably translates παρακαλεῖν[2], which means "to ask", but also "to summon" or "to exhort"[3];

—*tutatio* 1:16 means "protection", but the context requires "trustworthiness"; both meanings are covered by the Greek ἀσφά–λεια[4].

To these mistranslations, one may compare some possible instances of analytical translations, that is: translations of compound Greek words in which the constituent parts are separately rendered in Latin. To be sure, examples of this category are even less

---

[1] Charles, *The Assumption*, pp. xxxvii, 92.
[2] For this equivalence see, e.g., Matt. 8:5, 31, 34; 14:36; 18:29, 32.
[3] For this meaning of παρακαλεῖν, cf. Acts 2:40 καὶ παρεκάλει αὐτοὺς λέγων, Vulgate: *et exhortabatur eos dicens.*
[4] Rönsch, "Weitere Illustrationen", p. 222.

certain than the mistranslations. The following possible instances may be mentioned: *dimittere* 2:2 may reflect διατάσσειν or δια–τιθέναι, "to arrange"; *disdonare* 8:3 may reflect διαδιδόναι, "to divide"; *in campo* 5:6 may reflect ἔμπεδοι, "continually"[1]; *bonam viam exigere* 12:10 may reflect εὐοδοῦν, "to prosper"[2].

183. As has been said above (nr. 180), Greek participles are often rendered by *qui*-clauses in Latin[3]. In 1:6 προσκαλεσάμενος is translated with *qui vocavit ad se*. In As. Mos., *qui*-clauses are normally used attributively; the Latin of As. Mos. 1:6 means: "(the prophecy given by Moses) who called unto him". The context, however, requires that *qui vocavit ad se* is translated as a temporal subordinate clause (as the Greek participle): "when he called unto him"; see further nrs. 162-163.

184.   Greek final infinitives can be translated with *ut*-clauses in Latin[4] (see nr. 180: προεθεάσατό με ὁ θεὸς ... εἶναί με ... μεσί–την is translated with *excogitavit et invenit me ... ut sim arbiter* in 1:14). This may explain the position of *ut facias* in 1:10 *promitte secus industriam tuam omnia quae mandata sunt, ut facias quemadmodum sine quaerellam est*. The usual word-order in Latin would have been *promitte ut facias secus industriam tuam omnia quae mandata sunt &c*. If *ut facias* is considered as the rendering of a Greek final infinitive ([τοῦ] ποιεῖν), the word-order is natural.

        Greek final infinitives are occasionally also rendered by infinitives in Latin (see nr. 127).

185.   The phenomena mentioned in nrs. 182-184 may be considered as mechanical translations of Greek idiom, caused by a translator who ignored the effects of such automatic renderings on Latin syntax. Another instance of such mechanical translations may be: *dicentes tribus ad tribum, et homo de proximo suo* 3:10. This clause literally means: "one tribe speaking to another, and one man a b o u t his neighbor". But clearly, *de* in the second phrase must have the same meaning as *ad* in the first. In translation Latin,

---

[1] Hilgenfeld, "Die Psalmen Salomo's", p. 286; ἔμπεδοι is the masculine plural of the adjective ἔμπεδος.

[2] Hilgenfeld, "Die Psalmen Salomo's", p. 298.

[3] Fischer, "Limitations", p. 367.

[4] Fischer, "Limitations", p. 367-368.

de + accusative is often used to render a Greek instrumental dative. In 3:10, *de* may mechanically reflect an indirect object, denoted in the Greek version by a dative[1].

b. *The Supposed Greek Text of As. Mos.: a Translation from Hebrew?*

186. The extant Latin text of As. Mos. contains a number of "Hebraisms", often taken to be indications of a Hebrew original of the Greek text of As. Mos. But these Hebraisms are of an entirely different nature than the Grecisms mentioned in the preceding section, which can be regarded as proof of a Greek *Vorlage* of the Latin text. The Hebraisms in As. Mos. cannot prove a Hebrew original.

In his Introduction to *The Assumption of Moses*, p. xlii, Charles mentions eleven instances of what he considers to be reliable indications of a Hebrew original. Six of these must be deleted from the list, either because they have an uncertain textual basis, or because they are not certain examples of Hebrew (as opposed to Greek or Latin) idiom. The remaining instances can and must primarily be explained as consciously used biblical style-figures. In the following sections, Charles's proof-texts are briefly treated.

187. Two of Charles's instances must be dropped because of their uncertain textual basis: *circumibo* 2:7 is almost certainly corrupt; *testans ... invocabat ... testes* 3:12 is Charles's conjecture (the manuscript has the perfectly acceptable reading *testatus ... invocabat ... testes*).

188. Four of Charles's instances must be dropped because they are not actually Hebraisms: *patriae suae* in *terra patriae suae* 3:3 is either a genitive of possession or a genitive of definition (see nr. 110); *de isto* 3:13 reflects a typically Greek elliptical construction (ἀφ' οὗ, "since then"); *dividentur ad veritatem* 5:2 and *in sacerdotes vocabuntur* 6:1 are instances of Vulgar Latin (see nrs. 67 and 70).

---

[1] Rönsch, "Sprachliche Parallelen", pp. 93-96. Rönsch adduced two more instances of the same mistranslation, namely *dare de Jesum* 1:9 and *surgere de reges* 5:1, but in these instances, *de* has probably been used instead of *per* (see nr. 73).

189.   Charles mentions two etymological figures which he regards as
indicative of a Hebrew original: *in respectu quo respiciet* 1:18 and
facient facientes 6:1. However, etymological figures occur in
Greek and Latin texts that are no translations from Hebrew, as
well[1].

In As. Mos., they must primarily be understood as style-
figures, much used in non-Hebrew literature related to the Bible,
and meant to "evoke a biblicistic tone"[2]. For *in respectu quo
respiciet* 1:18 see Gen. 50:25 ἐν τῇ ἐπισκοπῇ ᾗ ἐπέσκεμμαι
ὑμᾶς; for the construction in general compare Luke 22:15
ἐπιθυμίᾳ ἐπεθύμησα. For the construction of *facient facientes* 6:1,
see Acts 7:34 ἰδὼν εἶδον.

The artificial character of the figure in As. Mos. is clearly illustrated by 6:1, which contains two contrasting etymological
figures: not only *facient facientes* (mentioned by Charles), but also
*sanctum sanctitatis: facient facientes impietatem ab sancto sancti-
tatis*, "they will act very impiously against the Holy of Holies".
The supposition of a Hebrew original underlying this sentence is
unnecessary.

190.   There is possibly only one instance of the biblical style-figure
of the "*vav*-apodosis", that is, the coordination of a main clause
with a subordinate clause by *et*: *et cum adpropiabunt tempora arguendi et vindicta surgit* 5:1[3]. The fact that this phenomenon occurs only once, in contrast to the considerable number of examples of the figure in, for instance, 4 Ezra, leads one to conclude
that this may simply be an anacolouthon, not rare in Greek and
Latin[4]. A second possible instance of *vav*-apodosis is found in 2:3
postquam intrabunt in terram suam ... et postea dominabitur.
However, lacunae in the text make the syntax of this sentence very
uncertain. Moreover, *et* in this sentence can also be explained as
abundant, since *postea* is not unusual as the (pleonastic) correlative

---

1 Schwyzer, *Griechische Grammatik* II, pp. 388, 700; Blaß-Debrunner, §§ 198,6; 422.

2 Bergren, *Fifth Ezra*, p. 300.

3 Not mentioned in Charles's list, *The Assumption*, p. xlii, but treated by Wallace, "The
Semitic Background".

4 Schwyzer, *Griechische Grammatik* II, p. 406; Hofmann-Szantyr II, p. 731:
"anakoluthische Rückfall in die Parataxe"; Ernout-Thomas, § 425, call it "*atque (et)* tem-
porel". The phenomenon occurs both in vulgar (Plautus, Terence) and in classical Latin
(Virgil, Livy, Curtius Rufus, Tacitus).

in the main clause of *postquam* introducing a subordinate clause[1]. The cases of *vav*-apodosis do not require the supposition of a Hebrew original.

191.   The use of the simple genitive as a genitive of quality is a popular biblical style-figure in Jewish and Christian Greek literature[2]. Charles mentions *tribus sanctitatis* 2:4. Some instances As. Mos. from may be added: *persona cupiditatum* 5:3; *sanctum sanctitatis* 6:1; *sedes regni* 10:3; *voluntas voluntatis* 11:13.

192.   Finally, Charles gives two examples of Hebrew idiom: (*dicentes*) *homo de proximo suo* (רעהו אל איש, "one to another") 3:12[3]; *implebuntur manus* (יד מלא, "to consecrate"[4]) 10:2. There is no need to take these expressions as proof of a Hebrew original: they are simply biblical idiom[5].

193. Although Charles has defended the hypothesis of a Hebrew original more energetically than any other scholar, he does not succeed in proving his theory. He can only show that the writing has a distinct biblical flavour, which is not surprising in a pseudepigraphon. We need not, therefore, occupy ourselves further with the rest of his arguments, such as alleged mistranslations from Hebrew and reconstructed puns in the supposed Hebrew original, which evidence has an additional value only.

    Hilgenfeld, in his attempt to prove that the original language of As. Mos. was Greek, has listed in his various editions of the text a total of 26 instances of words and constructions which he believes show that there cannot have been a Hebrew text underlying the Greek *Vorlage* of the Latin version[6]. However, the defence of

---

[1] Hofmann-Szantyr II, p. 598.

[2] Blaß-Debrunner § 165. In classical Latin, the genitive of quality is not unusual, but it is mostly provided with an additional adjective (type: *homo magnae eloquentiae*; see Hofmann-Szantyr II, p. 68); in later and Christian Latin, the simple genitive (type: *deus majestatis*, Hofmann-Szantyr II, p. 70) became popular as a biblical style-figure as well. See further Hilhorst, *Sémitismes*, pp. 110-113.

[3] The Septuagint most often renders this idiom by ἕκαστος τῷ πλησίον (or πρὸς τὸν πλησίον), but see also Judg. 6:29; 10:18; 2 Ki. 7:3, 9 καὶ εἶπεν ἀνὴρ (or ἄνθρωπος) πρὸς τὸν πλησίον.

[4] In As. Mos. 10:2, *manus* is the plural form, whereas the Hebrew expression occurs only with the singular יד, but the Septuagint often has the plural πληροῦν τὰς χεῖρας; see for instance Exod. 32:29; Num. 7:88; 1 Chron. 29:5; cf. T. Levi 8:10.

[5] So also certain formulas introducing direct speech; see nr. 150.

[6] Hilgenfeld, *Novum Testamentum*, p. 96; "Die Psalmen Salomo's", p. 276; *Messias Judaeorum*, p. 110.

such a thesis encounters all the difficulties of the theoretical impossibility of proving that something did not exist. Nevertheless,
there is some value in indicating that certain words and constructions in the supposed Greek text of As. Mos. have no direct counterpart in Hebrew. Since there is no basis in the extant Latin text
of As. Mos. for assuming a Hebrew original, such words and constructions underline the real possibility that the book was originally written in Greek. I shall give four examples of words and
constructions that are likely to have occurred in the Greek text of
As. Mos., which are unlikely to have had a Hebraic counterpart,
unless the Greek text was a free rendering of the Hebrew.

194.   In 11:16, the author of As. Mos. makes Joshua call Moses "the
inscrutable lord of the word", *inconpraehensibilis dominus verbi*.
The word *incomprehensibilis* enjoyed great popularity among
Christian Latin authors. In the Vulgate, however, it is used only
four times, and always predicatively (e.g. "the ways of the Lord
are inscrutable"), never attributively (as in As. Mos. 11:16, e.g.
"the inscrutable ways of the Lord"). As a translation from Hebrew, the word occurs only once in the Vulgate, in Job 9:10 (MT:
אֵין חֵקֶר)[1]. The Septuagint of Job is a notoriously free translation[2].

195.   In As. Mos. there are several words used for "knowing beforehand": *praevidere, providere, pronoscere*, and, in the Gelasian
quotation of 1:14, προθεᾶσθαι. In the entire Vulgate and Septuagint similar words occur only twice as translations of Hebrew
words[3].

196.   In 1:3, *Fynicis* is used to refer to Canaan, either as a noun
(*Phoenice*) or as an adjective (*Phoenix*). The Septuagint translates
Hebrew כְּנַעַן and its derivatives five times with Φοινίκη and its
derivatives (see the commentary). But the use of the Greek name
Φοινίκη/Φοῖνιξ instead of the transliteration Χανάαν, which is far
more common in biblical literature, suggests that the Greek text
underlying the Latin version of As. Mos. was composed in Greek
rather than translated from Hebrew.

---

[1] The other instances are 4 Ezra 8:21; Rom. 11:33. In Jer. 32(39):19, the recensions vary.
The situation is similar for synonyms of *incomprehensibilis*, namely *inscrutabilis, investiga-
bilis, inaestimabilis*.

[2] See, e.g., Heater, *A Septuagint Translation Technique*, p. 131.

[3] Gen. 15:13 has *praenoscens*, which is used in an etymological figure (hence for the sake
of variation, not meaning "to know beforehand"); in 2 Ki. 19:27 *praescire* is used; *providere*
is used only in the meaning "to provide" or "to be mindful (sc. of the future)".

197.   Finally, *habere* is used three times in As. Mos. as a transitive verb denoting possession. Hebrew does not have a verb for this function, but mainly uses a *lamed*-construction (הָיָה, שׁ, אֵין + -לְ). According to I. Soisalon-Soininen, there are 209 of these *lamed*-constructions in the Hebrew Pentateuch, of which only seven are rendered in the Septuagint with ἔχειν; as a rule, the Septuagint and the Vulgate render the *lamed*-constructions in the Pentateuch with the corresponding Greek and Latin dative of possession[1]. In As. Mos., there are four instances of the dative of possession (see nr. 116). That *habere* occurs three times is statistically significant compared with the instances of ἔχειν and *habere* in literal translations from Hebrew in the Bible. This use of *habere* in As. Mos. does not point, therefore, in the direction of a Hebrew original, although it obviously does not exclude it.

198. What we have observed in nrs. 180-197 leads to the following conclusion. The "Hebraisms" in the supposed Greek text of As. Mos. do not prove that Hebrew was the language in which the book was originally written. On the other hand, the linguistic phenomena typical of Greek (as opposed to Hebrew) do not conclusively prove that As. Mos. was originally written in Greek either. Ultimately, the possibility that the Greek text underlying As. Mos. was a free rendering of a Hebrew original cannot be ruled out altogether. The evidence for assuming a Hebrew original, however, is extremely weak and unconvincing, whereas there can be little doubt that As. Mos. once existed in Greek. Exegetical comments based on the supposition of a Hebrew original must therefore be dismissed as insufficiently founded.

---

[1] Soisalon-Soininen, "Der Gebrauch des Verbs EXEIN".

PART THREE

INTRODUCTION
THE HISTORY OF RESEARCH ON AS. MOS.

I. EARLY SCHOLARLY INTEREST IN AS. MOS.;
ITS EARLIEST EDITIONS FROM 1824 TO 1897

a. *From the 16th Century to the Editio Princeps*

In 1861 a fifth- or sixth-century Latin palimpsest from the Ambrosian
Library in Milan was published by A.-M. Ceriani. It included a long
fragment of an ancient Jewish book, hitherto considered to be lost. The
text appeared to consist mainly of a speech purporting to be delivered
by Moses at the moment of his impending death. A quick glance under
the heading "Moyses" in Fabricius' *Codex pseudepigraphus* of 1713
(second edition 1722-1723), in which all known traces of the lost apocrypha of the Old Testament had been collected, enabled Ceriani to
identify the text as a portion of the Assumption of Moses.

Until the publication of the Latin fragment of As. Mos., little was
known about the writing apart from its title, *Ascensio Mosis*, mentioned in Ps.-Athanasius' *Synopsis scripturae sacrae*[1]. Moreover, early
modern Biblical scholars knew that Origen in his *Principles* III, 2, 1[2]
had observed that Jude 9 drew on a book which, according to Rufinus'
translation, was entitled *Moysis Ascensio*[3]. Sixtus of Siena (1520-
1569)[4] in his *Bibliotheca sancta* of 1566 linked the information pro-

---

[1] For the text of this list, which is not earlier than the 6th century, see, e.g., Migne, *PG* 28,
cols. 284-437, especially col. 432B. For the date of this list and its attribution to Athanasius,
see Denis, *Introduction*, p. xii.

[2] Ed. Crouzel and Simonetti, *SC* 268, p. 152.

[3] Erasmus in his *Annotationes in Novum Testamentum* of 1516 briefly noted that Jude 9
was taken from some Jewish apocryphon. Later Erasmus went deeper into the matter; see the
Annotationes as printed in 1535[5] (ed. Clericus, *Erasmi Opera Omnia* VI, Leiden 1705, col.
1090, footnote 16). Here he recorded, *inter alia*, that, according to Origen, *Principles* III [2,
1], Jude 9 went back to a book "de adscensione Mosis".

vided by Origen and Ps.-Athanasius to passages in other ancient Christian authors (including Ps.-Oecumenius and Clement of Alexandria). Their comments amplify Jude's account, and Sixtus believed that the evidence thus collected went back to As. Mos. (see further the commentary on the lost ending).

Cornelius a Lapide (Cornelius van der Steen, 1568-1637) wrote that Sixtus had also stated that Pope Gelasius reckoned the *Ascensio Mosis* among the apocrypha[1]. However, a Lapide must have confused Ps.-Athanasius' *Synopsis* with Ps.-Gelasius' *Decretum de libris recipiendis et non recipiendis*, that is, the famous Gelasian Decree[2]. Both works are lists of canonical and apocryphal books. The former includes As. Mos. among the rejected books, the latter does not mention As. Mos. Sixtus correctly mentions Athanasius' *Synopsis* as the document in which As. Mos. is rejected[3]; he does not mention the Gelasian Decree.

The fifth-century ecclesiastical historian Gelasius of Cyzicus (who must be distinguished from Pope Gelasius, to whom the Decree was ascribed) quoted twice from As. Mos. in his *Acts of the Nicene Council*.[4] Perhaps a Lapide was aware of the quotations from As. Mos. in these *Acts*, causing him to confuse Athanasius' *Synopsis* with the Decree of the other Gelasius. The first two books of Gelasius' *Acts of the Nicene Council* containing the quotation from As. Mos. had recently been discovered. They were edited by R. Balforeus, and printed in Paris in 1599[5]. A reprint of this edition was published by Commelin at Heidelberg in 1604.

Apart from the references in Jude, Origen and in the lists of accepted and rejected books of the Bible, the quotations in the *Acts* by Gelasius of Cyzicus are the only certain traces of As. Mos. in early ec-

---

[4] The biographical and bibliographical details in this section are mainly taken from Jöcher, *Allgemeines Gelehrten-Lexicon*.

[1] *Commentaria in Epistulam S. Judae* (1648), ed. 1860, p. 956b: "Vide Sixtum Senensem verbo *Mosis Ascensio*, ubi docet hunc librum a Gelasio Pontifice relatum inter apocryphos".

[2] For the text of this 6th-century Italian list, see Dobschütz, *Das Decretum Gelasianum*, pp. 346-352.

[3] Sixtus Senensis, *Bibliotheca sancta*, ²1575, p. 98: "Athanasius in Synopsi hanc Mosis Ascensionem una cum alia huic affini scriptura, cui titulus est, Testamentum Mosis, inter Apocrypha rejicit" (the same words in the enlarged edition of 1626, p. 109b).

[4] For the text of Gelasius' quotations, see *Gelasius Kirchengeschichte*, II, 17, 17 and II, 21, 7, ed. Loeschcke and Heinemann, *GCS* 28, pp. 74 and 86; cf. Denis, *Fragmenta*, pp. 63-64.

[5] Γελασίου τοῦ Κυζικηνοῦ Σύνταγμα τῶν κατὰ τὴν ἐν Νικαίᾳ ἁγίαν σύνοδον πραχθέντων.

clesiastical literature, as will be shown below in the commentary on the lost ending. The earliest modern author I have found to quote these testimonies is J.A. Fabricius, *Codex pseudepigraphus* (1713). It is unlikely that Fabricius discovered the Gelasian passages himself, but he does not reveal to whom he owed the reference to Gelasius[1].

The incorporation of the Gelasian quotations in Fabricius' collection enabled Ceriani to identify the fragment he published as As. Mos. He furthermore noted that he did not know whether As. Mos. was identical to the Hebrew book *Petirat Mosheh*, because he had not seen the latter. A summary of the *Petirat Mosheh*, composed by E. Bernard and published in 1700 (see below), is also included in Fabricius' collection. In Fabricius' time, it was widely accepted that As. Mos. and the *Petirat Mosheh* were identical. As early as 1612, J. Drusius (1550-1616) mentioned the existence of a *Dibre ha-Yamim shel Mosheh* (*The Life of Moses*) and a *Petirat Mosheh* (*The Death of Moses*)[2]. He conceded that he had not seen the latter, but nevertheless believed it to be the same book as the Ἀνάληψις Μωσέως. H. Grotius (1583-1645) presented this identification as certain[3], although Grotius himself appears to have been unacquainted with the *Petirat Mosheh*[4].

It seems that by the time of the publication of the commentary on Josephus' *Antiquities* by Edward Bernard (1638-1697) in 1700[5], the identification of Ἀνάληψις Μωσέως with the *Petirat Mosheh* was gen-

---

[1] The idea of consulting the Greek text of Gelasius may have been suggested to Fabricius by a passage in Alphonsus of Pisa (Pisanus), *Nicaenum concilium primum generale in IV libros distributum*, Bk. III, vol. I (1572, [2]1581; see Grausem, "Pisanus", col. 2128), where the *Analipsis Mosis* is said to have been referred to by Origen, Clement and Athanasius. Fabricius does not mention Pisanus' work (which I have been unable to consult), but it is mentioned by J. Rainoldus, *Censura librorum apocryphorum* (1611), cols. 135-136, a passage referred to by Fabricius in the footnote to his quotations of Gelasius' *Acts of the Nicene Council*, see Fabricius, *Codex pseudepigraphus* ([2]1722: I), p. 844.

[2] Drusius, *Annotationes in totum Jesu Christi Testamentum* (1612); see *CS* [3]1698, *ad Jud.* 9.

[3] Grotius, *Annotationes in Novum Testamentum* (1641-1650); see *CS* [3]1698 *ad Jud.* 9.

[4] Grotius refers to both the *Dibre ha-Yamim* and the *Petirat Mosheh*. He asserts that *Dibre ha-Yamim* does not contain a passage similar to Jude 9. But he also claims that *Petirat Mosheh* was lost long before *Dibre ha-Yamim* was written. Both books, however, were published in one volume in 1629 by Jean Gaulmyn in Paris, where Grotius lived when he composed his *Annotationes*; see G. Gaulmyn, *De vita et morte Mosis libri tres*. These works had been printed previously in Constantinople (1516) and Venice (1544). See Strack-Stemberger, *Einleitung*[7], p. 301.

[5] E. Bernard, *Flavii Josephi Antiquitates*, p. 321, quoted by Fabricius, *Codex pseudepigraphus* I, pp. 840-842.

erally accepted, since Bernard liberally quoted from the latter work, calling it the *Analepsis Moyseos* without further explanation.

The relation between As. Mos. and *Petirat Mosheh* was investigated thoroughly in 1726 (for the first time, it seems) by the Roman Catholic scholar Augustin Calmet. Calmet provided an extensive summary of the *Petirat Mosheh* as well as of yet another Hebrew book, the *Midrash shel Petirat Mosheh*, edited by Gaulmyn, and compared these works with Jude 9. The Hebrew books do contain the account of a fight between angels involving Moses, but Calmet rightly concluded that their story is different from the one the author of Jude refers to[1]. Ceriani's discovery of the real As. Mos. confirmed Calmet's view that As. Mos. and the *Petirat Mosheh* are different books.

b. *The Editio Princeps of As. Mos.*

Before Ceriani's publication of the entire fragment in 1861[2], a small part of the Ambrosian fragment of As. Mos. had been published by A. Peyron, in his *Ciceronis orationum fragmenta inedita* of 1824. On pp. 131-134, Peyron edited some samples of the lower text of a palimpsest, codex C 73 of the Biblioteca Ambrosiana, including a few lines of Jubilees, 26:14-23. He mistook the lines of Jubilees for a passage of Genesis. Peyron also included some lines of what he called "apocryphal books of the Old Testament". These lines later became known as As. Mos. 4:5-5:1. At two places the transcription differs slightly from Ceriani's edition (see the critical notes on *misereator* line 69, and on *sua* line 73). Peyron dated the lower text to the fifth century[3].

---

[1] Calmet, "Dissertation sur la mort, et la sépulture de Moyse", p. 755: "Voilà le précis des deux Livres donnez par M. Gaulmin, qui contiennent l'un & l'autre le récit de la mort de Moyse, quoiqu'avec assez de diversitez. Mais ni l'un, ni l'autre ne raconte la dispute de saint Michel avec le démon pour le corps de Moyse. Ce qui fait juger que le Livre de *L'Assomption de Moyse*, connu par les anciens Peres Grecs, étoit différent de ces deux *Pétirath*, & qu'apparamment ce Livre Grec est perdu" (cf. the reprint of the Latin translation, "De Moysis obitu", in Migne [ed.], *Scripturae sacrae cursus completus* VII [1838], col. 806).

[2] *Monumenta sacra et profana* I, pp. 55-62; the manuscript's description on pp. 11a-12a; some notes on readings p. 64a-b.

[3] *Ciceronis orationum fragmenta*, p. 131; cf. Ceriani, *Monumenta*, p. 12a: "ecquis tanto judici refragaretur?". The library's catalogue dates the manuscript to the sixth century (see Paredi, *Inventario Ceruti*, p. 234); Lowe, *Codices latini* III (1938), p. 14, dated the lower text to the second half of the sixth century, as he did on p. 500 of his *Palaeographical Papers* II; on p. 311 of the first volume he dated it to the seventh century; Collura, *La precarolina*, p. 44, dated it to the sixth century.

When Ceriani published the entire fragment, he fortunately refrained from making conjectural emendations. He saw it as his sole task to reproduce the text of the codex as faithfully as he could[1]. Ceriani described the external features of the manuscript, indicated uncertain readings by italics, and illegible passages by dots[2]; the only addition he made to the manuscript's text was to omit the abbreviations its scribe had used. Also, Ceriani warned against renewed experiments with chemical substances in order to make the lower text of the palimpsest more legible—accusing, it seems[3], Peyron of having damaged the parchment with careless experiments of this sort. At the same time, however, Ceriani warmly thanked the Head of the Milano Record Office, for his competent assistance in making the text of the codex legible with the aid of chemicals[4].

At the request of one of the first scholars who investigated As. Mos., G. Volkmar, Ceriani examined the manuscript once again in order to check whether some of the readings proposed by Volkmar were possible. A few corrections and additions were thus made. I shall record them in my edition, though Ceriani later distanced himself from them[5].

---

[1] Ceriani, *Monumenta sacra*, I, p. 12a: "A conjecturis enim summopere abhorreo, quae, ut plurimum, non textum redintegrant, sed editoris commenta illi obtrudunt. Mei tantum officii id arbitratus sum, ut maxima qua potui fide codicem exhibeam ex iterata membranarum inspectione". In his 1862 review of Ceriani's edition, Ewald seems to object, if not to Italians in general, to Ceriani's simple approach: to Ewald, the edition is "mehr ... eine etwas eilige Ankündigung von künftigen verdienstlichen Arbeiten denn als eine streng wissenschaftlich vollendete Arbeit selbst" (p. 8).

[2] The dots do not indicate the number of illegible letters, but, in a somewhat vague way, the dimensions of the illegible passages (see Ceriani in Volkmar, *Mose Prophetie*, p. 154).

[3] Ceriani's introduction, written in Latin, is often rather vague, sometimes incomprehensible, a fact that excited Ewald's ire; see "Monumenta sacra", p. 9: "[wir wollen] uns jetzt nicht über das schlechte Latein beklagen welches hier von jenseits der Alpen her zu uns herüberschallt: mögen die heutigen Italer nach dem Beispiele der übrigen gebildeten Völker in der Christenheit das lateinische Schreiben aufgeben, wenn sie nur dem Christenthume selbst und der Wissenschaft auch in allen solchen Fächern desto eifriger zu dienen lernen wollen; denn lernen müssen sie dies allerdings erst".

[4] Ceriani, *Monumenta sacra*, p. 12b: "Quidquid salvis membranis ["without ruining the leaves"] effici potuit, puto factum ab amico D. Antonio Ponzio, addicto Archio Diplomatico Mediolanensi, qui artem subsidiorum evanidos characteres et rescriptos codices legendi diligentissime excoluit. Isti debent lectores plures nostri codicis paginas".

[5] *Monumenta sacra et profana* V (1868), p. 8: "Doctor Volkmar in fine libri sui collationem, quam rogatus illi scripseram, inseruit verbis meis servatis. Nemo credet me tam perverse uti mea lingua, ut illic est repraesentata; Doctorem Volkmar video ex contextu mea

(cont.)

Ceriani identified the text as the *Assumptio Mosis* on the basis of the quotation by Gelasius Cyzicenus (see above), corresponding to As. Mos. 1:14. On the contents of As. Mos., however, Ceriani hardly commented; he raised some questions, for instance about the original language of As. Mos., but he did not try to answer them. Soon, however, a considerable number of critical editions and studies appeared.

In 1866, A. Hilgenfeld published the first critical edition of As. Mos. in his *Novum Testamentum extra canonem receptum*[1], soon to be followed by the editions by G. Volkmar (1867), M. Schmidt and A. Merx (1869), and O.F. Fritzsche (1871). In his first edition, prepared with the help of five other scholars (including the same Schmidt and Merx)[2], Hilgenfeld introduced the division of the text into twelve chapters that is still in use[3]. Both in Hilgenfeld's and in Volkmar's editions, the number of conjectural emendations is limited; apart from filling out several illegible passages, most changes in the text are "corrections" of vulgar, unclassical spellings into classical orthography. To this, Schmidt and Merx rightly objected, arguing that in the case of the document at issue an editor should not interfere with the orthography, even if it deviates very much from the classical standards[4]. Notwithstanding this outstanding theoretical insight, Schmidt and Merx themselves did not entirely escape the temptation of normalizing the spelling. Moreover, they went much further in emending the wording of the text by conjectures. Finally, Fritzsche's edition offers a carefully established text, with fine emendations and a prudent evaluation of all formerly suggested conjectures. Fritzsche also introduced the division of Hilgenfeld's chapters into verses, which is still in use.

---

intellexisse, et ipse ut Italice scriberem dixerat; cuinam tribuenda sit corruptio nescirem, sed verba ut nunc sunt, tamquam mea non agnosco."

[1] This work was reprinted in a slightly revised form in 1884. In his periodical *Zeitschrift für wissenschaftliche Theologie* of 1868, Hilgenfeld presented a critical retroversion of the text into Greek, reprinted in *Messias Judaeorum* (1869).

[2] The other three were A. von Gutschmid, R.A. Lipsius and B. Weiss (Hilgenfeld, *Novum Testamentum*, pp. 96, 97).

[3] Volkmar's alternative division into nineteen chapters has not been adopted by later scholars.

[4] "Die Assumptio Mosis", p. 113; so already Ceriani, *Monumenta sacra*, I, p. 12a: "neque refictores nos decet esse versionis, sed editores"; cf. Clemen, *APAT* II, p. 316: "Zu verbessern sind nur wirkliche Schreibfehler (wie sie sich allerdings auch in anderen Codices häufig finden, so daß sie manchmal von Vulgarismen schwer zu scheiden sind)".

c. *The Origin of As. Mos.: Place, Language, Date*

Scholarly discussion on the contents of As. Mos. began with Ewald's review of 1862 of Ceriani's edition of the manuscript[1]. In this review (which was in fact extremely hostile to Ceriani), Ewald addressed the literary-historical questions regarding As. Mos. The original language and date of the writing were discussed at great length by later researchers, but Ewald's concisely formulated views on these matters (see below) were largely accepted by the end of the nineteenth century.

Hardly any discussion was devoted to the geographical origin of As. Mos. Apart from Hilgenfeld, who held that the author of As. Mos. lived in Rome, the great majority of scholars assumed that the author of As. Mos. lived in Palestine[2].

The identification of Palestine as the author's homeland also played a large role in the discussion on the original language of As. Mos. All commentators agreed that the extant Latin text of As. Mos. is a translation from a Greek text. Ewald furthermore claimed that this text in its turn was a translation as well. He argued that the original language of As. Mos. must have been Hebrew because of the many "strong Hebraisms" contained in the book[3]. Schmidt and Merx added to this argument that it is unlikely that a Jewish Palestinian author would have chosen Greek, the language of the abhorred pagan rulers, as the vehicle of his message, instead of his native tongue, Aramaic[4].

In the following decades, these two arguments were repeated several times in essentially the same form, and they gained almost general acceptance[5]. Even Hilgenfeld, who claimed that Greek was the original language of As. Mos., more or less subscribed to the second argument

---

[1] "Monumenta sacra et profana".

[2] Later, Bousset, *Die Religion des Judentums*, 1903, p. 116 ([2]1906, p. 133), suggested on the basis of 4:8 that As. Mos. originated in Babylon; see further Schwartz, "The Tribes" (1980), p. 221.

[3] Ewald, "Monumenta sacra", p. 6: "Die stärksten ja die grellsten Hebraismen wovon die griechische Vorschrift strotzen mußte, zeigen sich noch in dieser Afterübersetzung. Die Urschrift war also sicher hebräisch".

[4] Schmidt and Merx, "Die Assumptio Mosis", pp. 112-113. Schmidt and Merx preferred Aramaic to Hebrew because, they asserted, they had translated the book into both Hebrew and Aramaic, and the Aramaic translation produced a far more natural text. In 1955, Wallace, "The Semitic Origin", showed that it is not possible to decide on linguistic grounds whether Hebrew or Aramaic was more probably the original language.

[5] A number of scholars, including Volkmar and Schürer, considered the matter unsettled.

by asserting that the author of As. Mos. lived in Rome, because Greek could not have been the original language of a Palestinian Jewish book. If the book originated from Palestine, it was thought that Hebrew as the sacred tongue, or Aramaic as the vernacular of the Palestinian Jews, must have been the original language of As. Mos.

Ewald dated As. Mos. to the first third part of the first century C.E. on the basis of the 34 years mentioned in 6:6, a number that corresponds exactly with the duration of Herod's reign as indicated by Flavius Josephus. According to Ewald, the rule of Herod's sons, which is subsequently mentioned, is the last recognizable historical allusion in As. Mos.

Many scholars after Ewald tried to use more evidence from As. Mos. in order to achieve a more precise or an altogether different dating. Generally speaking, four main arguments feature in the debate at this stage: (1) the figures occurring at various places in As. Mos., apparently indicating dates and/or periods of time (e.g. 7:1-2, a very badly damaged passage, in which calculations of some sort are apparently given); (2) the identification of the *rex regum terrae* in chapter 8; (3) the partial destruction of the temple according to 6:9; (4) the identification of the *homines pestilentiosi* in chapter 7:3-10.

(1) The interpretation of numbers given in apocalypses and related writings is a hazardous enterprise, and this applies also to As. Mos. Especially in the nineteenth century, the various calculations that were made in fact show no more than a gross underestimation of the difficulties involved, in spite of rare warnings such as Colani's (as early as 1868)[1]. Hilgenfeld, Volkmar, Schmidt and Merx, and Rönsch[2] all consider the numbers to indicate one way or another real years. It must be said, however, that their calculations mostly presuppose a certain

---

[1] In "L'Assomption de Moïse", pp. 85-87, Colani particularly emphasized that it is unknown which chronology the author used. Schmidt and Merx, "Die Assumptio Mosis", p. 115, assume that the author "folgt—und darin liegt die Lösung des Zahlenräthsels—als Zeitgenosse des Josephus die übliche Rechnung seiner Zeit, wie sie in Josephus Verzeichniss der Hohenpriester vorliegt", but Colani rightly objected, that the author of As. Mos. could have used any chronology, known or unknown to us, e.g. the rabbinical one. In that case, the author expected the eschaton in 350 years: "Rien dans notre Apocalypse ne s'y oppose, comme rien non plus l'indique." Cf. also Drummond, *The Jewish Messiah* (1877), p. 80, who wrote on the "four hours" (7:1), that they are "rather a riddle for the exercise of a fruitless ingenuity than any ground for reasonable confidence", and, with self-knowledge, Volkmar, p. 35: "Da giebt es zu rathen".

[2] Rönsch, "Xeniola ... Chronologisches und Kritisches", pp. 542-562.

date established by other arguments, so that these scholars either have to tamper with the numbers[1], or else resort to extremely intricate calculations[2], unconvincing even to those who have the willingness and endurance to follow them.

(2) A second argument in the dating of As. Mos. depends on the identification of the *rex regum terrae* in chapter 8. This chapter is interpreted either as the description of a historical persecution, or as a prediction of a future persecution, modelled after the persecution of Antiochus IV Epiphanes[3]. Volkmar, followed by Colani[4], identified this king as the emperor Hadrian. They argued that the description is too precise to be a prediction. Furthermore, they held that there have been only two persecutions, that of Antiochus IV, and that of Hadrian. The persecution described in As. Mos. 8 is situated after Herod's rule and Varus's war (chapter 6). Therefore, Hadrian's persecution must be the one referred to[5].

(3) Such a dating, however, requires an explanation of what is said about the "king from the West" in 6:9, who "will burn a *part* of their temple". If As. Mos. is to be dated to the 130's, this clause must, it would seem, point to the destruction of the temple by Titus in 70. Then, it is peculiar that the temple's desolation be described as partial[6].

Several attempts were made to resolve this difficulty. Volkmar suggested that the destruction of the temple was described not in 6:9, but in the calculation of 7:1-2, and that the author apparently found that it needed no further comment[7]. According to Colani, in his article of 1868, the author of As. Mos. was not at all interested in the destruction of the temple, just as he had little appreciation for its rebuilding. The temple's pollution, caused by the arrival of the Romans under Varus, had made the temple worthless; the author of As. Mos. would claim,

---

[1] Of course, numerals are most liable to corruption; therefore, the possibility that they need emendation must be acknowledged—as must the speculative character of such alterations.

[2] So, e.g., Schmidt and Merx, pp. 115-119; Wieseler, "Die jüngst aufgefundene Aufnahme Moses", pp. 626-629.

[3] So Hilgenfeld and Schmidt and Merx. See further de Faye, *Les apocalypses juives* (1892), pp. 71-72.

[4] "L'Assomption de Moïse", pp. 74-75.

[5] Hausrath, *Neutestamentliche Zeitgeschichte* IV ([2]1877), p. 79, considers the *rex regum terrae* to be Vespasian/Titus, and the *ultio altera* (9:2 l. em.) to be Domitian's persecution.

[6] The thesis of a date before 70 has often been defended on the basis of 1:17, where it is said of the *locus* (interpreted as the temple) that it is to exist until the end of time. It is doubtful, however, that the temple is meant by this *locus*; see the commentary.

[7] *Mose Prophetie und Himmelfahrt*, p. 35.

however, that it was dispensable anyway. Even without the temple, the people would still live under God's care, as long as they kept the commandments[1]. The author would therefore have considered it unnecessary to mention the temple's destruction in 70 C.E.

Later, in 1916, Hölscher, equally defending a *post* 70 date, surmised that the temple's destruction was indeed only partial: even today, remains of the Herodian temple in Jerusalem exist, and rabbinical sources continue to speak of "our house" when they mean the destroyed temple. Furthermore, though there may have been no sacrifices in the temple anymore, its ruins were still used as a place of prayer[2].

(4) Most scholars are unconvinced by these arguments, and eventually, the late date fell out of vogue[3]. The debate later centered on the question at which moment in the *vaticinium ex eventu* the author of As. Mos. himself is situated, that is, the moment at which the *vaticinium* turns into a real prediction. The mainstream of research asserted that the author's own time is depicted in chapter 7, the rule of the *homines pestilentiosi et impii, docentes se esse justos* (7:3)[4]. They are the author's opponents, and if they can be identified, they may help in dating As. Mos. Unfortunately, the identifications have varied from Pharisees, Sadducees and Essenes to Sicarians, the younger Herodians and the Roman procurators, and none has proven convincing. These suppositions are mere guesses and allow one to conclude only that the abusive descriptions found in chapter 7 can refer to any group[5].

---

1 "L'Assomption de Moïse", pp. 90-93. Taxo's words in 9:5 should be understood accordingly: "*Haec* [sc. *mandata Dei*, as opposed to the temple] *sunt vires nobis!*" In 1874 M. Vernes, who adopted most of Colani's points of view, proposed an even simpler solution for the silence of As. Mos. on the destruction of the temple in 70: the book is too obscure and incoherent to justify the expectation of a regular exposition (*Histoire des idées*, p. 290).

2 "Über die Entstehungszeit", pp. 124-125. Clark, "Worship in the Temple" (1959/1960), has attacked the assumption of the crucial importance of the events from 70 C.E. Clark has argued on good grounds that the Jerusalem cult continued after that date, until the Jews were definitively expelled from Jerusalem in 135.

3 Hölscher withdrew his suggestion in the sequel to the first part of his article "Über die Entstehungszeit". Instead he followed Steuernagel and Schaefer, who had proposed to him to emend *partem aedis* into *portam aedis*, the destruction of the gates of a city meaning its capture (Jer. 17:27; 51:58; Neh. 1:3; 2:3, 13, 17). As far as I know, the last authors to defend a *post* Bar Kochba date were Zeitlin, "The Assumption of Moses" (1947), and Haacker, "Assumptio Mosis" (1969). Zeitlin does not deal with the problem of the omission of the temple's destruction at all; Haacker regards As. Mos. as a Samaritan writing.

4 A number of scholars considered the real prophecy to begin no earlier than at the theophany in ch. 10, Taxo being a contemporary of the author.

5 Reuss, *Geschichte der heiligen Schriften* (1881), p. 705: "Jeder sagt doch seinen Gegnern solches nach."

d. *Other Contributions*

Apart from editions and annotated translations, a number of articles appeared in this period, the more important of which may be mentioned here. First of all, there were the many articles by H. Rönsch elucidating the "vulgar" nature of the Latin used. His exegetical proposals[1] are less helpful. An intelligent overall interpretation was offered by Colani in 1868[2] (see above), whereas Wieseler in the same year anticipated much of the later discussion on the purpose of As. Mos. in general[3]. Also in 1868, A. Geiger expressed his dissatisfaction with the enthusiastic reception of the "bits and pieces of a lost Assumption of Moses" that had been found. He particularly protested against textual speculation[4] and pan-Essenism[5]. The latter reproach was directed especially against Schmidt and Merx, who had identified the background of the author of As. Mos. as Essene, but on insufficient grounds. P.E. Lucius, in his book on Essenism of 1881, asserted that the essence of the Essenian movement was its rejection of the Temple cult[6]. He also thought that the author of As. Mos. rejected the Temple

---

[1] E.g., in "Xeniola ... Chronologisches und Kritisches", 1874.

[2] Colani linked the discussion between Joshua and Moses in the second part of As. Mos. with the prophecy in the first part. Moses would be the type of the Mosaic cult, Joshua would speak on behalf of the people, bereft of its leader: though Moses dies (i.e., though the cult is polluted and therefore no longer existant), God will care for those who are as faithful and obedient as Taxo.

[3] On pp. 631-632 of his "Die jüngst aufgefundene Aufnahme Moses", Wieseler surprisingly defines As. Mos. with words that only need punctuation, not updating: "Es ist und soll nichts Anderes sein als eine prophetische Auslegung besonders des mosaischen Worts, ein prophetischer Midrasch im Geiste und nach dem Bedürfnisse der damaligen Gegenwart, zeigend daß immer und so auch jetzt, wie Mose einst weissagte, daß die mosaischen Gebote besonders auch durch Abfall von dem einigen wahren Gott nach der Seite des Heidenthums hin übertretende jüdische Volk von diesem gestraft, daß Gott aber das zur Erweckung von Buße hinreichend gezüchtigte Volk jetzt, wie er verheißen, nach Ablauf der vorher bestimmten Jahrwochen der Bedingung der Beobachtung seiner Gebote glücklich machen und seine Gottesherrschaft aufrichten werde."

[4] "Apokryphische Apokalypsen", p. 42: "So ist man in neuester Zeit wieder mit wahrem Heißhunger über einen geretteten Brocken einer verschollenen *Assumptio Mosis* hergefallen, es sucht ihn Einer dem Andern als sein werthvolles Eigenthum abzujagen, eine Beziehung und kritische Conjecturensammlung stellt sich der andern in voller Waffenrüstung entgegen, und das Resultat bleibt—verlorne Mühe."

[5] Geiger, "Apokryphische Apokalypsen", p. 42: "[Die Essäer] werden, als ein in der Dämmerung schwebende Gebilde, überall herangezogen, um andere Dunkelheiten durch sie zu erklären."

[6] *Der Essenismus*, pp. 101-102.

cult. However, Lucius did not jump to the conclusion that the author of
As. Mos. must therefore have been an Essene (as Schmidt and Merx
had proposed), because in view of the scarce evidence available, he
reckoned with the possibility of related, but distinct, currents within
Judaism[1].

---

[1] *Der Essenismus*, p. 119: "Widerlegen lässt sich wohl diese Hypothese nicht, aber auch
nicht bis zur Evidenz erheben, so lange wir nichts Genaueres wissen über die apokalyptischen
Tendenzen und deren Träger im spätern Judenthum. Es könnten [sich] ja recht wohl die
apokalyptische und die essenische zwar wahlverwandte, aber doch nur parallele Richtungen
gebildet haben".

II. Towards Consensus:
The Editions of R. H. Charles (1897, 1913)
and C. Clemen (1900, 1904)

Two new publications summarized all previous discussion and put forward opinions and arguments that gained almost general approval for a long period.

R.H. Charles published his *The Assumption of Moses* in 1897. In it, he gave the text of the Latin manuscript, alongside a critically emended text, as well as a translation into English, provided with detailed exegetical annotations. Also, Charles presented an elaborate and conveniently arranged survey of the literary-historical questions. His translation and introduction reappeared in a revised form in the second volume of his *The Apocrypha and Pseudepigrapha of the Old Testament* in 1913 (pp. 407-424).

C. Clemen provided a German translation with an equally helpful introduction in Kautzsch's *Apokryphen und Pseudepigraphen des Alten Testaments* II, of 1900 (pp. 311-331). In 1904 Clemen re-edited the text of the Latin manuscript on the basis of a renewed examination of the manuscript and a collation with Ceriani's edition. Clemen's edition contains the unemended text of the manuscript, with short notes, mainly on the vulgar characteristics of the Latin used.

Charles's work has been of great importance and far-reaching influence. It is not always as critical as it intends to be, and at times it is somewhat hasty and careless. His edition of As. Mos. is marred by drastic emendations, frequently based on the Hebrew original Charles presupposed.

The introduction to his commentary contains a survey of other apocryphal books connected with Moses, including those of which only the titles are known, and a review of earlier editions and critical investigations. Charles then proceeds to describe the manuscript, its main scribal errors and its linguistic peculiarities. A comparison with the Latin of codex *k* of the Gospels (codex Bobiensis) led him to date the Latin translation of As. Mos. no later than the fifth century[1].

---

[1] Cf. however Hoogterp, *Etude sur le latin*, p. 17: "k est la copie directe d'un archétype de la fin du 3me siècle."

With regard to the literary-historical questions, Charles propounded four important theses, of which three were to become standard positions for many decades.

(1) The Greek text which underlies the Latin fragment is itself a translation from Hebrew[1]. Although this was not a new thesis, Charles was able to give it greater credibility by citing a number of examples of Hebrew idiom which he claimed could not have occurred in an original Latin or Greek text. Clemen doubted the worth of Charles's evidence. He objected that the argument of Hebraizing idiom was not at all conclusive, and that no patent mistranslations from Hebrew or Aramaic could be discerned with certainty in the extant Latin fragment of As. Mos.[2] Regrettably, Clemen's warnings have largely been neglected, and the evaluation of Wallace, who in 1955 called the evidence brought forward by Charles "overwhelming"[3], is illustrative of the direction taken by many later studies of As. Mos.[4]

(2) In his *Geschichte des jüdischen Volkes* (1886-1890, [3-4]1901-1909), E. Schürer suggested that the Latin fragment was in fact not the Assumption of Moses, but the Testament of Moses, the title of which is mentioned alongside the Assumption of Moses in Ps.-Athanasius' *Synopsis* and Nicephorus' *Stichometry*[5]. According to Schürer, the Testament and the Assumption of Moses were two parts of one work. Charles modified this suggestion, and argued that the Testament and the Assumption of Moses were originally independent compositions, which were at a later stage merged into one book. The extant Latin text would be a part of this composite work, namely the part which was originally the Testament of Moses[6]. Clemen accepted this explanation, although he took care to interject phrases like: "Unmöglich ist das nicht ... denkbar ist es ... aber sicher ist alles das natürlich keineswegs"[7].

---

[1] Charles, *The Assumption*, pp. xxxviii-xlv; cf. *APOT* II, p. 410.

[2] Clemen, *APAT* II, p. 315: "Hebraismen und Aramäismen sind ja für sich überhaupt noch nicht beweisend ... Entscheidend wären nur offenkundige Übersetzungsfehler oder dem jetzigen Text zu Grunde liegende Korruptionen des semitischen Ausdrucks; aber dergleichen läßt sich ... in Wahrheit nirgends nachweisen."

[3] Wallace, "The Semitic Origin", p. 321.

[4] Since Charles, no one has ever actually tried to argue the case for a Semitic origin anew; Wallace and Laperrousaz, *Le Testament de Moïse*, pp. 17-25, are content to discuss the question whether the original language was Hebrew or Aramaic.

[5] On Ps.-Athanasius' *Synopsis*, see above. For the text of Nicephorus' *Stichometry*, see Zahn, *Geschichte des Neutestamentlichen Kanons* II, 1, pp. 295-301.

[6] Charles, *The Assumption*, pp. xlv-l; cf. *APOT* II, pp. 407-409.

[7] Clemen, *APAT* II, p. 312.

Charles's main argument for his proposal was the fact that the Latin fragment on several occasions unequivocally speaks of Moses' death, whereas the title of the book, Ἀνάληψις Μωσέως, would imply that Moses was considered not to have died, but to have been taken up to heaven. However, it has since been made abundantly clear that ἀνά-ληψις and *assumptio* do not necessarily mean "assumption into heaven". The words may very well have meant "the taking away", i.e., the death (of Moses). Moreover, it is possible to speak of someone's death as the ascension of his soul into heaven[1].

(3) A less successful theory was that of the dislocation of chapters 8-9. Charles noted that these chapters describe the Antiochan persecution, whereas chapters 5-6 describe the Hasmonean and Herodian periods. He argued that chapters 8-9 were accidentally dislocated, and proposed that they be returned to their proper place, before chapter 5. This somewhat naive solution was rightly rejected by Clemen, who recognized, as earlier commentators had done, that the description in chapters 8-9 had just used the "colours" of the Antiochan period in order to prophesy the future as a time of climactic disaster[2]. Charles's hypothesis was definitively refuted by C.C. Lattey (1942) and J. Licht (1961) (see below, section III).

(4) The fourth thesis defended by Charles concerns the ideological background of the author of As. Mos.[3] As was usual in his day, Charles took as his model Josephus' classification of Jewish philosophy: Sadducees, Pharisees, Essenes and Zealots. Charles gave various reasons why the author of As. Mos. could not have been a Sadducee, Essene or Zealot. By a process of elimination, Charles concluded that the author must have been a Pharisee, adding that he must have been of the quietistic sort (a type, by the way, not mentioned by Josephus), very much resembling the Hasidim of the early Maccabean times.

The expression "Pharisaic quietist" (Clemen: "pharisäischer Quietist"[4]) or "quietistic Pharisee" has often been applied to the author of

---

[1] Van Stempvoort, "The Interpretation of the Ascension" (1958-1959), pp. 32-33; see especially Lohfink, *De Himmelfahrt Jesu* (1971), pp. 63-69. The identification of the Ἀνάληψις Μωσέως as the Hebrew *Petirat Mosheh* proposed in the 17th century suggests that the early critics were well aware that ἀνάληψις can mean "death".

[2] Clemen, *APAT* II, p. 313.

[3] Charles, *The Assumption*, pp. li-liv; cf. *APOT* II, p. 411.

[4] *APAT* II, p. 315.

As. Mos. ever since[1], notwithstanding the better understanding which has developed during the twentieth century, both of Josephus and of the variety of Jewish spiritual life in the Hellenistic and Roman era.

Clemen is a far more cautious scholar than Charles, but on the whole, he is sympathetic to most of Charles's proposals.

The works of Charles and Clemen were the most thorough that had yet been published. It is not unfair to say, however, that the lasting influence their work has exerted is somewhat disproportionate. To a certain extent, their influence must be due to the publication of their annotated translations in the monumental collections of the Old Testament Apocrypha and Pseudepigrapha in England and Germany respectively (Charles's *APOT* of 1913, and Kautzsch's *APAT* of 1900). For a number of decades, these collections were the sole sources of this kind of Jewish literature for many students and theologians. Charles and Clemen are not responsible for that.

Charles and Clemen were closely followed in the annotated translations of As. Mos. by W. J. Ferrar (second impression 1918), by P. Rießler (1927), and, much later, by E. Brandenburger (1976).

---

[1] Laperrousaz, *Le Testament de Moïse*, p. 95, has argued for an Essene origin of As. Mos., but he agreed at least that he was a quietist: "c'était un Essénien quiétiste".

III. WANING OF INTEREST (CA. 1900-CA. 1970). A FEW DISSENTERS

In the period following the publication of the works by Charles and Clemen, few studies appeared that cast new light on As. Mos. In 1925 G. Kuhn issued a number of exegetical observations, many of them based on the supposed Semitic original of As. Mos. P. Rießler's poetic translation of 1928 does not seem to have been intended as a contribution to scholarly research into As. Mos. Some shorter articles were published in the 40's and 50's on the figure of Taxo, which are briefly treated in the appendix to this introduction. S. Zeitlin's treatment of As. Mos. in the *Jewish Quarterly Review* of 1947/1948 is extensive, but of little use. The new exegetical solutions proposed in it are far-fetched and unconvincing[1]. Zeitlin, by the way, was one of the last scholars to propose a date after 70[2]. D.H. Wallace's article of 1955 on the original language of As. Mos. has been mentioned above. A. Kahana's translation of As. Mos. into Hebrew published in 1956 can be seen as an interesting experiment[3]. It must be concluded that scholarly interest in As. Mos. was waning. Little of lasting value was written during this period, with the exception of the contributions discussed below.

In 1916, G. Hölscher wrote an article on the date of origin of As. Mos., which contains serious criticism of the widely accepted arguments. In particular, Hölscher showed that the similarities between the Roman intervention described in 6:8-9 and the war of Varus in 4 B.C.E. as described by Josephus are only superficial. Hölscher's own dating of As. Mos. (131 C.E., during the Bar-Kochba revolt), however, is no more convincing. As noted above, Hölscher stated that As. Mos.

---

[1] For instance, Zeitlin's interpretation: "Taxo's statement to his seven sons that they should fast for three [days] meant that they should suffer for 300 years" ("The Assumption of Moses", p. 33).

[2] Zeitlin, "The Assumption of Moses", p. 11, maintained that the author in 1:2 gives the date of Moses' death according to the *Anno mundi*-era. "Only after the destruction of the Second Temple did this manner of designating the era come into vogue. Thus, we may say with certainty that this book ... could have been composed only *after* the destruction of the Second Temple". Zeitlin does not refer to the problem of the "partial" destruction of the temple.

[3] According to Rowley, *The Relevance*, p. 153, a translation of the Latin text into Hebrew had also been made by Kaminetsky and was published in: *Ha-Shiloah* 15 (1905).

6:8-9 refers to the destruction of the temple by Titus[1], but he does not succeed in explaining the characterization of that destruction as "partial" in 6:9. Hölscher's dating is supported with ingenious calculations based on the symbolical numbers in As. Mos.[2] In 1919 Clemen reacted to Hölscher's proposals, refuting his dating with ease, but failing to respond to his criticisms[3].

M.R. James published an important little book on *The Lost Apocrypha of the Old Testament* in 1920, in which he carefully considered Charles's suggestion about the composite character of As. Mos. Charles, it may be remembered, had argued that the extant Latin text unequivocally speaks only of Moses' death, and concluded that this text was the Testament of Moses, an originally independent book, later amalgamated with the Assumption of Moses, which must have included the account of Moses' ascension into heaven, now lost. On the basis of the Greek quotations and of related traditions about the end of Moses' life in early ecclesiastical literature, James reconstructed the broad outlines of the narrative which the lost ending of As. Mos. might have contained. James conceded that the complexion of the Latin text does not resemble this reconstructed narrative, but he declined to conclude from their different characters that the two books were originally separate writings. Instead, he revived the suggestion made by Rönsch in 1874[4], namely, that the Testament of Moses is identical with the Book of Jubilees (see further below, section V,a).

In 1942, C.C. Lattey addressed the problem of the position of chapters 8-9[5]. Charles had suggested transposing chapters 8-9, which would deal with the Antiochan persecution and the "Maccabean" martyrs, and inserting chapter 8-9 between chapters 5 and 6, their chronologically correct position. Lattey accepted the transposition of chapter 8, but objected to transferring chapter 9 along with 8. In 9:7, Taxo affirms that he expects his and his sons' blood to be avenged. "Then comes

---

[1] "Über die Entstehungszeit", p. 112.
[2] "Über die Entstehungszeit", p. 153: "Es ist schwerlich Zufall, daß sich drei chronologische Rätselspiele unserer Apokalypse zu so vollkommener Harmonie lösen lassen. Ihre Erklärung ergibt, daß der Verfasser der Apokalypse im Jahre 131 n. Chr. schrieb und daß er das Weltende für das Jahr 159 n. Chr. erwartete."
[3] Clemen, "Die Entstehungszeit der Himmelfahrt des Mose".
[4] *Das Buch der Jubiläen*, pp. 480-482.
[5] Lattey, "The Messianic Expectation in the Assumption of Moses".

chapter X, which evidently goes on to speak of the consummation that will follow"[1]. This demonstrates the close relationship between chapters 9 and 10, and argues against the transfer of chapter 9. Taxo's role is "to be a suffering Messiah, and his death is to bring about a glorious consummation"[2]. Also, Lattey drew attention to the vicarious effect of Taxo's death. Lattey's article, in spite of some idiosyncracies[3], was important in recognizing the eschatological process as expected in As. Mos.

In 1961, J. Licht published an article on the instrumental role of Taxo in provoking the coming of God's kingdom[4]. Moreover, in an appendix to this article, Licht made a tentative suggestion with regard to the literary history of As. Mos. Lattey was unconvincing in his argument for the displacement of chapter 8. Licht, however, maintained that chapters 8 and 9 are just as closely bound to each other as chapters 9 and 10. Licht viewed As. Mos. 6-7 as adaptations of an apocalypse originally written at the beginning of the Hasmonean revolt, and reworked in post-Herodian times. As. Mos. 8-9, in the original form of the document, would have described the persecution under Antiochus IV and would thus have "suggested that the deeds of the Hasidean Martyrs had the eschatological significance of provoking Divine vengeance."[5] This suggestion has had important consequences for modern scholarly discussion of the document after it was taken up by G.W.E. Nickelsburg in 1972.

---

[1] Lattey, "The Messianic Expectation", p. 12.

[2] Lattey, "The Messianic Expectation", p. 17; cf. Hengel, *Die Zeloten*, p. 272.

[3] In order to explain the displacement of chap. 8 Lattey adduces Thomas Aquinas, and he objects to Taxo's "hunger-strike, a death so voluntary that it must surely be reprobated as a suicide" (p. 17).

[4] Licht, "Taxo, or the Apocalyptic Doctrine of Vengeance".

[5] Licht, "Taxo, or the Apocalyptic Doctrine of Vengeance", pp. 102-103.

IV. RESEARCH SINCE 1970

a. *Revival of Interest; New Translations*

Interest in As. Mos. revived around 1970. In 1968, G. Reese wrote his dissertation on the view of history in various Jewish writings, including As. Mos. The dissertation was not published[1], but a summary was published by D. J. Harrington in 1973[2]. Although his literary history of As. Mos. is not very useful, Reese's work contains many helpful exegetical observations.

In 1970, an annotated translation of As. Mos. into French was published by E.-M. Laperrousaz[3], which provided an extensive critical account (to which the present survey owes much) of the history of research into As. Mos. His thorough treatment of the literary-historical questions is the most significant contribution to the study of As. Mos. since Charles, even if Laperrousaz' book cannot be called a real commentary. Especially laudable was Laperrousaz' decision to reprint Ceriani's edition of the manuscript, which now became readily accessible to a wider circle of researchers. The publication of Laperrousaz' work may have been a major factor in the revival of scholarly interest As. Mos. in the 1970's.

Since Laperrousaz' book, a number of annotated translations of As. Mos. appeared. Mention has been made above of the annotated translation into German by E. Brandenburger of 1976. J. Priest's translation in Charlesworth's collection *The Old Testament Pseudepigrapha* (1983)[4] is on the whole acceptable. However, his treatment of the literary-historical questions and his annotations are in some cases somewhat superficial. Sweet's translation is included in H.F.D. Sparks' collection of *Old Testament Pseudepigrapha* (1984). This volume (and consequently Sweet's translation of As. Mos. as well) is of limited value because of the total lack of explanatory footnotes. A Spanish annotated

---

[1] G.W.E. Nickelsburg generously provided me with a photocopy of Reese's chapter on As. Mos.

[2] "Summary", pp. 69-70.

[3] Republished, with a strongly abridged introduction, in *La Bible de la Pléiade, Ecrits intertestamentaires* (1987).

[4] "Testament of Moses", *OTP* II, pp. 919-939.

translation with an extensive introduction by A. Vegas Montaner was published in Diez Mácho's collection in 1987.

In 1989, Schalit's *Untersuchungen zur Assumptio Mosis* appeared. Schalit had worked on his commentary for more than twenty years[1], but died before completing the first part, which deals only with As. Mos. 1. Schalit's criticisms of earlier scholarship are usually sound. His own exegetical proposals, however, are often far-fetched, and his presentation of the evidence less than felicitous.

b. *The Milieu of Origin of As. Mos.*

K. Haacker in 1969, suggested that As. Mos. is a Samaritan writing[2]. To support his suggestion, he adduced a considerable number of passages from As. Mos. paralleled in the Samaritan Chronicles and in the Teaching of the Samaritan theologian Marqah[3]. On closer inspection, it appears that these passages are paralleled in many Jewish writings as well, so that they cannot be regarded as conclusive evidence of a Samaritan origin[4]. The main arguments Haacker propounded for such an origin, however, are the founding of a temple by Joshua, which seems to be implied in 1:17[5], and the fact that As. Mos. does not mention any other prophet than Moses.

These arguments may be answered as follows. The "place" in which Joshua has to hide Moses' prophecy according to As. Mos. 1:17 is probably not a temple, but a secret location (see the commentary). The fact that no prophet other than Moses is mentioned is not sufficiently significant. In a review of history as concise as that given in As. Mos., the prophets could be omitted as factors of minor importance in the history of Israel's unfaithfulness, which is sharply contrasted to the

---

[1] In 1969, R. Oost (Groningen) abandoned his plan to write a commentary on As. Mos., after having made preparatory investigations esp. into chapter 10, because it became known that Schalit was preparing a commentary.

[2] "Assumptio Mosis—eine samaritanische Schrift?"; cf. Schäfer and Haacker, "Nachbiblische Traditionen" (1974).

[3] These Samaritan sources date from the 4th century C.E. onwards; see Purvis, "Samaritan Traditions", p. 93. Haacker, "Assumptio Mosis", pp. 403-405, dated As. Mos. after 135 C.E.

[4] Cf. Purvis, "Samaritan Traditions", p. 117: "As for the theological understanding of Moses and Joshua, these were ... characteristic of at least one circle of Samaritan thought. There is no reason to maintain, however, that such views were the exclusive property of Samaritan theologians".

[5] Cf. Haacker and Schäfer, "Nachbiblische Traditionen", p. 157.

grandeur of the one great Prophet and of the law he has mediated. It should also be noted that there are clear indications that the author of As. Mos. knew prophets other than Moses.

In 1972, J.D. Purvis added even more comparative material from Samaritan sources, but rightly concluded that the similarities are not indicative of a close relationship, especially since the traditions at issue concern such an important figure as Moses[1].

In 1970 Laperrousaz, in his survey of the history of research on As. Mos., discussed the various milieus to which the author of As. Mos. was said to belong. Laperrousaz himself defended an Essene origin for As. Mos. His argumentation, however, is weak. Apart from Schmidt and Merx, he mentions a number of scholars who linked As. Mos. to the movement behind the newly discovered Dead Sea Scrolls, including A. Dupont-Sommer who first put forward this thesis in 1950[2]. S. Mowinckel in 1951[3] also regarded the author of As. Mos. as a member of the sect of Qumran, mainly because of his identification of Taxo (9:1) with the Essene מחוקקק[4]. To support the thesis of an Essene origin for As. Mos., he also pointed to the retreat of Taxo and his sons into the desert and to the sectarian character of As. Mos. M. Delcor added to these details Moses' instruction to Joshua in As. Mos. 1:17 to conceal the books he gives him into jars, a procedure well attested in the Qumran caves[5]. Laperrousaz rejected Mowinckel's hypothesis concerning Taxo, and relativized the references to Taxo's retreat into the desert and to the storage of books in jars[6], but once more resorted to Josephus' "parties", and after excluding for various reasons the Zealot, Pharisaic and Sadducean philosophies, was left with the Essenes[7]. The

---

[1] "Samaritan Traditions on the Death of Moses".

[2] *Aperçus préliminaires*, p. 115.

[3] In 1951, Mowinckel published *Han som kommer*, better known in the English translation of 1956, *He That Cometh*.

[4] See below, in the appendix to this introduction.

[5] "Contribution à l'étude", pp. 64-65.

[6] Laperrousaz, *Le Testament de Moïse*, p. 94, calls these references "interesting".

[7] Janssen, *Das Gottesvolk*, pp. 101-108, argued for understanding 4:7-8 (where it is said that the temple is rebuilt by some parts of the tribes, but that the two tribes are sad because they cannot offer sacrifices) as the description of the schismatic group to which the author of As. Mos. belonged. Janssen made no effort to identify this group with one of Josephus' philosophies, but was content to call it a "Sondergruppe" (p. 107). An abstract of Janssen's book was published by Harrington in an appendix to his "Interpreting Israel's History" (1973), pp. 66-68.

109

theological agreements between As. Mos. and the Essenes that Laperrousaz noted are, however, of far too general a nature to allow such a precise conclusion[1].

In fact, Reese argued in 1968 that the author of As. Mos. was not a member of any sect[2]. Reese explained the withdrawal of Taxo and his sons into the desert not as a reference to specific sectarian practices, but as a literary and theological topos[3]. The rest of the theology expressed in As. Mos., too, is perfectly traditional, and it does not allow the identification of the milieu of origin of As. Mos. with any particular ideological denomination[4]. A great advantage of the assumption of a non-sectarian milieu for As. Mos. is that one does not have to explain how a sectarian writing could have turned up in the Christian church and maintained itself well into the fifth century.

c. *The Literary Integrity of As. Mos.*

After the publication of Laperrousaz' introduction and translation, another stimulus for renewed attention for As. Mos. was no doubt the work of G.W.E. Nickelsburg. In *Resurrection, Immortality, and Eternal Life in Intertestamental Judaism* (1972), Nickelsburg devoted a section to As. Mos. which became influential and was much discussed. Nickelsburg addressed the question of the literary history of As. Mos. anew, taking Licht's suggestion (see above, section III) as his lead. In 1973, a Society of Biblical Literature (SBL) seminar on As. Mos. was held, the papers of which were published in the same year. A large part of this collection is devoted to the questions raised by Nickelsburg in his dissertation. J.J. Collins, participating in this discussion, at first criticized Nickelsburg's arguments, but he eventually acceded to them. For a period, Licht's and Nickelsburg's view of the literary history was accepted by many scholars, although it never won the wide approval that the theories of Charles once enjoyed. In the 1980's, however, Nickelsburg's point of view has met with increasing doubt.

---

[1] Laperrousaz, *Le Testament de Moïse*, pp. 94-95 mentions: interest in the temple cult, Israel's living among the stars in the eschatological future, and God's all-encompassing sovereignty.

[2] Reese, *Die Geschichte Israels*, p. 124, subscribed to Charles's identification of the author of As. Mos. as a Pharisee, but the Pharisees cannot be called a proper "sect".

[3] Reese, *Die Geschichte Israels*, pp. 105-107.

[4] Reese, *Die Geschichte Israels*, pp. 121-123.

Licht had convincingly shown that chapters 8-9, which reflect the well-known traditions surrounding the Antiochan persecution and the beginning of the Maccabean revolt, are inextricably bound up with chapter 10, the description of the theophany and the establishment of the kingdom of God. According to Licht, chapters 8-9 must therefore not be transposed before chapter 6, where allusions are made to king Herod and his sons. This again poses the problem why Antiochus and the Maccabeans seem to have been described after the Herodians, and immediately before the advent of God's kingdom. Licht tentatively suggested that chapters 6-7 were interpolations added in Herodian times, intended to update the book.

Before Charles, Hilgenfeld concluded that the traditions on Antiochus and the Maccabeans were used and digested by the author of As. Mos. as more or less mythical material to build a scenario of the time of the end[1]. In 1970, Laperrousaz again argued that the Antiochan material was simply used to produce an eschatological tableau[2].

In 1972, however, and again at the SBL seminar in 1973, Nickelsburg presented a number of serious arguments in favor of Licht's theory about the literary history of As. Mos.[3].

(1) The first argument, taken over from Licht, is based on the insight that chapters 8-9 are logically connected with chapter 10. It is furthermore assumed that chapters 8-9 describe historical facts, and not the events expected in the eschatological future. Nickelsburg challenged Laperrousaz' view of chapters 8-9 as parts of an eschatological tableau by adducing "the apocalyptic premise ... that the author stands at the end of time". Since, according to Nickelsburg, the author of As. Mos. describes in chapters 8-9 the Antiochan persecution, which the author (in accordance with his "apocalyptic premise" just mentioned) evidently regards as the time immediately preceding the end, it can be deduced that he lived during the persecution described[4]. In this view, chapters

---

[1] Hilgenfeld, "Die Psalmen Salomo's", p. 305, on 8:2-3: "Wer sieht denn nicht, dass diese Schilderung über alle Wirklichkeit weit hinausgeht, bloss der Befürchtung angehört? Schon Antiochos IV. Epiphanes hatte die Beschneidung verboten ... Der römische Kaiser, so erwartet unser Verf., soll nun gar bei beschnittenen Kindern durch Aerzte eine Vorhaut erziehen lassen."

[2] *Le Testament de Moïse*, p. 122.

[3] Nickelsburg's theory supports his view that the description of the eschatological process in As. Mos. 10 draws "on a form of the material in Daniel 12:1-3 more primitive than the Danielic form", *Resurrection*, p. 30.

[4] *Resurrection*, p. 45.

8-9 describe events which chronologically precede those referred to in chapter 6. Yet they must not be transposed before chapter 6, because of their close connection with chapter 10. Therefore, it must be concluded that chapter 6 is a later interpolation.

(2) Nickelsburg also produced a form-critical argument. "The Assumption of Moses is structured according to a definite historical scheme, which occurs elsewhere in contemporary Jewish literature, and whose roots are found in the latter part of Deuteronomy—of which the Assumption of Moses is a rewriting". This scheme is presented by Nickelsburg as follows[1]:

1. Sin	ch.	5 (2)	Deut. 28:15
2. Punishment		8 (3:1-4)	28:16-68
3. Turning Point		9 (3:5-4:4)	30:2
4. Salvation		10 (4:5-9)	30:3-10

(3) Finally, Nickelsburg attempted to underpin his theory of the literary history of As. Mos. with arguments of a historical nature. During the SBL seminar, Nickelsburg stressed the unique specificity of the description of the Antiochan persecution, which would be best explained if regarded as an eyewitness's report[2].

I shall return to Nickelsburg's arguments in section V.

d. *Genre*

In 1976, E. Cortès, and in 1980, E. von Nordheim paid extensive attention to the formal characteristics of As. Mos.[3], and provided a thorough basis for the classification of As. Mos. as a formal "testament", or rather "farewell discourse".

The form of As. Mos. agrees with what is known from other examples of the genre of the farewell discourse. In the introduction 1:1-9 it is related that Moses summons Joshua, and addresses him; the words *vocavit ad se*/προσκαλεσάμενος are characteristic of the genre. In 1:10, Moses begins his speech with "a kind of prelude", which ends with the

---

[1] *Resurrection*, p. 44.

[2] "An Antiochan Date", p. 35.

[3] Cortès, *Los discursos de adiós*, pp. 140-146; Von Nordheim, *Die Lehre der Alten*, I, pp. 194-207.

characteristic announcement of Moses' impending death (1:15) and instructions with regard to the preservation of the speech Moses will presently be delivering (1:16-18). The speech itself is a prophecy concerning the future of the people from the entrance into the land until the coming of the kingdom of God (2:1-10:10). At the end of his speech, Moses commands Joshua again to preserve the prophecy, and again announces his death[1]. Then it is said that Joshua interrupts Moses' speech with a lament and a confession of his own incompetence to succeed Moses (chapter 11). This passage is an expansion of the basic pattern of the genre of the farewell discourse. Chapter 12 tells how Moses comforts Joshua and admonishes him (and the intended reader) to remain faithful to the law. The fragment closes with a reference to the covenant and God's oath which guarantee the final salvation. In the expansion of chapters 11 and 12, the problem of continuity is dealt with, as U.B. Müller noted in 1974[2]. Moses will leave, but the law and God's promise will remain, and will enable Joshua to be a worthy successor to Moses[3].

In view of the almost exemplary formal structure, Von Nordheim concluded that one could assume that the lost ending of As. Mos. conformed to the testament format as well. Moreover, in chapter 12 the discussion between Moses and Joshua has come to a satisfactory conclusion. According to Von Nordheim, it is therefore likely that the lost ending contained not much more than a rather short account of Moses' death and burial[4].

With regard to the contents and purpose of As. Mos., Von Nordheim stressed that the book, like all farewell discourses[5], is primarily concerned with moral instruction. Moses' prophecy contains little explicit paraenesis, yet, according to Von Nordheim, the main

---

[1] Von Nordheim, *Die Lehre der Alten*, I, p. 202, attempted to squeeze this passage into the testament scheme by labelling 10:11 and 13 as admonition.

[2] Similar points were already made by Colani in 1868; see above. Priest completely misses the point when in "Testament of Moses", p. 919, he considers chap. 11 to be merely "a few responses of Joshua, which serve to facilitate the flow of Moses' speech".

[3] Müller, "Die Parakletenvorstellung". Oost and Kolenkow made similar points with regard to the intercessor of 4:1 and Taxo: these figures, should be seen as representatives of the "Mosaic succession".

[4] Von Nordheim had in mind the particular passage on the death of Moses in the Byzantine *Palaea historica*. See on that passage the commentary on the lost ending.

[5] *Die Lehre der Alten*, I, p. 233: "Das Herz der Testamentsform schlägt ... in der Verhaltensanweisung!"

purpose of As. Mos. is to convey an ethical message[1]. It has been noted that Von Nordheim is here trying to force As. Mos. into the pattern of the Testaments of the Twelve Patriarchs, strongly emphasizing the similarities, while underemphasizing the differences[2].

It cannot be denied that there is an ethical element in As. Mos. The ethical point in Moses' prophecy (As. Mos. 2-10) was treated by A.B. Kolenkow in 1973. She drew attention to the *Doppelschema* that occurs in what she calls "blessing testaments"[3]. In such testaments, someone's last words consist of an account of some of the speaker's experiences and of the results of his actions. This account serves to illustrate the necessity of the sequence of sin and punishment, and of piety and reward. This necessity is projected by the speaker into the future, and thus serves as an admonition to the readers to act according to God's will.

Similarly, the author of As. Mos. presents to his readers the pre-exilic and exilic history of Israel with which they are already familiar[4]. His account is based on the Deuteronomistic pattern of history (Sin-Punishment-Repentance-Salvation), and is intended to prove the reality of that pattern. In chapters 7-10, the pattern is projected into the eschatological future, which the author believed to be near. The ethical implication is clear. According to chapters 9-10, God will bring salvation to Israel when a few will have remained steadfast during the most dreadful afflictions. The forecast of such a righteous judgment at the end of the imminent eschatological events is an admonition to remain steadfast, even in the tribulations the author expects to be coming soon[5].

---

[1] Von Nordheim, *Die Lehre der Alten*, I, p. 206: "Der Zweck der ganzen Schrift ist damit nicht die Offenbarung des Zukünftigen an sich sondern die Anleitung zu einem dementsprechenden Verhalten".

[2] See Lebram, review of Von Nordheim, col. 415, and Hollander, *Joseph as an Ethical Model*, p. 6, who also notes that Cortès' conception of the genre is rightly far less rigid. A strictness similar to that of Von Nordheim has been displayed by scholars who have tried to define the "apocalypse" formally and who have denied that As. Mos. can be called an apocalypse, because it is a farewell discourse; see esp. Collins, *Apocalypse*, pp. 45-46. As a consequence of this rigid distinction in some recent books on Jewish literature, As. Mos. is discussed alongside, for instance, the Testaments of the Twelve Patriarchs and the Testament of Job, rather than among those books with which it has most in common.

[3] "The Assumption of Moses as a Testament"; cf. Kolenkow's study on this matter in general, "The Genre Testament" (1975).

[4] The pseudo-prophetic character of Moses' speech causes history to be related in the future tense, but we may leave that aside for the moment.

[5] Cf. Reese, *Die Geschichte Israels*, p. 110, who stresses the actual importance of the elaborate description of the people's repentance in As. Mos. 3: "In der Erinnerung an die

(cont.)

C. Münchow, in his book on ethics in eschatological writings (1981), has drawn attention to the tension between the necessity of the course of history as predicted by Moses and the connection between sin and punishment, theologically formulated in As. Mos. 12: in the process of vindication, human merits are excluded, but ethical responsibility is emphasised[1]. The importance of this observation is that it shows the coherence of As. Mos. 2-10 and 11-12, which has been denied by some and neglected by many.

Vorgänge im Exil wird offenbar, wie das Volk beschaffen sein muß, wenn Gott ihm sein Erbarmen zuwenden soll."

[1] Münchow, *Ethik und Eschatologie*, p. 73: the author of As. Mos. "legt mit dem Hinweis auf die Treue und Barmherzigkeit Gottes (12:7) dar, warum das Volk Israel nach den Jahren der Bedrückung und Sünde (7:1 ff.) eine Zeit des Heils erwarten kann. Er betont zugleich die ethische Verantwortlichkeit des Menschen"; cf. p. 74: the covenant is both the basis of God's righteous punishment and the guarantee of salvation. Compare also Reese, *Die Geschichte Israels*, pp. 119-120; Von Nordheim, *Die Lehre der Alten* I, p. 199.

V. SUMMARY AND CONCLUSIONS

a. *Title*

The long fragment of the Jewish book under discussion was known in the early Christian church as the Ἀνάληψις Μωσέως and *Ascensio* or *Assumptio Mosis*.

Two arguments have been adduced to identify the book with the Διαθήκη Μωσέως or *Testamentum Mosis*: (1) The fragment designated as *Assumptio Mosis* does not in fact portray the ascension (*assumptio*) of Moses into heaven; (2) The fragment displays the characteristics of the testament genre. It has been noted above, however, that the first argument is not valid. The terms ἀνάληψις and *assumptio* do not necessarily mean a living person's "ascension (into heaven)". Indeed, according to some contemporary concepts of afterlife, these terms can refer to the *post mortem* ascent of the soul. The second argument equates a modern generic label with an ancient title. This is a hazardous enterprise, as is illustrated by the fact that the book which is commonly called *Testament of Abraham* does not fall within the generic category of the testament[1]. Thus the attempt to identify our Latin text with the *Testamentum Mosis* must be dismissed.

Although there is also little positive evidence for the identification of the fragment under discussion as the *Assumptio Mosis*, it cannot be ignored, as James has rightly emphasized in his *Lost Apocrypha* of 1920[2]. Gelasius quotes our writing and mentions as its title Ἀνάληψις Μωσέως. That is the only evidence, and we must not dismiss it simply because "Testament of Moses" would in the eyes of modern scholarship be a more appropriate title. On the other hand, there are three indications that suggest that "Testament of Moses" was a title associated with the book of Jubilees[3]. (1) The *Catena* of Nicephorus quotes Jub. 10:21, mentioning as its title ἡ Διαθήκη[4]. (2) Jubilees is not included in Ps.-Athanasius' *Synopsis* (see above, section I, a); in that list, the *Testamen-*

---

[1] Delcor, *Le Testament d'Abraham*, p. 42.
[2] *The Lost Apocrypha*, p. 50.
[3] Cf. Denis, *Introduction*, pp. 136, 160-161.
[4] James, *The Lost Apocrypha*, pp. 49-50; for the text of the scholion see VanderKam, *The Book of Jubilees* I, p. 267

tum Mosis precedes the *Assumptio Mosis*. (3) The codex in which the fragment of As. Mos. occurs also contains the Latin fragments of Jubilees.

The identification of Jubilees with Test. Mos. has been rejected because of the length of Test. Mos. as indicated in the *Stichometry* of Nicephorus[1], but many of Nicephorus' numbers are not in agreement with the actual size of the books in question and cannot be considered absolutely trustworthy.

b. *Date*

Ewald's arguments for the dating of As. Mos. in the early first century C.E. seem to recommend themselves.

In 6:6, it is stated that a *rex petulans* will rule for 34 years. This number agrees exactly with the number of years Herod the Great ruled (37-4 B.C.E.). In 6:7-8, mention is made of *nati qui breviora tempora dominabunt* (l. em.) These children of the rash king are most naturally taken to be Herod's sons, Archelaus, Antipas and Philip. Actually, only Archelaus ruled for a relatively short time (4 B.C.E.-6 C.E.), Antipas and Philip ruled for considerable periods (4 B.C.E-39 C.E. and 4 B.C.E.-34 C.E. respectively), but the author of As. Mos. may have had little interest in the latter two, who had no power in Jerusalem and Judea[2]. After his demise, Archelaus was not succeeded by any of his (or Herod's) sons, and Judea came under direct Roman rule. From 37 to 44 C.E. another Herod, Agrippa, was king over the whole of Palestine, but it does not seem that his short rule was included in the author's considerations[3], because it seems to make sense to refer to Herod's 34 years only if the memory of his rule was still relatively fresh. It cannot be established with certainty whether Archelaus' demise had already taken place when As. Mos. was written, because the characterization of the Herodians' rule as "short" may either be a prediction or an assessment *ex eventu*. It can be concluded with reasonable probability that As. Mos. was written not too long after Herod's death,

---

[1] See Wintermute, "Jubilees", p. 41.

[2] Reuss, *Geschichte der Heiligen Schriften*, p. 705.

[3] Hilgenfeld, *Novum Testamentum*, p. 96, dated As. Mos. after Agrippa's death.

which is the last recognizable historical event referred to in As. Mos. The first quarter of the first century C.E. seems a reasonable date[1].

As Hölscher has shown, the supposed correspondence between the attack of the *occidentes rex* (6:8) and Varus's war in 6 C.E. is not convincing. As a consequence, it is not clear whether the Roman intervention alluded to in 6:8 was something the author was expecting or something he had recently experienced. In 7:1 (a heavily damaged passage), it is said that "after these events ... the times will suddenly end". The author of As. Mos. therefore describes the rule of the sinners in 7:3-10 as part of the eschatological scenario[2]. If the Roman intervention alluded to in 6:8 belongs to the author's past, chapter 7 describes the author's present. If the author expected that intervention, he expected it soon, and the description in chapter 7 deals with the circumstances he saw coming in the near future. The passage 6:8-7:10 describes the author's present and possibly immediate future, but it does not give a clue for the dating of As. Mos.

c. *Geographical Origin and Original Language*

As. Mos. in all likelihood originated in Palestine. The book speaks of no city other than Jerusalem, and the dispersed Jews play no part whatsoever[3]; furthermore, the Temple cult is consistently treated as a historical reality: As. Mos. never speaks of it metaphorically, as might be expected if the author did not live in the close vicinity of the Temple. Perhaps one may add that in 1:4, the location of Amman is designated as *trans Jordanem*, which may indicate a Palestinian perspective.

The Latin text of As. Mos. is a translation from Greek. Two arguments have been adduced to defend the hypothesis that As. Mos. was not originally written in Greek, but in Hebrew or Aramaic: (1) it is unlikely that a Palestinian Jew would write a book on a sacred subject in

---

[1] See also Rhoads, "The Assumption of Moses", p. 58, who situates As. Mos. in the historical circumstances of the first half of the first Christian century, and concludes that it is plausible that the book was written in that period: "The Assumption may thus bear witness to a spirit and a milieu which pervaded the Jewish nation from 4 B.C. to A.D. 48".

[2] It is not clear whether the author considered the cesura he described in 7:1 as an event in the (immediately) future or as a past event. It is possible to imagine a gradual transition between the time preceding the beginning of the end and after it.

[3] For a different view, see Schwartz, "The Tribes" (1980), and the commentary on 4:7-9.

any language other than his vernacular (Aramaic) or the sacred language (Hebrew); (2) the text contains a large number of Hebraisms.

In recent years, however, it has become clear that Greek was widely used as a spoken and written language in Palestine, also in Judea and Jerusalem, and it is not at all impossible that it was used for sacred literature as well[1].

The linguistic argument is very difficult to handle. Hebraisms on their own cannot prove that the original language was Hebrew. Hebraizing idiom in a Greek text (or in a Latin text translated from Greek) can be explained in three different ways[2]: (1) the author wrote in Greek, but imitated the Greek of the translations of the Old Testament, which he regarded as a language fit for sacred subjects. The Hebraizing words and phrases can in that case be called "Biblicisms" or "Septuagintisms" instead of Hebraisms in the strict sense of the word[3]; (2) the author wrote in Greek, but his native language was Hebrew or Aramaic, which affected the Greek he used[4]; (3) the Greek text is a translation from Hebrew.

The possibility that the Greek text in its turn went back to a Hebrew or an Aramaic original cannot entirely be ruled out, but there is no solid evidence to substantiate it. In our linguistic and exegetical discussions regarding As. Mos., we must, therefore, avoid arguments based on a supposed Hebrew or Aramaic original. Moreover, I have tried to argue in the final section of the grammatical notes (see above), that As. Mos. is more likely to have been written in Greek than in Hebrew or Aramaic.

d. *Milieu*

It cannot be ascertained to which Jewish denomination, if any, the author of As. Mos. belonged. On the one hand, little is known of what

---

[1] From the vast amount of literature on this subject I refer especially to Sevenster, *Do You Know Greek?*; Mussies, "Greek in Palestine and the Diaspora"; Rajak, *Josephus*, ch. 2, "The Greek Language in Josephus' Jerusalem", pp. 46-64; Horsley, "The Fiction of 'Jewish Greek'", pp. 19-26; Hengel, *The 'Hellenization' of Judaea*, ch. 2: "The Linguistic Question and its Cultural Background", pp. 7-18.

[2] Cf. Beyer, "Woran erkennt man", p. 31.

[3] This matter was already thoroughly discussed by De Zwaan, "The Use of the Greek Language" (1922).

[4] His native language may even have been a Palestinian Greek dialect "infected" by the local Aramaic vernacular; cf. Horsley, "The Fiction of 'Jewish Greek'", pp. 9-10.

exactly distinguished the religious "parties" Josephus described (and how the differences worked out in everyday life[1]), and it is far from certain that Josephus gives a complete description of the ways in which the Jews of his day could express their theological and anthropological concepts. On the other hand, the theology of As. Mos. is rather unspecific. Although the author rejects the validity of the temple cult as performed by the officiating priests, he cannot on that account be connected with the Essene movement or the community in Qumran, because certain characteristics which might be regarded as distinctive for those groups, such as a pronounced dualism, are lacking in As. Mos.

The description of the rulers in 7:3-10 is not helpful either. It refers no doubt to people whom the author and his readers knew well, and who were their opponents, but their exact identity cannot be established. It seems that the author of As. Mos. belonged to a group in society with limited actual power, and the possibility must therefore be acknowledged that he has spoken in this passage with disdain about "the gentlemen in power" in general terms, irrespective of any religious or political distinctions among the rulers. The impression that this is the case is strengthened by the fact that the author seems to describe here things he himself expected in the near future. From that perspective, the question whether the rulers described in 7:3-10 belong to the Pharisaic or Sadducean or any other sect may be of little importance[2].

e. Genre

Formally, the book must be classified as a "farewell discourse". The narrative framework presents Moses and his successor Joshua in dialogue at the occasion of Moses' impending death. Within this frame-

---

[1] The description of the pestilentious men in 7:3-10 has been used as negative evidence for the identification of the author's ideological background: if in 7:3-10 the Pharisees are described, it is argued, the author himself is likely to be a Sadducee (and inversely). True, the Pharisees and Sadducees had, according to Josephus, contrasting opinions on various issues. But does that mean that they were enemies?

[2] Cf. Reese, *Die Geschichte Israels*, p. 104: "Von Kap. 7 läßt sich ... über die Person des Vf. soviel sagen, daß er der herrschenden Oberschicht nicht angehört, vielmehr unter ihr und ihre Maßnahmen zu leiden hat. Er fühlt sich nicht Anhänger einer Partei, sondern als Angehöriger des Gottesvolkes, das unter der frevelhaften Herrschaft der Mächtigen seufzt und voll Sehnsucht nach der Offenbarung der Herrschaft Gottes sich ausrichtet." I have suggested previously that the author of As. Mos. may have belonged to a Levitical schismatical group ("Taxo", p. 209), but I now see that one does not have to be a Levite to reject the Temple cult and, accordingly, to hope for a pure cult in the near, eschatological future.

work, a prophecy is placed in Moses' mouth. This prophecy concerns the vicissitudes of God's people, Israel, from its entrance into the promised land until the final, eschatological consummation. A major part of this prophecy is naturally a *vaticinium ex eventu*, in which the author interprets Israel's history, using the Deuteronomistic pattern of history. According to this pattern sin is necessarily followed by punishment, and repentance is required if salvation is to be obtained. The author has used this pattern because he wished to show to his readers that the miserable circumstances of their lives should be interpreted as the result of apostasy from God, and that they should remain steadfast in their faithfulness to God's commandments, especially in view of the yet greater troubles to come. Eventually, as the author makes the great prophet Moses affirm, God will bring salvation to the faithful.

The fact that As. Mos. is primarily a "farewell discourse" does not necessarily imply that the ending of As. Mos. was relatively short. It is certainly conceivable that As. Mos. ended with a longer account of Moses' death and burial. It should be remembered that the ending of Deuteronomy, on which As. Mos. depends (see commentary on 1:5-6), contains rather mysterious clauses about the circumstances of Moses' death and burial, around which a considerable corpus of traditions was woven. It is indeed improbable that a first century C.E. writing about the last moments of Moses' life on earth would bypass the opportunity to pick up these traditions in some form[1].

f. *The Literary Integrity*

There is no reason to doubt the literary integrity of the work. The arguments Nickelsburg has produced (see section IV,c) are less than convincing. They may here be briefly answered.

(1) The theory that an apocalyptic author always describes his own time as immediately preceding the end of time is unfounded. In his discussion with Nickelsburg, Collins drew attention to the very common apocalyptic practice of describing "final woes" before the final salva-

---

[1] The Ascension of Isaiah has often been regarded as composed of two earlier books; see e.g. Von Nordheim, *Die Lehre der Alten* I, pp. 208-219. There are, however, very strong arguments for assuming that the Ascension of Isaiah is an original literary unity. If so, Asc. Isa. 6-11 is an excellent example of an extensive sequel to a generically complete testament (the "Testament of Hezekiah", Asc. Isa. 1-5).

tion is treated. Chapter 8 can easily be interpreted as such a description of final woes[1].

(2) The form-critical argument as used by Nickelsburg to question the literary integrity of As. Mos. is by no means conclusive.

First, Nickelsburg claims that the Deuteronomistic pattern of history has its roots in the latter part of Deuteronomy. This cannot be proven. The pattern is also exemplarily developed in Lev. 26 and Deut. 4. Moreover, as Nickelsburg himself admits, it is a dominant pattern in much of the Jewish literature of the Hellenistic period. The author of As. Mos. certainly did not have to resort to Deut. 28 and 30 to find an appropriate pattern for the history he was planning to write.

Secondly, As. Mos. is not a rewriting of the latter part of Deuteronomy. If one insists on using the word "rewriting", As. Mos. is a rewriting of Israel's history. The author has situated Moses' last words in the appropriate scene, Moses' farewell, which is described in Deut. 31. The author has adopted the general outline of the scene in Deut. 31. For the rest, remarkably few references to the latter part of Deuteronomy occur in As. Mos.[2]

Finally, Nickelsburg seems to believe that a basic pattern, such as the Deuteronomistic, cannot be varied by an author who uses it. But of course, an author can do whatever he likes with it. Chapters 5, 8-10 display the same pattern as chapters 2-4. If chapters 6 and 7 are excised, the structure of Moses' prophecy is perfectly symmetrical[3]. But that is no reason to excise chapter 6-7[4].

(3) The great detail in which chapter 8 depicts the persecution cannot hide the traditional and general character of the description. Whether the author of As. Mos. wanted to refer to the present or to the future, he has used ancient, traditional language. This means that, if the description was meant to refer to the author's present, it did not need to correspond perfectly with the events that were actually taking place. I will not claim that the traditional character of chapter 8 precludes

---

[1] "The Date and Provenance", pp. 20-21.

[2] Harrington, "Interpreting Israel's History", pp. 65-66, mentions "several direct quotations (sc. from Deut. 31-34) which undergird the whole structure". Most of these are to be found in the framework of As. Mos., which explicitly corresponds to the scene set in Deut. 31; others occur so often in the Hexateuch that they cannot be called direct quotations from this passage. The remaining one or two quotations are only allusions to the Song of Moses (Deut. 32).

[3] See also Harrington, "Interpreting Israel's History", pp. 64-65.

[4] So also Collins, "The Date and Provenance", p. 18.

that it reflects the author's own time. But conversely, its detailed character must not lead to the conclusion that it does indeed allude to actual events[1].

With regard to the literary integrity of As. Mos. 5-10 my conclusions are as follows.

In As. Mos. 5-6 the sinfulness and the terror of the Hasmoneans' and Herod's reigns are described. These are things that belong to the author's past. According to 6:8-9, the author of As. Mos. expected or had recently witnessed a Roman intervention in Palestine, the punishment for the sins described in chapters 5-6. It is then explicitly stated in 7:1 that this intervention signals the beginning of the end of time. Chapter 7 depicts the author's own time, or at least the immediate future. The author offers an extensive eschatological scenario, which consists of unsurpassed sinfulness (7:3-10), and a divine revenge as has never before been executed (chapter 8). Then follows a description of the faithfulness and the zeal of a Levite named Taxo and his sons (chapter 9), and the advent of God's kingdom, following Taxo's violent death, which is apparently expected to placate the Lord (10:1-10). Chapters 8-10 give a picture of the future as the author expected it to unfold. It appears that chapters 8 and 9 do not directly reflect the Antiochan persecution. In these chapters, the author has digested the traditions underlying the legendary accounts of the Antiochan persecution found also in 1, 2 and 4 Maccabees and in Josephus, Ant. Jud. XII, and the author has used them to make them fit his own ends. The figure of Antiochus IV (already pictured in Dan. 11 as a mythical tyrant) has been used as a model for the Enemy of the End of Times.

Supposing the literary integrity of As. Mos., the following schema[2] of the pattern of history presented in Moses' prophecy can be drawn.

---

[1] It may be noted in passing that some of the details in chap. 8 are, from a historical point of view, perfectly impossible, such as the enforcement of the operation aimed at restoring the prepuce on circumcised boys (8:3). One only needs to compare similar statements in 1 Macc. 1:60-61; 2 Macc. 6:10, 4 Macc. 4:25 and Josephus, Ant. Jud. XII 256 to see that some details of the traditions concerning the Antiochan persecution are very persistent, but also tend to be exaggerated.

[2] This is indeed a *schema*. As. Mos. 2:3-9 does not solely consist of a description of sin, and in 5:1-6:7 sin and punishment overlap.

Sin	2:3-9	5:1-6:7	7
Punishment	3:1-3	6:8-9	8
Repentance	3:4-4:4		9
Salvation	4:5-9		10

As. Mos. begins with a section that characterizes the writing as a "farewell discourse", thereby indicating to the readers that the book they have in their hands will contain a speech by Moses on the occasion of his impending death. Moses' speech in As. Mos. 2:3-10:10 is pseudepigraphically presented as a prophecy, in this case a prediction of Israel's future from the entrance into the land until the end of days. Its climax is the eschatological salvation of Israel after a long, dreadful history of sin, failure and misery.

The book has much in common with such writings as Daniel, 4 Ezra and 2 Baruch, books that are usually named "apocalypses". This is not the place to enter into the discussion on the definition of "apocalypse". The term "apocalypse" has become so problematic, that M.E. Stone once suggested that it should be dropped altogether[1]. Indeed, the word is yet another instance of an ancient title which does not conform to modern literary classifications[2], leading to unnecessary confusion. In this commentary, I shall try to avoid the word "apocalypse". As. Mos. is a formal farewell discourse; Moses' speech is a (pseudo-)prophecy; the book is full of traditions commonly called apocalyptic.

g. *Purpose*

The purpose of the book can be said to be twofold. First, it intends to strengthen its readers in their faithfulness to the law, that is, to the conditions attached to the covenant which eventually guarantees Israel's salvation. Second, it wants to comfort readers who might despair in the face of the disastrous condition of Israel, both politically and religiously, by interpreting the present as the final stage of history and by pointing to the salvation awaiting the faithful of Israel in the very near future.

---

[1] "Lists of Revealed Things", p. 443 (*Selected Studies*, p. 408).
[2] Comparable instances are "testament" (see above), "midrash" and "pesher".

Appendix: Taxo (9:1)

The identity of *Taxo* (9:1) has fascinated scholars for a long time. Almost thirty proposals made since the publication of the manuscript of As. Mos. are listed in this appendix. A number of them were discussed by Charles in 1897[1], and by Rowley in 1944 and 1963[2]. None of these proposals is entirely satisfactory, most of them are unconvincing, a rather large number are nonsensical. I will make little comment on the proposals made, but primarily outline them in a more or less orderly way.

Taxo has been identified as a historical figure, contemporary with the author of As. Mos., by a number of scholars, who used various sorts of *notariqon* to underpin their identification.

Ewald (1867) recognized in Taxo Judas the Galilean. To support his proposal, Ewald did not apply the *notariqon*-technique of *gematria*, that is, the technique by which rabbis occasionally equated words with one another on the basis of their identical numerical value[3]. Ewald asserted, however, that the numerical value of the name Taxo must certainly have agreed with that of the name of this Judas, but that calculations could not be made, because the name of Judas' father is unknown[4]. Volkmar (1867) identified Taxo as Rabbi Aqiba; he equated the numerical value of ταξο with 431, which number is also the sum of אקבא רבון[5]. Colani (1868) saw in Taxo Rabbi Judah ben Baba, who in a cave in the desert consecrated seven pupils as rabbis, and who was killed by the Romans[6]; Colani, too, supported his identification by *gematria* (but see below). Torrey (1943) claimed that Taxo was Mattathias, the father of the Maccabees. The numerical value of מקשו, 415, is identical to the numerical value of חשמונא, Aramaic for "the Hasmonean"[7].

Another sort of *notariqon* is the rabbinical technique of *ab-bag*[8]. Ab-bag stands for the method of replacing each letter of a word by the letter following it in the alphabet. It was applied by Burkitt (1900), who in this way changed תכסו into אלעז, which is easily emended into אלעזר, that is: Eleazar, the old martyr known from the Maccabean traditions[9].

---

[1] *The Assumption of Moses*, pp. 35-36.

[2] *The Relevance of Apocalyptic*, third edition, "Note C. The Figure of Taxo in the Assumption of Moses", pp. 149-156.

[3] Bacher, *Die exegetische Terminologie* I, p. 127: גמטריא לחשבון.

[4] "Das Judenthum in Palästina", pp. 111, 117.

[5] *Mose Prophetie*, pp. 59-60. For those who might object that אקיבא is usually written *plene*, Volkmar was prepared to add another 10 to the sum, by emending either ταξφ′ or rather ταξιο′.

[6] "L'Assomption de Moïse", pp. 80-81.

[7] "'Taxo' in the Assumption of Moses". In 1945, Rowley, "The Figure of 'Taxo'", refuted Torrey's thesis (see further Torrey's weak defence, "'Taxo' Once More", and Rowley's final answer in *The Relevance of Apocalyptic*, pp. 153-155).

[8] Bacher, *Die exegetische Terminologie* I, p. 127: גמטריא לתמורת האותיות.

[9] "Moses, Assumption of", p. 449b.

Hausrath in 1877 reversed the method of *ab-bag* (see above): he proposed to emend Taxo into Tacmo *via* Hebrew: תכמו would have been corrupted into תכסו. If the letters of תכמו are replaced by the letters preceding them in the alphabet, שילה is obtained. In Gen. 49:10, one reads: "until Shiloh will come", a phrase which is traditionally interpreted as a messianic prophecy[1]. According to Charles, "Rosenthal [1885] ... points out that שילה is numerically equal to משה"—the name Shiloh hidden in Taxo is therefore a reference to the second Moses (Deut. 18:18)[2].

Gematria was also used by Hilgenfeld (1866) in support of his identification of Taxo as the Messiah. He proposed to restore Taxo into the Greek number τξε', which the translator would have misunderstood for a real name[3]. The Greek number corresponds to the numerical value of המשיח. Rönsch in 1874 transliterated תחשו, which gives 714. He multiplied this number by 7[4] (a week of years), so that 4,998 is obtained. Other calculations had led Rönsch to the conviction that the author of As. Mos. believed the number of years which the creation would last was 5,000 (see the commentary on 1:2-4). In this line of thought, Taxo denotes the year of the Messiah[5].

In 1875, Furrer calculated, in a way which he does not explain, that both תגשו and משה add up to 39; thus, Taxo is a genuinely rabbinic hidden reference to Moses[6]. Von Nordheim (1980) reports that Schalit, too, suspected that the name Taxo would refer, through *gematria*, to Moses[7].

At-bash[8] was applied in a most curious suggestion made by Heidenheim in 1871 (in *at-bash*, the first letter of the alphabet is replaced by the last, the second by the last but one, and so forth). He transliterated Taxo with the Hebrew letters טעכזו. Through *at-bash*, one obtains נלעפ (the ע from טעכזו has disappeared in this piece of jugglery, probably because Heidenheim considered it as a *mater lectionis*). Then, one has to alter the order of the letters (which procedure was, according to Heidenheim, perfectly normal among the rabbis) to obtain פלעני, that is, "someone".

The latest proposal in this vein was made by Van Henten in 1987, who suggested understanding Taxo as תΑאΩ, the first and final letters of both the Hebrew and the Greek alphabet. According to Van Henten, this name indicates that Taxo and his sons represent the end of the Jewish people in history, and the beginning of Israel's new existence in God's kingdom; also, they keep the law from א to ת[9].

Already in 1868, Colani warned against this kind of speculation, especially since it often involved an alteration of the text. Colani jested that this method could be applied

---

[1] Hausrath, *Neutestamentliche Zeitgeschichte* IV ([2]1877), p. 77.

[2] Charles, *The Assumption*, p. 36, referring to Rosenthal, *Vier apocryphische Bücher*, pp. 31-32 (*non vidi*).

[3] *Novum Testamentum*, p. 105.

[4] Cf. Clemen, *APAT* II, p. 326: "freilich weshalb?".

[5] "Xeniola theologica", p. 445.

[6] "Das Wort Taxo".

[7] Von Nordheim, *Die Lehre der Alten* I, p. 201.

[8] Bacher, *Die exegetische Terminologie* I, p. 127: גמטריא לתמורת האותיות.

[9] Van Henten, "Traditie en interpretatie", pp. 28-29.

with ease to support the identification of Taxo with Emperor Barbarossa[1] (a challenge which Drummond took up in 1877[2]), but he nevertheless admitted[3] that he had tried to relate the name "Taxo" numerically to the name of Rabbi Judah ben Baba (with whom he identified Taxo). Colani's attempt succeeded, but he added: "Tout cela, bien entendu, est un jeu, rien qu'un jeu ... parfaitement illusoire"[4].

Two other theories, which I have not able to verify, are reported by Schürer. Philippi (1868) identified Taxo and his sons as Jesus Christ and his disciples[5]; Loeb (1880) as Rabbi Joshua ben Hananiah[6]. I do not know whether either of these based their speculations on some kind of *notariqon*.

A number of scholars identified Taxo with a historical figure without making use of *notariqon* techniques. Charles (1897) regarded Taxo as a contemporary of Judas the Maccabee; in the supposed Hebrew text, Judas would have been designated as הקנא, "the zealous", which would have been misread by the Greek translator as חתקסו[7]. Klausner in 1928 considered Taxo to be the nameless old man described in Josephus, *Bell. Jud.* I 312-313 and *Ant. Jud.*, XIV 429 (see the commentary to 9:6)[8]. Rowley in 1945, defended the view that Taxo was a historical figure, contemporary with the author of As. Mos., but someone who was very soon forgotten, so that he no longer figures in the traditions that have come down to us, and can therefore not be identified.

Other explanations of the name Taxo assume that it is a symbolical name, a word which actually means something, and characterizes the bearer of the name. The theory most widely accepted is also the oldest of this kind. In 1866, Langen tentatively suggested that Taxo represents the Greek τάξω, which would be a translation of something like אערך, "I shall prepare", a name which would agree with Taxo's function as the forerunner of the Messiah[9]. In 1869 Schmidt and Merx improved this suggestion, understanding τάξων, "the one who will put things right", and compared his function with that of the ἐπιμελητής of the Essenes (see Josephus, *Bell. Jud.* II 134)[10]. In this form, Langen's suggestion has won much acclaim. Clemen (1900), Jeremias (1935), Van der Woude (1957) and Hahn (1963), specifically identified this

---

[1] "L'Assomption de Moïse", pp. 82.

[2] Drummond "emended" ταξο into ταρο, which has the numerical value of 471, identical to the numerical value of ברברוסא, Barbarossa.

[3] "L'Assomption de Moïse", p. 82: "il serait puéril de le cacher".

[4] "L'Assomption de Moïse", p. 83.

[5] Schürer, *Geschichte des jüdischen Volkes* III (⁴1909), p. 299, referring to Philippi, *Das Buch Henoch*, pp. 166-191, esp. pp. 177, 182.

[6] Schürer, *Geschichte des jüdischen Volkes* III (⁴1909), p. 304, referring to I. Loeb, "Le taxo de l'Assomption de Moïse", *L'Univers israélite* 35. Schürer himself seems to have taken the reference from E. Renan, *Journal asiatique* 16 (1880), p. 45.

[7] *The Assumption*, p. 36. Charles later, in *APOT* II, p. 421, followed Burkitt's suggestion.

[8] *Jesus of Nazareth*, pp. 143-144.

[9] Langen, *Das Judenthum*, pp. 110-111.

[10] "Die Assumptio Mosis", pp. 124, 148.

τάξων with *Elias redivivus*, whose coming is prophesied in Mal. 3:23-24[1]. Rießler (1927) again referred to the Essene ἐπιμελητής, but derived Taxo simply from the present participle τάσσων. Mowinckel (1953) retranslated τάξων into מחוקק, the "expounder of the Law" of Gen. 49:10, a figure that also occurs in the Damascus scroll[2]. Serious objections against the interpretation of Taxo as τάξων were raised by Kuhn in 1925: first, it is peculiar that the future participle would have been used, instead of the simple τάσσων; and second, if the figure is characterized by his name as an "orderer", one would expect that his actions would somehow agree with this characterization, which is not the case[3].

In 1943, Zeitlin proposed to understand the name Taxo as a Latinization of the Greek word τόξον, meaning "rainbow", a word that "occupied a conspicuous place in the early Jewish theology". Zeitlin recognized in this "Rainbow" Rabbi Joshua, who opposed Bar Kokhba's insurrection[4].

A mistranslation from Aramaic is supposed by Carrière (1868). He believed that the Greek translator had misread the original Aramaic. He translated די שומה תקסא/תכסו, but, according to Carrière, the original reading was probably דישים תכסא, "who will give an order", or: "who will raise the banner", that is: "who will draw a line of conduct"[5].

In 1921, Klausner identified Taxo with Mattathias. He did not use *notariqon* to underpin this theory, but assumed a corruption in the supposed Hebrew text: מתיה would have been mistaken for תכסה[6].

Kuhn (1925) argued that Taxo's name and his actions should be in accordance with each other. Since טקשו "or something similar" does not make sense, Kuhn suspected that those letters are a corruption of קושט, "truth, honesty", or קשים, "the Reasonable"[7].

Aptowitzer in 1927 also assumed a mistake by the translator. The original Hebrew text would have read ששמו מכסה, "whose name is hidden", that is: a simple man. But the translator would mistakenly have read a ט instead of the מ of מכסה, and "Taxo" was the incomprehensible result[8]. To this solution, one must compare the

---

[1] Jeremias, "Ἠλ(ε)ίας", p. 935; Van der Woude, *Die messianischen Vorstellungen*, pp. 85-86; Hahn, *Christologische Hoheitstitel*, (³1966), pp. 355-356.

[2] Mowinckel, "The Hebrew Equivalent"; cf. *He That Cometh*, pp. 300-301. Gen 49:10 was also referred to by Hausrath, who conjured Taxo into Shiloh.

[3] "Zur Assumptio Mosis", p. 129.

[4] "The Assumption of Moses", pp. 5-9.

[5] "Note sur le *Taxo*".

[6] *The Messianic Idea*, pp. 326-327 (quoted from the English translation of 1955 of the third Hebrew edition. This part of Klausner's book goes back to an originally separate work published in 1921).

[7] "Zur Assumptio Mosis", p. 129.

[8] Aptowitzer, *Parteipolitik der Hasmonäerzeit im rabbinischen und pseudepigraphischen Schrifttum*, Vienna 1927, pp. 238-239, quoted by Beek, *Inleiding in de joodse apocalyptiek* (1950), p. 132.

one proposed in 1905 by Kaminetsky, who suggested an original תכסה, "you must hide"[1].

In 1882, Wieseler proposed to take the word *taxo* for what it means in Latin, namely "badger"[2]. Badgers live in holes, and in 2 Macc. 10:6 it is related that faithful Jews celebrated the Feast of Tabernacles ἐν τοῖς σπηλαίοις (= *in speluncis*; cf. As. Mos. 9:6) θηρίων τρόπον, "in caverns, like animals do"; see also 2 Macc. 5:27; cf. 1 Macc. 2:29; 2 Macc. 6:11; Josephus *Ant. Jud.* XIV 421-422; Heb. 11:38. Even more important than these instances is 1 En. 96:2, which Wieseler failed to quote: "And in the days of the distress of the sinners your young will mount up and rise like eagles [cf. As. Mos. 10:8], and your nest will be higher than that of vultures; and you will go up and like badgers enter the crevices of the earth and the clefts of the rock for ever before the lawless." Finally, Wieseler adduced some evidence for the possibility that someone could be nicknamed "Badger": Θασσί in 1 Macc. 2:3, which may be explained as תחשי[3], "the one like a badger"; and Αὐαράν in 1 Macc. 2:5, that is חורן, "caveman" (חור meaning "cave"[4]). The advantages of this solution are clear: the word can be explained from the language of the text it stands in, no emendation is necessary, and it makes perfect sense if linked with the caverns mentioned in As. Mos. 9:6. The only problem that remains is the question why Taxo, if he is a figure expected to appear in the future, should be named so emphatically "Badger"; possibly, an explicit reference to 1 En. 96:2 or a similar text has been intended, but this cannot be proven.

---

[1] In *Ha-Shiloah* 15 (1905), p. 47, quoted by Rowley, *The Relevance of Apocalyptic*, p. 153.

[2] Zeitlin, "The Assumption of Moses", p. 5, quotes Deane, *The Pseudepigrapha. An Account of Certain Apocryphal Sacred Writings of the Jews and Early Christians*, Edinburgh 1891, p. 119, who also proposed to translate Taxo as "badger".

[3] This explanation, however, is not at all certain; cf. Abel, *Les Livres des Maccabées*, pp. 31, 50

[4] So also Michaelis and Grimm, but not so Abel, *Les Livres des Maccabées*, p. 31.

PART FOUR

COMMENTARY

THE STRUCTURE OF AS. MOS.

1:1-9a INTRODUCTION
The description of the scene of Moses' farewell discourse (with reference to Deut. 31)

1:1-4 Chronological and geographical situation

1:5-9a Introduction of the main figures, Moses and Joshua

1:9b-10:15 MOSES' SPEECH

A. A PREAMBLE TO MOSES' FORECAST OF THE FUTURE
1:9b-2:2 Moses' Instructions to Joshua. Israel as the Purpose of God's Creation

1:9b-15 Before delivering his prophecy, Moses reveals to Joshua the aim of God's creation

1:16-18 Moses gives instructions to Joshua concerning the preservation of Moses' prophecy until the end of time

2:1-2 Moses instructs Joshua with regard to the entrance into the land and the nation's constitution

B. MOSES' FORECAST OF THE FUTURE
2:3-4:9 Sin, Punishment, Repentance, Salvation

2:3-9 *Sin*

2:3-5 The secession of the ten tribes and the sanctification of the two tribes

2:6-9 The apostasy of the two tribes

3:1-3 *Punishment*

The coming of the king from the East

3:4-4:4 *Repentance*

3:4-9 Recognition of God's righteousness and of the people's sinfulness; an appeal to the covenant

3:10-14 The remembrance of Moses' warnings; recognition of the trustworthiness of his words; realization of the punishment

4:1-4 The intercessor's prayer

4:5-9 *Salvation*

> 4:5-6 God remembers his covenant and displays his mercy
>
> 4:7-9 The return of parts of the tribes; the sadness of the faithful; the disappearance of the ten tribes

5:1-6:9 Sin and Punishment

5:1-6:7 *Sin*

> 5:1-6 The post-exilic Jewish society characterized as entirely sinful
>
> 6:1 The unholy rule of the priest-kings (the Hasmoneans)
>
> 6:2-6 The terror and sinfulness of Herod's rule, a deserved punishment
>
> 6:7 The short rule of Herod's sons

6:8-9 *Punishment*

> The coming of the king from the West

7:1-10:10 The Eschatological Scenario

7:1-2 The time of the end begins; a calculation concerning the time of the end

7:3-10 *Sin*

> The rule of the pestilential men

8:1-6 *Punishment*

> The coming of the king of the kings of the world
>
> The prohibition of Judaism and the enforced transition to paganism

9:1-7 The *Zeal for the Law* of Taxo and his sons

> 9:1-3 The introduction of Taxo and his sons; his recognition of the disasters as a divine punishment
>
> 9:4-7 Their innocence, and their zeal for the law; their trust in God

10:1-10 *Salvation*

> 10:1-2 The appearance of God's kingdom; the devil's death; the vindication of Taxo
>
> 10:3-7 God arises; nature's reaction; the destruction of the nations and their idols
>
> 10:8-10 The exaltation of Israel into heaven

C. 10:11-15 CONCLUDING WORDS

Indication of the time left between Moses' death and the fulfilment of his prophecy; encouragement for Joshua

11:1-12:13 A DIALOGUE BETWEEN MOSES AND JOSHUA ON LEADERSHIP AND PROVIDENCE

A. 11:1-19 JOSHUA'S COMPLAINT

    11:1-4 Joshua expresses his fear of the future

    11:5-19 Joshua contrasts Moses' grandeur to his own alleged incompetence

        11:5-8 The impossibility of designing a monument large enough to glorify Moses

        11:9-11 The impossibility of proceeding without Moses' leadership and intercession

        11:12-15 Joshua's assertion of his own incompetence to lead the people as Moses led them

        11:16-19 Eulogy of Moses, placed in the mouth of the kings of the Amorites, who will, according to Joshua, be secure of their victory after Moses' death

B. 12:1-13 MOSES' ANSWER TO JOSHUA'S COMPLAINT

    12:1-3 Moses reassures Joshua with regard to the latter's competence

    12:4-5a God has known and determined everything from the outset of creation

    12:5b-9 Moses' and Joshua's success, as well as the people's wellbeing, depend on God's mercy and magnanimity alone

    12:10-13 Faithfulness to the law will eventually pay off; God's covenant and his oath guarantee that his people will never be entirely destroyed

THE LOST ENDING OF THE ASSUMPTION OF MOSES

No longer extant. It must have contained an account of Moses' death and his burial (probably by angels), which the devil at first tries to prevent. Possibly, the ascension of Moses' soul into heaven was also related.

1:1-9a

INTRODUCTION

As. Mos. 1:1-9a forms the introduction to the book as a whole. Two sub-sections may be distinguished: 1:1-4, which indicates in a very exact manner the date and place of the event to be related in As. Mos.; and 1:5-9a, which introduces the scene in which the event is set, as well as the main themes of As. Mos. as a whole.

The dates in 1:1-4 clearly hint at the moment of Moses' impending death: the departure from Egypt, in 1:3b-4a interpreted as the return to Canaan, has been completed. The readers are well aware that Moses will not take part in the entrance into the land (1:4b).

In 1:5-9a Joshua is depicted as the perfect successor to Moses, and he is selected by the Lord to lead the people into the land.

a. *1:1-4*

In the first section of the introduction, the date of the scene of Moses' prophecy is indicated in four different ways. Texts in the apocalyptic tradition sometimes give the exact time and place of the revelation, e.g., Dan. 7:1; 8:1; 9:1; 10:1; 1 En. 60:1; 4 Ezra 3:1; 2 Bar. 1:1 (cf. Ezek. 1:1-3). In As. Mos., the purpose of this elaborate dating may be to emphasize that Israel has reached a crucial point in history: the moment immediately prior to the crossing of the Jordan (1:4), that is, to the capture of the promised land (2:1).

1 ⋯

2 which is the two thousand fivehundredth year since the creation of the earth 3 a (but according to those who live in the East the number is the … and …th), b and the …th since the departure from Phoenicia, 4 a when the people left; b after the departure that took place through Moses, until Amman over the Jordan.

1:1
The first three lines of the manuscript, presumably containing the book's title, are completely lost, and it is impossible to reconstruct them in detail. Two elements, though, are likely to have formed part of these lines: the word *profetia* and the year of Moses' death. On the basis of these two elements, Clemen suggested that the first lines may have read something like *liber profetiae Moysis, quae facta est anno vitae*

ejus Cmo et XXmo, "the book of the prophecy of Moses, which was given in the 120th year of his life"[1].

The words *Liber profetiae* are chosen because the genitive *profetiae* in 1:5, gives the impression of resuming an earlier genitive[2]. Furthermore, 1:1 must have contained some date, since 1:2 continues with *qui est ... annus,* that is, an alternative date. The occasion on which this prophecy is given is Moses' impending death, to which he alludes in 1:15; 10:14, and probably 12:5, and which took place in the 120th year of his life (see e.g. Deut. 34:7).

1:2-4

In this passage, four alternative dates are given to specify the year of Moses' death.

(1) It is equated with the 2,500th year since the creation of the world (1:2). This equation is, as far as is known, unique in Jewish chronology[3], apart perhaps from the date given for the crossing of the Jordan in Jub 50:4. There it is said that the revelation on Mount Sinai took place after 49 jubilees, 1 week and 2 years, or 49 x 49 + 7 + 2 = 2,410 years since the days of Adam; after this revelation it would take another 40 years before Israel would be purified, so that it could enter into the land. That is, from Adam until the crossing of the Jordan 2,410 + 40 years = 50 jubilees of 49 years. If one reckons with jubilees of 50 years, 2,500 years is 50 jubilees, as well[4]. It seems possible, therefore, that the figure in As. Mos. is in fact the same as that in the book of Jubilees[5]. It should be noted, however, that As. Mos. does not use the jubilees-system elsewhere.

In 10:12, Moses announces to Joshua that the period from the moment he is speaking until the coming of God is "250 times". Rönsch suggested that these 250 times should be taken as the equivalent of 2,500 years, so that Moses' death would take place exactly in the middle of the world's history[6]. The suggestion is tempting but very uncertain.

(2) In 1:3a, the number of years since the creation according to "those who live in the East" is given[7]. There is no reason to consider this passage as a gloss, as all commentators except Hilgenfeld suppose. Which number the "Eastern chronology" gave to the event related is not known, because the figures, originally written in red ink,

---

[1] *APAT* II, p. 317; *Die Himmelfahrt,* p. 4. Clemen's reconstruction is the simplest of all the proposals made.

[2] See, however, Kuhn, "Zur Assumptio Mosis", who sees in the phrase *profetiae quae facta est* an awkward rendering of a Greek absolute genitive construction, προφητείας γενομένης.

[3] See e.g. Klein, "The Text of Deuteronomy"; Schalit, *Untersuchungen,* pp. 7-12, lists eight different ancient chronologies.

[4] In two ways: 50 x 50 = 2500, or, in the calculation of Jub 50:4, 49 x 50 + 7 + 2 + 40 = 2499.

[5] So Dillmann in Rönsch, "Die Leptogenesis", p. 92.

[6] Rönsch, "Die Leptogenesis", p. 92, "Xeniola theologica", p. 544. So also Schalit, *Untersuchungen,* pp. 12-13, cf. p. 125.

[7] Rönsch, "Xeniola theologica", p. 556, rightly discerned two dates in 1:3a-b. Other commentators read 1:3 as a single dating: "in the...th and...th and...th year since the departure from Phoenicia", but see Clemen, *APAT* II, p. 317.

have become illegible. Since the number is unknown, it is equally impossible to determine which "people in the Orient" were meant[1].

(3) The third way to indicate the date is "the ...th year since the departure from Canaan, when the people left" (1:3b-4). These two clauses are to be taken together: *cum exivit plebs* cannot be connected with the following *post profectionem*, because such a connection would mean that Israel "departed after the Exodus". If, on the other hand, *cum exivit plebs* is taken to indicate the agent of "the departure from Canaan", it neatly emphasizes the contrast intended. The departure of Jacob and his sons for Egypt is also used as a dating device in Jub. 34:9.

Fynicis is probably a translitteration of the Greek name of Phoenicia (the classical nominative is *Phoenice*; see further grammatical note nr. 196) and denotes Canaan[2]. For the use of the genitive to denote the point of departure, see grammatical note nr. 111.

The year "since the departure from Phoenicia" is to be seen directly in relation to the next indication:

(4) "after the departure that took place through Moses" (1:4), which is of course the Exodus from Egypt. By mentioning the departure of Jacob and his sons from Canaan, the capture of the promised land by the sons of Israel is interpreted as a return[3]: Jacob left the land, but had been given the divine promise that his seed would inherit it. These two dates, the departure (to Egypt) and the return (to the land), announce the exile-return schema[4]. In the Deuteronomistic view (which dominates As. Mos.) this schema is considered to be the rhythm of Israel's history.

The last indication of time in 1:4 serves to point to the central importance of the things about to happen. "After the departure which took place through Moses", taken together with the geographical position of the Israelites (near Amman over the Jordan), indicates that the Exodus at this point is completed, and that therefore Moses' task is completed. Reaching Amman (so the Septuagint; MT: Ammon) is the termination of Israel's wanderings. According to Deut. 2:19 Israel is not to attack the Ammonites,

---

[1] Hilgenfeld, *Novum Testamentum*, p. 111, concluded from the mention of "those who are in the East" that the author of As. Mos. himself came from the West, that is, from Rome; for the same reason, Charles, *The Assumption*, p. 54, bracketed this verse as a redactional gloss. However, "East" and "West" are relational concepts, and wherever the author lived (in Rome, in Palestine, in Antioch, or in Alexandria), there always are people in the East. If he lived in Palestine, for instance, he may have wanted to indicate the chronology of Babylonian Jewry.

[2] This identification was first made by Volkmar, *Mose Prophetie*, p. 17: "Φοινίκη ... ist der richtige, wenn auch in LXX nicht aufgenommene Ausdruck für Kanaan" (cf. Von Gutschmid, in Hilgenfeld, *Novum Testamentum*, p. 111). Schalit, too, asserts that Φοινίκη does not occur in LXX nor in Josephus as a translation of "Canaan". Both scholars, however, are wrong in this respect, cf. Hatch-Redpath, *Concordance. Supplement*, p. 155: Φοινίκη = כנען Exod. 16:35; כנעני Josh. 5:1; Φοινίκες = כנען Josh. 5:12; כנענים Job 40:25 (30); Φοίνισσα = כנענית Exod. 6:15.

[3] Cf. Volkmar, *Mose Prophetie*, p. 17.

[4] Cf. Reese, *Geschichtsdarstellung* , pp. 119-120, and Janssen, *Das Gottesvolk*, p. 101: "Der Verfasser der Himmelfahrt Moses sieht sich wieder am Anfang stehen wie einst Israel vor dem Einzug in das heilige Land... Dieser letzte Umbruch [sc. the rapidly approaching time of salvation] hat seine Entsprechung, seinen Antitypos, in dem Einzug Israels in das heilige Land unter Moses und Josua."

but instead it must conquer the land of the Amorite Sihon, king of Hesbon (Deut. 2:24), which is the beginning of the capture of the promised land[1]. On the other hand, it is implied that the entrance into the land is at hand, and that therefore Joshua's mission is about to begin. By recalling these facts (cf. Deut. 31:1-6) the author prepares his readers for the scene that will now follow: Moses' death and his succession by Joshua.

b. *1:5-9a*

In this section, Joshua is introduced as Moses' successor (1:7). Joshua is said to have been elected by God (1:6, cf. 10:15), who deemed him to be worthy of the momentous task to lead the people into the land and to take care of the service in the tabernacle (1:7). Explicit references to Deut. 31:14-23 are found in As. Mos. 1:5 and 9a.

5 (*sc.* the book) of the prophecy, which was given by Moses according to the book of Deuteronomy, 6 when he called unto him Joshua, the son of Nun, a man deemed worthy by the Lord 7 to be the (*sc.* Moses') successor for the people and for the tabernacle of the testimony with all its holy objects, 8 and to lead the people into the land that was given to their fathers, 9 a so that it would be given to them on account of the covenant, and on account of the oath—the things he (*sc.* Moses) said in the tabernacle, namely that he (*sc.* God) would give it (*sc.* the land) through Joshua.

1:5-6
The prophecy which Moses will utter presently (2:3-10:10) is said to be given *in libro Deuteronomio*[2]. This is a concise way to say that this prophecy is mentioned in Deuteronomy, not that the prophecy is contained in that biblical book (see grammatical note nr. 176)[3]. The prophecy which the author of As. Mos. ascribes to Moses is an example of the traditional apocalyptic topos of the "secret revelation", which is used to suggest that prophets of the past received more revelations than they published in the

---

[1] See Schalit, *Untersuchungen*, pp. 62-64. See further 11:11, mentioning the Amorites as the first enemies to counter. Charles, *The Assumption*, p. 55, bracketed this verse because "Moses could not have spoken of Amman as across the Jordan: only a dweller in Jerusalem could have so described it" but Moses is not speaking yet (Clemen, *APAT* II, p. 318).

[2] Schmidt and Merx, "Die Assumptio Mosis", p. 137, bracketed this verse as a "Randbemerkung". They were followed by Charles, *The Assumption*, p. 55, who added: "In a book of Hebrew origin the phrase in libro Deuteronomio could not have been original". I fail to see why *Deuteronomium* cannot be the Greek indication for a book (cf. Barn.10:2) which might have been indicated in a potential Hebrew original in the appropriate Hebrew way; cf. Schalit, *Untersuchungen*, p. 69.

[3] Nor that the contents of this prophecy are "eigentlich schon" contained in Deuteronomy (against Volkmar, *Mose Prophetie*, p. 13; Clemen, *APAT* II, p. 318).

scriptures[1] (see further the commentary on 1:16-18). The prologue to the book of Jubilees is connected to the scene on Sinai in a similar way: "This is the account of the division of the days of the law ... as the Lord gave it to Moses on Mount Sinai, when he went up to receive the stone tablets of the law and of the commandments, in accordance with God's command, as he said to him: 'Go up to the top of the mount'." See also the prologue to Apoc. Mos.: διήγησις ... ἀποκαλυφθεῖσα παρὰ θεοῦ Μωϋσῃ τῷ θεράποντι αὐτοῦ ὅτε τὰς πλάκας τοῦ νόμου ἐκ χειρὸς αὐτοῦ ἐδέξατο διδαχθεὶς παρὰ τοῦ ἀρχαγγέλου Μιχαήλ.

The passage to which As. Mos. 1:5 refers is probably Deut. 31:14. The words *qui vocavit ad se Jesum* 1:6a are a translation of the aorist participle προσκαλεσάμενος (see grammatical note nr. 180). This participle should probably be translated temporally (see grammatical note nr. 183): "the prophecy which was given by Moses, according to the book of Deuteronomy, namely, when he called Joshua unto him". That moment is reported in Deut. 31:14. According to that passage, the Lord said to Moses: "Behold, the days approach when you must die; call Joshua (κάλεσον Ἰησοῦν), and present yourselves in the tent of meeting (καὶ στῆτε παρὰ τὰς θύρας τῆς σκηνῆς τοῦ μαρτυρίου), that I may commission him (καὶ ἐντελοῦμαι αὐτῷ)". These words appear to have been the starting-point of the author of As. Mos.: the roots (προσ-) καλεῖν (קרא) and ἐντέλλεσθαι (צוה), and a formula concerning impending death belong to the stock vocabulary of the farewell discourses[2], to which genre As. Mos. formally belongs. Except for ἐντέλλεσθαι (Lat.: *mandare*, but see *omnia quae mandata sunt* 1:10), these formulaic phrases have been adopted in As. Mos. 1:6 and 15[3].

Furthermore, in 1:9, the tabernacle (*quod locutus est in scenae*) is mentioned, which may be another reference to Deut. 31:14 (στῆτε παρὰ τὰς θύρας τῆς σκηνῆς τοῦ μαρτυρίου).

Finally, the announcement in Deut. 31:14 that God would instruct Joshua (ἐντελοῦμαι αὐτῷ) is instead followed by an account of God speaking to Moses[4]. Perhaps the author of As. Mos. interpreted the announcement as a reference to a revelation not recorded in the scriptures themselves, so that it was natural for him to set Moses' prophecy in this framework.

Joshua is called a man *probatus Domino*, that is, "approved of by the Lord"; cf. Acts 2:22 Ἰησοῦν τὸν Ναζωραῖον, ἄνδρα ἀποδεδειγμένον (Vulgate: *approbatus*, codex Bezae *probatus*) ἀπὸ τοῦ θεου; cf. also As. Mos. 12:9, where the entire creation is described as being approved of by the Lord (*provata a Deo*). The translation "deemed worthy" is chosen to express the connection of *probatus* with *ut sit successor* 1:7 (cf. 10:15 *Te elegit Deus esse mihi successorem*) and with *ut et inducat* 1:8. *Ut sit successor* can also be constructed with *qui vocavit ad se* ("He called unto him Joshua ... so that he would be [his] successor"), but the enumeration of Joshua's momentous future tasks in 1:7-9 suggests the connection with *probatus*. 1:6b-9a is then to be seen as an attributive adjunct, in which Joshua's role and significance is defined.

---

[1] So Volkmar, *Mose Prophetie*, p. 19.

[2] See, e.g., Cortès, *Los discursos de adiós*, pp. 54-63.

[3] Cf. also As. Mos. 1:15 with Deut. 31:16.

[4] According to the Massoretic text, God addresses Joshua in Deut. 31:23. In the Septuagint, however, Deut. 31:23 is put in Moses' mouth.

1:7

In 1:7-8 Joshua is described as Moses' successor[1] in the affairs of the people and of the tabernacle of the testimony with its holy objects. The enumeration of his tasks introduces the main themes of As. Mos.: Israel and the temple[2], the land and the covenant.

The "testimony" (testimonium; Vulgate also testificatio) consists of the commandments of the Lord which were placed in the ark, according to Exod. 25:16; 25:21; 40:18 (according Deut. 10:5; 1 Ki. 8:9 the tables of the law were placed in the ark); therefore the ark is called the "ark of the testimony" in e.g. Exod. 25:22; 26:33, 34; 30:6. This ark in its turn is set in the tabernacle (Num. 7:89), and the tabernacle may therefore also be called the "tabernacle of the testimony" (cf. Exod. 38:21; Num. 1:50, 53; esp. Exod. 40:2-3). For σκηνὴ τοῦ μαρτυρίου cf. further Vitae Prophetarum 12:13; Eupolemus, in Eusebius Praeparatio IX 34, 7; Acts 7:44. The phrase omnia sancta illius is used in relation to the tabernacle in Num. 1:50; 4:16; 18:3; 1 Ki. 8:4; Hebr. 9:21.

According to Num. 1:50; 3:6-8; 18:3-4; 1 Chron. 23:28, 32 the care of the tabernacle was allotted to the Levites, more specifically to Eleazar, Aaron's son and successor (Num. 4:16; in Num. 32:28; 34:17; Josh. 14:1 and elsewhere, Joshua and Eleazar cooperate as leaders of the people). In As. Mos. Aaron and Eleazar do not feature; Aaron's high priestly office is obviously thought to have been fulfilled by Moses (cf. As. Mos. 11:17). This may indicate that in As. Mos., Joshua is considered to be a Levite, therefore a successor of Moses in all respects (see also the commentary on 1:16). It is in any case the first instance in As. Mos. of the merging of several figures (in this case Joshua and Eleazar) into one (see further the introduction to 3:1-3, and the commentary on 4:1).

1:8-9a

In 1:8 Joshua's next task is mentioned: he must lead the people into the land (cf. As. Mos. 11:11). On the basis of the well-known formula (ἡ γῆ, ἣν ὤμοσεν τοῖς πα-τράσιν αὐτῶν δοῦναι αὐτοῖς, occurring about twenty times in the Pentateuch alone), I have adopted the conjecture by Schmidt and Merx, reading terram datam patribus eorum, "the land that was given to their fathers", instead of the manuscript's impossible terram datam ex tribus eorum[3]. This conjectured reading must be regarded as a short version of the full expression that occurs in As. Mos. 2:1 and 3:9. Indeed, the subordinate clause in 1:9 must be taken as if the full form of the formula had been used. The following comparison of 1:8-9 may serve to clarify this point:

---

[1] Charles, The Assumption, p. 56, has vigorously argued for the interpretation of διάδο-χος (underlying successor) as a rendering of the Hebrew מְשָׁרֵת, "minister". But there is no need to see in the word successor any other meaning than "successor".

[2] The scene testimonii is the prefiguration of the temple, see the metaphor for the building of the temple in 2:4 figet palum scenae suae l. em.

[3] Schmidt and Merx, "Die Assumptio Mosis", p. 127 of their edition conjectured datam patribus eorum, but in their annotation p. 137, they declared that they would explain the corruption by omission of a line. The original would have read the solemn datam ex [testamento pa]tribus eorum.

As. Mos. 1:8-9	As. Mos. 2:1	Josh. 1:6[1]
ut inducat plebem	*intrabunt per te*	σὺ γὰρ ἀποδιαστελεῖς τῷ λαῷ τουτῷ
in terram datam	*in terram quam ... promisit ...*	τὴν γῆν ἣν ὤμοσα
patribus eorum	*patribus eorum*	τοῖς πατράσιν ὑμῶν
ut detur illis per testamentum	*dare illis*	δοῦναι αὐτοῖς

From a grammatical point of view, however, we must understand *ut detur* to be a continuation of *ut inducat*. But possibly *ut detur* renders an infinitive δοῦναι dependent on the Greek underlying *datam*; see grammatical note nr. 184.

In As. Mos. 3:9, the contents of this oath are quoted: *ne umquam deficiat semen eorum a terra quam dedisti illis*. There (as in 11:17 and especially 12:12-13), the covenant and the oath guarantee that the possession of the land is meant to be everlasting.

At first sight, *quod locutus est in scenae* is to be read as an attributive relative clause determining *jusjurandum*, "the oath that he had spoken in the tabernacle". But *testamentum* and *jusjurandum* are a word-pair in As. Mos., which must not be separated, and which consistently refers to the covenant with the fathers. Therefore, we must punctuate: *ut detur illis per testamentum et per jusjurandum, quod locutus est in scenae dare de Jesum. Quod locutus est* must then be taken as loosely resuming the earlier references to the prophecy Moses is about to give: "the things he (Moses) said in the tabernacle". The scene to which this refers is probably the one described in Deut. 31:23 (see the commentary on 1:5-6a).

---

[1] This is one of the instances of the formula; one may compare Deut. 11:9; 26:3; 31:7; Judg. 2:1 and many other instances.

1:9b-2:2
MOSES' INSTRUCTIONS TO JOSHUA
ISRAEL AS THE PURPOSE OF GOD'S CREATION

In As. Mos. 1:9b Moses' address to Joshua begins. In 2:3-10:10, Moses
prophesies the future of Israel from their occupation of the land until
the coming of God's kingdom. 1:9b-2:2 forms a preamble to this
prophecy.

In this passage the author first makes Moses admonish Joshua to keep
the law (1:9b-10). Before Moses delivers his prophecy (which is announced in 1:11), a digression is made on the purpose of the creation
of the world, which includes a twofold explanation of why this is revealed only now: it was necessary that first the nations should be rejected and that the covenant with Israel should be mediated by Moses
(1:12-14).

Subsequently, Moses' imminent death is mentioned (1:15) as the occasion to hand to Joshua Moses' testament, a prophecy which must
serve as a witness to the reliability of the law in the end of days. In
order to be able to perform that function, the prophecy must undergo
conservational treatment and be stored in a secret place (1:16-18).

Finally it is related how Moses instructs Joshua to lead the people
into the land, and to establish it there according to what pleases the
Lord (2:1-2).

a. *1:9b-15*

Moses' address to Joshua begins with an admonition to keep the law impeccably. A
Botenformel signals that the following speech is the word of God, even though the
prophecy proper, that is, the forecast of the future, begins only in 2:3. As. Mos. 1:12-
14 comments on the divine purpose of the creation and on Moses' role in achieving
that aim.

9 b Saying to Joshua: "Keep this word, 10 and promise to do impeccably
everything that is commanded, according to your zeal. 11 Therefore,
thus says the Lord of the world. 12 —For he created the world on behalf of his people, 13 a but he did not also reveal this purpose of the creation from the beginning of the world, b so that the nations would be
put to disgrace on their account, c and, through their deliberations
among themselves, to their own humiliation disgrace themselves. 14

Therefore, he has devised and invented me, I who have been prepared from the beginning of the world to be the mediator of his covenant. 15 But now, I will reveal it (*sc.* the purpose of God's creation) to you, because the time of the years of my life is fulfilled, and I will go to the resting-place of my fathers, and before the entire people ... —

1:9b-10

In these lines Moses commands Joshua to keep the law (*verbum hoc* and *omnia quae mandata sunt*) perfectly[1]. Such commandments, in similar wordings, occur quite often in Deuteronomy and in the first chapters of the book of Joshua[2]. As. Mos. 1:9b-10 may be compared especially to Josh. 1:7-8[3], in which passage it is related how God commands Joshua to "keep the law so as to act accordingly" (φυλάσσεσθαι καὶ ποιεῖν), and not to deviate from it in any way ("to the left nor to the right", cf. *quemadmodum sine quaerellam est* , i.e., ἀμέμπτως, "impeccably"[4]); furthermore, to study the book of the law day and night ("zealously", *secus industriam tuam*[5]), so that, as it is said again, he may keep everything that has been written in it.

The syntax of As. Mos. 1:9b-10 is somewhat complicated because the object and an adverbial adjunct of the subordinate clause are positioned in the main clause: *promitte secus industriam tuam ... mandata ... ut facias*. Probably, the *ut*-clause renders a Greek infinitive (ποιεῖν), retaining, however, the infinitive's position (see grammatical note nr. 184).

1:11-12

Moses utters a formula which commonly introduces prophetic speech (the *Botenformel*[6]): "Therefore, thus says the Lord". However, he does not immediately proceed to deliver his prophecy, but first comments on the purpose of creation (1:12-15). The *Botenformel* appears to be completely fossilized as a result of a development already

---

[1] On *dicendo* instead of *dicens*, see grammatical note nr. 129; on the biblical character of this formula introducing direct speech, see grammatical note nr. 150.

[2] See e.g. φυλάσσεσθαι (πάσας) τὰς ἐντολάς (προστάγματα κτλ.) ὅσα ἐγω; ἐντέλλομαι σοι σήμερον Deut. 4:2, 40; 5:10; 6:2; 28:1, 13; with λόγους Deut. 29:9 (8); 32:46; cf. Deut. 33:9 and Exod. 12:24 (ῥῆμα). Very often, φυλάσσεσθαι is complemented with ποιεῖν or καί with a form of ποιεῖν.

[3] Both passages are elaborately compared by Schalit, *Untersuchungen*, pp. 117-124.

[4] For the equivalence of *sine querela* and ἄμεμπτος, ἀμέμπτως, see the Vulgate of Wisd. 10:5, 15; 18:21; Phil. 2:15; 3:6; 1 Thess. 2:10; 3:13; 5:23. In all these instances, *sine querela*/ἄμεμπτος is closely connected to righteousness and the law; see esp. Luke 1:6 ἦσαν δὲ δίκαιοι ἀμφότεροι ἐναντίον τοῦ θεοῦ, πορευόμενοι ἐν πάσαις ταῖς ἐντολαῖς καὶ δικαιώμασιν τοῦ κυρίου ἄμεμπτοι.

[5] The Septuagint of Josh. 1:8 reads μελετήσεις for "you shall study", cf. *industria* As. Mos. 1:10 = μελέτη (Schalit, *Untersuchungen*, p. 120).

[6] See, for instance, Westermann, *Grundformen*, p. 71. Charles, *The Assumption*, p. 5, makes *ideo* refer to the preceding clauses: "These things said the Lord of the world"; cf. Priest: "For this is what the Lord of the world has decreed".

in process in Old Testament prophecy: the formula came to introduce anything a prophet said, even if his words did not claim to be a divine oracle[1].

Moses reveals (*nunc palam facio* 1:15) that the world has been created on behalf of God's people, Israel; cf. 4 Ezra 6:55, 59; 7:11; 2 Bar. 14:19[2]. These parallels show that this concept should not be taken as some kind of metaphysical conviction about the reasons and motifs for creation, but rather as a strong expression of the idea of Israel's election. In 4 Ezra 6:38-59, a section on the creation and the election[3], it is said that God created the "first" world "on our behalf" (*propter nos creasti primogenitum saeculum* 6:55; *propter nos creatum est saeculum* 6:59). From the same section, it is clear that this refers to Israel's election: the nations are compared to "nothing" on the one hand (*istae gentes quae in nihilum deputatae sunt*, 6:56), and Israel to a "firstborn, only-begotten" son on the other (*nos autem populus tuus quem vocasti primogenitum, unigenitum* 6:58; see also the commentary on 11:12 below).

In As. Mos. 1:12, too, the claim that God created the world on behalf of Israel probably refers to its election. If one believes that Israel is the people which God in the very beginning of creation chose to love, to the exclusion of all other nations, it is not too much to say that the world was created on their behalf. This strong emphasis on the chosen people as the aim of creation serves, as in As. Mos. 12 and in 4 Ezra and 2 Baruch, to reassure the readers that Israel's history will have a happy ending, even if not for the entire people (cf. As. Mos. 12:12-13).

1:13a

That God created the world on behalf of Israel is summarized by *ea intentio creaturae* in 1:13. The manuscript has *inceptio creaturae*, and several attempts have been made to vindicate this reading. Some scholars consider that *inceptio* refers to Israel itself as the "firstling" of creation[4]. But a paraphrase of 1:12-13a forces one to understand the word *inceptio* as "intention", or "plan, design", as Schmidt and Merx proposed[5]:

> Although God created the world on behalf of his people, he did not also reveal this <?> of the creation from the beginning of the world.

This proposal was adopted *via* Charles in the *Thesaurus* s.v. *inceptio*[6]. But it is the only instance of this meaning of *inceptio*, and how *inceptio* may have developed into this meaning is unclear[7]. Therefore, it is more likely that *inceptio* is a corruption of

---

[1] Westermann, *Grundformen*, p. 135: "Allmählig überwiegt diese Stellung [sc. at the beginning of a speech of a prophet] der Botenformel, so daß sie nun schlechthin als Einleitungsformel des ganzen Prophetenwortes erscheint. Schließlich erstarrt die Formel so, daß sie auch Worte einleitet, die gar nicht Botenworte zu sein beanspruchen."

[2] Cf. a similar statement concerning the church in Hermas, *Vis.* II 4, 1.

[3] Cf. Stone, *Fourth Ezra*, pp. 181, 188-189.

[4] They derive *inceptio* from the root αρχ, and consider it to be a somewhat unlucky translation of ἀπαρχή, "firstling" (*inceptio* does not occur in the Vulgate; *incipere* is the Vulgate's equivalent of ἄρχειν [and compounds, though not ἀπάρχειν] or μέλλειν).

[5] "Die Assumptio Mosis", p. 138: "*Inceptio* ist 'das Vorhaben'".

[6] *ThLL* VII, 1, col. 875:12-15: "hoc propositum creationis".

[7] There is the slight possibility of a mistranslation. *ThLL* VII, 1, col. 874:82-83 calls attention to *inceptio* listed as an equivalent of ἐπιβολή in Pseudo-Philoxenus' glossary (ed. Goetz, *Corpus Glossariorum* II, p. 307:16). This Greek word has exactly the meaning we need for our text, namely "plan, design", in for instance Polybius V,35,2: κατὰ τὴν ἐξ

(cont.)

intentio. The corruption of T into C is paleographically not surprising; moreover, the immediate context relatively often mentions the "beginning" of the creation and of the world, so that the corruption of *intentio* into *inceptio* can be plausibly explained.

1:13b

In 1:13b the reason is given why God has kept the purpose of his creation a secret for such a long period: it was his intention that the nations would, to their humiliation[1], convict themselves by their disputes[2], or rather, deliberations (*disputatio* can be understood as a translation of διαλογισμός[3], meaning "deliberation" [in the Vulgate usually *cogitatio*]; see further grammatical note nr. 183).

The verb *arguantur* is qualified by the phrase *in eam*. It is not entirely clear what *in eam* refers to. If *in eam* refers to Israel (*in eam* sc. *plebem* from 1:12), *in eam* can either be taken as the complement of the agent: "so that they will be convicted by Israel"; or causal: "so that the nations will be convicted on account of Israel"[4]. To the last interpretation may be compared Ps. 105(104):14 (= 1 Chron. 16:21), which stands in the context of Israel's wandering through the desert: "He allowed no one to oppress them; he rebuked kings on their account (ἤλεγξεν περὶ αὐτῶν βασιλεῖς)". If *in eam* refers to the *intentio*, then it is likely that the first clause means: "so that the nations will be convicted on account of this plan"[5]. The meaning must then be that the nations' ignorance concerning Israel's exceptional status forms a deliberate part of God's plan[6].

The nations' deliberations are, almost by definition, not God's (cf. Ps. 33[32]:10-11). For a similar rejection of acting on one's own accord see Isa. 55:7-9 and the commentary to 2:5. The entire clause can be compared to passages such as Ps. 2; 33(32):10-11; 56(55):6; see especially Lam. 3:60-61:

> εἶδες πᾶσαν τὴν ἐκδίκησιν αὐτῶν εἰς πάντας διαλογισμοὺς αὐτῶν ἐν ἐμοί. Ἤκουσας τὸν ὀνειδισμὸν αὐτῶν, πάντας τοὺς διαλογισμοὺς αὐτῶν κατ᾿ ἐμοῦ.

1:14

From the very start of his creative work, God provided that Moses should be the mediator of the covenant he had planned to establish with Israel. The Greek quotation in Gelasius' *Acts of the Nicene Council* (see the apparatus to lines 17-19) uses the expression προεθεάσατό με. In the Latin text, the words *excogitavit et invenit me* are

---

ἀρχῆς ἐπιβολὴν καὶ πρόθεσιν, "according to the original plan and purpose". Polybius quite often uses ἐπιβολή as a synonym of πρόθεσις, see Mauersberger, *Polybius-Lexikon* I, p. 912. For πρόθεσις with regard to creation, see Lampe, *Patristic Lexicon*, p. 1149.

[1] See grammatical note nr. 179.

[2] Coincidentally, words similar to these have been used in Rom. 2:15, as remarked by Lipsius in Hilgenfeld, *Novum Testamentum*, p. 112; cf. also Loman, *Quaestiones*, p. 481. However, Rom 2:15 has a meaning quite contrary to that of As. Mos. 1:13b (Scholten, *Bijdragen*, p. 113, contradicting Loman).

[3] So Kuhn, "Zur Assumptio Mosis", p. 125.

[4] For these two meanings of *in* in As. Mos., see grammatical note nr. 70.

[5] Cf. perhaps Eccl. 3:10-11.

[6] So Kolenkow, "The Assumption of Moses", p. 73: "God did not reveal it before the time of Moses ... because God's intent was to deceive and thus convict the Gentiles".

used. *Excogitare* and *invenire* are near-synonyms[1]; possibly, the translator of As. Mos. used these two words to render a single Greek word; see further grammatical note nr. 170.

The issue here is not Moses' preexistence[2], as Tiede has convincingly argued. The phrase *qui ab initio orbis terrarum praeparatus sum* must be compared with similar expressions elsewhere in As. Mos. In these passages, mention is made of the predetermination of the aim of creation (1:13), of the place where Moses' prophecy is to be preserved (1:17), and even of the primordial predetermination of all history (12:4). Tiede concludes: "the author of the TM [= As. Mos.] is primarily interested in affirming that God had already designated a mediator of his covenant before he had actually created anything"[3].

Itaque must therefore be given its full consecutive meaning, referring directly to the preceding sentence: "in order that the nations be condemned, for that reason (*itaque*) I, Moses, was prepared from the beginning of creation to mediate the covenant". 1:13-14 may be read as antithetical parallel clauses:

> Just as God did not reveal the plan of creation from the beginning,
>> so that the nations be condemned,
> Likewise, he provided me from the beginning,
>> so that his covenant be mediated to Israel.

The primeval election of Israel (established in the covenant mediated by Moses) stands in contrast to the secrecy of God's plan and the condemnation of the nations. The antithesis of 1:13 and 1:14 is accordingly not secrecy *versus* revelation, but condemnation *versus* election.

1:15

At this juncture of Moses' speech, he announces to Joshua his impending death. "To die" is expressed with the common euphemism "to go to the resting-place of one's fathers"[4]. As. Mos. here probably depends on Deut. 31:16, in which passage God is said to announce to Moses: Ἰδοὺ σὺ κοιμᾷ μετὰ τῶν πατέρων σου. According to Schalit, *transire* is a word used in Jewish and Christian sepulchral language, but see also the Vulgate of John 13:1 *sciens Jesus quia venit ejus hora ut transeat ex hoc mundo ad Patrem*; in As. Mos. 10:4 the simplex *ire* is used[5]. In the same context of Moses' death, LAB 19 uses this and related expressions three times, e.g. *Ecce ego dormio cum patribus meis, et eam ad populum meum* LAB 19:2; see further 19:6 and 12. The reason for Moses' death is the "completion" of his lifetime. These words are also closely paralleled in LAB 19:8 *Ecce ego complevi tempus vite mee, et complevi annos CXX*.

Moses' impending death is the occasion of his farewell address to Joshua. Moses is reported to say that the subject matter of his testament is the revelation of God's plan: *Et nunc palam facio tibi* resumes 1:13a *non coepit ... et ab initio orbis terrarum palam facere*—God did not want to reveal the goal of creation in the beginning, but

---

[1] Cf. the definition of *excogitare* in *ThLL* V, 2, col. 1274:74: "cogitando invenire".

[2] So Charles, *The Assumption*, p. 6.

[3] Tiede, "The Figure of Moses", p. 90.

[4] Many instances are found in Schalit, *Untersuchungen*, pp. 162-164.

[5] Schalit, *Untersuchungen*, p. 162.

Moses has known it, and because he himself is about to die he will now pass this knowledge on to Joshua, his successor (who in turn is to keep it a secret, see below).

Moses' statement about his impending death is concluded by what seems to be an incomplete sentence[1] about something that must happen in the presence of the entire people. The manuscript has a lacuna, which must be partly occupied by a *tu* that is necessary in 1:16 (see below). A possible supplement is *moriar*: "I shall die in the presence of the entire people". Alternatively, some word indicating Joshua's installation as Moses' successor may have been used, for instance: "I shall appoint you in the presence of the entire people". In that case, Moses' death and his succession by Joshua are contrasted in a way similar to the contrast in As. Mos. 10:14-15; cf. also Deut. 31:7 καὶ ἐκάλεσεν Μωυσῆς Ἰησοῦν καὶ εἶπεν αὐτῷ ἔναντι παντὸς Ἰσραήλ· Ἀνδρίζου καὶ ἴσχυε κτλ. It must be said that a word meaning "to appoint" also requires an object and an object complement (e.g. *indicabo te successorem*), and there may be no room for all that.

Some confusion, however, about the extent of the lacuna exists. In his edition Ceriani indicated a blank space without dots because, as he later wrote to Volkmar, the manuscript in this passage is "conservatissima", and shows no traces whatsoever of lost letters. Ceriani concluded that the word preceding *autem* (1:16) must have been written in red ink (which leaves no traces when washed off), and he suggested to Volkmar to assume a "Tu", written with an initial. Volkmar in his turn concluded that the lacuna cannot have contained more than the word "tu"[2], but this is contradicted by Clemen[3]. According to Clemen, the lacuna takes up more than half of a line. Perhaps, the blank space was purposely left open by the scribe, for instance because he had trouble in reading his *Vorlage*. In that case, the room the lacuna offers has no bearing on the room a proposed supplement requires.

b. *1:16-18*

In this section, the author relates that Moses hands a writing (*scribtura*) to Joshua, who has to bring these books (the writing seems to be referred to in the plural) in order, anoint them and store them in jars. These jars must in their turn be hidden in a secret place, where they will remain until the day of penitence, at the end of time. The writing is a copy of the prophecy Moses is about to give, and it is intended to verify at the end of Israel's history that the course of that history proved to be in perfect accordance with the Lord's promises and threats as laid down in the covenant.

16 You, however, receive this writing, which serves to confirm the trustworthiness of the books which I will hand to you, 17 and you must

---

[1] Rönsch, "Sprachliche Parallelen", pp. 82-83, suggested that the sentence is complete: "I will go to the resting-place of my fathers, even in the presence of the entire people". This is a possible solution, but the resulting phrase is rather short and abrupt. In "Weitere Illustrationen", pp. 220-221, therefore, Rönsch proposed to fill the lacuna following *plebem* with *eam* (= *ibo*) or *eo*.

[2] Volkmar, *Mose Prophetie*, p. 154, cf. Schmidt and Merx, "Die Assumptio Mosis", p. 138.

[3] *Die Himmelfahrt* (1904), p. 5.

order them, embalm them, and put them in earthenware jars in a place which he made from the beginning of the creation of the world, 18 a so that his name be invoked; b until the day of repentance, in the visitation with which the Lord will visit them in the fulfilment of the end of days.

1:16

The Latin word *tutatio* means "protection". At first sight, therefore, the writing which Moses gives to Joshua according to 1:16 would contain instructions aimed at "protecting the books" which Moses will hand to Joshua. These *libri* are almost certainly the books of the law. In Deut. 31:23-26 (part of the scene to which As. Mos. 1 is explicitly linked) it is related that Moses addressed Joshua, promising him God's help in leading the people into the land, and that he (Moses) subsequently wrote down the law, and gave the book of the law to the Levites, whom he instructed to put it in the ark of the covenant, so that it might serve as a witness against the people. The author of As. Mos. has simplified this account, and makes Moses address Joshua and hand him the books of the law simultaneously.

The *scribtura* is the prophecy given by Moses according to 2:3-10:10. The *scribtura* occurs again in 10:11 and 11:1. From the latter passage, it appears that Moses has told Joshua a prediction contained in a writing: *Et cum audisset Jesus verba Moysi tam scripta in sua scriptura, omnia quae praedixerant &c.* This clearly refers to Moses' prophecy in 2:3-10:10. In 10:11, in the conclusion of his speech, Moses is said to summon Joshua to "preserve these words and this book": *Nam tu, Jesu Nave, custodi verba haec et hunc librum.* The concept of a prophecy delivered in writing as well as in speech is common in the testamentary and apocalyptic traditions[1].

If, however, the *scribtura* Joshua receives in 1:16 is Moses' prophecy given in 2:3-10:10, *recognoscere tutationem* in 1:16 cannot mean "to preserve" materially, because As. Mos. 2:3-10:10 gives no instructions how to do this[2]. Therefore, Rönsch was probably right, when he suggested that *tutatio* is a mistranslation of the Greek ἀσφάλισις (or rather, ἀσφάλεια)[3]. Ἀσφάλεια can mean "protection", like *tutatio*, but it can also mean "reliability", especially of statements[4], a translation which suits the present context excellently. *Recognoscere tutationem* may be a translation of ἐπιγι-νώσκειν τὴν ἀσφάλειαν; see for this expression Luke 1:4 (Vulgate: *cognoscere veritatem*; Vetus Latina: *agnoscere firmitatem*)[5].

---

[1] Russell, *The Method and Message*, pp. 120-121; Cortès, *Los discursos de adiós*, pp. 366-369. A remarkable parallel to As. Mos. is found in the introduction to the Apocalypse of Paul (ed. Tischendorf, *Apocalypses apocryphae*, pp. 34-35). There it is told how this apocalypse was found under the foundations of a noble man's house in Tarsus at the end of the fourth century.

[2] Cf. Schalit, *Untersuchungen*, p. 172.

[3] "Weitere Illustrationen", p. 222.

[4] In *ThGL* I, 2309B, the following usages are mentioned: ἀσφάλεια λόγου; ἀσφαλὴς ῥήτωρ; λόγου νοῦν ἔχοντος καὶ ἀσφαλείας.

[5] In Luke 1:4 a concept similar to that in As. Mos. 1:16 is found, although if there has a different application: the story of Jesus is well-known from several books, but Luke has made a new, historical investigation into the matter for the benefit of Theophilus, enabling the latter to confirm that everything he has learnt from the earlier books is indeed reliable; see further Fitzmyer, *Luke I-IX*, pp. 289-290, 300-301.

As. Mos. 1:16 can then be translated as follows: "But you, receive this writing in order that the reliability of the books that I will hand over to you be confirmed." The *scribtura*, Moses' prophecy in As. Mos. 2:3-10:10, makes it possible to verify the reliability of the law. Moses' prophecy describes Israel's future, and shows that the people will abandon the law, that is, break the covenant. In accordance with the conditions of the covenant, laid down in the law (the *libri quos tibi tradam*), they will be punished; the reliability which is particularly stressed, however, is God's faith to the covenant, which ensures that God will bring salvation to the faithful.

1:17-18

The relative pronoun *quos* apparently refers to the *libri quos tibi tradam* in 1:16. Moses' discourse, therefore, seems to continue to speak about the books of the law. However, it is much more likely that the passage 1:17-18a deals with the preservation of the *scribtura* of 1:16, that is, Moses' prophecy, which in the time of the end must serve to verify the reliability of the books of the law. The arguments for this supposition are as follows.

First, the books which are mentioned must undergo preservational measures, obviously because they must remain intact for a very long time. *Chedriare* must mean "to embalm with cedar-oil" (see grammatical notes nrs. 43 and 181). The embalming of books was a well-known method in Antiquity of preserving books[1]. Similarly, the storage of books in jars (*et reponis in vasis fictilibus*) is attested throughout the ancient world (not just in Qumran), and it equally is regarded as a preservational method[2]. It is not easy to understand why the books of the law should be embalmed and stored in jars, apparently without anyone being able to consult them. Moses' prophecy, on the other hand, is intended to be publicly revealed in the time of the end, so that measures to keep it intact for a long period make perfect sense.

Second, the books must be deposited in a "place which he (*sc.* God) made in the beginning of creation". This *locus* is often interpreted as the temple in Jerusalem, where the books of the law should be kept, and parallels from rabbinic sources are adduced to show that the temple has indeed been regarded as the starting-point of the creation[3]. But of course, Joshua cannot bring the books of the law into the temple in Jerusalem: even if the temple was made at the beginning of the creation, as some rabbinic sources imply, that does not mean that it already stood in Jerusalem. The author of As. Mos. himself alludes in 2:4 to the building of the temple, even after the separation of the tribes[4]. Moreover, it is said of this *locus* that it will exist until the final consummation; but in 3:2 the author of As. Mos. shows himself well aware that the tem-

---

[1] A considerable number of proof-texts in Schalit, *Untersuchungen*, pp. 184-185, who concludes that the embalming of the books with cedar-oil is done "damit sie gegen Feuchtigkeit, Wurmfrass und ähnliche Schäden geschützt sind und dem Zahn der Zeit trotzen können".

[2] Schalit, *Untersuchungen*, pp. 197-198. For *reponere* meaning "to store", see 4 Ezra 7:77 *etenim est tibi thesaurus operum repositus apud Altissimum, sed non tibi demonstrabitur usque in novissimis temporibus.*

[3] A thorough treatment of the relevant passages in Schäfer, "Tempel und Schöpfung".

[4] Wieseler, "Die jüngst aufgefundene Aufnahme Moses", p. 630, therefore suggested that the sanctuaries in Gilgal or Silo may have been meant, because these were sanctuaries that Joshua had witnessed, even founded.

ple was destroyed by the Babylonians. If, on the other hand, the vague allusion to a certain "place" is connected with Moses' prophecy mentioned in 1:16, As. Mos. 1:16-18 appears as a quite normal instance of the apocalyptic and testamentary[1] tradition of the secret revelation: the *locus* is a secret place that was made in the beginning of creation[2], where Moses' prophecy must be stored until the end of time[3].

This tradition occurs in several variants: the revelation may be kept secret for a (long) period of time (see for instance Dan. 8:26; 12:4, 9), or it may be revealed to only a few (see for instance 1 En. 82:1-2; 4 Ezra 14:46). This literary convention, closely related to the pseudepigraphic character of most of these works, serves on the one hand to justify to the readers why a revelation, allegedly received by a pious man in ancient days, was not known previously. On the other hand, the emphasis on the limited extent of its audience (the wise, the pious) may serve as a *captatio attentionis* of the intended readers. Finally, if it is said that the book is to become public at the end of time, that is a signal to the readers that the final consummation is at hand.

The question remains to be answered, however, how the masculine plural relative pronoun *quos* can refer to the feminine singular *scribtura*. In view of the general state of the manuscript, the emendation of *quos* into *quam* may not be too drastic[4]. But the word *ordinare*[5] and the plural *vasa fictilia* seem to suggest, too, that what Moses gives to Joshua is indeed thought of as something plural. The author may have thought of the *scribtura* as *libri*[6], and for this reason have chosen the relative *ad sensum: quos.*

Jer. 32:10-14 is useful in illuminating the scene in As. Mos. 1:16-18. This passage[7] (which is missing in the Septuagint) describes how Jeremiah purchases a field, symbolizing that "houses and fields and vineyards will be possessed again in this land" (Jer. 32:15). The deed of purchase is put in an earthenware vessel because it needs to remain undamaged for many years (Jer. 32:14)[8]; after these many years, the jar will

---

[1] Kolenkow, "The Assumption of Moses", p. 73.

[2] The phrase *quem creavit ab initio creaturae &c.* is to be understood as a reference to God's predetermination of history, as in 1:14. The reader is assured of the fact that Moses' revelation as well as its long-time concealment are not coincidental events occurring at some random moment during the turbulent course of history, but premeditated decisions of God.

[3] So Volkmar, *Mose Prophetie*, p. 22.

[4] There may have been attraction of the preceding *quos* (1:16).

[5] The exact meaning of *ordinare* is unclear; the general meaning of this verb is "to bring in order". With regard to books, it often means "to compose, to write", but that meaning must here be excluded. In the third letter of Ps.-Seneca to the apostle Paul (ed. Haase), it seems to mean "to arrange scrolls according to their proper order": *quaedam volumina ordinavi et divisionibus suis statum eis dedi.*

[6] In Greek, writings can be referred to in the plural; see Schwyzer, *Griechische Grammatik* II, p. 43: "ἐπιστολαί von éinem Brief Thuk. I 132, 5; ἀντίγραφον und –φα für éine Abschrift (Mayser II 1, 43)". See also Polycarp, *Ad Philipp.* III 2 ἐπιστολάς, said of Paul's Epistle to the Philippians. Deissmann, *Licht vom Osten*, p. 28, pointed to 1 Ki. 21(20):8-9, where the Septuagint render ספרים first by βιβλίον, then by βιβλίοι; cf. Isa. 37:14.

[7] There are grave difficulties in interpreting this passage, but the main point is clear; see Deissmann, *Licht vom Osten*, pp. 28-29, and Koffmahn, *Die Doppelurkunden*, pp. 16-20.

[8] To this one may compare LAB 62:10, where Jonathan suggests to David that they mix their tears in a vessel (*vas*), so that they may serve as a testimony. This image probably derives from Ps. 55(56):9.

have preserved the contract, serving as proof of the reliability of God, who had promised the restoration of the people after the desolation by the Chaldeans (Jer. 32:43-44).

According to 1:17, Joshua must store Moses' testament in a secret place, making sure that it can withstand the ravages of time. This must be done so that God's name may be invoked up to and including (*usque in*) the "day of repentance", when the writing will be publicly revealed. One may compare especially Dan. 12:4 Θ: καὶ σύ, Δανιήλ, ἔμφραξον τοὺς λόγους καὶ σφράγισον τὸ βιβλίον ἕως καιροῦ συντελείας (Vulgate: *signa librum usque ad tempus statutum*), ἕως διδαχθῶσιν πολλοὶ καὶ πληθυνθῇ ἡ γνῶσις.

From the last phrase of 1:18 (*in consummatione exitus dierum*), it is clear that the day of repentance is the eschatological Day of the Lord. The designation of this day as the day of repentance is, as far as I could ascertain, unique. In the Old Testament and related literature it is more commonly called the day of judgement, punishment, wrath, or the like; sometimes, when attention is centered on the righteous ones, the day of salvation or mercy[1].

The Lord's coming is called his visitation. *Respectus* probably renders ἐπισκοπή (so in Wisd. 2:20; 4:15; 14:11; cf. *conspectus* Sir. 16:18; 18:20), although the Vulgate usually prefers *visitatio*. This word may be used in a general sense, or have specific regard to either the righteous or the sinners[2]. Since there are no clear indications that the author of As. Mos. specifically had a specific group in mind, it may be best to regard *respectus* in its general sense.

c. 2:1-2

Taking the events recorded in the book of Joshua as a starting-point, the author now makes Moses give instructions to his successor with regard to the occupation of the land. The instructions concern the occupation, the division and the constitution of the land: Joshua must establish the land's polity in accordance with the Lord's pleasure. The style of this passage is solemn, characterized by the pairing of synonymous words and phrases: *decrevit et promisit* (2:1); *dabis unicuique et stabilibis sortem* (2:2b); *constabilibis regnum et magisteria locorum* (2:2c).

1 But now, they will enter through you into the land which he decided and promised to give to their fathers. 2 a And in it (*sc.* the land) you must give blessings; and you must give to each of them their share in it, b and you must found for them a kingdom, and arrange for them local rule according to their Lord's wish in justice and righteousness.

---

[1] Volz, *Die Eschatologie*, pp. 164-165.
[2] Volz, *Die Eschatologie*, pp. 165-166.

2:1

The manuscript has a blank space preceding *intrabunt*. Neither the photographs, nor Ceriani's edition allows us to establish whether words are lost or whether the scribe of the manuscript left some room deliberately (cf. the commentary to 1:15). Possibly, the scribe wanted to indicate a new paragraph. There is in any case a transition: in 1:12-15, Moses is depicted as elaborating on the aim of creation, on Israel's role therein, and on the function of the prophecy that is presently to be delivered. Now, he is seen to move on to giving instructions to Joshua with regard to the occupation of the land. If words are lost, a transitional formula such as *nunc autem*[1] or *mox autem* may have stood here.

Since the testament scene in As. Mos. explicitly refers to Deut. 31:14-23, As. Mos. 2:1 is probably derived from Deut. 31:23 (cf. Deut. 31:7). In Deut. 31:23, Joshua is commanded to lead the people into the land; cf. LAB 20:2. More often, God is said to bring in the people himself (e.g. Lev. 18:3; Num. 14:31; Deut. 7:1; 8:7; 28:37). The latter is probably the intention in As. Mos., as well, as may be concluded from the periphrastic expression *intrabunt per te* (not: *introduces eos*).

The land into which Joshua must lead the people is specified as "the land which the Lord has promised to give to the fathers" (cf. Deut. 31:7). In As. Mos. 2:1, this promise is expressed by two verbs, *decrevit et promisit*, in accordance with the elevated style of this passage (see grammatical note nr. 170).

2:2a

In the Old Testament records of Joshua's exploits, blessing is not very dominant. Yet the book of Joshua does relate a few instances in which Joshua blesses parts of the people in connection with the division of the land: Josh. 14:13; 22:6, 7; cf. Josh. 8:33 (9:2 d) and LAB 21:10.

The object of *dare* is probably *sortem*, which is the object of *stabilire* as well (see further grammatical note nr. 171). *Sors* (Greek: κλῆρος or κληρονομία) has two meanings between which a clear distinction cannot always be made: on the one hand, it indicates the action of casting lots by which the land is partitioned among the people; on the other hand, a part of the land as far as it has been allotted to one particular group may also be called that group's *sors*, its territorial property[2]. In As. Mos. 2:2b, the latter nuance is intended, but the use of *sors* doubtlessly implies a reference to the way in which the division was executed. LAB 20:9 closely parallels As. Mos. 2:2a: *Et dedit Ihesus in sortem terram populo, unicuique tribui secundum sortes, iuxta quod preceptum fuerat ei*. See also Deut. 31:7 κατακληρονομήσεις αὐτὴν (sc. τὴν γῆν) αὐτοῖς (Vulgate: *tu eam sorte divides*). The casting of lots in order to divide the land among the tribes is a favorite topic in the Book of Joshua (see Josh. 1:6; 14:2; 16:1; 17:1, 6, 8 and many more instances; see also Num. 26:55; 33:54; 34:2, 13; 36:2; Deut. 1:38).

The author sustains the solemn style of this passage by joining more or less synonymous words together in one commandment. Accordingly, *stabilire* is a rather insignificant word, meaning something vague as "to found", possibly with the

---

[1] Hilgenfeld, *Novum Testamentum*, p. 100.
[2] Foerster, "κλῆρος κτλ.", p. 757.

connotation of solidity[1]. *Stabilire* is used in the Vulgate for "to lay foundations" in e.g. Prov. 3:19 (ἑτοιμάζεσθαι, said of the foundation of the heavens; in Zach. 5:11 *stabilire* is used of the foundation of a house: *Et stabiliatur, et ponatur ibi super basem*). It is also relatively often used with *regnum, thronus* or a dynasty as object; see 1 Sam. 20:31; 2 Sam. 7:13, 26; 1 Chron. 17:11, see also 2:2b.

2:2b

Constabilibis eis regnum and *magisteria locorum dimittes illis* in 2:2b are apparently used as synonymous phrases. *Regnum* and *magisteria locorum* may have an abstract and a concrete meaning, indicating a territory[2] or the activity of ruling. The former meaning would best fit the historical events the author evidently refers to: according to the biblical records, Joshua did not establish the kingship in Israel. Under his leadership, however, the tribes were settled in the land (for *stabilire*, see the commentary on 2:2a; on the semantical equivalence of *stabilire* and *constabilire*, see grammatical note nr. 167).

On the other hand, the author of As. Mos. simplifies history on other occasions, describing certain events from the perspective of their outcome. Thus in 2:4 he makes the temple be built after the division of the tribes, simply, it seems, because the Jerusalem temple eventually ended up with the two tribes. From that perspective, he might make Moses command Joshua to found a "kingdom" as well.

As far as I know, *magisterium* does not occur in the Latin versions of the Bible. Lipsius[3] has proposed to regard *magisteria locorum* as an analytical translation of τοπαρχίαι, "districts". This would be a synonym of *regnum* as "territory". Then, 2:2b refers to the division of the land into districts as one of the aspects of Joshua's work, most elaborately described in the Book of Joshua. However, according to the dictionaries, *magisteria* means the "office or post of a leader"[4], and would then be synonymous with the meaning "kingship" for *regnum*. It seems that "making arrangements in justice and righteousness" (see below) is more appropriately said of the way in which the land must be ruled than of the establishment of a country with its districts. To 2:2b, one may now compare to Deut. 16:18: Κριτὰς καὶ γραμματοεισαγωγεῖς (MT: ושטרים שפטים; Vulgate: *judices et magistri*) καταστήσεις (cf. As. Mos. 2:2b *constabilibis*) σεαυτῷ ἐν πάσαις ταῖς πόλεσίν σου (MT: שעריך; Vulgate: *portae*), αἷς κύριος ὁ θεός σου δίδωσίν σου, κατὰ φυλάς, καὶ κρινοῦσιν τὸν λαὸν κρίσιν δικαίαν (cf. As. Mos. 2:2b *in judicio et justitia*).

Judging from the context, *dimittere*, classically, "to send away"[5], must mean "to arrange, make arrangements". In our context, the word may have to be explained as an analytical translation (see grammatical note nr. 182) of a Greek compound verb

---

[1] Cf. Vulgate 1 Chron. 17:11 *stabiliam regnum ejus*, LXX ἑτοιμάσω τὴν βασιλείαν αὐτοῦ; in As. Mos. 12:13 *stabilitum est testamentum illius* (sc. *Dei*) the notion of steadfastness predominates; but contrast As. Mos. 2:5 *X tribus stabilient sibi ... regna*, which must mean no more than "to found" (Niermeyer, *Lexicon*, p. 986a). *Stabilire* with *regnum, rempublicam* or *urbem* is normal, classical Latin, see Forcellini IV, p. 468c.

[2] For this meaning the Vulgate uses also the cognate *regio*; cf. As. Mos. 4:6.

[3] In Hilgenfeld, *Novum Testamentum*, p. 100.

[4] Lewis-Short, p. 1097b; cf. also Niermeyer, pp. 625b-626a, where more nuances are recorded for Medieval Latin; they all relate, however, to such an office or to the authority derived from it.

[5] In 4:6 *dimittere* is used meaning "to let go", i.e. "to allow to leave".

with δια⁻ (e.g. διατάσσειν, διατίθεσθαι), and *mittere* must be taken as "to set"[1], an equivalent of *ponere*; indeed, the Latin *disponere* would have been perfectly understandable.

Judicium et justitia are a word-pair, probably rendering κρίσις (κρίμα) καὶ δικαιοσύνη, as they do in the Vulgate. The two words are frequently found in combination throughout the Old Testament and related literature, both juxtaposed and in parallelism; see Gen. 18:19; 1 Ki. 10:9; 2 Chron. 9:8; Isa. 5:16; 9:7(6); 33:5; 56:1; Jer. 22:3; 23:5; Ezek. 45:9; 1 Macc. 2:29; Ps. Sol. 17:19. In Jer. 9:24 it is explicitly said that God "wishes" justice and righteousness (ὅτι ἐν τούτοις τὸ θέλημά μου, Vulgate: *haec enim placent mihi*), cf. Ps. 33(32):5 and Prov. 21:3.

---

[1] Niermeyer, *Lexicon*, p. 698a; cf. French *mettre*.

2:3-3:3
SIN AND PUNISHMENT

The events leading up to the exile are summarized very schematically. The outlines are clear. After the people's entrance into the land, they will be ruled by princes and kings (2:3a-b). In the end, the ten and the two tribes will go their separate ways (2:3c). The ten tribes will organize themselves according to their own regulations (2:5). The Lord will build his temple in the kingdom of the two tribes, who at first, as a holy nation, will offer their sacrifices there (2:3d-4, 6), but who will eventually, like the ten tribes, abandon the Lord (2:7-9). As the instrument of God's punishment, a king from the East will come, destroy their city and lead the people into exile (3:1-3).

These outlines agree with the overviews of history found in the typically Deuteronomistic passages of the Pentateuch, for instance Deut. 4:25-27[1]: "When you will have begotten children and grandchildren, and lived a long time in the land, and you will then act lawlessly (ἀνομήσητε) and make idols (cf. As. Mos. 2:8-9)... then your days will no more be long in the land, but you will surely be exterminated, and the Lord will disperse you among the nations (cf. As. Mos. 3:3)".

It is difficult to interpret this passage in depth because the description is so concise. Knowing that his readers were well-acquainted with this period of history, the author found it unnecessary to go into great detail. However, the resulting sketchiness of the description has led to a lack of clarity[2].

The division of the pre-exilic period into periods designated by numbers of "years" is hard to interpret. The time of the common rule over the twelve tribes is designated as eighteen years (2:3). After these eighteen years, in the nineteenth year, the ten tribes will secede (2:3), and a period of twenty years will begin during which the two holy tribes will offer sacrifices (2:6). The entire pre-exilic period is therefore covered by a period of thirty-eight years, to which an unspecified

---

[1] Reese, *Die Geschichte Israels*, p. 94. Compare also the correspondance of As. Mos. 3:4-4:4 with (e.g.) Deut. 4:29-30.

[2] Cf. Brandenburger, "Himmelfahrt", p. 70: "Bei der beabsichtigten Periodisierung—Konsolidierung des Reiches Juda, glückhafter Fortbestand und Niedergang—hat man sich an Hauptmerkmale gehalten, einiger Abweichungen ... nicht achtend."

number of years, possibly one or two, indicated in 2:3a may have to be added, resulting in a total of thirty-nine or forty years. All of this, however, is very uncertain.

a. *2:3-5*

The author of As. Mos. quickly glosses over the first period of the people living in the land. He merely notes the period of common rule, and devotes most attention to the separation of the ten and the two tribes. He seems to regard the two tribes as no less sinful than the ten tribes. In cases where the two tribes might appear to surpass the ten tribes in holiness, the author stresses that this is due to divine initiative.

3 a ..., however, after they will have entered into their land in the ...th year, b and afterwards, they will be ruled by princes and kings for eighteen years, c but in the nineteenth the ten tribes will break themselves loose. d And the two tribes will separate themselves and transfer the tabernacle of the testimony. 4 a Then the heavenly God will fasten the pole of his tabernacle and the tower of his sanctuary, b and the two (*sc.* tribes) will be appointed as holy tribes. 5 The ten tribes, however, will establish for themselves kingdoms according to their own ordinances.

2:3a

The manuscript is partly illegible: one word is missing before *autem*, which always stands in second position[1]. Schmidt and Merx's suggestion to supply *fiet* fits both the lacuna and the context[2], but something like *Tunc* or even *Plebs* is equally possible.

The transition from commandment to prophecy is marked by adversative *autem*, and by the switch from second singular forms, directly addressing Joshua (*tu benedicis, dabis, stabilibis* etc. in 2:2) to third plural forms, speaking about the future actions of the people (*intrabunt, se abrumpent, descendent* etc. in 2:3). However, the transition is smooth, and the prophecy is closely connected with Moses' instructions to Joshua by the repetition of *intrare* (2:1 *intrabunt per te*, 2:3 *postquam intrabunt*).

Another lacuna follows ANNOS, which contained some numeral. It has been proposed that *annos* is an accusative indicating a period of time[3]. It should be noted, however, that elsewhere in As. Mos. duration is denoted by the ablative or by *per* + accusative[4], not by the accusative alone. Therefore, the *s* is preferably interpreted as the first letter

---

[1] See grammatical note nr. 143.

[2] *Fiet* ("And it will come to pass") is then continued by *et postea dominabitur* ("that the land/people will be ruled"). This would be a Hebraizing construction, (ו ... ויהי), but cf. grammatical note nr. 190. Schmidt and Merx were followed by Charles and Clemen.

[3] Von Gutschmid in Hilgenfeld, *Novum Testamentum*, p. 100, supplemented *annos VII*; Volkmar, *Mose Prophetie*, p. 23, *annos quinque*.

[4] See grammatical notes nrs. 73 and 108.

of an ordinal number. In 2:3b and 2:6 mention is made of periods of eighteen and twenty years respectively. If *anno s<ecundo>* is read, it would appear that the entire pre-exilic period is divided into thirty-nine or forty "years" (on the meaning of these "years", see the commentary on 2:3b). This reading is tempting since forty is a perfect number. It is, however, mere speculation.

One way or another, 2:3a indicates the period between Moses' speech and the events prophesied in 2:3b. That is, 2:3a must relate to the period of Joshua's leadership. 2:1-3 can be paraphrased as follows:

> Joshua, you must lead the people into the land and divide the land among them, etc.
> But hear the things that will happen after they will have entered into their land in the
> <Nth> year.

2:3b

After the period of Joshua's leadership, they (*sc.* the people) "will be ruled by princes and kings for eighteen years". Elsewhere in As. Mos., *annus* seems to indicate quite plainly "year", without a symbolic reference to something else[1], but this is clearly not the case in chapter 2[2]: the numbers of *anni* in 2:3 and 6, eighteen and twenty, presumably cover periods before and after the division between the two and the ten tribes mentioned in 2:3c-d, though it is not clear exactly how they do so.

It is often assumed that the eighteen "years" indicate the rules of the judges and kings before the division of Israel. Some scholars confidently put the number of the judges at fifteen and that of the kings at three (including Saul)[3], so that the number of years is equal to that of the number of judges and kings. They consider this interpretation corroborated by two facts: the numeral *XVIIII* is used, which agrees with the number of kings over the Northern kingdom, and the number *XX* matches the number of kings over the Southern kingdom.

In fact, however, the biblical record as well as post-biblical tradition are obscure about the exact number of judges that officiated before Saul. The agreement of the numeral eighteen with the number of judges and kings before the separation cannot therefore be substantiated. Likewise, the numeral nineteen in 2:3c does not match the number of kings over the Northern tribes (there were, according to the biblical record, twenty kings in the North). Moreover, *XVIIII* should be interpreted as an ordinal (see below). The number twenty in 2:6 does agree with the number of kings over Judah, but 2:6 is concerned with the temple service.

Finally, the identification of *anni* with periods of rule seems to be based on a misunderstanding of an analogy to which Von Gutschmid referred. Von Gutschmid suggested that the *anni* of As. Mos. should be interpreted in the same way as the "hours" in 1 En. 89:72 and 90:5[4]. In these instances, however, the "hours" no more

---

[1] 1:2 "the twenty-five hundredth year since the creation of the world"; 1:15 "the years of my life"; 3:11 "in the desert during forty years"; 3:14 "they will be slaves during seventy-seven years"; 6:6 "he will execute judgement on them such as the Egyptians did for thirty-four years".

[2] Other symbolic indications for periods of time are used in As. Mos., as well: *horae* 7:1; *tempora* 10:12. As with the years in chapter 2, it is impossible to determine their exact value.

[3] For instance Charles, *The Assumption*, p. 9: "The 'chiefs and kings' are the fifteen judges and the three kings, Saul, David, and Solomon"; Volkmar, *Mose Prophetie*, p. 23, relativized: "gleichviel wie der Verf. 15 Richter gezählt hat".

[4] Von Gutschmid in Hilgenfeld, *Novum Testamentum*, p. 112.

designate exact numbers of kings than the years in As. Mos. They serve to divide history into phases in a purely schematical way. In 1 Enoch a differentiation is made between the rulers ("shepherds") and the duration of their reigns ("hours"); both the shepherds and their hours eventually add up to seventy[1], but the rule of one shepherd does not automatically equal one hour.

All in all, it seems safest to interpret the "years" in As. Mos. 2:3-7 not as the respective reigns of the judges and kings, but more simply as a division into relative periods of the time between the entrance into the land and the exile. What exactly the proportions stand for I dare not guess.

Principes and *tyranni* can be understood as different types of rulers following each other (e.g. "judges" and "kings"). But it is equally possible that the words are here used more or less synonymously, as *princeps* and *judex* in Jub. 47:9: *Quis te constituit principem aut judicem super nos?*; cf. 1 En. 89:48 and Jub. 31:15. In the Vulgate, *princeps* is the usual equivalent of κριτής and ἄρχων; οἱ κριταί are sometimes parallel to οἱ πρεσβύτεροι (Ezra 10:14; 3 Ezra 9:13; in Deut. 21:2; 29:10[9] ἡ γερουσία), sometimes to οἱ ἄρχοντες (2 Chron. 1:2 [cf. 1 Chron. 28:1]; Ps. 148:11; Sir. 41:18). Τύραννος is not used pejoratively[2]; in the Vulgate its equivalents include: *princeps* Prov. 8:16; *rex* Wisd. 6:10, 22; 8:15; *tyrannus* Wisd. 14:16; Sir. 11:5 (cf. Wisd. 12:14 οὔτε βασιλεὺς ἢ τύραννος Vulgate *neque rex neque tyrannus*, see also Hab. 1:10).

2:3c-d

The manuscript's text of 2:3c is certainly out of order, but it is not hard to reconstruct a satisfactory reading. Generally, the intention is clear: after the eighteen years in 2:3b, *XVIIII* is likely to be an ordinal; mention is made of secession (the verb [*se*] *abrumpere*, "to break away", is used[3]), and the numeral *X* in this context makes the assumption that the ten tribes are the logical subject of *abrumpere* inescapable. The statement in 2:3c must therefore be, in paraphrase, that there will be a secession of the ten tribes in the nineteenth year. "During nineteen years" is not a reasonable alternative, since *se abrumpere* has a punctual meaning and cannot be used to indicate duration[4].

In answer to the secession of the ten tribes, the two tribes are said to "leave": *descendent* ("they will descend") must probably be understood as the classical *discedent* ("they will leave")[5]; *discedere* and *descendere* were practically homophonous and often confused in Latin manuscripts (see grammatical note nr. 3). The image is rather obscure. The schism is presented as if the tribes first live together in a certain part of

---

[1] Black, *The Book of Enoch*, pp. 275, 277-278.

[2] There is therefore no need to see in the use of this word an expression of the author's "rabbinisch-republikanischen Groll gegen alle weltliche Königsherrschaft" (so Volkmar, *Mose Prophetie*, p. 27).

[3] The verb *abrumpere* is very rare in the Vulgate; in Lev. 13:56 it is the equivalent of ἀπορρηγνύειν (or -ρήσσειν), which elsewhere can mean "to rebel", cf. Josephus, *Bell. Jud.* II 283.

[4] Against Clemen, *APAT* II, p. 320, who translates: "19 Jahre hindurch werden sich zehn Stämme losreißen".

[5] So Schmidt and Merx, "Die Assumptio Mosis", p. 128 (who translate διαστήσονται, "spalten sich", emending the two tribes of As. Mos. 2:3d into twelve).

the land. At some point, the ten tribes depart from the two tribes. The latter subsequently leave that place as well, taking with them the ark of the covenant. This reflects the tendency of the author of As. Mos. to use geographical or even theatrical imagery: in 3:4 it is said that the tribes "will go into the fields", and in 4:1, an intercessor is described as "entering".

It is posible that here *descendent* is a synonym for the *se abrumpent* of the ten tribes[1], and is intended to bear the same negative connotation. If this is so, then the two tribes are held equally responsible for the division[2]. This seems indeed to be the intention of the author of As. Mos.[3]. By blaming the two tribes for the division as much as the ten, the author of As. Mos. insists on the sinfulness of the whole people. As related in 2:7b-9, after the division the two tribes will eventually be as sinful as the ten tribes[4]. This insistence on the sinfulness of the whole people recurs in 3:3 and 3:7.

With regard to the two tribes' replacing the tabernacle of the testimony, Charles[5] suggested a correspondence with either 2 Sam. 6, where it is related how David "and all the house of Israel" (2 Sam. 6:15) moved the ark from Kirjath-Jearim to Jerusalem, or 1 Ki. 8, which records the transferral of "the ark, the tabernacle and the holy vessels" (1 Ki. 8:4) from the city of David to the newly built temple. It seems, however, simpler to view the transferral of the tabernacle to Jerusalem as part of the departure of the two tribes[6].

The transfer of the tabernacle to Jerusalem infringes upon the chronology set out in the Bible, since it is here situated after the schism rather than before. However, in 2:4a, Solomon's building of the temple also comes after the division. Apparently, the author of As. Mos., did not want to introduce too many complications and described this part of history from the perspective of its eventual result, namely, that after the division of Israel, the ark and the only divinely recognized temple were in Jerusalem. A comparable simplification can be found in Ps. 78(77):67-69, in which passage the Lord is said to have chosen the tribe of Judah and Mount Zion after having rejected the temple in Shiloh and the tabernacle of Joseph.

---

[1] For this metaphorical meaning of *discedere*, see the numerous examples in *ThLL* V, 1, cols. 1285:49-1286:28 (also used absolutely, "to defect"). *Discedere* in this meaning is a synonym of *abscedere = accedere* in As. Mos. 2:7b.

[2] This is in marked contrast to the usual interpretations of the division of David's kingdom, see, e.g., 1 Ki. 12:19 καὶ ἠθέτησεν Ἰσραὴλ εἰς τὸν οἶκον Δαυὶδ ἕως τῆς ἡμέρας ταύτης; 2 Ki. 17:21; Isa. 7:17, quoted in CD VII 12.

[3] Janssen, *Das Gottesvolk*, p. 103, asserts that the ten tribes are made responsible for the division, whereas the two tribes are said to be holy tribes. Janssen denies that 2:3d refers to the division of Israel and Judah, and claims that the schism is not mentioned before 2:5 ("The ten tribes will establish for themselves kingdoms"). However, he offers no alternative explanation for 2:3d-4. Reese, *Die Geschichte*, p. 94, writes similarly: "Die Reichsspaltung schildert der Vf. als eine eigenmächtige Absonderung der zehn Stämme des Nordreiches", and to support this, Reese equally stresses 2:5. In practice, these interpretations follow the same procedure as Volkmar's, namely a transposition of clauses. For 2:5 is to be seen as a contrast to 2:4, and not as a further comment on 2:3d.

[4] This is acknowledged by Reese, *Die Geschichte*, p. 94, who senses in 2:4 a certain bias in favour of Judah, but adds: "Wie [der Vf.] in Wahrheit über Israel und Juda denkt, hat er in 3,4ff ausführlich dargelegt."

[5] *The Assumption*, pp. 9, 61.

[6] So Clemen, *APAT* II, p. 320.

2:4a

If the proposed reading is accepted, "the heavenly God"[1] is said in this sentence to "fasten the pole[2] of his tabernacle and the tower of his sanctuary". This must refer to the building of the temple by Solomon (though it must be noted that here it is emphatically said that God is the one who takes action; for As. Mos.' chronological order, see commentary to 2:3d). The allusion to the construction of the temple stresses the continuity between the formerly travelling tabernacle and the now steady temple; compare especially Isa. 33:20: "Your eyes will see Jerusalem, a quiet habitation, an immovable tent, whose stakes will never be plucked up, nor will any of its cords be broken". From 2:8-9 it appears that from now on, the tabernacle and the temple are identical (*ponent idola scenae ... et in domo Domini facient sceleste*)[3]. For the solidity and durability of the temple[4], see 1 Ki. 8:13 (the text of this passage is uncertain[5]); cf. Ps. 132[131]:14.

The "tower of his sanctuary" (*turrim* 1. em.; the manuscript reads the incomprehensible *ferrum*[6]) may be another hint at the permanence and strength of the Lord's temple[7]. The use of this image is possibly inspired by Isa. 5 ("The Lord has built a tower in the middle of his vineyard" Isa. 5:2). But the image may have been more common: it is used for the temple in 1 En. 89 and 91[8] (cited and allegorized in Barn. 16), and for the church in Hermas, *Vis.* III 2, 4-3, 5; *Sim.* IX. In Ps. 61(60):4-5 the psalmist calls God his "hope and strong tower against my enemies; I shall live in your tabernacle in eternity". The temple and towers (βάρεις) are also associated in Ps. 48(47):4, 14; Lam. 2:5, 7.

---

[1] Cf. *Dominus caelestis* As. Mos. 4:4 and *Caelestis* in 10:3; cf. further ὁ κύριος τοῦ Ἰσραὴλ ὁ οὐράνιος Ezra 6:15; οὐράνιος θεός Sib. Or. III 19, 174; Οὐράνιος Sib. Or. III 247, 261; cf. also 2 Chron. 36:23; Ezra 1:2; 5:11; 6:9; Dan. 2:18 ὁ θεὸς τοῦ οὐρανοῦ; 3 Macc. 2:2 βασιλεὺς τῶν οὐρανῶν.

[2] *Figere palum*, MS *facere palam*; the conjecture is first made by Rönsch, "Weitere Illustrationen", pp. 223-225, who adduces many parallels for *figere tabernaculum* and for *figere palum/clavum/paxillum*.

[3] Koester, *The Dwelling of God*, p. 18: "in [some] Psalms, the terms 'tent' ... and 'tabernacle' ... are poetic descriptions for the temple or Mt. Zion, and Ps 46:4 [5] may speak of Jerusalem itself as 'the holy tabernacle of the Most High'"; see further *ibid.* pp. 21-22.

[4] In Isa. 22:23, 25 the image of fastening a tent-pin (יָתֵד עַקֹם; absent from LXX, reflected in 22:25 by στηρίζεσθαι) is used to indicate the durability of David's house; cf. Sir. 14:24-25; Ezra 9:8.

[5] In 1 Ki. 8:13 MT has מָכוֹן לְשִׁבְתְּךָ עוֹלָמִים; corresponding words are absent from LXX, but OLPM† add ✳ἕδρασμα τῇ καθέδρᾳ σου αἰῶνος‹, and the Vulgate has *firmissimum solium tuum in sempiternum*.

[6] Rönsch's attempt to explain *ferrum* ("Sprachliche Parallelen", pp. 86-87; "Weitere Illustrationen", pp. 223-225) as a contrast to *palum* (iron vs. wood) is unsuccessful, in spite of Jer. 1:18.

[7] Πύργος and οἶκος are variant readings in Sir. 49:12(14): Ἰησοῦς υἱὸς Ἰωσεδέκ, οἳ ἐν ἡμέραις αὐτῶν ᾠκοδόμησαν οἶκον (A† πύργον) καὶ ἀνύψωσαν ναὸν ἅγιον κυρίῳ.

[8] E.g. 1 En. 89:50 "And the Lord of the sheep stood upon that tower, and they offered a full table before him."

2:4b-5

As a corollary to the definitive establishment of God's habitation in the temple in Jerusalem, the two tribes[1] are said to be "constituted" as the holy tribes (cf. Exod. 19:6; Ps. Sol. 17:26), in contrast to the ten tribes, of whom it is said in 2:5 that they will establish for themselves kingdoms according to their own regulations.

The sanctification of the two tribes is entirely God's work, just as the building of the temple was. The two tribes' holiness is therefore not a merit of theirs, but due to an action by God, and is to be seen in connection with the temple, which is understood to be within the two tribes' territory; cf. Ps. 78(77):67-71. Although the two tribes may seem to be holy, in apparent contrast to their guilt concerning Israel's division in 2:3c, their holiness is a result of the presence of God's habitation in their midst. *Ponentur tribus sanctitatis* may therefore be best understood as an assignment (*ponere* = τιθέναι): "the two tribes will be appointed as the holy tribes", that is: from this moment on, the two tribes (and not the twelve tribes as a whole, see 2:5) will be expected to be holy. For this concept cf. Lev. 11:44-45: "You shall be holy, for I am holy".

This presentation of the new relation between the two and the ten tribes is part of the continued reduction of the Lord's people that the author of As. Mos. observed. In view of the definitive rejection of the ten tribes in 2:5 (see below), the sanctification of the two tribes may be seen as a redefinition of "Israel, the Lord's holy nation". This is no final redefinition: in 4:8 the "two tribes" themselves are defined anew, resulting in a drastic reduction of their number. The author of As. Mos. presents Israel's history in terms of a constant decline; with that ideological approach in mind, 2:4b can be compared with Isa. 4:3 "And the remainder in Zion and the rest in Jerusalem, they shall be called holy".

In parenthesis (introduced by *nam*, see grammatical note nr. 146), the organization of the ten tribes is briefly described as a self-founded kingdom: they will found (*stabilient*, see the commentary on 2:2a) their kingdom *secus ordinationes suas*, "according to their own arrangements", which apparently are not the Lord's (cf. 2 Ki. 17:8); contrast 2:2, where Moses is said to instruct Joshua as follows: *constabilibis eis regnum et dimittes illis secus quod placebit Domino*. The clause also stands in strong contrast to 2:4, where the regulations concerning the two tribes are described as entirely determined by God.

By this short comment, the ten tribes are written off. They are once more introduced in 3:4-9, but solely as the antagonists of the two tribes. There, the author of As. Mos. seemingly defends the ten tribes against the accusation of having caused the exile of the two tribes, but instead of defending the ten, the author accuses the two themselves (cf. 2:3d). The role of the ten tribes in 3:4-9 is therefore entirely secondary. It seems that in 4:9, a difficult passage, their disappearance is more or less predicted.

---

[1] The subject of this clause must be taken from the predicate: *ponentur duae* (sc. *tribus*) *tribus sanctitatis* (see grammatical note nr. 171).

b. *2:6-9*

In 2:6-9 the apostasy of the two tribes is prophesied. In his description the author uses the well-known prophetic and Deuteronomistic reproofs (cf. for instance again Deut. 4:25) against the sins committed in the time of Israel's and Judah's kings, with their typical emphasis on the cult of "foreign" gods and idolatry.

₆ And they will offer sacrifices for twenty years. ₇ And in the seventh they will surround themselves with walls, and as the ninth will have elapsed they will also abandon the covenant of the Lord, and defile the alliance the Lord made with them. ₈ And they will sacrifice their children to foreign gods, and erect idols in the tabernacle and serve them, ₉ and they will act disgracefully in the house of the Lord, and sculpt many idols of all kinds of animals.

2:6
Following the parenthesis 2:5, in which the apostasy of the ten tribes is predicted, the two tribes once again are the grammatical subject of 2:6-9, as is shown by the mention of the "tabernacle" and the "house of the Lord" in 2:8 and 9. In 2:6 it is said that they will offer sacrifices for twenty years. It must be repeated here that the identification of *annus* with a period of rule is not at all cogent, even though modern chronology indeed counts twenty kings of Judah after the separation of the Northern and Southern tribes (see the commentary on 2:3b). The period indicated may rather be compared with LAB 19:7 *Demonstrabo tibi locum, in quo mihi servient annos DCCXL*. Of course, these 740 years in LAB are in no way numerically related to the twenty years of As. Mos. But in whatever way the author of As. Mos. arrived at his number of years, it seems that he wanted to indicate the time during which the temple functioned rather than the number of kings who ruled in Judah (*adferent victimas*, not *dominabitur* as in 2:3b).

2:7
The manuscript's *circumibo* can in no plausible way be fitted into the present context, in spite of the several suggestions made. Most scholars explain *circumibo* as a translation of περιελεύσομαι, "I shall protect", as in Jer. 31:21(38:22) LXX[1], or from the Hebrew סבב על[2]. The question is of course who the subject of this verb may be. Grammatically, it can only be Moses, but it is most unlikely that Moses himself would "protect nine kings". Therefore it is often assumed that the author of As. Mos. in-

---

[1] Hilgenfeld, "Die Psalmen Salomo's", p. 280; the Vulgate reads *femina circumdabit virum*.

[2] As in Deut. 32:10 (LXX ἐκύκλωσεν, Vulgate *circumduxit*), see Schmidt and Merx, "Die Assumptio Mosis", p. 139; Charles, *The Assumption*, p. 10; p. 62 "אסובב"; in his notes Laperrousaz, *Le Testament*, p. 115, equally explains *circumibo* as "to protect", but his translation reads "J'en ferai le tour" (= "I will inspect, visit").

tended God to be the subject—which is equally unconvincing[1]. Furthermore, lists containing the nine kings of Israel whom God would have had protected, drawn up for instance by Hilgenfeld[2], are as little convincing as any list containing the seven kings who would have built walls.

The numerals *VII* and *VIIII* need not be cardinals ("during 7, during 9 years"), but can also be ordinals ("in the seventh, in the ninth year"). If the manuscript's *circumibo* is altered into *circumito* (*circumito* [sc. *anno*] *nono*), an absolute ablative construction is obtained: "when the ninth year will have elapsed". One major advantage of this solution is that the omission of the noun *anno* supposed to accompany *VIIII = nono* is much less offensive than the omission of the noun *annos* in case *VIIII* is taken to be a cardinal. The clauses 2:6-7 may then be read as follows:

> *Et adferent victimas per annos viginti, et septimo circumvallabunt muros, et circumito nono et adcedent ad testamentum Domini.*

This interpretation is corroborated by the apparent condemnation by the author of As. Mos. of the building of walls, which can be seen as a prelude to the complete betrayal of the covenant ("in the seventh they will build walls, and once the ninth is over, they will also[3] abandon the covenant"). The interpretation of Israel's history given in As. Mos. depicts a constant decline in human moral and religious behaviour. If the author believes that the building of walls is wrong, then this review of history appears to be consistent; there is then no exception of seven "years" to the process of moral and religious decline. The condemnation of building walls agrees with the negative assessment of the same activity in 4:7.

"To elapse" would in Latin be more properly expressed by *praeterire*. For the active use of the passive participle, cf. *praeteritos ... annos* in Vergil, *Aeneis* VIII 560. *Circumire* may have received the meaning "to elapse" in As. Mos. because of the Greek περιέρχεσθαι[4]; in other meanings *circumire* is an equivalent of περιέρχεσθαι[5]. Possibly, one may compare the use of *circulus* indicating the completion of a period of time in the Vulgate of Lev. 25:30 *si non redemerit et anni circulus fuerit evolutus* (Septuagint: ἐὰν δὲ μὴ λυτρωθῇ, ἕως πληρωθῇ ἐνιαυτὸς ἡμερῶν); 2 Chron. 36:10 *cumque anni circulus volveretur* (Septuagint: καὶ ἐπιστρέφοντος τοῦ ἐνιαυτοῦ); cf. also Judg. 11:40; 1 Sam. 1:20; 1 Chron. 20:1; 2 Chron. 21:19; these instances show various Greek terms, but all seem to indicate that a full period has been completed.

By building walls, the two tribes will show themselves to be lacking trust in the Lord; but only the Lord can protect the people, not man-made walls; cf. Hos. 8:14; Ezek. 13:10, and the extensive use of the latter passage in CD IV 12, 19; VIII 12, 18; XIX 24, 31; cf. also 4QTest 26. Note that, unlike in 2:4, the initiative for building the walls is not the Lord's: God himself will fasten the pole of his tabernacle and the

---

[1] E.g. Brandenburger, "Himmelfahrt", p. 70: "Der Verfasser fällt von der Sache her in die Gottesrede."

[2] *Novum Testamentum*, p. 112.

[3] *Et = etiam*, see grammatical note nr. 140.

[4] Cf. *ThGL* VII, p. 822B s.v. Περιέρχομαι: "Circumeo, Circumagor, i.e. Praetereo, de tempore".

[5] Goetz, *Corpus Glossariorum* II, p. 101:13; esp. p. 402:41: *perago circumeo* &c.; *peragere* can also mean "to complete" with regard to temporal categories.

tower of his sanctuary—but the two tribes, apparently not relying on the Lord, will build walls.

The description of the two tribes' total apostasy is introduced by the general[1] verdict that they will abandon the covenant of the Lord. *Adcedere ad* must be understood here as the seemingly opposite *abscedere ab*; the form *adcedere ad* is due to phonetic developments (see grammatical notes nrs. 28 and 67). *Abscedere* is a synonym of *discedere* (see the commentary on 2:3c-d), and means "to fall off, to defect", see 1 Tim. 4:1 Vetus Latina *abscedent a fide*, Vulgate *discedent*, Greek ἀποστήσονται[2].

Parallel to abandoning the covenant by the two tribes it is said that they will "pollute the *fides*[3] which the Lord made with them". The word *fides* (in practically all respects equivalent of πίστις[4]) is notoriously hard to translate. In 4:8 *fides* is used again, and from both instances it appears that in As. Mos. *fides* is not used to indicate some attitude, but something more objective. Perhaps we are to understand that the two tribes will pollute (betray) the "trust" which God vested in them, the trust which is exchanged when a pact is concluded[5]. As a parallel to *testamentum*[6], the word may be taken as a metaphor, and means possibly as much as *foedus*. Πίστιν ποιεῖσθαι is a common Greek metaphorical expression for making a treaty (Liddell and Scott, p. 1408a). In 1 En. 55:2, reference is made to Gen. 9:12. In Gen. 9:12, the rainbow which God made is called (in the Septuagint) σημεῖον τῆς διαθήκης; 1 En. 55:2 reads: "and it will be between me and them faithfulness (*haymanota*)". A paraphrase of 2:7b then is:

> The two tribes will break the covenant and betray the trust on which it was based.

2:8-9
In four short clauses, the sins of the two tribes are enumerated. They are the "sins of Jeroboam": child offerings, idolatry, "disgraceful behaviour" in the temple and therio-

---

[1] Following Schmidt and Merx, many scholars add before *adferent* the numeral *IV* to the numbers *VII* and *VIIII* in 2:7a, in order to arrive at a total of twenty (2:6); this shows all the more how hazardous it is to unconditionally assume an interpretation of numbers which is not at all certain.

[2] Cf. *abscessio*, often a translation of ἀποστασία, see *ThLL* I, cols. 146:83-84; 147:9-17.

[3] *Fidem* is Schmidt's and Merx's emendation of the manuscript's *finem*, which does not seem to make any sense. For *quem* in lieu of *quam*, see grammatical note nr. 90.

[4] Freyburger, *Fides*, pp. 33-34, 319. In the Vulgate, *fides* is an equivalent of πίστις in many instances, e.g. 1 Sam. 26:23; 1 Chron. 9:22; Ps. 33(32):4; Wisd. 3:14; Jer. 5:1; Hos. 2:20; and throughout the New Testament.

[5] Freyburger, *Fides*, pp. 83-84: "On peut donc définir le *foedus* comme l'acte consistant pour les deux parties, à 'échanger leur foi', *dare et accipere fidem*, chacune devant 'donner sa foi' et 'recevoir' celle du partenaire. Le 'crédit' des uns et des autres est dès lors 'lié'." This definition, relating to covenants in pagan antiquity, is valid for the Jewish concept of *foedus/testamentum*, as well, cf. Jaubert, *La notion d'Alliance*, pp. 43-50, esp. pp. 49-50.

[6] Laperrousaz, *Le Testament*, p. 115, and Priest, "Testament of Moses", p. 928, interpret *fides* as a "promise", and support their suggestion by pointing out that elsewhere in As. Mos., *testamentum* is paralleled by *jusjurandum* (see 1:9; 3:9; 11:17; cf. 12:13). However, the latter observation must rather be taken as an objection to the translation "promise" than as support for it.

latry. The child offerings refer to the well-known practice of "making children pass through the fire"; see 2 Ki. 16:3; 17:17; 2 Chron. 28:3; Ezek. 20:26, 31; Hos. 11:2. In Ezek. 16:20 and Ps. 106(105):37 (cf. Jub. 1:11), the terminology "to offer one's children" is used. The "foreign gods" are the gods of the Canaanites. Idolatry is the cardinal sin which the Old Testament historians considered to have caused the exile. Terms for idolatry came to be used for outrages other than the worship of foreign gods, as well (so in As. Mos. 5:3, see the commentary), but in 2:8 it is used in its proper sense. No specific sin seems to be indicated by "to do scandalous things"[1]. Finally, the carving of images of "all kinds of animals" is mentioned; for the terminology employed see Deut. 4:25 ἐὰν ποιήσητε γλυπτὸν ὁμοίωμα παντός. For the variety of species involved, cf. Ezek. 8:10.

c. 3:1-3

In this passage, the author makes Moses announce the punishment that necessarily follows sin. The words used concentrate on this main issue, combining the punishment of Israel with that of Judah. As 3:3 emphatically states, this king will come both for the two tribes and for Israel as a whole (*omnem plebem eiciet ... et duas tribus ducit secum*). There were in fact two kings from the East to cause the ruin of the ten tribes as well as that of the two tribes: indeed, the ten tribes as well as the two tribes were to be punished by a king from the East, Sennaherib of Assyria and Nebuchadnezar of Babylonia respectively.

1 In those days a king from the East will come to them, and his cavalry will cover their land, and 2 he will burn their city with fire, including the holy house of the Lord, and he will carry off all holy objects; 3 and he will expel the entire people and lead them to his fatherland, and he will lead the two tribes with him.

3:1

The punishment will be executed by "a king from the East". The author of As. Mos. clearly imitates Old Testament prophecies, in which it is not unusual to predict the coming of a hostile power as from one or another quarter of the compass, usually the East or the North: see for instance Jer. 1:15; 4:6; 6:22; the device is elaborately employed in Dan. 11.

The geographical provenance of the agents of God's punishment ("the East") is used by the author of As. Mos. as a lead in the rhythm of history. When after the restoration the people resume their sinful behaviour, punishment will naturally have to come again, and it will come by the agency of a king "from the West" (6:8), i.e., the Romans. Finally, the eschatological punishment is executed by the "king of the kings of the earth" (8:1), whose title is clearly intended as a climax. This rhythm is sup-

---

[1] *Scelus* is used in As. Mos. as a word for "crime": 5:1, parallel to *iniquitas* 5:6; 7:7 (the word belongs to the group of ἀνομία, ἀδικία, ἁμαρτία, etc., see for instance Exod. 34:7; Num. 14:18; Job 13:23). Cf. also Deut. 4:25 ἀνομήσητε.

ported by the description of the punishment by the king from the West, a description
which to a certain extent parallels that of the actions of the king from the East (see the
commentary on 6:8).

For cavalry "covering the land", one may compare Jer. 8:16; Ezek. 26:10-11; Dan.
11:40; Hab. 1:8 (cf. 1QpHab III 10).

3:2-3

The rest of the king's actions are entirely described as we know them from the biblical
records: their city (Jerusalem) will be burnt down, together with the Lord's holy
house, the temple's holy objects will be stolen, and the entire people will be led into
capitivity; see 2 Ki. 25:9, 13-17, and 2 Chron. 36:18-20. The account in Chronicles is
shorter than that in Kings, but includes all elements contained in As. Mos. 3:2-3
(compare also As. Mos. 3:14, where the duration of the exile is prophesied, with
Jeremiah's prophecy recorded in 2 Chron. 36:21c; such a chronological indication is
absent in the Book of Kings).

The use of the word *colonia* was taken by Volkmar[1] as evidence for a late dating of
As. Mos., namely *post* 135 C.E., when Jerusalem was transformed into the *colonia
Aelia Capitolina*. This is not a convincing argument since *colonia* is used "(simply) as
city" by Petronius and Commodian[2]. Moreover, it could be that the use of *colonia* in
3:2 reflects the influence of the translator: nothing warrants the assumption that it renders κολωνία and not πόλις. It should also be noted that in As. Mos. *urbs* does not
occur, whereas *colonia* is used three times (3:2; 5:6; 6:9). There are no occurrences of
oppidum, civitas or *municipium*.

It is stated emphatically that the two tribes are to be included in the punishment, no
doubt as a result of their sins. These sins are related in 2:7-9, and at first sight there
seems to be no reason to declare that the two tribes are included among the exiles. By
this statement, however, the author looks ahead to the discussion between the two and
the ten tribes in 3:5-7. There, the two tribes put the blame for their exile on the ten
tribes. But the exile itself is the very proof of the two tribes' own guilt, for the exile is
the punishment God threatened to execute if the children of Israel abandoned the
covenant. If, therefore, the two tribes are led in exile, this points to their own guilt
(3:7), since God is a righteous judge (3:5). The aim of the author's elaborate treatment
of this argument is probably to convince his readers of his interpretation of their own
days as a time of divine punishment, and of the necessity to repent.

---

[1] *Mose Prophetie*, p. 70.

[2] Souter, *Glossary*, p. 60a; see Petronius 44:12, 16; 47:9; Commodian, *Carmen apologe-
ticum* 976, 989.

REPENTANCE, INTERCESSION, AND SALVATION

In 3:4 it is described that the two tribes will call unto the ten tribes and go into the fields. The description of the events which follow is an extensive adaptation of the so-called confessional prayers, one of the most fixed forms of Jewish literature from the exile up to the present. There is no need to postulate a distinct exemplar of this form as the source of As. Mos. 3:4-4:4. The form is so familiar that it is not necessary to postulate some specific literary *Vorlage*. The authors of literary works containing a confessional prayer frequently handle the form in a free manner, filling in the structural outline according to their individual requirements. The constituting elements of confessional prayers which consistently recur are as follows[1]:

(1) They are prayers offered in a time of distress: the one who prays recognizes that this distress is a deserved punishment from God because of his (and/or his people's) sins and those of their ancestors. National confessions are usually partly or entirely made by intercessors.

(2) When they occur in a narrative context, confessional prayers are described as accompanied by rites of mourning and remorse, and by elaborate praying-gestures, often depicted in some detail to stress the humility of the one who prays. These rites and gestures, and the humility of the one who prays are often referred to in the prayer itself, as well.

(3) Apart from initial and final doxologies, they are structured according to the following pattern[2]:

> (a) an anamnetical section, or historical paragraph, describes the sins committed; in national confessions often a review of Israel's history (sometimes contrasted with God's forgiveness) is given; in individual confessions there may be a retrospect on the life of the one who prays;

---

[1] Cf. Harvey's short description of the "rigid structure" of the confessional prayers (*Le plaidoyer prophétique*, p. 158):
> "I. Reconnaissance de la rectitude de l'agir divin et de la culpabilité d'Israël.
> II. Reconnaissance des bienfaits passés de Yahvé et des ingratitudes passées d'Israël.
> III. Reconnaissance des malheurs présents comme punition et des fautes, récentes comme passées, qui les ont provoqués.
> IV. Supplication en vue de l'avenir et demande de pardon."

[2] See Giraudo, *La struttura letteraria*, pp. 156-159.

(b) an epicletical section, or the plea itself, calls on God's will to forgive; it is often introduced by עַתָּה/καὶ νῦν or similar transitional formulas;

(c) either section, or both of them, may be supported by a solemn scriptural quotation, which serves to reinforce the plea for pardon, either by stressing the sense of guilt, or by reminding God of his former promises.

The prayers meeting this description include the following:

National: Ps. 106(105); Isa. 63:7-64:12; Dan. 9:4-19; Ezra 9:6-15; Neh. 1:5-11; 9:6-37; Esth. 4:17 l-z; Bar. 1:15-3:8; Pr. Azar.; 4 Ezra 8:20-36; 3 Macc. 2:1-20; cf. 1QS I 24-II 1; CD XX 27-31; LAB 30:4.

Individual: Ps. 51(50); Tob. 3:1-6; 8:5-7, 15-17; Pr. Man.; Jos. As. 12-13.

As. Mos. 3:4-4:4 is clearly inspired by this form. It contains all the elements mentioned, although they are only partly cast in the form of a prayer. The mourning rituals of covering oneself with dust and of fasting are modified and employed to depict the miserable condition of the tribes in exile. The confession of sin proper takes the form of a discussion between the two and the ten tribes about who is to blame for the exile[1]. A reference to God's righteousness provides the answer: since all of the tribes have been punished, they have to acknowledge that all have sinned. They then remember the threats Moses uttered in God's name and laid down in the law, according to which such punishment (including exile) befalls the sinners. After a short comment on the fulfilment of the punishment, the plea for mercy is presented as a new prayer, said by an intercessor, independent from the tribes' prayer (this accounts for some duplication of the tribes' prayer). The intercessor refers to the covenant in order to move God to mercy. The structure of As. Mos. 3:4-4:4, which agrees with that of the confessional prayers, may be presented as follows.

---

[1] A comparable adaptation of the traditional form of confessional prayer is found in 4 Ezra's dialogues with the angel Uriel (cf. Boyarin, "Penitential Liturgy"). In LAB 30:4, the terminology of the confessional prayers is used to relate how Israel decided to repent, and which expectations they connected with their repentance.

NATIONAL CONFESSION
3:4b   mourning rites
3:5a   praise of God's righteousness
3:5b-7   confession of sins
3:8-9   epiclesis with quotation: appeal to the covenant
3:10-13   anamnesis with quotation
INTERCESSION
4:1   prayer gestures
4:2a   praise of God
4:2b-3   anamnesis: covenant and exile
4:4   epiclesis

a. *3:4-9*

In this section, the first part of Israel's penitence, rituals of mourning are performed: A discussion follows, in which the two tribes try to exculpate themselves, but which results in the acknowledgment that Israel's distress is a punishment for the sins of the entire people. Finally, an appeal for mercy is made on account of the covenant with the fathers.

4 Then the two tribes will call upon the ten tribes, and they will retire into the fields like a lioness, covered with dust, starving and thirsting. 5 And they will cry: 'Righteous and holy is the Lord! Truly, because you have sinned, we and our children have been carried off just like you.' 6 Then the ten tribes will weep, hearing the reproaches of the two tribes, and they will say: 7 'What can we say to you, brethren? Has not this distress come over the entire house of Israel?' 8 And all tribes will weep, crying unto heaven, and saying: 9 'God of Abraham, and God of Isaac, and God of Jacob, remember your covenant, which you made with them, and the oath, which you swore by yourself, that their seed would never be absent from the land that you gave to them!'

3:4

Pulverati in 3:4 must be explained as "covered with dust". It has often been emended into *pulveratis* in order to match *campis*[1]; *campi pulverati* would then be a more or less poetical characterization of the desert. If one retains *pulverati*, however, it refers to the Israelites (see grammatical note nr. 98), and probably reflects one of the common rituals of mourning and repentance, namely sprinkling ashes or dust on one's head, a corollary of fasting (*esurientes et sitientes* 3:4), weeping and crying (3:8), confessing and praying. In confessional prayers, the ritual of sprinkling ashes or dust on some-

---

[1] The proposal was made by Volkmar (p. 25). Schmidt and Merx dismissed it as "höchst ergötzlich" ("hilarious", p. 140), but it was followed by most scholars.

one's head occurs in Dan. 9:3; Neh. 9:1; Esth. 4:17 k; Jos. As. 10:16; 13:4; cf. also Job 42:6; Jonah 3:6; VAE 31, 36, 40[1]. *Esurientes et sitientes* is the equivalent of fasting, described in Dan. 9:3; Ezra 9:5; Neh. 1:4; 9:1; Bar. 1:5; Jos. As. 10:20; 13:8[2]; LAB 30:4; cf. also Jonah 3:5, 7.

The words *pulverati, esurientes et sitientes* belong to the terminology for the rituals of mourning and repentance, but they are used here to describe the desolate situation of the tribes in exile. The rituals are changed into quasi-historical events. The two tribes are said to "call unto" the ten tribes, apparently to come to them in the fields[3], where the discussion in 3:5-13 takes place. This probably refers to the well-known motif of the retreat into the desert, often described as made in order to avoid impurity and transgressing of the Law[4]. Such a retreat is not standard in the other descriptions of penitence[5]. Perhaps 3:4 is inspired by the lamentation in Ezek. 19, which would account for the combination of these three words with the image of the lioness. In Ezek. 19:2 Israel is compared to a lioness that nourished its cubs, which were eventually brought to Babylon[6]; in 19:10 this mother animal is likened to a vine in a fruitful land, which was uprooted, cast down and dried by the east wind (19:12; cf. perhaps As. Mos. 3:1, *ab oriente rex*), and which is now planted in the wilderness, in a dry and thirsty ground[7] (LXX ἐν γῇ ἀνύδρῳ, Vulgate *in terra invia et sitienti*). The combination of the elements of both comparisons (the lioness as mother, the dry desert) may have led to the imagery in As. Mos. 3:4 *ut liena in campis, pulverati, esurientes et sitientes*.

The author of As. Mos. has a certain tendency to evoke geographical circumstances (see the commentary on 2:3c-d). Clemen has noted a connection with 4 Ezra 13:40-42[8]. According to that passage, the nine tribes have left the heathen nations, among whom they had been exiled, and went to a distant, isolated land (*Arzareth*), where they might keep the commandments as they had not done before in their own land.

---

[1] In VAE, the word *pulver* is used.

[2] In this instance, the fasting explicitly causes hunger and thirst.

[3] For *se ducere* meaning simply "to go", see grammatical note nr. 36.

[4] Hengel, *Die Zeloten*, pp. 255-259.

[5] On some occasions, the penitents do gather at some specific place, usually near or in the temple, or, if they are alone, in some kind of isolation: Neh. 9:2-4; LAB 30:4; Jos. As. 10:9; in Tob. (LXX) 3:10 Sarah retires into her father's upstairs room, but with the intention of hanging herself; likewise, in LAB 19:8, Moses ascends Mt. Abarim, but his prayer there is an attendant circumstance.

[6] The manuscript reads *ut liena in campis pulverati esurientes et sitientes cum infantibus nostris*. In the edition, I have followed Schmidt and Merx in transposing *cum infantibus nostris* to 3:5, *quia enim vos peccastis et nos pariter adducti sumus vobis {cum infantibus nostris}*. If the phrase were to be retained in its position in the manuscript, the word *nostris* could not be satisfactorily explained, and should be emended into, e.g. *suis* (referring to the lioness; see Rönsch, "Sprachliche Parallelen", p. 90). This would match with the supposed derivation of the image from Ezek. 19, but it is hard to imagine how a quite natural word like *suis* could have been corrupted to *nostris*. For the explicit inclusion of children in the exile, see the commentary on 4:3.

[7] The image of desert and thirst for Israel's exile can be found elsewhere, e.g. in Ps. 107(106):40; cf. 2 Bar. 77:14.

[8] *APAT* II, p. 321.

3:5-6

The two tribes put it to their brethren of the ten tribes that their exile is due to the sins of the ten tribes. For this concept, one may compare 2 Bar. 77:4:

> And because your brothers have transgressed the commandments of the Lord, he brought retribution over you as well as over them; and he did not spare the one, but made the other go into exile, as well, and he did not leave a single one behind.[1]

However, it does not seem that the author of As. Mos. finds this point of view correct, as Carlson suggested[2]. Whereas 2 Bar. 77:4 shows that this concept existed, it is clear that the author of As. Mos. rejects it. This appears from the following points:

(1) In 2:6-9 the apostasy of the two tribes is described without restrictions[3].

(2) The ten tribes defend themselves successfully: they confront the two tribes with the fact that the distress has come over Israel as a whole—that therefore Israel as a whole has been punished[4]. The two tribes react to this by joining in with the ten in their plea for mercy (*omnes tribus plorabunt &c.* 3:8 f.). It is emphatically stated that the scriptural quotation which explicates the acknowledgment of the righteousness of God's punishment is said *tribus ad tribum*, that is "each tribe to the other"[5].

(3) Only if all tribes, including the two, are guilty, can 3:5a, *justus et sanctus Dominus*, make sense. The alleged innocence of the two would make such praise dubious, if not cynical.

Thus it is clear that 3:6-7 is a dramatic periphrasis of the confession of sin, by which the author counters the idea that one may be punished for the sins of someone else. The confession of sin is the hallmark of the confessional prayers; the acknowledgment of God's righteousness[6] is never absent, since it is the pious reversal of the confession. Also, the immediate juxtaposition of God's righteousness and the people's sin is common to confessional prayers; see Tob. 3:2-3; Pr. Azar. 28; 4 Ezra 8:31-36; Ps. Sol. 9:2; CD XX 28-30; cf. also Ps. Sol. 10:5.

---

[1] Cf. T. Dan 5:7-8, where Dan predicts that his offspring will be sinful and therefore be punished. Their sin is identified as association and joining together with the Levites. Because of their connection with the Levites, they will be carried off into capitivity with them (διὰ τοῦτο ἀπαχθήσεσθε σὺν αὐτοῖς ἐν αἰχμαλωσίᾳ 5:8).

[2] "Vengeance and Angelic Mediation", p. 92.

[3] There can therefore be no question of the tribes' "comparative innocence", as suggested by Licht, "Taxo", p. 98.

[4] So Hölscher, "Die Entstehungszeit", p. 122, cf. Reese, *Die Geschichte Israels*, p. 96: "In diesem Abschnitt sollen Juda und Israel gemeinsam unter die große Katastrophe gestellt werden, vor der es irgendeine Ausnahmestellung ... nicht geben kann".

[5] Other confessional prayers that insist on the universality of Israel's sins are: Dan. 9:7-8, 11; Neh. 9:32; Bar. 2:1, 26.

[6] The invocation of God as righteous etc. is, of course, not restricted to the confessional prayers. (For the phrase *justus et sanctus Dominus*, see the identical phrase in Deut. 32:4 LXX δίκαιος καὶ ὅσιος κύριος.) However, this "vindication formula ... tends to recur in those passages in which the sins of Israel are brought to light and confessed to the accompaniment of much weeping and prostration" (Staples, "Rev. xvi 4-6", p. 285).

3:7

The clause *quid faciemus vobis, fratres* is difficult to understand. In Job 7:20, the accused protagonist in his anger speaks to God: εἰ ἐγὼ ἥμαρτον, τί δύναμαί σοι πρᾶξαι, ὁ ἐπιστάμενος τὸν νοῦν τῶν ἀνθρώπων, or, in the Vulgate (which syntactically sides with MT): *Peccavi; quid faciam tibi, o custos hominum?*, and can be paraphrased as: "All right, suppose I have sinned; what do you want me to do about it, you watcher of men?". If As. Mos. 3:7 is to be interpreted accordingly, the ten tribes are said to accept the two tribes' claim that the two are exiled because of the ten tribes' guilt[1]. If this were the case, however, the connection with the next clause (in which reference is made to the relation between guilt and punishment) would be quite unclear. Perhaps it is possible to explain *facere* here, as in 5:3, as "to say"[2]. Then the clause is reminiscent of Ezra 9:10, τί εἴπωμεν, ὁ θεὸς ἡμῶν, μετὰ τοῦτο; and expresses a mood of shame, self-humiliation and desolation. The rites of repentance derive from those of mourning[3], and they may also include a period of dumbness; see Job 2:11-3:1; 40:4 (42:6); Lam. 2:10. For examples taken from confessional prayers, see Pr. Azar. 33; Jos. As. 12:6. From the perspective of this ritual, and in view of the quasi-historical presentation in As. Mos. 3:4-4:4 observed earlier, it seems less relevant that the clause in Ezra 9:10 is directed to God.

If, however, we do not understand *facere* in 3:7 as "to say", the future tense of *faciemus* becomes problematic[4]; a perfect tense[5] would then be more obvious, directly denying the two tribes' allegation: "What have we done to you?"[6]. This interpretation, however, would require a very dubious text-critical intervention.

The ten tribes defend themselves by pointing to the connection between act and consequence (here: guilt and punishment), which is valid for all tribes. Since all tribes find themselves in exile, all tribes, we are to understand, must be guilty. The word *tlibsis* is used, a transliteration of the Greek θλίψις. This is also the word used in Deut. 4:30(29) to describe the situation which causes the Israelites to return to the Lord: καὶ ζητήσετε ἐκεῖ τὸν θεὸν ὑμῶν καὶ εὑρήσετε, ὅταν ἐκζητήσετε αὐτὸν ἐξ ὅλης τῆς καρδίας σου καὶ ἐξ ὅλης τῆς ψυχῆς σου ἐν τῇ θλίψει σου. Cf. for this specific use of θλίψις Deut. 28:53, 55, 57; see also Deut. 31:17, 21[7].

---

[1] In Petronius 58, the expression *quid faciat* serves as an (ironical) exculpation formula, "he cannot help it". Heräus, in Friedländer, *Petronii Cena Trimalchionis*, p. 299, translates *quid faciat, crucis offla?* as "Was kann man auch von einem Galgenstrick anders erwarten?".

[2] See grammatical note nr. 52.

[3] Lipiński, *La liturgie pénitentielle*, p. 28.

[4] Priest, "Testament of Moses", p. 928, understands the future tense to express the will of the ten tribes to restore the solidarity of all tribes, asking: "What is there that we can do together with you?", namely, in order to restore the tribes' well-being. This proposal seems to strain *vobis*, which stands without a preposition that would indicate such a sociative aspect more precisely. Furthermore, in this way the ten tribes would in fact comply with the accusation raised against them.

[5] *Fecimus*, suggested by Hilgenfeld, "Die Psalmen Salomo's", p. 282.

[6] Cf. Reese, *Die Geschichte Israels*, p. 96, referring to Boecker, *Redeformen*, pp. 31-34: "Eine 'Beschwichtigungsformel'".

[7] Schlier, "θλίβω κτλ.", p. 142. The word is similarly used in Neh. 9:27, 38; Esth. 4:17 r; Ps. 106(105):44 (θλίβεσθαι); Isa. 63:9.

3:8-9

Apparently convinced by the answer of the ten tribes to their allegations, the two tribes cry together with the ten unto heaven[1]. They appeal to the covenant and to God's oath made to the fathers, who are mentioned by name from the outset. The names of the three patriarchs are also mentioned in Bar. 2:34; Pr. Azar. 34-36; cf. Pr. Man. 8. The appeal to the covenant occurs very often in Jewish prayers[2]. In the confessional prayers (though only in the national ones), it is very prominent, and is almost never omitted, see Dan. 9:4 = Neh. 1:5 = Neh. 9:32; Neh. 9:8, 15, 23; Bar. 2:34-35; Pr. Azar. 34; Ps. Sol. 9:10. The appeal to God to remember[3] his oath is the plea proper. As a structural element of the confessional prayer, the content of God's oath is referred to with great emphasis and solemnity in 3:9b. This quotation is not literal, but *ad sensum*: God's promise to the patriarchs that their posterity would live in the land forever is repeatedly recorded throughout the Pentateuch. More specifically, Reese[4] pointed to Exod. 32:13, where a combination of elements similar to those in As. Mos. 3:9 is found: the mention of the names of the patriarchs, God's oath "by himself" and the promise of the eternal possession of the land[5]. In confessional prayers a comparable appeal to a similar oath is found in Pr. Azar. 36; cf. Bar. 2:35.

b. *3:10-14*

In 3:10-14 Moses forecasts that the tribes will remember that he predicted the things that have happened to them. The reference is to such passages as Lev. 26 and Deut. 4; 28-30, in which the Deuteronomistic pattern of history is exemplarily set out[6]. As. Mos. 3:10-13 prophesies that the way out of distress prescribed in those passages will indeed be followed: in the land of their exile, Israel will return to God. In Deut. 4:29-31 it is said:

---

[1] "To cry" of course again is a mourning rite, a fact which does not need substantiation here. There is no need to identify "heaven" with "God", as Schmidt and Merx, "Die Assumptio Mosis", p. 141, and Charles, *The Assumption*, p. 11, suggested. The prayer is simply given a spatial direction: it must go up, to heaven, in order to reach God (Jos. As. 12:1). Cf. Raguel's daughter Sara, who in Tob. (LXX) 3:11 prays with her arms stretched out to the window.

[2] See Johnson, *Prayer*, p. 46: "The inducement which the Jews employed most regularly in their prayers was a reminder of God's past promises. Again and again the petitions of the Apocrypha and Pseudepigrapha call on God to remember the covenant he made with the ancient patriarchs".

[3] See the commentary on 3:10, and cf. 4:5.

[4] *Die Geschichte Israels*, p. 97.

[5] Exod. 32:13: μνησθεὶς Ἀβραὰμ καὶ Ἰσαὰκ καὶ Ἰακὼβ τῶν σῶν οἰκετῶν, οἷς ὤμοσας κατὰ σεαυτοῦ καὶ ἐλάλησας πρὸς αὐτοὺς λέγων Πολυπληθυνῶ τὸ σπέρμα ὑμῶν ὡσεὶ τὰ ἄστρα τοῦ οὐρανοῦ τῷ πλήθει, καὶ πᾶσαν τὴν γῆν ταύτην, ἣν εἶπας δοῦναι τῷ σπέρματι αὐτῶν, καὶ καθέξουσιν αὐτὴν εἰς τὸν αἰῶνα. For *jurare per te/se*, cf. also Gen. 22:14; Jub. 18:15; LAB 47:3; Heb. 6:13.

[6] Reese, *Die Geschichte Israels*, p. 97. Esp. in Deut. 4, all elements of the allusion in As. Mos. 3:12-13 occur: Moses is described as a mediator of God's commandments (Deut. 4:5, 14); he warns Israel not to transgress these commandments; he calls heaven and earth as his witnesses that otherwise, they will go into exile (Deut. 4:23-27).

But if you will seek the Lord from there, you will find him, if you seek him with all your heart and with all your soul. When you will be in tribulation and all these things will have come over you in the future, and when you will return to the Lord your God and listen to his voice—for the Lord your God is a merciful God—, then he will not forsake you, and not destroy you; and he will not forget the covenant which he swore to your fathers.

A similar picture is found in Lev. 26:40-42, with specific stress on the necessity of confessing sins and self-humiliation.

To regain God's favour, the sinful Israelites must remember that what they have done has been contrary to God's will[1]. The miserable situation in which they find themselves is proof of God's power and active involvement. That same power and concern warrants that repentance will not stay unanswered; again, history proves that this is so (see As. Mos. 4:5-6).

10 Then, on that day, they will remember me, each tribe saying to the other, and each man to his neighbour: 11 'Is it not this, the things which Moses formerly testified to us in his prophecies? Moses, who suffered many things in Egypt, and in the Red Sea, and in the desert, during forty years. 12 And having testified, he also called on heaven and earth to be witnesses, lest we should transgress his commandments, which he had mediated to us. 13 But since then, these things have come over us, in accordance with his words and his solemn confirmation, which he testified to us in those days, and which have come true up to our expulsion into the land of the East.' 14 And they will be slaves there for seventy-seven years.

3:10

Following the discussion in 3:4-9, it is said that the tribes will realize their own guilt, saying to one another that Moses had warned them not to transgress God's commandments. They now acknowledge that they are being punished, in a way which agrees perfectly with Moses' predictions. The recognition of that fact leads to the communal confession in 3:11-13, introduced by the words: "Then they will remember me". *Tunc ... die illo* is a tautological indication of time; see also *novissime post haec* 8:5b and cf. *tunc illo die* 9:1 l. em. In the confessional prayer, "to remember the Lord" is tantamount to confessing one's sinfulness[2].

---

[1] In order to corroborate his plea, the author of Neh. 1:8-9 makes Nehemia explicitly quote from Deut. 30, where a nearly automatic mechanism Repentance-Return is described (similarly Bar. 2:29-35). It must be noted that, although repentance is a condition that has to be met with before God will have mercy, it does not, so to speak, force God to end the punishment. Repentance is a humble recognition of one's sinfulness, a moral reversion on account of which God autonomously changes his wrath into grace (see Sjöberg, *Gott und die Sünder*, pp. 215-220).
[2] "To remember" equals the acknowledgment of having previously forgotten (*sc.* the wondrous deeds of God towards his people); see Giraudo, *La struttura letteraria*, pp. 106-108.

(cont.)

The communal character is strongly emphasized. The expression *homo de proximo suo* in 3:10 ("one to another"[1]) in itself indicates the public character of the confession of sin[2], as well as the universality of these sins[3]. But it is provided with an additional, otherwise unknown, parallel expression, *tribus ad tribum*, which deliberately refers to the preceding discussion and reflects its outcome: "all tribes will say to one another, each man will speak to his neighbor &c."

3:11-13

As said above, the tribes will recognize their misery to be the fulfilment of the threats that accompanied the covenant, and which were announced by Moses in his prophecies (3:11)[4]. The recognition of the trustworthiness of God's words (cf. the commentary to 1:16) features in most confessional prayers in the form of a solemn quotation of a scriptural passage that has come true; so in Dan. 9:13; Ezra 9:11-12; Bar. 2:2-5, 24-25, 29-35[5]. In As. Mos. 3:11-13 there is no formal quotation, but there are clear references to what Moses predicted. The closest formal parallel to As. Mos. 3:11-13 is Bar. 2:7: ἃ ἐλάλησεν κύριος ἐφ' ἡμᾶς, πάντα τὰ κακὰ ταῦτα ἦλθεν ἐφ' ἡμᾶς[6].

In a relative clause, Moses is pictured as having suffered much in Egypt, the Red Sea and during the forty years in the desert[7]. This additional comment may be a trace of the tradition of the violent fate of the prophets. In the confessional prayers, it is found in Neh. 9:26; in other examples of the form we encounter the related concept of disobedience to the prophets[8]. In Josephus (*Ant. Jud.* IV 194-195), it is described how Israel mourned after Moses announced his impending death: they displayed deep regret, remembering the risks their general had run (κινδυνεύσειε), and his dedication

---

The counterpart of the people's remembrance is God's remembrance; see As. Mos. 3:9 and 4:5.

[1] On this construction, see grammatical notes nrs. 69, 167, 185, 192.

[2] Many national confessions have a distinct public (liturgical) character. Ezra prays in the presence of a large crowd in the temple (Ezra 9:4-5); Levites pray before the Israelites in Neh. 9:1-5; see also Bar. 1:10-14; LAB 30:4. In 1QS I 24-25, confessions are probably done individually, yet in public and with others.

[3] In CD XX 17-18 (in the immediate vicinity of the confessional prayer XX 27-30), it is prescribed that members of the community should uncover each other's (אִישׁ אֶל רֵעֵהוּ) sins in order to support each other (אִישׁ אֶת אָחִיו) in righteousness. This of course expresses the inner solidarity of the community.

[4] The word used is *testari*, that is, μαρτυρεῖν, "to give witness", or "to notify"; in this context it may be understood as "to prophesy" or "to predict", since Moses' announcements are concerned with Israel's future.

[5] Not all quotations listed here contain "real" quotations; sometimes they are only allusions or quotations *ad sensum*; nonetheless, these instances all are formally presented as quotations ("as has been said" and the like).

[6] Almost identical to this clause is Dan. 9:13 κατὰ τὰ γεγραμμένα ἐν διαθήκῃ Μωσῆ πάντα τὰ κακὰ ἐπῆλθεν ἡμῖν. Cf. finally 2 Bar. 84:2-5 and the comments made by Laperrousaz, *Le Testament*, pp. 76-79.

[7] A similar statement, without the element of suffering, however, is made in Acts 7:36. There is no reason to suppose a literary relationship between these two texts (against Charles, *The Assumption*, pp. lxiii-lxiv, and also Laperrousaz, *Le Testament*, pp. 67-70).

[8] See Steck, *Israel*, pp. 110-137: "Die Überlieferung (sc. des deuteronomistischen Geschichtsbildes) in Sündenbekenntnissen und Bußgebeten des Volkes".

to their salvation[1]; they also repented that they had angrily spoken against him in the desert (ὧν τε ἐπὶ τῆς ἐρήμου μετ᾽ ὀργῆς ὁμιλήσειαν αὐτῷ μετανοοῦντες ἤλγουν). The mention of Moses' hardships adds to his authority as a prophet.

After this interruption, 3:12 resumes 3:11a[2]. Moses foretells that the exile will be recognized as the θλίψις he announced in Deuteronomy: *Nonne hoc est quod testabatur nobis tum Moyses in profetis?*[3] In 3:12 a solemn allusion to the scriptures points to the connection between act and consequence. Moses, the mediator of God's (*illius*[4]) commandments (see 1:14), had invoked heaven and earth as witnesses, that the people should not transgress the commandments, see for instance Deut. 4:23-27[5].

In 3:13, very strong emphasis is given to the exact correspondence between prophecy and fulfilment: "Since then (*sc.* when Moses gave his warning), these things have come over us in accordance with his (*sc.* God's[6]) words and his confirmation, such as he (*sc.* Moses) testified them to us in those times, and they have come true up to our expulsion to the land of the East". In this way, the absolute trustworthiness of God's word is stressed. For *de isto* meaning "since then", see grammatical note nr. 188.

3:14

In confessional prayers, the confession of sin is normally followed by a plea for mercy. In 3:14, these two elements are separated from each other by the mention that the tribes will be slaves for a period of 77 years, obviously the exile (3:14). *Servire* (here: "to be slaves", δουλεύειν) is an ordinary designation of Israel's condition during the exile, see Ezra 9:9; Neh. 9:36; cf. Jer. 25:11; 2 Macc. 1:27; T. Judah 23:5; T. Iss. 6:2; T. Napht. 4:2.

Scholarly opinion is divided on the question why the exile is said to have lasted 77 years, instead of the traditional 70 years (see Jer. 25:11-12). The earlier commentators have been especially ingenious in their attempts to explain the higher number of years[7]. The simplest explanation is probably that 77 is an approximation of 70 and

---

[1] Cf. also LAB 19:5, where Moses speaks: *vos autem scitote laborem quem laboravi vobiscum, ex quo ascendistis de terra Egipti.*

[2] It does so by repeating the verb *testari*; for the inversion of *et* (*testatus et,* that is: "And having testified"), see grammatical note nr. 139.

[3] On *profetis = profetiis,* see grammatical note nr. 11.

[4] *Illius* refers to God, see grammatical note nr. 60.

[5] For the invoking of heaven and earth as witnesses, see e.g. Isa. 1:2; Jer. 2:12; Ps. 50(49):4; 2 Bar. 19:1; LAB 19:4. Since heaven and earth were witnesses when the covenant was made (according to e.g. Deut. 30:19; 31:28; 32:1), they are often invoked in the texts containing prophetical accusations against the people's breaching of the covenant; see Harvey, *Le plaidoyer prophétique,* p. 16: "Ce sont les témoins de la première alliance qui sont appelés, dans le *rîb* complet, à servir de témoins ou de juges".

[6] *Ipsius* refers to God (see grammatical note nr. 60).

[7] The most remarkable proposal was made by Schmidt and Merx, "Die Assumptio Mosis", pp. 141-142, who assume a play with letters and figures (LXXVII = עז): "Es heisst einmal wörtlich das, was Lat. bietet ... dann aber unter Anwendung der Abkürzung עז = עבדת הרז Götzendienst auch: Diejenigen, welche Götzendienerei Aehnliches treiben, Jahre hindurch. Um עז zu gewinnen, setzte der Verfasser den Juden sieben Jahre Exil zu." Rönsch, "Xeniola theologica ... Chronologisches und Kritisches", p. 551, took the 77 years to be 77 weeks of years. The *servitus* of the exile would thereby have been extended up to the author's

(cont.)

suggests a higher degree of completeness. In the context, the factor of completeness makes sense: it reinforces the idea that the appeal to God's mercy can be supposed to lead to a favourable result: the more complete Israel's suffering, the more justified its expectation of rescue.

The years of the exile are mentioned here because the fulfilment of the Lord's prediction of punishment of Israel is a circumstance which enhances the intercessor's chances of success. On several occasions, confessional prayers refer to the execution of the punishment. In Dan. 9, too, the realization of Israel's punishment is a reason for Daniel to confess his and his people's sins and to pray for mercy. Daniel's prayer however was not (immediately) successful; for the angel's answer to Daniel, see commentary on 4:6-9.

The third person plural *servient* comes somewhat unexpectedly, but agrees with the third person plural forms occurring from 3:4 *invocabunt* to 3:10 *reminiscentur*. Moses is speaking.

c. 4:1-4

In this passage, an intercessor is introduced, who prays on behalf of the people. His prayer (4:2-4) continues the theme of the twelve tribes' confession, and provides their prayer with an appropriately concluding plea for forgiveness. The intercessor's prayer consists of a doxology (4:2a), a short anamnetical section, contrasting the covenant and the exile (4:2b-3), and a plea for forgiveness (4:4).

1 Then someone will enter who is above them, and he will spread his arms and bend his knees, and pray for them, saying: 2 a 'Lord, King of All in the throne on high, who rulest the world, who wanted this people to be your elect people. b Then you wanted to be called their God, according to the covenant which you made with their fathers. 3 But (now) they have gone as captives into a foreign land, with their wives and children, and to the gate of the gentiles, where there is great sadness. 4 Behold, and have mercy on them, heavenly Lord!'

4:1
At the end of the exile, an intercessor "will enter" and pray for the tribes[1]. He is characterized as an intercessor by the technical term *orare pro*, which is the Vulgate equivalent of (1) ἐξιλάσκεσθαι περί or ἐπί (approximately 12 times in Leviticus and Numbers, cf. T. Levi 3:5 and Ps. Sol. 3:8); (2) (προσ)εύχεσθαι περί or ὑπέρ (approximately 18 times in the other books of the Old Testament, about 11 times in the

---

time: "Das Joch der Knechtschaft wird von da an immerfort und endlos auf uns lasten, eine lange, lange Reihe von Jahrwochen hindurch, zu deren Bezeichnung die gewaltige Zahl 77 kaum ausreicht."

[1] Spreading one's arms and kneeling (4:1b) are common prayer gestures. The very same words are used in Ezra 9:5; 3 Macc. 2:1.

New Testament); (3) on a few occasions of similar words (κατεύχεσθαι, ζητεῖν περί etc.).

It is not clear precisely where he "enters". Does he enter into a (liturgical) room[1], or into the field where the exiles are (cf. 3:4), or εἰς αὐτούς (cf. εἰς ὑμᾶς Acts 20:29), or εἰς τὸν κόσμον (Heb. 10:5; 1 Clem. 38:3)? Equally vague is his characterization as "someone who is above them". Usually, and probably rightly, this is taken as a figure of speech, indicating the intercessor's social and moral eminence. His righteousness provides him with authority over the people, and for that reason his prayer on their behalf is likely to be especially effective (cf. Judith 8:31; 4 Ezra 7:111-112). In confessional prayers made by like Daniel, Azariah, Ezra and Nehemia, the righteousness of the intercessors is, of course, beyond dispute.

There has been some scholarly disagreement on the exact identification of the intercessor in As. Mos.[2]. Both Hilgenfeld, at first[3], and Volkmar[4] were content merely to refer to the similarity of As. Mos. 4:1-4 to Dan. 9:4-19 and 4 Ezra 8:20-36. Charles, however, resolutely identified the intercessor as Daniel[5], and he was followed by many others. Clemen expressed serious reservations about this identification[6]. He conceded that the words used in As. Mos. 4:1-4 are similar to those used in Dan. 9:4-19, but noted that the mere similarity of the words used does not justify the identification of *unus qui supra eos est* with Daniel[7]. The traditional form of the confessional prayer is already in use in Dan. 9. From that perspective, the similarity between Daniel and the intercessor in As. Mos. 4:1 is only superficial. In As. Mos., the one who prays in 4:1-4 asks for Israel's restoration, which immediately follows, in accordance with God's promise (4:5-6). In Dan. 9, the confessional prayer has a different function. Moreover, it does not seem that Jewish tradition has ever ascribed to Daniel a crucial role in the events of the exile.

Clemen himself suggested that the intercessor of As. Mos. could be Ezra, who, as a leader of Israel, can more appropriately be called *unus qui supra eos est*; see esp. the characterization of Ezra in Neh. 8:5 αὐτὸς ἦν ἐπάνω τοῦ λαοῦ. Also, Ezra is famous

---

[1] Cf. Neh. 9:3, 4, where Levitical intercessors take up their special positions in the Temple; see also Bar. 1:14. Perhaps one may even think of a heavenly room, God's throne hall, if the "one who is above them" can be an intercessory angel (so Kuhn, "Zur Assumptio Mosis", p. 126; Goldstein, "The Testament of Moses", p. 51; Camponovo, *Königtum*, p. 170).

[2] Reese, *Die Geschichte Israels*, p. 97, who proposed to identify the intercessor with Nehemiah, has rightly stressed that the primary intention of the author of As. Mos. was to indicate the specific function of the intercessor, rather than a certain individual.

[3] *Novum Testamentum* (1866), p. 112. In "Die Psalmen Salomo's" (1868), p. 301, Hilgenfeld changed his view, convinced that only Daniel could have been meant. In his 1884 edition of *Novum Testamentum*, Hilgenfeld reverted to the mere comparison with both texts (p. 132).

[4] *Mose Prophetie*, p. 27.

[5] *The Assumption of Moses*, p. 14.

[6] "Die Himmelfahrt Mosis", p. 322.

[7] This criticism was also raised by Reese, *Die Geschichte Israels*, p. 96, and Goldstein, "The Testament of Moses", p. 51. Goldstein finds As. Mos. 4:1-4 closest to passages from Isaiah; but *unus qui supra eos est* must refer, according to Goldstein, to an angel. Goldstein translates the phrase as "one who is in charge (or, concerned with) them" (אשר על), and compares it with Job 33:23. That the expression used there refers to an angel does not prove, however, that the intercessor is an angel in As. Mos., as well.

as an intercessor for Israel; see Ezra 9; 4 Ezra 8:20-36. There are considerable differences between Ezra in these passages and the intercessor in As. Mos. In Ezra 9, Israel has already returned to the land[1], and God's answer to Ezra in 4 Ezra 8 is an interpretation of the prayer, comparable to Dan. 9. Nevertheless, 4 Ezra appears to use an existing image of the scribe which seems to have been much more akin to the intercessor in As. Mos. 4:1 than to Daniel: Ezra is Israel's leader in exile; on his activity the people's fate is said to depend (4 Ezra 5:16-18; 12:40-45). In view of the priestly interests of As. Mos., one is tempted to note that Ezra was a Levite and priest (Ezra 7:1-5, 11; 10:10, 16), and that 4 Ezra 14 pictures him explicitly[2] as a new Moses. Both Ezra's priestly office and his Mosaic character qualify him as an intercessor[3].

4:2

In the doxology with which the intercessor begins his prayer, God's omnipotence is praised: he is called King of all, exalted in his throne[4]. This praise changes smoothly into the remembrance of Israel's election: with parallel relative constructions it is said that God rules the world and that he has wished Israel to be his chosen people. In this way, the praise to God is at the same time the foundation of the plea for mercy[5]. Whereas it is acknowledged, in the confession As. Mos. 3:4-13, that the distress has deservedly come over Israel, the intercessor appeals nonetheless to God's original intention with which he had once granted Israel an exceptional[6] status. Israel's misery is juxtaposed to the intimate bond of love and compassion between God and the patri-

---

[1] This is not to deny that Ezra plays an important role in Israel's return to the land according to the book of Ezra itself (chapters 7 and 8).

[2] Knowles, "Moses, the Law, and the Unity of 4 Ezra", has shown that 4 Ezra as a whole is structured according to the concept of Ezra as *Moyses redivivus*.

[3] According to a possible interpretation of As. Mos. 12:6, Moses is thought to intercede on behalf of Israel after his death. In that case, Moses himself would most likely be the intercessor of As. Mos. 4:1. *Unus qui supra eos est* can then be literally understood as "someone who is above them, namely in heaven". See further, however, the commentary on 12:6.

[4] Cf. Josephus, *Ant. Jud.* XIV 24: ὦ θεὲ βασιλεῦ τῶν ὅλων; Esth. 4:17 z ὁ θεὸς ὁ ἰσχύων ἐπὶ πάντας; 3 Macc. 2:3 τῶν ὅλων ἐπικρατῶν; Philo, *De vita Mosis* II 88 ἡγεμὼν τοῦ πάντος; cf. also Esth. 4:17 b ἐν ἐξουσίᾳ σου τὸ πᾶν ἐστιν; Jub. 31:13 *Deus cunctorum*; *alta sedes* indicates God's throne in heaven, cf. θρόνος ὑψηλός 1 En. 14:18; θρόνος ἐν οὐρανοῖς T. Job 41:4; Heb. 8:1 (Isa. 66:1 ὁ οὐρανός μοι θρόνος); cf. Rev. 4:2. "King" (*rex*, βασιλεύς) and "who rulest the world" (*qui dominaris saeculo*) are ordinary titles of God (cf. Κύριε κύριε βασιλεῦ πάντων κρατῶν Esth. 4:17 b). For the latter, see more specifically 3 Macc 2:2 Κύριε κύριε βασιλεῦ τῶν οὐρανῶν καὶ δέσποτα πάσης κτίσεως, ἅγιε ἐν ἁγίοις, μόναρχε, παντοκράτωρ; Sib. Or. III 19 κόσμον κρατέων.

[5] Cf. the doxologies in the confessional prayers, in which the plea is founded on the praise of God as "keeping the covenant and mercy" (Dan. 9:4; Neh. 1:5; 9:32), anticipating the plea for merciful restoration of the covenant; similarly, in Bar. 2:11, the prayer anticipates his plea for the termination of the exile by praising God as the one who led Israel out of Egypt.

[6] *Plebs excepta* 4:2; cf. Deut. 14:2 σὲ ἐξελέξατο κύριος ὁ θεός σου γενέσθαι σε αὐτῷ λαὸν περιούσιον (Vulgate: *peculiarem*) ἀπὸ πάντων τῶν ἐθνῶν τῶν ἐπὶ προσώπου τῆς γῆς (cf. Ps. 135[134]:4); 1 Ki. 8:53 σὺ διέστειλας (Vulgate: *separasti*) αὐτοὺς σαυτῷ εἰς κληρονομίαν ἐκ πάντων τῶν λαῶν τῆς γῆς.

archs, on which bond the covenant was based[1]. The election is similarly contrasted to the present misery in Esth. 4:17 m-o[2].

The combination of all these motifs (God's love for his elected people, the connection between God's and Israel's names, the reference to the enmity of the gentiles [cf. Ps. Sol. 9:1], and the appeal to God's compassion) is neatly paralleled in Ps. Sol. 9:8-9:

Καὶ νῦν σὺ ὁ θεός, καὶ ἡμεῖς λαός, ὃν ἠγάπησας· ἰδὲ καὶ οἰκτίρησον, ὁ θεὸς Ἰσραήλ, ὅτι σοί ἐσμεν, καὶ μὴ ἀποστήσῃς ἔλεός σου ἀφ' ἡμῶν, ἵνα μὴ ἐπιθῶνται ἡμῖν.
ὅτι σὺ ᾑρετίσω τὸ σπέρμα Ἀβραὰμ παρὰ πάντα τὰ ἔθνη καὶ ἔθου τὸ ὄνομά σου ἐφ' ἡμᾶς, κύριε, καὶ οὐκ ἀπώσει εἰς τὸν αἰῶνα.

4:3

The distress of the people is defined as the exile[3], which frequently provides the historical background of many confessional prayers. Apart from inciting God's compassion, the mention of the exile serves to point out that Israel, being in exile, has undergone its punishment, and that it may now hope for the remission of its sins, based on its repentance[4]. At the end of the confessional prayer, the realization of the punishment is often cited. In the epicletical section, Israel's miserable situation is again described in words quoting or recalling God's prophecies; see for instance Neh. 9:36-37, clearly alluding to Deut. 28:33; cf. Pr. Azar. 36-38, alluding to Deut. 4:27; 28:62 and Hos. 3:4 (cf. Bar. 2:13). Likewise, the intercessor in As. Mos. 4:3 alludes to several prophecies that foretold Israel's expulsion among the gentiles and its sadness while in exile, e.g. Lev. 26:33, 36, 39; Deut. 28:64-65. I do not know of an instance of *maestitia* (λύπη) used elsewhere to describe the exile[5], but related expressions are often used. One example may suffice: T. Zeb. 9:6 καὶ αἰχμαλωτεύσουσιν ὑμᾶς οἱ ἐχθροὶ ὑμῶν, καὶ κακωθήσεσθε ἐν τοῖς ἔθνεσιν ἐν πάσαις ἀσθενείαις καὶ θλίψεσι καὶ ὀδύναις ψυχῆς.

Allofili, found in As. Mos. 4:3, is a transliteration of the Greek word ἀλλόφυλοι. In the Septuagint, the word is used to indicate Israel's enemies, in particular the Philistines[6]. By using this strong word, the prayer highlights the suffering of the exile. It remains rather enigmatic why it is said that the people had to go to the gate of the gentiles. One is inclined to understand that the pagan gates had something particularly horrifying about them, but I have been unable to find in related literature some

---

[1] Cf. the instances in which the election is explicitly based on God's love: Deut. 4:37; 10:15; Mal. 1:2; Ps. Sol. 9:8.

[2] Somewhat differently in LAB 30:4, where the same contrast is used by Israel in its recognition of the divine punishment.

[3] For the explicit inclusion of wives and children among those who are prisoners (*captivi*), see 1 Macc. 1:32; 5:13, 23; 8:10; 2 Macc. 5:13; 3 Macc. 3:25; T. Judah 23:3; cf. Dan. 6:24

[4] See, for instance, T. Napht. 4:3.

[5] Compare, however, Antiochus' farewell in 1 Macc. 6:13 καὶ ἰδοὺ ἀπόλλυμαι λύπῃ μεγάλῃ ἐν γῇ ἀλλοτρίᾳ, Vulgate: *et ecce pereo tristitia magna in terra aliena*. In Deut. 28:65, the Vulgate uses the phrase *anima maerore consumpta* to reflect נפש/ דאבון τηκομένη ψυχή.

[6] In classical Greek, the word means simply "foreigner", although the Greeks' xenophobia probably gave the word a pejorative ring to them, as well.

clarification. Perhaps one should not lay too much emphasis on *ostium*, and simply understand the gate as the place where the Israelites used to pass their day, the only terrible thing being that it is not their own gate. In that case, 4:3 may be read as a *parallelismus membrorum*:

| in | terram | alienam |
| circa[1] | ostium | allofilorum. |

4:4

The intercessor concludes his prayer to the "heavenly Lord"[2] with a plea for mercy. *Respice et miserere* is an ordinary prayer formula, occurring literally in Jerome's versions *juxta LXX* and *juxta Hebraeos* of Ps. 25(24):16 and 86(85):16 (also Ps. 119[118]:132 *juxta Hebraeos* only). In various confessional prayers, however, similar formulas are passionately accumulated; most famous is Dan. 9:18-19, but see also Neh. 1:11; Bar. 2:14-17; 3:2; Jos. As. 13:1-9.

d. *4:5-6*

After the punishment is undergone, and the people have repented, God will not let the intercessor's prayer stay unanswered, but he will, as he had promised through Moses, let the people be restored in their land.

5 a Then God will remember them, on account of the covenant which he had made with their fathers, b and he will manifest his mercy in these days, too. 6 And he will give it into the heart of the king to have mercy on them, and to let them return to their land and region.

4:5a

In 3:9, the tribes are portrayed as asking the Lord to "remember the covenant which he had made with the fathers, and the oath he swore unto them that their posterity would never be absent from the land". In 4:5a it is said that the Lord will indeed "remember them on account of the covenant which he had made with their fathers"; this will prove God's faithfulness to his words: both to his oath and to his promise to redeem the penitent sinners, e.g. Lev. 26:42 καὶ μνησθήσομαι τῆς διαθήκης Ἰακὼβ καὶ τῆς διαθήκης Ἰσαὰκ καὶ τῆς διαθήκης Ἀβραὰμ μνησθήσομαι καὶ τῆς γῆς μνησθήσομαι; cf. Lev. 26:45; Deut. 4:29-30; 30:3. It must be stressed that the people's restoration, which results from God's remembering them, is not presented as some kind of reward for their repentance; it is based solely on the covenant with the fathers. By their penitence the tribes show that they themselves have no merits on account of which they may expect God to intervene. Although their self-humiliation is a condition to be fulfilled, it is in no way the cause or reason for God to remember them; the reason is to be found in God's autonomous promise to restore the covenant when the people repent.

---

[1] On the variation of *in* and *circa*, see grammatical note nr. 167.
[2] *Dominus caelestis*, cf. *Deus caelestis* As. Mos. 2:4.

4:5b

Remembering the covenant stands parallerl to the manifestation of God's mercy. See for instance Deut. 4:31, where it is said that God will "not forget the covenant with your fathers", because he is a "merciful God" (θεὸς οἰκτίρμων κύριος ὁ θεός σου); cf. Deut. 30:3. For the expression "to reveal mercy", see Isa. 56:1.

Unless the word *et* is to be deleted, the phrase *et temporibus illis* must be connected to the preceding clause; if it were to be connected to the following clause (*et mittit in animam regis* 4:6), there would be a senseless repeat of *et* ("And in those days, and he will etc."). Connected to the preceding clause, *et* is to be understood as *etiam* (see grammatical note nr. 140), and the phrase indicates the willingness of God to be repeatedly merciful: "He will be merciful on this occasion, too", i.e., "as he has been on several other occasions"[1]. This is reminiscent of passages such as Deut. 9:19 and 10:10, where Moses relates how God answered his prayer "again", καὶ ἐν τῷ καιρῷ ἐκείνῳ, but even more of the anamnetical section in Neh. 9, in which the inveterate sinfulness of the people is mentioned, but also God's unremitting willingness to forgive[2]. It must be admitted that in As. Mos. there is no earlier manifestation of God's mercy. Since, however, the author of As. Mos. intended 4:5-6 to prove to his readers God's faithfulness to his promise to redeem the penitent sinners (apparently in order to exhort them to repent), he may by the use of this "also" evoke the well-known instances of God's mercy prior to the moment when Moses is said to deliver this prophecy. At the same time, God's willingness to forgive the author's intended readers is implied.

4:6

In Moses' prophecy, God will end the exile through "the king"; the author of As. Mos. of course refers to the Persian king Cyrus. Again, God is the one who acts: he "gives it in the heart" of the king to set them free; that is, God "made the king want them to be free". The initiative is also ascribed to God in Solomon's prayer in 1 Ki. 8:50 καὶ δώσεις αὐτοὺς εἰς οἰκτιρμοὺς ἐνώπιον αἰχμαλωτευόντων αὐτούς, καὶ οἰκτιρήσουσιν (Vulgate: *ut misereantur*) αὐτούς. The Latin uses the expression *in animam mittere*, whereas the Vulgate commonly uses the expression is *in corde dare* (LXX: διδόναι ἐν καρδίᾳ, as in e.g. Exod. 35:34; 2 Chron. 12:14; Ezra 7:10, 27; Neh. 2:12; 7:5). The difference between *mittere* and *dare* is negligible; the use of *anima* instead of *cor* may have been caused by the semantic overlap of the words (both the heart and the soul being the seat of the will), and by their frequent juxtaposition in parallelisms.

This passage ends with an allusion to Cyrus's edict (2 Chron. 36:23; Ezra 1:2-4). Even the elevated style of that "document" seems to have left its traces in As. Mos. 4:6, namely in the combination of the synonyms *terra et regio* (see grammatical note nr. 170).

---

[1] Thus Clemen, *APAT* II, p. 322.
[2] See also Ps. 106(105):43 πλεονάκις ἐρρύσατο αὐτούς; cf. 3 Macc. 2:13.

4:7-9
THE TRIBES AFTER THE RESTORATION

After the king's permission to return, the subsequent fate of the various groups within the people is summarily related. The two and the ten tribes, temporarily reunited in 3:8-13, are again divided, but an additional division is made, and a third group, "some parts of the tribes" is distinguished:

> 1) *Ascendent aliquae partes tribuum et venient in locum ...*
> 2) *Duae tribus permanebunt in praeposita fide ...*
> 3) *X tribus crescent et devenient apud nationes in tempore tribulationum.*

It seems that, according to the author of As. Mos., those "parts of the tribes" who return to rebuild the "place" (apparently Jerusalem or the temple) are not the two tribes. Their return and the restoration of the "place" is contrasted to the faithfulness to the covenant which is reserved for the two tribes. Apparently, the author in this passage redefines the "two tribes": from this moment, only those who abide in the faith of the fathers may be called by that name. Once again the people of God is reduced to a smaller group, consisting of only a part of the "two tribes". If this is correct, the designation "two tribes" is an honorific one, and it is used in the same way in which for instance Paul uses the name "Israel" (cf. Rom. 9:6 οὐ πάντες οἱ ἐξ Ἰσραήλ, οὗτοι Ἰσραήλ). In contrast, "some parts of the tribes" is a derogatory designation. The fate of the ten tribes, prophesied in 4:9, is unclear, due to textual corruption; it seems, however, unlikely that the author of As. Mos. would view their post-exilic existence positively.

7 Then some parts of the tribes will go up, and they will come in the place that was appointed to be theirs, and they will rampart the place anew. 8 But the two tribes will hold on to the allegiance that was ordained for them, mourning and weeping, because they will not be able to bring offerings to the Lord of their fathers. 9 And the ten tribes will be more and more absorbed among the nations in a time of tribulations.

4:7
In this sentence, it is predicted that "some parts of the tribes" will return, and rampart the city anew. As has been remarked above, "some parts of the tribes" seems to be a pejorative designation of the ones who rebuild the walls: *pars* and *aliqui* are used in a

similarly derogatory way in 6:9 (see the commentary on that passage). In 2:7, the building of walls is considered as the first stage of apostasy; here, the renewed fortification of the city apparently disqualifies its makers to be counted among the "two tribes"; see below on 4:8.

There has been some debate on what place is meant with *locus*, Jerusalem or the temple, but Jerusalem is no doubt the most natural referent, since it is said that "they will rampart the place", which is more appropriately said of a city than of a temple. The emphatic formulation *locus constitutus suus* suggests that the place to which they will return was "appointed to be theirs"[1]; see Exod. 23:20 ἡ γῆ, ἣν ἡτοίμασά σοι; 2 Sam. 7:10 καὶ θήσομαι τόπον τῷ λαῷ μου τῷ Ἰσραήλ; cf. Num. 10:29; 1 Sam. 12:8.

Probably, *renovare* here means "to rebuild"; cf. Sir. 49:7(9) οἰκοδομεῖν καὶ καταφυτεύειν; Vulgate: *iterum aedificare et renovare*. It cannot be excluded, however, that it means "to re-dedicate". In the Vulgate of 1 Macc. 4:36 and 54, the verb *renovare* appears to have borrowed the meaning "to (re-)dedicate" from the Greek ἐγκαινίζειν. A related Greek noun is also used in connection with Jerusalem's walls in Neh. 12:27 ἐν ἐγκαινίοις τείχους Ἰερουσαλήμ (Vulgate: *in dedicatione autem muri Hierusalem*).

4:8

In 4:8, it is stated that the two tribes will be sad[2], because they will not be able to bring sacrifices. The return of "some parts" of the tribes to the city may be assumed to imply the restoration of the Jerusalem temple cult. The sadness of the two tribes is therefore often interpreted as a rejection of the validity of the restored temple. Such a rejection must be seen in connection with the building of walls around the city in 4:7 (cf. 2:7-9, where the fortification of Jerusalem is regarded as the beginning of apostasy).

This interpretation has, however, met with objections. D.R. Schwartz especially has protested against what he sees as a strained interpretation of *non poterint*[3]. According to Schwartz, the simple words "they will not be able" say nothing about cultic validity or rejection[4]. As an alternative, Schwartz suggests that the two tribes can be seen as the Jews who remained in Babylonia, but who kept in touch with the Jerusalem temple (as opposed to the ten tribes, the apostates from Northern descent). This geographical distance would prevent them from bringing sacrifices—the cause of their sadness[5]. However, assuming that As. Mos. was not written by a Diaspora

---

[1] In that case, *locus constitutus suus* would be equivalent to *locus quem constituit* (sc. Deus) *eis*; cf. 4:8 *praeposita fides sua*, equivalent to *fides quam praeposuit eis*.

[2] *Tristes et gementes*; cf. the Vulgate of Isa. 29:2 *tristis et moerens*; Ezek. 9:4 *gementes et dolentes*.

[3] Schwartz, "The Tribes of As. Mos. 4:7-9".

[4] So also Reese, *Die Geschichte*, p. 100. But cf. Goldstein, "The Testament of Moses" pp. 49-50, who suggested that at some time in the textual tradition a word like לרצון (to offer up sacrifices "acceptably") or its equivalent in Greek or Latin was lost; alternatively, the notion of acceptability is implied.

[5] Similarly, Doran, "T. Mos. 4:8" p. 492: "Rather than a rejection of the Second Temple, then, T. Mos. 4:8 describes the fidelity of the two tribes to the Temple worship while in exile, similar to the longing expressed in Psalm 137." The main parallel for such a concept

(cont.)

Jew[1], it is unlikely that the author would designate those who returned as "some parts" of the tribes, and those who stayed back as "the two tribes"; rather, he would have written: "the two tribes will return, but some parts of the tribes will remain in exile".

In fact, only the rejection of the rebuilding of the walls by some parts of the tribes as a sinful act, can explain why from 5:1 onwards punishment is expected. Schwartz attempted to neutralize this *vindicta* by claiming that it was "not seen as a punishment ..., but rather a necessary and foreordained part of the chain of events leading to the end of days"[2]. Yet although this punishment is foreordained, this is only the case because the Lord has also foreseen the sin to which it is a reaction. Obviously, the Lord would never have foreordained punishment for punishment's sake (cf. 3:10-13).

Reading 4:8 in connection with 4:7, the unavoidable conclusion is that the two tribes are distinguished from "some parts of the tribes" because the former "remain faithful to the prescribed allegiance" (*viz* to the covenant, see commentary on 2:7). That implies, however, that "some parts of the tribes" fail to be faithful to this allegiance to the covenant. Since these parts of the tribes appear to be the dominant group (it is they who will rebuild the walls), it is impossible for the faithful ones to bring sacrifice—it is no coincidence that it is said that sacrifices cannot be offered to the God of their fathers (see the commentary on 9:6). It can be concluded that the validity of the temple cult is indeed rejected by the author of As. Mos.

A rejection of the validity of the temple cult is found in a few other texts, esp. in 1 En. 89:73 (alluding to Mal. 1:7), and now also in 4Q390 ("Pseudo-Moses"); cf. Sib. Or. III 265-294. Objections have been made that the parallel from 1 Enoch is imperfect, since, in that passage, the temple cult is not altogether rejected—only the offerings are said to be impure and polluted[3]. In response, it should be noted that the rejection of the temple cult in As. Mos. probably concerns its impurity as well (cf. 5:4)[4]. However, the new text from Qumran provides an even closer parallel to As. Mos. 4:7-8[5]. In 4Q390 I, it is prophesied that the Israelites will act just as sinfully as their pre-exilic fathers, except for the first generation, which will rebuild the temple (4Q390 I 4-

---

(speaking, however, about the "nine" tribes), which neither Schwartz nor Doran quotes, is 4 Ezra 13:39-49, esp. 41-42 (Hilgenfeld, "Die Psalmen Salomo's", p. 284).

[1] As Bousset, *Religion des Judentums*, pp. 115-116, [2]p. 133, would have it; Schwartz, "The Tribes", p. 221, limits himself to commenting that he sees "no need" to assume a Babylonian standpoint.

[2] Schwartz, "The Tribes", p. 222.

[3] Similarly, it has been suggested that the author of As. Mos. only states that the glory of "second Temple" was less than that of the "first", as in 2 Bar. 68:5-6 (so Laperrousaz, *Le Testament*, p. 117; Priest, "Testament of Moses", p. 929). But then As. Mos. 4:8 would really be something of an overstatement (cf. Charles, *The Assumption*, p. 15).

[4] According to Goldstein, "The Testament of Moses", p. 49, the phrase *tristes et gementes* is taken from Ezek. 9:4 (Vulgate: *gementes et dolentes*), "where the words refer to the scrupulous minority, scandalized over the abominations of the majority".

[5] 4Q390 will be published, with a translation and commentary, by D. Dimant, in "New Light from Qumran on the Jewish Pseudepigrapha - 4Q390", in J. Trebolle Barrera and L. Vegas Montaner (eds.), *The Madrid Qumran Congress. Proceedings of the International Congress on the Dead Sea Scrolls, Madrid 18-21 March, 1991* (STDJ 11), Leiden 1993. I wish to thank Prof. Dimant who kindly permitted me to use 4Q390 before her edition could be published.

6). But, after that generation has passed away, they will violate every commandment that the Lord has given them (7-9)—וְהִשְׁאַרְתִּי מֵהֶם פְּלֵיטִים, "but I will cause to remain from among them a remnant" (10).

Permanere in means "to hold on to", and may be complemented by an abstract denoting a disposition of the mind or soul, or by the object of such a disposition: for instance, one can "hold on to the Lord" (*permanere in Domino*, e.g. LAB 21:10), or "persevere in the fear of God" (*permanere in timore Dei* e.g. Tob. 2:14). Similarly, one can "persevere in the faith"; see *permanere in fide* (ἐμμένειν τῇ πίστει) Acts 14:21[1]. *Permanere in fide* may therefore be translated as "to persevere in the allegiance (*viz* to the covenant)", or, which is effectively the same, "hold on to the covenant" (for *fides* as "covenant", see commentary to 2:7b).

The faith the two tribes hold on to is said to have been "laid before them"[2]; *praeponere* has probably been confused with *proponere* (see grammatical note nr. 46). *Proponere* is used in connection with the law and commandments in e.g. Exod. 21:1 and Deut. 4:44 (LXX: παρατιθέναι ἐνώπιον); Deut. 4:8 and 1 Ki. 9:6 (LXX: διδόναι ἐνώπιον); see esp., in connection with the covenant, Josh. 24:25 *percussit igitur Josue in die illo foedus et proposuit populo praecepta atque judicia in Sychem* (LXX differs); cf. also 4 Ezra 7:20 *anteposita ... Dei lex*.

4:9

Finally, in 4:9, the fortunes of the ten tribes are reported. The text is in disorder. First, it is said that the ten tribes will "grow" (*crescent*). This may be an allusion to the multitude of the Jews in the Diaspora (cf. Josephus, *Ant. Jud.* XI 133 αἱ δὲ δέκα φυλαί ... ἀριθμῷ γνωσθῆναι μὴ δυνάμεναι). But in such an interpretation, the clause seems to have little coherence with the context. Perhaps one may take *crescent et devenient apud nationes* as an "enumerative figure", coordinating what is logically subordinate: "they will more and more (*crescent*) be absorbed among the nations"[3].

The rest of 4:9 is conjectural. The manuscript offers *devenient apud natos in tempore tribum*, which makes no sense. It is relatively easy to correct *tribum* to *tribulationum*[4] (see the textual commentary to line 81), the emendation of *natos* into *nationes*

---

[1] See also Col. 1:23; 1 Tim. 2:15.

[2] Hilgenfeld, "Die Psalmen Salomo's", p. 284, retranslated *praeposita* as προκειμένη. Reese, *Die Geschichte*, pp. 100-101, in turn interpreted this as "vorhandene Treue" ("extant faith"). This hardly renders the clause more intelligible, *pace* 3:10-13. Moreover, Reese's appeal to Hilgenfeld's authority is unjustified, since Hilgenfeld only gives the literal rendering of *prae- (pro-) ponere*, and does not explicitate which of the many meanings of προκεῖσθαι would have been meant.

[3] So Clemen, *APAT* II, p. 323: "zehn Stämme werden immer mehr zu Heiden werden". For the enumerative figure, see Hofmann-Szantyr II, p. 783.

[4] Doran, "T. Mos. 4:8", p. 491, prefers to retain the manuscript's *devenient apud natos*, claiming that this clause could be translated as "'they go to stay with their children' [so already Volkmar, *Mose Prophetie*], a sense of domestic bliss that contrasts strongly with the sorrow of the two tribes." I doubt, however, that *devenire* can mean "to go to stay", and I am not sure whether the exceptionally high esteem for such domestic bliss is not anachronistic, or, if it is not, whether it is the proper opposite of the inability to sacrifice. Doran's suggestion to read 4:8-9 before 4:1 must be dismissed as speculative and based on a gross misunderstanding of 4:1-7 (p. 492: "4:1-7 ... sketch the decline after the return from the exile").

is the most likely one. The majority of scholars connect *devenient* with *apud nationes*, "they will end up among the nations". It is also possible to connect *devenient* with *in tempore tribulationum* (cf. 1 Macc. 6:11 *in quantam tribulationem deveni*). The fate of the ten tribes, thus interpreted, is not that they will become numerous among the nations, but that they will end up in a time of growing tribulation among the nations. The fact that *apud nationes* follows *devenient*, however, suggests that "they will more and more be absorbed among the nations in a time of tribulations" is what the author meant.

For the general meaning of 4:9, one may compare Neh. 9:27 καὶ ἔδωκας αὐτοὺς ἐν χειρὶ θλιβόντων αὐτούς, καὶ ἔθλιψαν αὐτούς κτλ.; cf. also Isa. 33:2.

5:1-6:9
THE PEOPLE'S SINFULNESS

Many interpreters of As. Mos. have assumed that chapter 5 is a continuation of the prophetically announced history of the people. Since chapter 6 recognizably refers to the Hasmonean and Herodian periods, chapter 5, in this view, must cover the temporal space between the restoration of the temple and the Hasmonean period. The kings, perpetrators of crime and executers of punishment (5:1), are accordingly identified as the last Persian kings[1], or as the Ptolemies and Seleucids[2], or as the earlier Hasmonaeans[3]; the division with regard to the truth (5:2) is interpreted as the conflict between Daniel's *maśkilim* and *rabbim*[4], or between the Pharisees and Sadducees[5]; the priests, who are in reality nothing but slaves (5:4) would be the Hellenizers[6], in particular Jason and Menelaus[7], or the Maccabaean priests[8], in particular John Hyrcanus[9], and so on.

Apparently, all the various identifications proposed are primarily intended to fill in the gap between the allusions to the return from exile (4:7) and to king Herod (6:2-6). It must be recognized, however, that the information chapter 5 supplies is simply too general and too vague to make such specific identifications.

In a brief discussion that has received little attention Laperrousaz argues convincingly that chapter 5 and chapter 6 are concerned with the same historical period, but that they view this period from a different perspective. Chapter 5 is a general characterization of the people's sinfulness; chapter 6 connects this sinfulness to the kings under whose

---

[1] Hilgenfeld, "Die Psalmen Salomo's", p. 302.

[2] Clemen, *APAT* II, p. 323; Rießler, *Jüdisches Schrifttum*, p. 1302; Reese, *Die Geschichte*, p. 101; Brandenburger, "Himmelfahrt", p. 72.

[3] Laperrousaz, *Le Testament*, p. 118.

[4] Schmidt and Merx, "Die Assumptio", p. 143.

[5] Charles, *The Assumption*, p. 16; Clemen, *APAT* II, p. 323; Rießler, *Jüdisches Schrifttum*, p. 1302; Brandenburger, "Himmelfahrt", p. 72; Laperrousaz, *Le Testament*, p. 118, for understandable reasons, adds the Essenes.

[6] Lucius, *Der Essenismus*, p. 114; Clemen, *APAT* II, p. 323.

[7] Heidenheim, "Beiträge zum bessern Verständniss", pp. 85-86; Rießler, *Jüdisches Schrifttum*, p. 1302; Reese, *Die Geschichte*, p. 102.

[8] Hilgenfeld, *Novum Testamentum* (1866), p. 102.

[9] Hilgenfeld, *Novum Testamentum* ([2]1884), p. 132; Priest, "Testament of Moses", p. 929.

rule this corruption is to take place[1]. This period is the relatively short time immediately preceding the eschatological events (described in As. Mos. 8-10), and is signalled by the words *et cum adpropiabunt tempora arguendi* (5:1). In this pre-eschatological chaos, the people and its leaders are entirely perverted, as chapter 5 attempts to show. With chapter 6, the author intends to make his readers recognize their own time as the final stage of the pre-eschatological chaos, described in chapter 5.

It can be concluded that it was not the author's intention to discuss all the people's vicissitudes in the time between the return from exile and his own age. He omits most of post-exilic history, and moves on at once to what is to him and his readers recent history. Apparently, he wishes to show that his own time mirrors the events that, in his view, led to the exile referred to in As. Mos. 3:1-3[2].

The author supports his interpretation of his own time as the pre-eschatological period by the use of one or more references to scripture, formally introduced by the clause *propter quod factum fuit* (5:3). I suspect that 5:4-6 are meant as an exegetical application of this appeal to the scriptures. This suspicion is corroborated by the numerous cross-references between 5:2-3 and 5:4-6. In 5:2-3 one finds four words which are echoed in 5:4-6:

5:2 dividentur ad *veritatem*	5:4 non enim sequentur *veritatem*
5:3 devitabunt *justitiam*	5:5 pervendent *justitias* accipiendo
5:3 accedent ad *iniquitatem*	5:6 implebitur colonia ... *iniquitatibus*
5:3 contaminabunt *inquinationibus* domum servitutis	5:4 altarium *inquinabunt*

The way in which the concepts introduced in 5:2-3 are given a new context in 5:4-6 is reminiscent of certain exegetical methods used in Qumran and other contemporary literature.

In 5:4-6, the sins introduced in the reference to scripture are ascribed to those groups within Jewish society of which they are typical. By enumerating these groups with their typical transgressions, the author

---

[1] Laperrousaz, *Le Testament*, p. 119: "Ce verset (sc. 6:1) n'annonce pas des événements devant se produire après ceux mentionnés dans les versets du chapitre V; mais, après avoir, en V, 1, fait allusion en termes assez vagues aux rois d'alors, puis, successivement, aux divers adversaires de son parti, l'auteur précise, ici, l'identité de ces rois sous le règne desquels se dérouleront les événements rapportés dans le chapitre V".

[2] Compare Kolenkow's remarks on the use of the *Doppelschema* in As. Mos., in "The Assumption of Moses as a Testament", p. 73.

of As. Mos. conveys an image of Jewish society as one that is diseased in all its branches[1]. The various groups are the kings, possibly the people, the priests, the teachers, and the judges (*reges ... ipsi ... sacerdotes ... doctores ... judices*). Similar schematic arrangements are found in Ezek. 22:25-29 (οἱ ἀφηγούμενοι ... οἱ ἱερεῖς ... οἱ ἄρχοντες ... οἱ προφῆται); Micah 3:11 (οἱ ἡγούμενοι ... οἱ ἱερεῖς ... οἱ προφῆται; cf. Micah 7:3); Zeph. 3:3-4 (οἱ ἄρχοντες ... οἱ κριταί ... οἱ προφῆται ... οἱ ἱερεῖς); cf. Neh. 9:34; Ezra 9:2; Jer. 6:13; Dan. 9:8; Bar. 1:15-16. It will be noted that in As. Mos. 5 no prophets occur, which accords with the tendency in As. Mos. to suppress all prophets but Moses[2].

a. *5:1-3*

In 5:1-3 the author of As. Mos. alludes to prophecies in the scriptures, intended for the time near the end, in order to characterize the time in which he and his readers live as "the times of the approaching judgement". In these days of pressure, the knowledge of the truth will be obscured, and injustice, defilement and idolatry will prevail.

1 And when the times of judgement approach, revenge will come through kings who participate in crime and who will punish them. 2 And they themselves will move away from the truth, 3 wherefore it has been said: 'They will avoid justice and turn to iniquity,' and: 'they will defile the house of their worship with pollutions,' and that 'they will go awhoring after foreign gods'.

5:1
The *tempora arguendi* are said to be "approaching"[3], which of course means that the time left before the advent of the time of the end is short. In 7:1 the point in time is indicated on which the "times will suddenly end". Chapters 5-6 must therefore be seen as the short time immediately preceding the eschatological events. It may safely be as-

---

[1] Cf. Isa. 9:14-15, where it is said that the Lord will destroy the people entirely, "head and tail": πρεσβύτην καὶ τοὺς τὰ πρόσωπα θαυμάζοντας (αὕτη ἡ ἀρχή) καὶ προφήτην διδάσκοντα ἄνομα (οὗτος ἡ οὐρά).

[2] It may be that As. Mos. 5:4-6 is in its entirety directed against the priests. The functions mentioned can all be fulfilled by priests, and parallels from biblical literature show that the reproaches made can be directed against priests as well; see further the commentary on 5:5-6. On the threefold function of the Levites (priests, judges and scribes), see T. Levi 8:17, and Hollander and De Jonge, *The Testaments*, p. 154, cf. pp. 106-107, 166; for the function of king, see As. Mos. 6:1.

[3] *Adpropiare*; apart from 1 Macc. 9:10, the Vulgate prefers the synonym *appropinquare*. For the use of these synonyms in connection with a point in time, see for instance Deut. 31:14; 1 Ki. 2:1; Lam. 4:18; Luke 21:20, cf. 10:9, 11 (the approaching Kingdom of God).

sumed that the author of As. Mos. wanted to suggest to his readers that they themselves lived in the time immediately preceding the judgement.

I have found no other instance of the words *tempora arguendi* (καιροὶ τοῦ ἐλέγχειν?[1]), but cf. 2 Ki. 19:3 ἡμέρα θλίψεως καὶ ἐλεγμοῦ καὶ παροργισμοῦ; Isa. 37:3 ἡμέρα θλίψεως καὶ ὀνειδισμοῦ καὶ ἐλεγμοῦ; see also the commentary on As. Mos. 1:18, and cf. καιρὸς ἐκδικήσεως in for instance Sir. 5:7(9) (Vulgate: *tempus vindictae*); 18:24 (Vulgate: *tempus retributionis*); or Jer. 26(46):21 ἡμέρα ἀπωλείας ἦλθεν ἐπ' αὐτοὺς καὶ καιρὸς ἐκδικήσεως αὐτῶν (Vulgate: *tempus visitationis*; similar Jer. 27[50]:27, 31).

As the final judgement approaches, retribution already have begun in the form of harsh rule by the kings of the people[2]. This retribution is probably the consequence of the apostasy described in 4:8 (see above). But this kingly rule will not only punish sin, it will also contribute to it: the kings will take part in crimes and will punish the sinful people as well; see 6:2 *rex petulans ... judicabit illis quomodo digni erunt*, and cf. also Ezek. 22:3 Ὦ πόλις ἐκχέουσα αἵματα ἐν μέσῳ αὐτῆς τοῦ ἐλθεῖν καιρὸν αὐτῆς.

Particeps probably renders κοινωνός, "associate", see 2 Macc. 5:20; Prov. 28:24; cf. Job 34:8; Sir. 13:1, 2; Rev. 18:4 (συγκοινωνεῖν). For kings being companions of criminals, cf. Isa. 1:23 οἱ ἄρχοντές σου ἀπειθοῦσι κοινωνοὶ κλεπτῶν (Vulgate: *socii furum*).

5:2

According to the majority of interpreters, the author in 5:2 alludes to emerging religious dissension: *dividentur ad veritatem* would then mean "they will be divided with regard to the truth". For this dissension, many commentators point to the antithesis between the Pharisees and the Sadducees[3]. Charles referred to 1 En. 90:6-7[4], in which he sees an allusion to the emergence of both parties in the same historical period as the dissension of As. Mos. 5:2[5]. But even if the *dividi ad* is to be translated with "to be divided with regard to the truth", any link to specific religious parties is unwarranted. Dissension in the period immediately preceding the end is a traditional motif, primarily used as a sign of the time of the end. In Jub. 23:16-19, for instance, violent struggle is expected to arise between all kinds of opposing groups[6], illustrating the total disruption of the social order; see also 4 Ezra 5:9; 6:24; 9:3; 13:30-31; 2 Bar.

---

[1] Thus the retranslation by Hilgenfeld, "Die Psalmen Salomo's", p. 284.

[2] Unless *cum* is to be read as *tum*, the apodosis is introduced by *et vindicta*, a semiticizing construction, see grammatical note nr. 190. For *de* denoting the agent, see grammatical note nr. 68.

[3] See above, in the introduction to this section. Hilgenfeld, "Die Psalmen Salomo's", p. 302, suggested that *dividere* referred to the diaspora, but it remains unclear how he understood *ad veritatem*.

[4] *The Assumption*, p. 16.

[5] 1 En. 90:6-7 speaks about young lambs who began to open their eyes and who cried to the sheep, who, however, were deaf and blind. The lambs are usually interpreted as a reference to the Hasidim in early Maccabean times, see also Foerster, "Die Ursprung des Pharisäismus", pp. 38-39, 44.

[6] Foerster, "Die Ursprung des Pharisäismus", pp. 42-43, connected this passage to the Hasidim as well, but a reading of the passage in its entirety excludes such an interpretation.

39:6; 70:3, 5; 1 En. 100:1-2; cf. T. Judah 22:1. The motif is also known to Isa. 3:5; Micah 7:6 (cf. Matt. 10:35); Zech. 14:13; Matt. 10:21.

However, the reflexive voice of *dividere* is preferably taken to mean "to distance oneself"; if *ad* is taken in its Vulgar Latin meaning of *ab* (see grammatical note nr. 67)[1], we may translate: "they[2] will move away from the truth". For this meaning of *dividere*, see for instance Ps. 55(54):22 LXX; or *separare*[3] in 2 Ki. 17:21; Wisd. 1:3 *perversae enim cogitationes separant* (χωρίζουσιν) *a Deo*; esp. Sir. 33:8 *a Domini scientia separati sunt*, LXX: ἐν γνώσει κυρίου διεχωρίσθησαν. The advantage of this second translation of *dividi* is that it seems to match the context of As. Mos. 5:2 better. In 5:3 *devitabunt justitiam* must mean that "they will distance themselves from righteousness". In 5:4 it is said that "they will not follow the truth", which is a clear reference to 5:2 (see below). But in 5:4 there is no mention of partisanship, only of a general abandoning of truth.

Veritas (ἀλήθεια) here is equivalent to the true religion[4], the right way to live one's life before God. In this meaning it stands parallel to δικαιοσύνη (1 En. 10:16; Jub. 20:9; cf. 30:18, 23), or to ἔλεος (as a human virtue, Ps. Sol. 17:15). In 1 En. 104:13, it is said that the righteous may learn from the books of Enoch πάσας τὰς ὁδοὺς τῆς ἀληθείας (cf. Wisd. 5:6). The clearest examples of this use of the concept are found in the Qumran texts, in which the members of the community are occasionally referred to as האמת אנשי (4QpHab VII 10; cf. אמת בני 1QS IV 5 and elsewhere). Truth has an absolute character, and it can be obtained through wisdom, insight and piety. The darkening of truth and insight is a concept which occurs elsewhere as a sign of the approaching end; see for instance 4 Ezra 5:1, 9; 13:30-31; 14:17; 2 Bar. 39:6; Jub. 23:21-22.

5:3

Literally translated, *propter quod factum fuit* means "wherefore it has happened, or has been done". *Propter quod* occurs often in the Vulgate, and it almost always corresponds to διό, "for which reason": the abandonment of the truth (5:2) must be the reason for which something *factum fuit*. However, if *facere* were in this instance to be translated with "to do, or to happen", a subject is clearly missing. Moreover, the perfect tense *factum fuit* would be difficult to explain.

From the very beginning therefore, commentators have attempted to interpret *facere* in a way that accounts both for the apparently missing subject and for the perfect tense. Above all, the perfect tense seems to be understandable only if the phrase is taken as a formula introducing a quotation; several suggested emendations (such as

---

[1] In *ThLL* IV, col. 1604:15-17 (cf. cols. 831:39-43 and 823:7-12), the author of the article "divido" suggests that *ad* should be understood as *adversus*, see the Vetus Latina of Num. 21:5 *detrahebat populus ad Deum et adversus Moysen* (κατελάλει ὁ λαὸς πρὸς τὸν θεὸν καὶ κατὰ Μωυσῆν).

[2] Probably correctly, Schmidt and Merx, "Die Assumptio Mosis", p. 143, read *ipsi* as having a certain emphasis: not only will there be punishment by criminal kings, but also they (that is, the people) will fail to keep the commandments.

[3] In the Vulgate, both *dividere* and *separare* are used as equivalents of διαχωρίζειν; see for *dividere* e.g. Gen. 1:4; 13:11, 14 (cf. 13:9 διαχωρίσθητι ἀπ' ἐμοῦ, Vulgate: *recede a me*); for *separare* e.g. Gen. 30:32, 40; 2 Chron. 25:10; Sir. 6:13.

[4] In 1 Tim. 2:7, ἀλήθεια stands parallel to πίστις.

dictum[1] or *fatum*[2]) point in that direction as well. Löfstedt in 1911 gathered a number of instances from late Latin literature (including As. Mos. 5:3) in which *facere* is perhaps loosely used for "to say", even for "to write"[3], so that an emendation would not be necessary.

Even if the text of the phrase *propter quod factum fuit* is not entirely in order, it is fairly certain that it introduces a quotation. It is not possible, however, to trace the source of the words following this formula in the Old Testament or in related literature[4]. This is no singular phenomenon. In the New Testament it occurs with some regularity that a formally introduced quotation is nowhere to be found in the Old Testament and related literature[5].

It may be that the quotation is from a book no longer known to us, or from a lost variant or version of an Old Testament book[6]. But it is more likely that the author of As. Mos. has not quoted correctly or precisely, either because he quoted by heart or because he quoted *ad sensum* (that is, not the exact wording of some scriptural passage, but the intention of one or more[7]). The sentence *Devitabunt justitiam et accedent ad iniquitatem* does not occur in the Old Testament as we have it, but such apostasy is, of course, expected by numerous Biblical writers[8]; see for instance Jer. 11:10:

> ἐπεστράφησαν ἐπὶ τὰς ἀδικίας (Vulgate: *iniquitates*) τῶν πατέρων αὐτῶν τῶν πρότερον, οἳ οὐκ ἤθελον εἰσακοῦσαι (cf. *devitare?*) τῶν λόγων μου, καὶ ἰδοὺ αὐτοὶ βαδίζουσιν ὀπίσω θεῶν ἀλλοτρίων (Vulgate: *post deos alienos*) δουλεύειν αὐτοῖς.

Compare also Deut. 31:29:

> οἶδα γὰρ ὅτι ἔσχατον τῆς τελευτῆς μου ἀνομίᾳ ἀνομήσετε (Vulgate: *inique agetis*) καὶ ἐκκλινεῖτε ἐκ τῆς ὁδοῦ, ἧς ἐνετειλάμην ὑμῖν, together with Deut. 31:16 λαὸς οὗτος ἐκπορνεύσει ὀπίσω θεῶν ἀλλοτρίων (Vulgate: *fornicabitur post deos alienos*).

It should be noted that the author of As. Mos. must have assumed that the source of these quotations were the books of Moses, unless he is inconsistent with regard to the attribution of the prophecy in his work to Moses.

Determining the end of the quasi-quotation assumed to be introduced by *propter quod factum fuit* poses another problem. The antithetical parallelism *devitabunt justitiam et*

---

[1] Volkmar, *Mose Prophetie*, p. 29.

[2] Schmidt and Merx, "Die Assumptio Mosis", p. 143.

[3] *Philologischer Kommentar*, pp. 165-166; this use of *facere* explains the meaning "to say" which the French word *faire* sometimes has (p. 165). Löfstedt warned that the instances he quoted are not certain; they derive their persuasive force from their accumulation.

[4] For introductory formulas containing the words *propter quod*, see the Vulgate of Eph. 4:8; 5:14; James 4:6 (*propter quod dicit*, διὸ λέγει; cf. Luke 11:49 *propterea et sapientia Dei dixit*, διὰ τοῦτο καὶ ἡ σοφία τοῦ θεοῦ εἶπεν; add 1 Clem. 15:5).

[5] See Fitzmyer, "The Use of Explicit Old Testament Quotations", p. 304.

[6] So for instance Hilgenfeld, *Novum Testamentum*, p. 112.

[7] Cf. on this matter Bonsirven, *Exégèse rabbinique*, pp. 38-41.

[8] *Justitia* and *iniquitas* are also contrasted in Ps. 45(44):8 (quoted in Heb. 1:9) and Ezek. 33:13.

accedent ad iniquitatem suggests that these two phrases belong together[1]. The passages from Jeremiah and Deuteronomy quoted above suggest that the phrase *fornicabunt post deos alienos* also forms part of the quotation; at least, it can be recognized as a real quotation. In that case, *quia*, which precedes this phrase, may be interpreted as another introduction of direct speech or a quotation, translating the so-called ὅτι *recitativum* (see grammatical note nr. 152). It is not at all exceptional for a quotation to include material from several passages.

If this is correct, the clause in between, *et contaminabunt inquinationibus domum servitutis suae*, must belong to the quotation as well. Then, the structure of 5:2-3 would be as follows:

> And they themselves will move away from the truth;
>> wherefore it has been said:
>> "They will avoid justice and turn to iniquity,"
>> and "defile with pollutions the house of their worship,"
>> and that "they will go whoring after foreign gods".

In 5:4, the introduction to this quotation (*et ipsi dividentur ad veritatem*) is resumed: *non enim sequentur veritatem Dei*). This, too, suggests that the quotation should be taken to include *fornicabunt post deos alienos*[2].

Domus servitutis suae, usually a designation for Egypt[3], must refer in this instance to the temple. On a few occasions, the Vulgate uses the word *servitus* for the servitude to God, in 2 Chron. 12:8 (where the *servitus* [LXX: δουλεία] to God is contrasted to that to the kingdom of the earth; cf. 1 Macc. 2:10 *servitus legis*, LXX: λατρεία πατέρων), and in Sir. 2:1. As far as I can ascertain, *servitus* only once unequivocally designates the cultic service to God, in Wisd. 18:21 (LXX: λειτουργία). On the other hand, the Greek word δουλεία can be used as a designation for the cultic service to God; it is connected to the "house of God" in 1 Chron. 25:6 (Vulgate: *ministerium*); Neh. 10:33(32) (Vulgate: *opus*), whereas λατρεία and λατρεύειν are more common designations (esp. used in connection with foreign deities), and λειτουργία/λειτουργεῖν the predominant terms; the latter are connected with the temple (the tabernacle, the house of God) on numerous occasions.

The reproach of the contamination of the temple by the Jews themselves is also found in Mal. 1:7; 2:11; Ps. Sol. 1:8; 2:3; 8:12, 22; Jub. 23:17, 21 (see further the commentary on 5:4).

Idolatry is expressed in terms of adultery (*fornicari*), as is often done in Biblical and related literature, possibly after the example of Hosea; see also 1 Chron. 5:25; Ps. 106(105):39; Jer. 3:9; Ezek. 6:9; chap. 23 (esp. 23:37-39).

---

[1] For a similar antithetical parallelism cf. 2 Tim. 4:4 καὶ ἀπὸ τῆς ἀληθείας τὴν ἀκοὴν ἀποστρέψουσιν, ἐπὶ δὲ τοὺς μύθους ἐκτραπήσονται.

[2] So Schmidt and Merx, "Die Assumptio Mosis", p. 143.

[3] E.g. Exod. 13:3, 14; Deut. 5:6; 6:13.

b. 5:4-6

The explicit use of a scriptural quotation (5:3) leads to the expectation that the author will subsequently interpret it: a quotation serves to establish and to legitimize an author's views on the events and circumstances he describes. In 5:4-6, the author substantiates his claims by relating the prophecies contained in the quotation to the circumstances which he sees as characteristic of his own time.

The author's exegetical method is mainly to take up key-words from the prophecies, and to connect them to the wrongs he denounces. For example, the prophecy that "they will avoid justice (*justitiam*)" (5:3) is applied to the teachers who will be financially compensated for their legal pronouncements (*justitias*). This exegetical method is well-known from Qumran and New Testament literature[1].

₄ For they will not follow the truth of God, but some people will defile the altar with the offerings they will bring to the Lord, (*sc.* people) who are not priests, but slaves born of slaves. ₅ For the scholars who will be their teachers in those times will favour the persons that please them, and accept gifts; and they will sell legal settlements, accepting fees. ₆ And so their city and dwelling-place will be filled with crimes and injustice against God, since those who will do them will be impious judges: they will continually judge according to their own liking.

5:4

The first half of 5:4, *non enim sequentur veritatem Dei*[2], resumes 5:2, *et ipsi dividentur ad veritatem*, thereby signalling the transition from the quotation in 5:3 to its application to the circumstances of recent history (from the author's perspective).

Priestly cultic practices are condemned in extremely radical terms. The cultic officers are designated as *quidam*, a derogatory word ("certain characters"; cf. Rom. 3:8 *sicut aiunt quidam* [τινες], and see further grammatical note nr. 63); the repugnance with which they fill the author is further expressed in the clause *qui non sunt sacerdotes sed servi de servis nati*. As. Mos. 5:4 can be paraphrased as follows: "the altar of God is polluted by people who call themselves priests, but who are in reality no more than slaves". Possibly, the basis for this accusation is given in the first half of 5:4, "they will not follow the truth" (cf. Isa. 65:2).

In the attempt to identify these priests who were slaves born of slaves, commentators have pointed to John Hyrcanus who, according to Josephus, *Ant. Jud.* XIII 291-

---

[1] Elliger, *Studien zum Habakuk-Kommentar*, p. 127, describes the exegetical principle "daß *einzelne Textworte direkt in die Auslegung* selbst hineingenommen werden", according to the interpreter's wish "die Übereinstimmung von Text und Auslegung auch äußerlich zu dokumentieren. Es sind solche Wortzitate, die man heutzutage etwa in Anführungsstriche setzen würde."

[2] For the expression "to follow the truth" (ἀκολουθεῖν τῇ ἀληθείᾳ), see T. Asher 6:1; cf. 2 Macc. 8:36 τοῖς νόμοις; Isa. 65:2 οὐκ ἐπορεύθησαν ὁδῷ ἀληθινῇ.

292, was admonished by the Pharisee Eleazar to give up the high-priesthood because his mother had been imprisoned during the reign of Antiochus Epiphanes[1]. It does not necessarily follow, however, that Josephus' apocryphal anecdote[2] is related to the serious denunciation of the priesthood in As. Mos. 5:4. Moreover, the phrase *servi de servis nati* does not mean that one of the priests' mother had been a captive, but that the entire priestly stock will consist of slaves[3].

It is equally unlikely that the author of As. Mos. in 5:4 would call the priesthood "slaves" because of its genealogical imperfections in a more general sense[4]. It is obvious that priests should be of Aaronic descent; but if they are not, that does not make them slaves. "Slave" should be taken here simply as a term of abuse[5], in accordance with the Hellenistic contempt for the unfree[6]. For this abusive use of the term "slave" one may compare Lam. 5:8 δοῦλοι ἐκυρίευσαν ἡμῶν, and the several occasions on which Alexander the Great's alleged divine offspring is rejected in the Sibylline Oracles, e.g. Sib. Or. III 383, where Alexander is called ἄλγος ἐκ γενεῆς Κρονίδαο νόθων δούλων τε γενέθλης, "a pain in the neck from the bastard family of Kronos, born of slaves"; cf. Sib. Or. V 7 (= XII 7); XI 197-198. That the priests were supposed to be slaves is not the reason why their office is here rejected. On the contrary: the author finds the cultic officers unfit for their dignified task, and therefore calls them no more than slaves.

The priesthood is rejected because of its members' moral misconduct, which renders their cultic actions impure, defiling the Lord's sanctuary. In some Old Testament and related texts, the concept is found that immolations to God, which may ritualistically be in perfect order, are nevertheless defiled because of the spiritual impurity of the ones who offer them. In Amos 5:21-24, for instance, the rich and festive offerings are rejected because of sinfulness (for comparable rejections, see Isa. 43:27-28 LXX; Jer.

---

[1] For instance Hilgenfeld, *Novum Testamentum*, p. 112; Volkmar, *Mose Prophetie*, pp. 32-33; others, such as Clemen, *APAT* II, p. 323, and Brandenburger, "Himmelfahrt", p. 73, rejected this identification, because the Maccabees are not introduced until ch. 6.

[2] Laperrousaz, *Le Testament*, p. 118, inflates Josephus' rather Herodotean story by calling it a "tradition selon laquelle la mère de Jean Hyrcan aurait été esclave sous le règne d'Antiochus Épiphane". The story is known also in bQidd. 66a; there, it is told in connection with Alexander Jannaeus, which shows that the story is more of a traditional tale than a genuine historical tradition (or, as Josephus himself puts it, ψευδὴς δὲ ὁ λόγος ἦν). Apart from that, Hyrcanus' mother was said to have been a captive (αἰχμάλωτόν σου γεγονέναι τὴν μητέρα), which is not quite the same as being a slave.

[3] In contrast, Paul claims the purity of his Jewish descent by saying that he is Ἑβραῖος ἐξ Ἑβραίων.

[4] Clemen, *APAT* II, p. 323, suggested tthat, because they lacked the proper Aaronic descent, the *servi* were Hellenistic priests; Charles, *The Assumption*, p. 19, took "slaves" to refer to the same priests because they were Antiochus' puppets, "being made and unmade by him at pleasure".

[5] So Lucius, *Der Essenismus*, p. 114: "Es möchte ... das Wort Sklave und Sklavengeborener als blosser Schimpfname aufzufassen sein, womit der Verfasser die Hohenpriester der Syrerzeit brandmarkt, ähnlich wie gewisse Pharisäer den Hyrkan vorwarfen, er sei der Sohn einer Sklavin ..., wie das Volk dieselbe Beschuldigung, er sei ein Sklavengeborener, gegen Alexander Jannäus schleuderte ..., wie das Volk und noch die späteren Rabbinen ... König Herodes als 'den Sklaven' zu schelten beliebten."

[6] Cf. Hengel, *Juden, Griechen und Barbaren*, pp. 78-79.

6:20; 7:30; Ezek. 5:11; Hos. 5:4-6; 6:6; Mal. 2:11-16; cf. Heb. 10:4). In Isa. 1:13 the sacrifices themselves are called an abomination. In Ps. Sol. 2:3 (cf. Ps. Sol. 1:8; 8:12, 22) it is explicitly stated that the offerings that are brought to God are polluted because of the bringers' transgressions, and that by bringing them the sanctuary is defiled: οἱ υἱοὶ Ἰερουσαλὴμ ἐμίαναν τὰ ἅγια κυρίου, ἐβεβηλοῦσαν τὰ δῶρα τοῦ θεοῦ ἐν ἀνομίαις. So also Jub. 23:22 et sanctificationem sanctam polluent in abominationibus veritatis et inmunditiis.

On some occasions, similar reproaches are specifically directed against the priests; see Ezek. 22:26 καὶ οἱ ἱερεῖς αὐτῆς ἠθέτησαν νόμον μου καὶ ἐβεβήλουν τὰ ἅγιά μου; similarly Zeph. 3:4. These last two examples are taken from passages which display the classification of sinners also found in As. Mos. 5 (see above). See further T. Levi 16:1-2 (an alleged quotation from a book of Enoch). In 1QpHab XII 6-10, Hab. 2:17 is applied to the wicked priest:

> And when it says: "Because of the blood spilt in the city, and the violence committed in the land", its meaning is: "the city", that is Jerusalem, where the wicked priest did works of abomination, and he defiled the sanctuary of God; and "violence committed in the land": these are the cities of Judah, where he robbed the goods of the poor."

See also CD V 6-7; perhaps 4QpNah I 11, and the commentary on As. Mos. 5:6.

Finally, there are some instances in which moral misconduct is equated not only with cultic pollution, but also with idolatry. See 1 Sam. 15:22-23[1], and Mal. 2:11:

> ἐγκατελείφθη Ἰούδας, καὶ βδέλυγμα ἐγένετο ἐν τῷ Ἰσραὴλ καὶ ἐν Ἰερουσαλήμ, διότι ἐβεβήλωσεν Ἰούδας τὰ ἅγια κυρίου, ἐν οἷς ἠγάπησεν, καὶ ἐπετήδευσεν εἰς θεοὺς ἀλλοτρίους.

See also Eph. 5:5 πλεονέκτης, ὅ ἐστιν εἰδωλολάτρης, and Col. 3:5 Νεκρώσατε οὖν ... τὴν πλεονεξίαν, ἥτις ἐστὶν εἰδωλολατρία; cf. T. Judah 19:1 ἡ φιλαργυρία πρὸς εἴδωλα ὁδηγεῖ; T. Levi 17:11, where idolatry is the first of a list of sins, also including greed; see further T. Judah 18:2, 5. Perhaps the idolatry of which the priests in Jerusalem are accused in 1QpHab XII 10-14, too, is to be understood in this way[2]. In T. Levi 9:9 it is said that the Levites will pollute the sanctuary because of the spirit of fornication that dominates them—fornication is often connected with idolatry (see the commentary on 5:3).

It seems, then, that the author of As. Mos. intends to say that the priests' immoral behaviour makes the sacrifices they bring to God impure; moreover, their sinfulness testifies to their disregard for the Lord's will, which is the same as idolatry. In this way it is shown that the prophecies quoted in 5:3 are fulfilled, even the prophecy concerning idolatry[3].

---

[1] The versions vary, but carry the same point.
[2] At least, the accusation, derived from Hab. 2:18, immediately follows the rejection of the immoral behaviour of the wicked priest in XII 6-10 quoted above.
[3] Cf. Laperrousaz' comment on 5:3, Le Testament, p. 118: "Ce verset ne dit pas que les Juifs en question ont réellement commis tous les crimes dont il rappelle la prédiction ... la raison selon laquelle l'autel est pollué est que les prêtres exercent illégitimement les fonctions sacerdotales du fait qu'ils sont 'des esclaves fils d'esclaves'."

5:5

Following the condemnation of the priests, the author denounces the teachers. With these "teachers", jurists are probably meant, teachers of the law. They are accused of partiality and of being open to bribery.

Two words are used to indicate the jurists, *magistri* and *doctores*. These words are nearly synonymous: in the Vulgate they are both used as equivalents of διδάσκαλος[1], more rarely of γραμματεύς (Num. 11:16; Josh. 23:2; 24:1; 2 Chron. 19:11; 34:13; cf. γραμματοεισαγωγεύς Deut. 16:18; 29:9; 31:28; γραμματικός Isa. 33:18)[2]. Schmidt and Merx[3] therefore suspected that the use of both words in As. Mos. was due either to the collation of two variants, or to the uncertainty of the translator as to which of both synonyms to choose. Clemen[4], however, rightly saw that the two words are not entirely synonymous.

In Latin, *magister* seems to be preferred within the context of teaching and learning; the opposite of "master" is "pupil". *Doctor*, on the other hand, is simply the name of a profession, namely the study and the instruction of the law. "Teacher" is then opposed to other professions or functions, in this case priests and judges (cf. the use of *doctor* in the lists of ministries in Acts 13:1; 1 Cor. 12:28-29; Eph. 4:11 and elsewhere). When διδάσκαλος is translated into Latin, the translator can choose either *magister* or *doctor*, because διδάσκαλος covers the meaning of both. We should translate "the scholars who will be their teachers"[5].

The reproach that is made against the doctors of the law is favouritism in their legal pronouncements. Apparently, the teachers are distinguished from the judges, and their *justitiae* should accordingly be distinguished from the judges' *judicare* (As. Mos. 5:6). Possibly, the doctors' *justitiae* are doctrinal legal pronouncements, whereas the judges' *judicare* refers to practical verdicts. "Laws" and "commandments" are "taught"; see for instance Deut. 5:31; Ezra 7:10 (3 Ezra 8:7); Ezek. 44:23-24; 3 Ezra 9:48; Sir. 45:17(21); Jub. 31:15-16.

On the other hand, the distinction between teachers and judges may not be very sharp, esp. if these two tasks are here considered priestly functions. On a number of occasions, priests are presented as teachers, in Deut. 33:9-10; Ezra in Neh. 8:9 Ἔσδρας ὁ ἱερεὺς καὶ γραμματεύς; Mal. 2:7 (the law is to be found on the lips of the priests, cf. T. Reub. 6:8); 1QSb III 22-23; CD XIV 7-8; or as judges, in Deut. 17:8-13; 19:16-18; 1 Chron. 23:4; 2 Chron. 19:8-10; 34:13 LXX; 1QSa I 24. In Deut. 16:18 κριταί and γραμματοεισαγωγεῖς are mentioned side by side.

The reproach here directed against the teachers of the law is found directed against the priests in Mal. 2:9 ἐλαμβάνετε πρόσωπα ἐν νόμῳ; Micah 3:11 οἱ ἱερεῖς μετὰ

---

[1] In the New Testament Vulgate, *magister* is, for the most part, a translation of the term of address for Jesus, διδάσκαλε. In a great number of instances in the Old Testament, *magister* is used to correspond to שר, "chief", in LXX often rendered with a compound with ἀρχι-.

[2] It must be added that *doctor* seems to be used adjectively in 2 Chron. 15:3 *sacerdos doctor* (ἱερεὺς ὑποδεικνύων).

[3] "Die Assumptio Moses", p. 144.

[4] *APAT* II, p. 323; Clemen translates: "Denn die Schriftgelehrten, die dann ihre Lehrer sind".

[5] Cf. Volkmar, *Mose Prophetie*, pp. 29-30; p. 143.

μισθοῦ ἀπεκρίνοντο; T. Levi 14:6: ἐν πλεονεξίᾳ τὰς ἐντολὰς κυρίου διδάξετε; against prophets in Isa. 9:14 (ἀφεῖλεν κύριος) ... προφήτην διδάσκοντα ἄνομα; against leaders and priests in Micah 3:11 οἱ ἡγούμενοι αὐτῆς μετὰ δώρων ἔκρινον, καὶ οἱ ἱερεῖς αὐτῆς μετὰ μισθοῦ ἀπεκρίνοντο[1]; against judges (the sons of Samuel) in 1 Sam. 8:3; cf. Amos 5:12; Isa. 5:23.

Compare finally Jub. 5:16, where it is denied that God, as a righteous judge, respects persons or accepts bribes (cf. e.g. Acts 10:34; Rom. 2:11).

The reproach is phrased in a mingling of two idiomatic expressions: 1) *mirari personam*[2]; 2) *accipere munera*, which are transformed into a single expression:

> *mirari*   (1) *personam*
>   (2) *acceptionem munerum.*

The literal Greek equivalents of the original expressions are 1) θαυμάζειν πρόσωπον, also λαμβάνειν πρόσωπον, and 2) λαμβάνειν δῶρα[3]. The expressions occur side by side in Deut. 16:18-19, an important passage in this connection, because it contains many of the elements present in As. Mos. 5 (see also the commentary on 2:2b):

> Κριτὰς καὶ γραμματοεισαγωγεῖς καταστήσεις σεαυτῷ ἐν πάσαις ταῖς πόλεσίν σου ... καὶ κρινοῦσιν τὸν λαὸν κρίσιν δικαίαν. οὐκ ἐκκλινοῦσιν κρίσιν, οὐκ ἐπιγνώσονται πρόσωπον οὐδὲ λήμψονται δῶρον· τὰ γὰρ δῶρα ἐκτυφλοῖ ὀφθαλμοὺς σοφῶν καὶ ἐξαίρει λόγους δικαίων.

Cf. also 2 Chron. 19:7. The expressions designate partiality and bribery. "The teacher of the Law [may] adapt his teaching to what his hearers may wish to hear. He may, in his teaching, overlook the sins of those on whose favor he depends"[4]. See especially Jude 16 (on the false teachers) θαυμάζοντες πρόσωπα ὠφελείας χάριν[5]; and contrast Luke 20:21, where Jesus is praised: διδάσκαλε, οἴδαμεν ὅτι ὀρθῶς λέγεις καὶ διδάσκεις καὶ οὐ λαμβάνεις πρόσωπον, ἀλλ' ἐπ' ἀληθείας τὴν ὁδὸν τοῦ θεοῦ διδάσκεις. Note the combination of impartiality with "teaching" and "truth".

With the genitive *cupiditatum*, determining *personas* (a biblical style-figure, see grammatical note nr. 191), the author has further corrupted the proper expression. One can compare the genitive construction with Dan. 9:23 Θ, 10:11 Θ, 19 Θ: ἀνὴρ ἐπιθυμιῶν[6]; Ezek. 23:6 Vulgate *juvenes cupidinis* (LXX: νεανίσκοι ἐπίλεκτοι); Sir. 21:25 *persona potentis* (not in LXX; cf. Job 34:19).

Finally, it is said that the teachers will sell their legal settlements. Literally, it is said that they will sell[7] *justitias accipiendo poenas*. The word *poena* should here be taken as "fee"; the meaning must be that paying for justice is bribery. The reproach of

---

[1] Cf. the reproach against the wicked priest in 1QpHab VIII 10-13, see also 1QpHab IX 4-5.
[2] See Ps. Sol. 2:18.
[3] Cf. the substantives προσωποληψία and δωροληψία.
[4] Bauckham, *Jude*, p. 100.
[5] For Jude 16, see again the commentary on 5:6.
[6] Cf. T. Reub. 1:10 ἄρτον ἐπιθυμίας, "pleasant food".
[7] For *pervendere* as a vulgar variant of *vendere*, see grammatical note nr. 44.

bribery is already made in this sentence by the reference to δωροληψία. The mingling of expressions (see above) in that part of the sentence may show that their meanings were not evident, and that an explanatory addition was needed.

Poena is used in Latin for fines or damage compensation, which is not exactly the same as the reimbursement of expenses one pays to a legal advisor. It is likely that *poenas* renders τιμάς[1]. Τιμή is nearly synonymous with ποινή (= *poena*), but also means "payment".

5:6

Finally, Moses is said to predict that the teachers' misconduct will result in misdeeds and the lack of justice among the people. The city and the land they inhabit will be "filled with crime and iniquity"; cf. Hab. 2:17, where it is said that disaster will come διὰ αἵματα ἀνθρώπων καὶ ἀσεβείας γῆς καὶ πόλεως καὶ πάντων τῶν κατοικούντων αὐτήν; Nah. 3:1 Ὦ πόλις αἱμάτων, ὅλη ψευδὴς ἀδικίας πλήρης. The judges, however, who should of course be the ones to uphold justice, will be wicked themselves (cf. perhaps Hab. 1:3-4).

The connection between the injustice which dominates the land and the judges who are criminals themselves refers back to the first part of the quotation in 5:3 *Devitabunt justitiam et accedent ad iniquitatem*.

For the text of this passage, which is in grave disorder, see the textual commentary to lines 92-93. One final remark on the text is called for. The clause *ut qui faciunt erunt impii judices* can be explained as translated above: "since those who will do (them, sc. all these crimes) will be impious judges". The adjective "impious" is rather superfluous here. Perhaps one may understand *impii* as the adverb *impie* (with which it is homophonous), and transpose it after *faciunt: ut qui faciunt impie erunt judices*, "since the ones who act impiously will be judges"[2].

It is said of the judges that they will pronounce sentence according to "anyone's liking". *Quisquae* (= *quisque*) may refer to the ones in whose favour the judges pronounce sentence (for "anyone", see grammatical note nr. 62). In that case, bribes are probably implied, and the reproach directed against the judges is the same as that directed against the teachers in 5:5.

Alternatively, *quisquae* may refer to the judges themselves ("any of them"), and then the reproach concerns the judges' arbitrariness: they will not pronounce sentence according to (God's) justice and law, but according to their own whims. See Micah 7:3 ὁ κριτὴς εἰρηνικοὺς λόγους ἐλάλησεν, καταθύμιον ψυχῆς αὐτοῦ ἐστιν[3]. Also comparable are the accusations against false prophets who pronounce victory or peace only in order to please the king and the people; see 1 Ki. 22:11-18; Micah 3:5; Jer. 6:14; 14:13-15 (esp. 14:14 προαιρέσεις καρδίας αὐτῶν αὐτοὶ προφητεύουσιν ὑμῖν); Ezek. 13:10, 16. See finally the fourth Psalm of Solomon, which describes the hypocrisy of the ἀνθρωπαρέσκοι, eager to condemn the sinners, but full of crimes

---

[1] Hilgenfeld, *Novum Testamentum*, p. 103.
[2] On *facere* + adverb instead of *agere* + adverb, see grammatical note nr. 52.
[3] MT and Vulgate deviate slightly from LXX.

themselves; the Lord will destroy the ἀνθρωπάρεσκον λαλοῦντα νόμον μετὰ δόλου (4:8)[1].

Acting according to "someone's liking" implies acting against God's will in Jude 16: (the false teachers) κατὰ τὰς ἐπιθυμίας αὐτῶν πορευόμενοι; cf. Jer. 18:12; T. Judah 13:2. This contrast is explicit in 2 Tim. 4:3; T. Asher 3:2. In CD II 20-21 it is said that those who err will be destroyed, "because they have done whatever pleased them (בעשותם את רצונם), and did not keep the commandments so as to do them"; cf. CD III 11-12. In CD VIII 7, moreover, the reproach that they are eager to gain property is added.

In campo means "in the field", which is problematic. Perhaps the translator associated the Greek word ἀγορα, the "market-place" where courts of justice were located, with *ager*, and rendered the word with *campus*, a synonym of *ager*. More attractive is Hilgenfeld's suggestion[2] to understand *in campo* as an analytical translation of the adjective ἔμπεδοι, "constantly" (see grammatical note nr. 182).

c. 6:1

As. Mos. 6 describes the concrete historical circumstances which are regarded as the fulfilment of the prophecies of sinfulness quoted and interpreted in chapter 5. The author probably describes the Hasmonean rulers, whom he regards as illegitimate priests. Because of their illegitimacy, he regards the sanctuary to be desecrated, in accordance with the prophecy in 5:3 and its application in 5:4.

1 Then, kings will arise for them to assume government, and they will proclaim themselves priests of the Most High God. They will act most impiously against the Holy of Holies.

6:1

The kings are said to be *imperantes*. Although the (seemingly attributive) use of the participle, as well as the context might suggest that *imperare* should be understood negatively (for instance: "tyrannical kings"), the word *imperare* in itself does not have a negative connotation. It can however, be used as a translation of καταδυναστεύειν (e.g. Wisd. 15:14), which means "to oppress"[3]. But the possibility should not be excluded that *imperantes* must be understood as a Grecism, namely a supplementary participle with verbs meaning "to begin"[4]. In that case, the translation must be: "Then kings will arise for them to assume government".

It is unclear whether *vocari* has been used here passively or reflexively. The expression *vocari ad* is regularly used to mean "to be called to an office or a condition". Accordingly, it would be said in As. Mos. 6:1 that the kings "will (also) be called to

---

[1] It is improbable, however, that these hypocrites, "sitting in the council of the holy" (4:1) are official figures.

[2] "Die Psalmen Salomo's", p. 286.

[3] It should be noted that καταδυναστεύειν is normally used of foreign rulers (cf. also Ezek. 34:27 where *imperans* corresponds to the Septuagint's καταδουλωσάμενος).

[4] Blaß-Debrunner § 414.

officiate as priests"[1]. A reflexive meaning, however, would convey more clearly the negative implication the author undoubtedly intends: "they will proclaim themselves priests of the Most High God (but illegitimately so)"; cf. 5:4 *quidam ... qui non sunt sacerdotes sed servi de servis nati*. Either way, the reference is probably to the Hasmonean rulers, the priests who assumed the title of king—it matches the tendency of As. Mos. to turn this around into kings assuming the title of priest.

These self-made priests will act impiously with regard to the holiness of the temple (cf. 5:3 *contaminabunt inquinationibus domum servitutis suae*). A strong contrast is made between the impious priests and the holiness of the temple by the juxtaposing of two etymological figures: *facient facientes* and *sanctum sanctitatis*[2]. *Impietatem facere* occurs twice in the Vulgate, in Mal. 3:15 and 19(4:1); the Septuagint has ποιεῖν ἄνομα in these cases. If *impietatem facere* in As. Mos. 6:1 is be a possible translation of ἀνομεῖν (for which there is no one-word equivalent in Latin), the etymological figure in Greek may have been something like ἀνομίᾳ ἀνομήσουσι (cf. Deut. 31:29[3]), which would make the contrast with *sanctum sanctitatis* even stronger.

Sanctum sanctitatis must be the well-known biblical designation of the innermost part of the temple, "the Holy of Holies", although it does not occur in this form in the Vulgate, which usually renders the expression *sanctum* or *sancta sanctorum*. But see also Ezek. 45:4 *sanctuarium sanctitatis*, and another variant in Jub. 23:22 *sanctificatio sancta*.

d. *6:2-6*

Following the prophecy of the rise of the Hasmoneans in 6:1, the author of As. Mos. makes Moses predict the particularly bad rule of a "petulant king" (6:2). This king is first characterized as a wicked man (6:2); his misdeeds are described (6:2-4), and his reign is said to be one of terror (6:5). A concluding note compares his rule to that of the Egyptians (6:6). The king is said to rule for 34 years (6:6), which enables us to identify him as Herod the Great (37-4 B.C.E.); the crimes predicted in 6:2-4 agree with what is known of Herod.

2 And a petulant king will succeed them, who will not be of priestly stock, a wicked and cruel man. And he will rule over them as they deserve. 3 He will kill their men of distinction, and he will bury their corpses at unknown places, so that no one knows where their corpses are. 4 He will kill old and young, and he will not spare. 5 Then there

---

[1] For *in* having adopted the final meaning of *ad*, see grammatical note nr. 70. The emendation of *summi* into *summos* ("they will call themselves high priests of God", Charles, *The Assumption*, p. 75) is not only unnecessary (cf. *summus Deus* in As. Mos. 10:7), but it also blurs the contrast between the self-made priests and the Most High God.

[2] This contrast illustrates the artificial character of the use of these figures, suggesting that they do not necessarily derive from a Hebrew or an Aramaic original; see grammatical note nr. 189.

[3] The Vulgate has *inique agetis*. For the use in As. Mos. of *facere* + adverb instead of *agere* + adverb, see grammatical note nr. 52.

will be bitter fear of him in their land. ₆ And he will judge them like the Egyptians for 34 years, and he will punish them.

6:2

The priest-kings will be succeeded by a king "who will not be of priestly stock". By this phrase, this king is distinguished from the illegitimate priests of 6:1. But the distinction is hardly positive, for the rest of the passage leaves no doubt with regard to the king's low moral standards: he is called *rex petulans, ... homo temerarius et improbus*, adjectives which are various expressions of shamelessness and lack of consideration[1]. Probably, the distinction is made in order to give a historical clue: the priest-kings (the Hasmoneans) were succeeded by a secular king, Herod, who indeed was not a Levite. As. Mos. 6:6 confirms the identification of the petulant king with Herod (see below).

The king's brutal character is evidenced by his most cruel government (see 6:3-4). The author of As. Mos. comments: he rules in the way the people deserve[2]. *Judicare* here obviously has an unfavourable overtone (which may explain why it is followed by a *dativus incommodi*; see grammatical note 116): his rule is also God's punishment of the people; see 5:1b-2a *reges participes scelerum et punientes eos*, and cf. 6:6.

6:3-4

In this passage, the cruelty of the king's rule is worked out in detail.

(1) The king "will kill their *principales* by the sword". The instrumental ablative *gladio* (ῥομφαίᾳ), or, alternatively, the instrumental prepositional phrase *in ore gladii* (ἐν στόματι ῥομφαίας), is a very common expression, indicating that someone's death is caused by violence. The king's victims are called *principales*, which is a very general indication of "important people" (cf. the Vulgate of Acts 25:23 *viri principales*, a translation of οἱ ἄνδρες οἱ κατ' ἐξοχήν). In Nah. 3:10 it is prophesied that the "grandees" (οἱ μεγιστᾶνες LXX; *optimates* Vulgate) will be killed; see also Hos. 7:16 *cadent in gladio principes eorum* (LXX: ἄρχοντες αὐτῶν); cf. Ps. Sol. 17:12.

(2) The king will "bury their corpses on unknown places". In my edition, I have adopted the common emendation of the manuscript's SINGULIET (SINGULI, ET?) into *sepeliet*.

An alternative suggestion, which has much to recommend it, was made by H. Rönsch[3]. He proposed to read *stinguet* for *singuliet*. *Stinguet* would then be an apocopated form of *extinguet*, "he will murder" (see grammatical note nr. 14). No doubt, *stinguet* is much closer to the manuscript's reading. Moreover, it seems more logical to say that someone will "murder" people at unknown places, so that it is not possible for their relatives to bury them. The complaint about the inability to bury the dead is a traditional one; see Ps. 79(78):3 (cf. 1 Macc. 7:17); Jer. 8:2; 14:16; 16:4, 6; 25:33[4].

---

[1] Cf. Caesar's description of the Germanic king Ariovistus, of whom it is said in *Bell. Gall.* I 31:12-13: *Ariovistum ... superbe et crudeliter imperare ... Hominem esse barbarum, iracundum, temerarium* (quoted in Forcellini IV, p. 678a).

[2] For the terminology used, cf. Apoc. Ezra 2:20 κύριε, ἀξίως ἐπάγεις ἐφ' ἡμᾶς.

[3] "Sprachliche Parallelen", pp. 88-89.

[4] If Rönsch's proposal to read *stinguet* is followed, Jub. 23:23 would furnish an additional, important parallel. In that passage the same elements as in As. Mos. 6:3-4 are found:

(cont.)

On the other hand, one should feel somewhat uneasy about the introduction of another vulgarism into the text. But even more important is the question whether one can say that *corpora*, "bodies" or "corpses", are "killed". Therefore, it seems wiser to stick to *sepeliet*, which gives good sense, and which is an ordinary form, ordinarily constructed.

(3) The enumeration of the king's actions ends with a very general crime: he will kill anyone, without the least reserve. As often in the biblical literature polar concepts are juxtaposed in order to express inclusiveness. In this case, old and young are contrasted (*major natu* is the common Vulgate equivalent of πρεσβύτερος). The same contrast is used in Ps. Sol. 2:8; in connection with massive killing: Deut. 28:50; Ps. Sol. 17:11.

These royal crimes are part and parcel of ancient despotism and cannot by themselves justify the identification of the petulant king with Herod. However, once this identification is made on the basis of 6:5, it is entirely possible to compare the description of 6:3-4 with some episodes from the life of king Herod, as described by Flavius Josephus.

Josephus reports that king Herod, as soon as he had captured Jerusalem, confiscated the wealth of the rich (οἱ εὔποροι) and killed forty-five leaders (πρῶτοι) of Antigonus' party (*Ant. Jud.* XV 5; cf. *Bell. Jud.* I 358); see also *Ant. Jud.* XIV 175 (cf. XV 4). In the last period of his reign he had Matthias and his companions burnt alive (*Ant. Jud.* XVII 167; *Bell. Jud.* I 655); Matthias had incited the young men of Jerusalem to pull down the eagle Herod had erected on the Great Gate of the temple. According to Josephus, this Matthias had been a most learned man, a great interpreter of the πάτριοι νόμοι, and he was much loved by the people (*Ant. Jud.* XVII 149; *Bell. Jud.* I 648-649). During his last illness, Herod commanded the notables of the entire country to be executed at the hour of his death (*Ant. Jud.* XVII 178; *Bell. Jud.* I 659-660); Christian tradition of course accuses him of the massacre of the innocent children of Bethlehem (Matt. 2:16). As Smallwood noted, the last two stories are "typical tyrant-legends", the former of which is elsewhere told in connection with Alexander Jannaeus[1]. The emergence of such legends testifies to Herod's bad reputation, especially at the end of his reign, and confirms the possibility that As. Mos. 6:2-6 indeed deals with this king.

To the secret killings described in As. Mos. 6:3, one may compare Josephus's account in *Ant. Jud.* XV 366, on Herod's measures to prevent revolt:

> No meeting of citizens was permitted, nor were walking together or being together permitted, and all their movements were observed. Those who were caught were punished severely, and many were taken, either openly or secretly, to the fortress of Hyrcania and there put to death (trans. Marcus-Wikgren).

6:5-6

As. Mos. 6:5-6 seems to be a concluding statement concerning the petulant king. In 6:5, his reign is summarily characterized as a rule of "terror" (*timor acervus*; cf. the use of φόβος in Sib. Or. III 178; IV 87; for *acervus* one may compare the characteriza-

---

the Lord will raise up sinners with no mercy for either young or old, who will shed much blood, and there will be no one who will bury.

[1] *The Jews under Roman Rule*, pp. 103-104.

tion of the Athenian governor's rule in 2 Macc. 6:3 χαλεπὴ δὲ καὶ τοῖς ὅλοις ἦν δυσχερὴς ἡ ἐπίτασις τῆς κακίας). In 6:6a a variation is made on the clause 6:2b— *judicabit illis quomodo digni erunt* becomes *faciet in eis judicia quomodo fecerunt in illis Aegypti per XXX et IIII annos*. In 6:6b (*et punivit eos*), the king's cruel actions described in 6:3-4 are summarized.

The Egyptians are mentioned, because they are regarded as exceptionally cruel oppressors. By recalling the Egyptians, whose rule the petulant king's government equals, the author closes the circle of Israel's fateful history (it should be remembered that the story of As. Mos. is staged right after the exodus from Egypt, and immediately prior to the entrance into the land, see 1:4[1]). The author implies that the people, in their condition of disgrace, have returned to the days prior to God's deliverance through the hand of Moses,[2]. During the petulant king's rule, the prophecy in Deut. 28:68 (cf. 28:60) has been fulfilled that the Lord would bring the people back to Egypt, along the road which he said they would never see again. Perhaps the mention of the bitter fear the king will cause (6:5) is to be seen in the same connection, as a fulfilment of the prophetic words in Deut. 28:66-67. In Deut. 28:66-68 it is said that the people will yearn for the evening in the morning and for the morning in the evening, ἀπὸ ("because of") τοῦ φόβου τῆς καρδίας σου, ἃ φοβηθήσῃ ... καὶ ἀποστρέψει σε κύριος εἰς Αἴγυπτον.

The main argument for identifying the petulant king with Herod the Great is the mention of the number of years this king reigned. Josephus informs us that Herod ruled for thirty seven years from the moment he was appointed king by the Romans, but that the period of his effective rule was thirty four years (ἀφ' οὗ μὲν ἀποκτείνας Ἀντίγονον ἐκράτησεν ἔτη τέσσαρα καὶ τριάκοντα, *Bell. Jud.* I 665; cf. *Ant. Jud.* XVII 191). If the textual transmission of As. Mos. has not caused damage to the number, the reference indeed seems unmistakable: in this era there was no other king who ruled for this exact number of years in Palestine. The other references in 6:2-8a fit Herod very well, so that the identification may be accepted.

The number of years of the government of Herod is specifically mentioned probably to enable that the intended reader to recognize the reference. This means that As. Mos. cannot have been written too long after Herod's death, at a time when the memory of his rule and the duration of it was still relatively fresh.

e. 6:7-9

In this section, Moses predicts what will happen after Herod has been succeeded by his sons. The petulant king's sons will rule for a short while, but punishment will soon be executed by the king from the West. Presumably, the author intends to make Moses prophesy the coming of Roman forces, who will act as the king from the East had done (see 3:1-3). However, the author also wants to make the Western king's ac-

---

[1] Cf. Janssen, *Das Gottesvolk*, p. 106: "der Verfasser [sieht] sich wie in der ägyptischen Gefangenschaft".

[2] Cf. von Rad, *Das 5. Buch Mose*, p. 126, commenting on Deut. 28:68: "etwas wie eine göttliche Liquidation der gesamten von Jahwe veranstalteten Heilsgeschichte".

tions appear relatively insignificant in view of the still worse persecution in the time of the end.

₇ And he will bring forth children who will succeed him. They will rule for shorter periods. ₈ Cohorts will come into their territory, and a mighty king from the West, who will defeat them, ₉ and lead them off in chains. And he will burn part of their temple with fire, some he will crucify near their city.

6:7

The petulant king will be succeeded by his sons[1]. It is not clear whether the plural *nati* refers only to those of Herod's sons who would rule successively in Jerusalem[2], or to all four sons among whom his kingdom was divided. *Partes* in 6:8 is ambiguous as well (see below).

Their government is said to last for *breviora tempora*. Ewald[3], and many after him, took these words to mean "a shorter while", that is, shorter than Herod's 34 years[4]. A less convincing understanding of *breviora tempora* was suggested by Volkmar[5]. The "shorter times" would have to be interpreted as an expression of the strong expectation of the arrival of the end. The rules of Herod's sons are signals that the end is no longer far off: the times will become shorter. The motif of an acceleration of the times is well-known from 4 Ezra and 2 Baruch; see 4 Ezra 4:26; 12:20, 30; 2 Bar. 20:1; 54:1; 83:1; 85:10; also Sir. 33:10; LAB 19:13; cf. Mark 13:20; Matt. 24:22. The phrase *breviora tempora dominabunt* (6:7) is however insufficient evidence to warrant the conclusion that the author uses here the tradition of the shortening of the final stage of history. He may equally well have thought that Herod's sons were likely to rule for shorter periods than their father. The fact that Archelaus reigned for only ca. 10 years (4 B.C.E.-6 C.E.) can only have confirmed him in this idea[6].

6:8-9

It is uncertain how the words *in partes eorum* (if this emendation is correct) should be constructed. If they are taken with *dominabunt* in 6:7, there seems to be a reference to the division of Herod's kingdom among his sons: "they will rule in their (respective) parts (of the inheritance)". The phrase, however, may also be taken as the complement of *chortis*[7] *venient*: "cohorts will come into their *partes*", that is, "into their region" (for *pars* or the plural *partes* meaning "region" or "country", see commentary on

---

[1] *Succedere* (l. em.) is constructed with the reflexive pronoun *sibi*, to which construction several commentators have objected. But the construction is perfectly classical, *sibi* referring to the subject of the clause.

[2] Reuss, *Die Geschichte der Heiligen Schriften*, p. 705: "Der [Verfasser] konnte ... an Archelaus und Agrippa denken, die ja allein für einen Jerusalemer Interesse hatten".

[3] "Monumenta sacra et profana", p. 5.

[4] See further the Introduction, section I,c and V,b.

[5] *Mose Prophetie*, p. 34. Volkmar prefers, however, to emend the underlying βραχυτέ-ρους into τραχύτερους, the times will become "noch schlimmer".

[6] Charles, *The Assumption*, pp. lvii.

[7] *Chortis = cohortes*; see grammatical notes nrs. 3 and 13.

3:13). In that case, there is no particular emphasis on Herod's inheritance being divided.

The king from the West is habitually identified with the Roman governor of Syria, Varus. This identification is based on the assumption that the partial destruction of the temple in Jerusalem, prophesied in As. Mos. 6:8b, is a *vaticinium ex eventu*, reflecting the rebellion against the commander of Jerusalem and the intervention by his superior, Varus, in 4 B.C.E. During this rebellion, parts of the temple premises were burnt down.

Objections to this identification can, however, be made on both historical and literary grounds.

(1) G. Hölscher has noted a number of incongruities between the reports on the events under Varus (to be found in the works of Josephus) and the description of the western king's actions in As. Mos. 6:8-9[1]. Hölscher overstresses the point that Varus was not a king and that he came from Antiochia, not from "the West"; it does not seem impossible that the author of As. Mos. regarded Varus as the representative of "the king from the West"[2]. On the other hand, Hölscher's criticisms do show that the description of the Roman intervention in As. Mos. 6:8-9 covers the events under Varus only superficially. An abstract from Josephus (*Bell. Jud.* II 45-75; *Ant. Jud.* XVII 254-298[3]) may serve to illustrate his point. Varus came to restore order in Jerusalem, where rebellion had broken out against the local commander, Sabinus. This Sabinus and his soldiers battled with the Jews in the temple court. The mob climbed on the roof of the porticoes surrounding the temple-court, to which Sabinus' soldiers subsequently set fire. After this, Sabinus' soldiers plundered "God's treasury", while they remained besieged in the temple court. Varus entered Jerusalem with two legions, relieved Sabinus, rounded up the rebels and crucified about two thousand of them.

(2) Such historical incongruities are not decisive. It is conceivable that the author of As. Mos., who clearly tends to simplify history, has refrained from giving the details in this instance as well. It must then also be recognized that the description of the Western king's actions is in fact of a rather general and traditional kind: defeat, captivity, destruction and executions. Between 100 B.C.E. and 100 C.E. there were numerous Roman interventions, all of which contain the four elements listed above. Moreover, on a general level, the description of the Eastern king's actions in As. Mos. 3:1-3 contains practically the same elements, as does the description of the king of the kings of the world in 8:1-5.

The only outstanding element is the explicit mention of the temple's destruction being partial. This is a surprising detail, which requires an explanation other than the author's aspiration to historical precision. As appears from As. Mos. 7:1, the Western king's actions are seen as the breaking point in history: after his appearance, "the times will end". Hölscher comments: "Es ist nicht wahrscheinlich, daß jener gelegentliche Brand des Tempelhallendachs im Jahre 4 v. Chr. dem Apokalyptiker so bemerkenswert erschienen wäre, daß er ihn als Vorzeichen des nahenden Weltendes hätte

---

[1] "Über die Entstehungszeit", p. 111.

[2] Clemen, "Die Entstehungszeit des Himmelfahrt des Mose", p. 73.

[3] Cf. Smallwood, *The Jews under Roman Rule*, pp. 110-113. Smallwood accepts the identification of As. Mos. 6:8-9 with Varus' war.

ansehen sollen"[1]. It is possible, however, that the author did interpret the event in such a manner, but it is then unlikely that he would have said that just a "part of the tempel will be burnt". In that case, he could just as well have said: "they will set the temple on fire".

A similar point must be made with regard to the phrase *aliquos* (τινες) *crucifigit*. According to Josephus, two thousand rebels were crucified by Varus. Josephus possibly exaggerated the number, but regardless of the exact number who were crucified, one would not expect an author who wishes to emphasize the importance of the event to say that only "some will be crucified".

These two qualifiers, *pars* and *aliqui*, must therefore not be seen as indicating how small the effects of the Western king's actions actually were, but as hints to the author's intended readers not to overestimate the importance of the events described[2]. That is to say, the author's description does not allow us to gauge the actual extent of the events described. The partial destruction of the temple and the execution of a limited number of people are the divine answer to the pre-eschatological chaos caused by the general sinfulness. After that, the times will come to an end (*ex quo facto finientur tempora* 7:1), and real trouble will begin: the rule of the pestilential men (7:3-10), followed by the advent of the eschatological enemy, the king of the kings of the earth, who will crucify all Jews, and torture even the renegades (8:1-2).

If this is so, the author sees himself at the end of history. To him, the eschatological times are near. But the eschatological times will not start with the advent of God's kingdom (10:1-2). Unparalleled sinfulness and great woe will first come over the world, making the present chaos and imminent destruction into mere trifles by comparison.

Taking all this into consideration, one may conclude that 6:8-9 reflects the violent Roman interference in Judean affairs at the beginning of the first century C.E. The passage may also contain remote reminiscences of the actions taken by Varus. But the image the author gives of the Roman intervention is of a general, simplified nature. The author does not aim to do justice to the details of history. To him, the Roman intervention is already history; it is his present as well as the final stage of history; things will only become worse in the near future.

---

[1] Hölscher, "Über die Entstehungszeit", p. 112.

[2] Therefore Hölscher's suggestion ("Über die Entstehungszeit", pp. 124-127) that the temple cult continued after 70 C.E., and that therefore the destruction referred to in As. Mos. 6 (which, according to Hölscher, is the destruction by Titus) is correctly characterized as partial, is equally off the mark. Hölscher withdrew the suggestion in the second part of his article, p. 158, published some months later.

A CALCULATION CONCERNING THE TIME OF THE END

It is clear that 7:1-2 was a crucial passage, but little is left of it in the manuscript. Still legible is the announcement that from this moment on (*ex quo facto*; see grammatical note nr. 136) the "times will end". *Momento* may belong to this phrase; if so, the times will end "suddenly" (see also the commentary on 8:1a-b). Further, there is mention of four hours (*horae IIII veniant*), of "beginnings" and "endings" (*initiis tribus ad exitus ... propter initium*), and of several numbers, both cardinals and ordinals. The rest is so illegible that it is impossible to reconstruct meaningful phrases. Any attemptt to interpret this passage is futile because of the extremely poor state of conservation of this part of the text.

Two general remarks, however, can be made. First, the phrase *ex quo facto finientur tempora* expressly indicates to the intended readers that the circumstances under which they are presently living and which have been described in chapters 5 and 6 lead directly to the beginning of eschatological events. At the same time, it points to the imminent denouement of history as described in chapters 7-10. The latter is anticipated in 5:1, where the description of the author's recent history and his present is headed by the phrase *cum adpropiabunt tempora arguendi*.

Second, the numbers mentioned in 7:1-2 suggest that this passage contained some kind of calculation about the proportional duration of this stage of history. The occurrence of ordinals among the numbers included strongly suggests that the numbers are fractions. That must mean that the numbers do not indicate a specific number of days or years that must elapse until the final consummation, but divide history into constituent parts of varying proportions. It cannot be established, however, whether the duration of eschatological events is related to the duration of the world's history (or part of it), or whether the eschatological scenario is divided into interrelated periods of time.

THE SINFUL RULERS OF THE TIME OF THE END

In 7:3-10 the author of As. Mos. describes the wicked men who will rule during the first stage of the eschatological events. Whether these men were actually ruling when As. Mos. was being written, or whether the author expected their rule in the (immediate) future is not clear. It can be assumed, however, that the author's description relates to specific people, contemporaries of the author and his readers. It cannot be said, however, that his description "is drawn from life"[1]: the description is heavily biased, consisting of a list of invectives, similar to those that can be found in various Jewish and Christian writings of the time. A long, hateful tirade occurs, in which the rulers are depicted with the most vicious characteristics conceivable[2]. But no names or even functions are given, and although the readers were probably expected to recognize the description, it is impossible for us to know whom exactly the author of As. Mos. had in mind[3].

The men who figure in 7:3-10 are characterized only in a general way. Since the author's main objection boils down to the accusation of hypocrisy, it is likely that they shared his values, but that they did not, in the author's opinion, live according to those values. They belonged to the ruling classes (7:3, 8). The accusations of intemperateness (7:4, 8) are probably exaggerated, but it is unlikely that they regarded a display of plainness and poverty as exceptionally virtuous. They held themselves to be just (7:3), which may here mean that they regarded themselves as part of God's people; they highly valued charity (7:6) and purity (7:10). The author of As. Mos. denies them all these quali-

---

[1] Charles, *The Assumption*, p. 23.

[2] The translator has used relatively many Vulgar Latin expressions, presumably colloquialisms; see grammatical note nr. 41.

[3] Schmidt and Merx, "Die Assumptio Mosis", p. 121, argued on the basis of the speech against the Pharisees in Matt. 23:1-36 that the persons described in As. Mos. 7 are Pharisees; cf. Geiger's criticism, "Apokryphische Apokalypsen", p. 44: "Die Pharisäer werden von unsern Kritikern noch immer in der gallsüchtigen Weise vorgeführt, wie sie der leidenschaftliche Parteieifer des Evangelisten in heftiger Strafrede zeichnet". Charles, *The Assumption*, p. 24, on the other hand argued that the author cannot have intended the Pharisees, because the rulers in As. Mos. 7 are presented as openly gluttonous drunkards, whereas the Pharisees were "decidedly ascetic". But Charles, too, fails to distinguish here between a matter-of-fact description and a description inspired by hate.

ties, but it is unlikely that he and the "rulers" had fundamentally different views on these matters[1].

The ethics which underly 7:3-10 are essentially the common stock of contemporary moral teaching, pagan and Jewish[2]. The only typically Jewish issue in the list is perhaps the preoccupation with ritual purity expressed in 7:10 (*dicent: "Noli ne me tange, ne inquines me"*)[3]. The vices mentioned are: mischief and impiety (7:3), hypocrisy (7:3, 4, 6, 7), anger, deceit, self-satisfaction (7:4), debauchery (7:4, 8), oppression of the poor (7:6), murder, quarrel, secrecy, crime, iniquity (7:7), arrogance (7:8), impurity and insolence (7:9).

As. Mos. 7:3-10 can be compared, as regards form and content, to the Hellenistic form of the ἔκφρασις[4]. This form consists of descriptions of types of persons (e.g. the perfect man, the fool) by enumerating their characteristic virtues or vices[5]. Related to this form are the lists of virtues and vices (*Tugend- und Lasterkataloge*), in which virtues and vices are enumerated without being connected with the description of typical characters[6]. These two forms were popular in pagan and Jewish ethical literature of the Hellenistic period, as well as in the New Testament Epistles and other early Christian literature (especially the Testaments of the Twelve Patriarchs). One of the longest lists of vices is in fact found in Philo's *De sacrificiis* 32. There, Philo enumerates almost 150 characteristics of the "pleasure-lover" (φιλήδονος; see, in the same work, §§ 22-23, 27[7]). See further e.g.

---

[1] See Reese, *Die Geschichte Israels*, p. 104: "Von Kap. 7 läßt sich ... über die Person des Vf. soviel sagen, daß er der herrschenden Oberschicht nicht angehört, vielmehr unter ihr und ihre Maßnahmen zu leiden hat. Er fühlt sich nicht Anhänger einer Partei, sondern als Angehöriger des Gottesvolkes, das unter der frevelhaften Herrschaft der Mächtigen seufzt und voll Sehnsucht nach der Offenbarung der Herrschaft Gottes sich ausrichtet."

[2] Cf. Malherbe, *Moral Exhortation*, p. 138: "In their content [the vice lists] tended to represent generally held views". For every vice listed in As. Mos. 7:3-10 parallels in pagan and Jewish literature (including the Old Testament) can be found; see esp. the wealth of material found in Van der Horst, *The Sentences of Pseudo-Phocylides*; Hollander and De Jonge, *The Testaments of the Twelve Patriarchs*; Niebuhr, *Gesetz und Paränese*.

[3] According to Vögtle, *Die Tugend- und Lasterkataloge*, p. 208, ἀκαθαρσία and related concepts (μοίχος, πορνεία etc.) do not figure in the pagan catalogues of vices.

[4] Cf. Vögtle, *Die Tugend- und Lasterkataloge*, pp. 101-102.

[5] Berger, "Hellenistische Gattungen", pp. 1201-1202: "die Ekphrasis ... stellt das Nebeneinander von Eigenschaften dar ... Kennzeichen der Gattung ist besonders die Dominanz von katalogartigen Reihen."

[6] Berger, "Hellenistische Gattungen", p. 1089: "Kataloge von Tugenden und Lastern [entstehen] aus Beschreibungen (Ekphraseis) 'typischer' Personen".

[7] Berger, "Hellenistische Gattungen", p. 1090: "Die Kataloge [*sc.* in *De sacrificiis* 20-45] sind von ermüdender Vollständigkeit".

Wisd. 14:22-26, 1QS IV 9-14; Sib. Or. II 254-262; III 36-43; 763-765;
IV 31-34. Much material, from Jewish, early Christian as well as pagan
literature, has been collected by Vögtle, *Die Tugend- und Lasterkataloge* (1936).

The ἔκφρασις of As. Mos. 7:3-10 describes the author's opponents
with the characteristics of the typical sinner; for this polemical application of the form compare 1 En. 10:20; 91:5-7; 94:6; 95:2-7; 96:7; 2
Bar. 73:4; Jub. 21:21; 23:14[1]; cf. 2 Tim. 3:1-7; T. Levi 14:5-6; 17:11.

3 a And pestilent and impious men will rule over them, b who proclaim
themselves to be righteous. 4 And they will excite their wrathful souls;
they will be deceitful men, self-complacent, hypocrites in all their
dealings, and who love to debauch each hour of the day, devourers,
gluttons, 5 . . . . . . 6 who eat the possessions of . . ., saying they do this
out of compassion . . . 7 murderers, complainers, liars, hiding themselves lest they be recognized as impious, full of crime and iniquity,
from sunrise to sunset 8 saying: 'Let us have extravagant banquets, let
us eat and drink. And let us act as if we are princes'. 9 And their hands
and minds will deal with impurities, and their mouth will speak
enormities, saying in addition to all this: 10 'Keep off, do not touch me,
lest you pollute me ...'

7:3

The author says that impious men described in 7:3-10 "will rule" (*regnabunt*). There
are no indications about which functions, if any, these men would fulfil. Probably,
regnare must be taken to refer to the "ruling classes", the elite (compare the equally
vague designation ἄρχοντες[2], especially known from the New Testament). It has
been claimed that in the first century only the priests or other members of the San-
hedrin could have been referred to by the word *regnare*[3]. However, such a concept of

---

[1] Vögtle, *Die Tugend- und Lasterkataloge*, pp. 100-102.
[2] In the LXX, ἄρχειν can translate משׁל, equivalent to the Vulgate's *dominari*. The Vulgate consistently renders the New Testament's ἄρχων with *princeps*. *Regnare* is equivalent to
ἄρχειν in Judg. 9:22 (Hebr.: שׂור).
[3] Geiger, "Apokryphische Apokalypsen", p. 45-46. The phrase *impii docentes se esse
justos* was taken by Geiger as a pun on the name "Sadducees" (cf. צדיקים, "*justi*"), a pun
Geiger adduced as additional evidence that this passage is directed against the Sadducees. But
of course, an opponent's piety or impiety is an author's personal evaluation, which we cannot
verify on the basis of historical criteria. Compare also the rather naive comment by Charles,
The Assumption, p. 26, on *impii*: "A natural description of the Sadducees from the standpoint
of a Pharisee. It could not, however, be used of a Pharisee".

the Judean polity in this period assumes more of a regulated and institutionalized society than is probably warranted.

Pestilentiosus is a Vulgarism, an extended form of *pestilens* (see grammatical note nr. 41). In the Vulgate, *pestilens* is used to render λοιμός, as an adjective meaning "unhealthy", figuratively "bringing destruction", more generally "mischievous"; see 1 Macc. 10:61 (*viri pestilentes ... viri iniqui*, Septuagint: ἄνδρες λοιμοί ... ἄνδρες παράνομοι); 15:3, 21; see also Prov. 29:8, and cf. *pestifer* Acts 24:5. In 1 Sam. 30:22 λοιμός is paired with πονηρός (Vulgate: *pessimus et iniquus*). Impiety (ἀσέβεια) is the general denominator of sinfulness, both in the pagan and in the Jewish conception[1] (see also As. Mos. 6:1; 7:7; 9:3); in lists of vices, ἀσεβής occurs in e.g. Philo, *De mutatione nominum* 197; *De sacrificiis* 22; *De posteritate Caini* 52; Sib. Or. III 36.

The accusation of impiety is compounded by the accusation of hypocrisy: they are impious whilst they proclaim themselves to be righteous. Hypocrisy is the dominant theme of the description in As. Mos. 7:3-10; see 7:4, 6, 7, and compare the speeches against the scribes and Pharisees in the Gospels, esp. Matt. 23:28: "To the people you seem from the outside to be righteous (δίκαιοι), but on the inside you are full of deceit and lawlessness (μεστοὶ ὑποκρίσεως καὶ ἀνομίας)"; cf. also Isa. 5:21: οὐαὶ οἱ συνετοὶ ἐν ἑαυτοῖς καὶ ἐνώπιον ἑαυτῶν ἐπιστήμονες, and Rom. 1:22 φάσκοντες εἶναι σοφοὶ ἐμωράνθησαν.

Docere does not necessarily refer to the activity of teaching (διδάσκειν)[2]. It is also used in the Vulgate as an equivalent of ἀναγγέλλειν, "to proclaim" (see e.g. Deut. 24:8; Josh. 4:22; Isa. 2:3), or even simply "to say"[3].

7:4

The sinful rulers will "excite the anger of their spirits". *Ira animorum suorum* is a biblical construction, in which an emotion or a quality of mind is combined with the genitive ψυχῆς (or πνεύματος, as in Ps. Sol. 18:7 ἐν σοφίᾳ πνεύματος; T. Jos. 7:2 πόνος καρδίας ... καὶ οἱ στεναγμοὶ τοῦ πνεύματός μου) in order to express a strong personal commitment; see for instance ὀδύνη ψυχῆς Isa. 38:15(14); T. Judah 11:4; T. Zeb. 9:6; πικρία ψυχῆς Sir. 7:11(12); ταπείνωσις ψυχῆς Ps. Sol. 3:8; T. Judah 19:2. Anger is one of the affections generally condemned in the Hellenistic period[4].

---

[1] Foerster, "σέβομαι κτλ.", esp. pp. 186-188.

[2] Volkmar, *Mose Prophetie*, p. 105, identified the impious rulers as the Sadducees, apparently because of the word *docentes* ("eine sadducäische *Volks-*, ja *Lehrer-* oder Rabbinen-Partei"). It is not clear why these teachers, according to Volkmar, must be Sadducees. Laperrousaz, *Le Testament*, p. 121, translates, without justification, "prétendront", so also Priest, "Testament of Moses", p. 930, "who represent themselves". No doubt, this reflects the general sense, but *docere* does not mean "to pretend".

[3] Schniewind, "ἀγγελία κτλ.", p. 61: "fast = εἰπεῖν". Hilgenfeld, *Novum Testamentum*, p. 104, emended *docentes* into *dicentes*; however, it is unlikely that a simple and clear *dicentes* should be corrupted into the more difficult *docentes*.

[4] Van der Horst, *The Sentences of Pseudo-Phocylides*, p. 153. See, in connection with the mind, Horace, *Epist.* I, 2, 62 *ira furor brevis est: animum rege*; see also Hollander and De Jonge, *The Testaments of the Twelve Patriarchs*, pp. 280-282.

Next¹, they are called *dolosi*. *Dolosus* renders δόλιος, "deceitful", "wily", generally regarded as a particularly nasty vice; in the lists of vices and ἐκφράσεις of sinners, δόλος and δόλιος occur in e.g. Wisd. 14:25; Sib. Or. III 36-37 (αἳ γένος αἰμοχαρὲς δόλιον κακὸν ἀσεβέων τε // ψευδῶν διγλώσσων ἀνθρώπων καὶ κακοηθῶν); Rom. 1:29; 1 Pet. 2:1. *Sibi placentes* can be compared with φίλαυτος in the list of vices in 2 Tim. 3:2. Aristotle regards φιλαυτία as the opposite of φιλαγαθία². In *De specialibus legibus* I 333, Philo calls φιλαυτία "the great evil"; Cain is called φίλαυτος (as opposed to φιλόθεος) in *De sacrificiis* 3; *Quod deterius* 32, 68, 78; *De posteritate Caini* 21³. *Ficti* means "hypocrites". According to Wisd. 1:5, the Holy Spirit of discipline avoids insincerity (δόλος; Vulgate: *fictum*); cf. δόλος (Vulgate: *fictio*) in the list of vices in Wisd. 14:25.

The last sin mentioned in this section is immoderateness. Immoderateness is a major vice in pagan and Jewish moral teaching. Here, as in 7:8, immoderateness is concentrated on eating and drinking⁴. Much emphasis is laid on the all-encompassing character of the pestilent men's sinful behaviour (see also 7:7): they are hypocrites in "everything" they do, and they like to have banquets on "every" (or "any") hour of the day; cf. Isa. 5:11 οἱ ἐγειρόμενοι τὸ πρωὶ καὶ τὸ σίκερα διώκοντες, οἱ μένοντες τὸ ὀψέ (Vulgate: *qui consurgitis mane ad ebrietatem sectandam et potandum usque ad vesperam*).

Devorator, "devourer", and *gula*, "throat" (here *pars pro toto*, "glutton"), are vulgar abuses (see grammatical note nr. 41). *Devorator* is used in the Vulgate of Luke 7:34, a passage in which the author of the Gospel quotes popular objections against Jesus: *ecce homo devorator et bibens vinum* (φάγος⁵ καὶ οἰνοπότης), *amicus publicanorum et peccatorum*; cf. the Vulgate of Luke 15:30 on the prodigal son: *devoravit* (καταφαγών) *substantiam suam cum meretricibus*. Gluttony is a major vice condemned in the list of vices in 2 Pet. 2:13-14, but the partial resemblance of this list to As. Mos. 7:4 must not lead to the assumption of a direct literary connection between these two texts⁶.

7:5

7:5 is largely illegible. In the manuscript, seven lines are almost entirely lost. It is very probable, however, that the list of accusations continued, but precisely in what strain is impossible to determine. Possibly, mention was made here of sexual misbehaviour, a vice rarely lacking in Jewish moral instruction⁷, but absent in the remainings of As.

---

¹ After *et hi sucitabunt*, the clause *qui erunt &c.* is most naturally understood as a rendering of a Greek participle such as ὄντες; cf. grammatical note nr. 183.
² Grundmann, "ἀγαθός κτλ.", p. 17; for more pagan evidence, see Vögtle, *Die Tugend- und Lasterkataloge*, p. 201.
³ Bultmann, "καυχάομαι κτλ.", p. 648.
⁴ Cf. Foerster, "ἄσωτος, ἀσωτία", pp. 504-505, and Niebuhr, *Gesetz und Paränese*, pp. 93, 117-120, 132-133, 152 (on the Testaments of the Twelve Patriarchs; see also Hollander and De Jonge, *The Testaments of the Twelve Patriarchs*, pp. 208-211), p. 220 (on 4 Macc. 2:7).
⁵ The Vulgate of the parallel Matt. 11:19 translates *vorax*.
⁶ Against Charles, *The Assumption*, p. lxiii.
⁷ Cf. Vögtle, *Die Tugend- und Lasterkataloge*, pp. 107-111; Niebuhr, *Gesetz und Paränese*, pp. 92-93, 161 on the Testaments of the Twelve Patriarchs, pp. 177-185 on the Si-

(cont.)

Mos. 7:3-10. The last word of 7:5 probably is *delentes* (in the manuscript, *elentes* is legible), "destroying". In Ps. Sol. 4:11-12 a corrupted man is described who "destroys a house" (ἠρήμωσεν οἶκον ἕνεκεν ἐπιθυμίας παρανόμου κτλ.).

7:6

In 7:6 the rulers are said to be "eaters of possessions". An important parallel for this remarkable image[1] is Mark 12:40, on the scribes οἱ κατεσθίοντες τὰς οἰκίας τῶν χηρῶν. This passage probably has induced Deane to restore *viduarum* instead of the more usual conjecture *pauperum*[2] preceding *bonorum comestores*. In any case, a contrast is made between the rulers' debauchery and the poverty of other people; for the same contrast see Ezek. 16:49; Ps. Sol. 4:11-12; 1 En. 96:4-8; 99:2; 102:9; Sib. Or. III 41, 242. The contrast seems to imply that the rulers' craving for luxury is at the expense of those who are not as well off. Perhaps that implication was made explicit by the illegible word at the end of 7:6. There, Ceriani and Clemen read QU . . . SEET. Of these letters, only SE is certain; if the letters ET stand for the conjunction *et*, *se* can hardly be anything else than the ending of an adverb (*-se*), determining the clause in 7:6. *Qu(a)estuose*, "eager for gain" might be a possibility[3] (cf. Jude 16 θαυμάζοντες πρόσωπα ὠφελείας χάριν, Vulgate: *quaestus causa*).

The hypocrisy of the rulers is accentuated by placing into their own mouth the absurd claim that this is their way of showing charity to the poor. Works of charity (ἐλεημοσύνη) are also charged with the odium of hypocrisy in Matt. 6:2. Lack of charity and not caring for the poor seems to be a specifically Jewish concern[4]. It is contained in the list of vices in Wisd. 14:26 (χάριτος ἀμνηστία); cf. Wisd. 2:10.

7:7

The next three character traits in 7:7, *exterminatores, quaerulosi, fallaces* are among the commonest in the lists of vices. For the accusation of murder, see Wisd. 14:25 (αἷμα καὶ φόνος); 1 En. 99:15; Sib. Or. III 36 (αἱμαχαρής), 379 (combined with ἔρις, cf. Rom. 1:29); V 431; T. Asher 2:7; 4:2; cf. Matt. 23:34-36. *Querulosus* is a rare word, meaning "full of complaints". According to 2 Bar. 73:4 "judgements, condemnations and contentions" will be condemned in the end of time. In the Vulgate of the list of vices in Jude 16, *querulus* is the translation of μεμψίμοιρος, a synonym of γογγυστής, "grumbler, malcontent"[5]. *Fallax* probably renders ψευδής (see Prov. 17:4; 26:28); ψεῦδος and cognate words occur in lists of vices, e.g. in Sib. Or. III 37. For *celantes se, ne possent cognosci impii* compare Ps. Sol. 1:7 αἱ ἁμαρτίαι αὐτῶν ἐν ἀποκρύφοις; see also Ps. Sol. 4:5; 8:9; using the metaphor of darkness and light John 3:20 πᾶς γὰρ ὁ φαῦλα πράσσων μισεῖ τὸ φῶς καὶ οὐκ ἔρχεται πρὸς τὸ

---

bylline Oracles (see esp. p. 179, footnote 63). See further Hauck and Schultz, "πόρνη κτλ.", pp. 587-589; Van der Horst, *The Sentences of Pseudo-Phocylides*, pp. 110-111.

[1] The image is mitigated in a number of manuscripts of the synoptic parallel Luke 20:47 (D P R Θ f[13] pc): κατεχόμενοι τὰς οἰκίας.

[2] Deane, *Pseudepigrapha*, quoted by Clemen, *APAT* II, p. 325. *Pauperum* was conjectured by Volkmar, *Mose Prophetie*, p. 145, and followed by most editors.

[3] The possibility was suggested to me by H.J. de Jonge.

[4] Cf. Van der Horst, *The Sentences of Pseudo-Phocylides*, pp. 65, 118-119 and elsewhere.

[5] In the Greek Apocalypse of Baruch 8:5; 13:4, γογγυσμός occurs in lists of vices.

φῶς, ἵνα μὴ ἐλεγχθῇ τὰ ἔργα αὐτοῦ. *In scelere pleni et iniquitate* again refers to a vice often recorded in the lists, which also have the tendency to describe the vices as having gained absolute control (e.g. Rom. 1:29 μεστοί, πεπληρωμένοι).

Ab oriente usque ad occidentem here indicates a period of time ("from sunrise to sunset"). The phrase can be connected with the preceding (*in scelere pleni et iniquitate ab oriente usque ad occidentem*), but a less strained syntax is obtained if the phrase is connected with the following *dicentes*, "saying from sunrise to sunset: 'Let us have extravagant banquets &c.'"; cf. 7:4 *omni hora diei amantes convivia*, and see the commentary on that passage.

7:8

The sinners are now presented as speaking themselves, inciting each other to debauchery and gluttony. The direct speech serves to stress the deliberateness and impudence of their sinful behaviour. This device is used also in Wisd. 2:6-8: Δεῦτε οὖν καὶ ἀπολαύσωμεν τῶν ὄντων ἀγαθῶν ... οἴνου πολυτελοῦς καὶ μύρων πλησθῶμεν ... μηδεὶς ἡμῶν ἄμοιρος ἔστω τῆς ἡμετέρας ἀγερωχίας (Vulgate: *luxuria*), see also Isa. 22:12-13; 56:12 (both instances equally in connection with debauchery); 1 En. 97:8-9; 102:6-11; 103:5-6; 104:7.

The hendiadys *discubitiones et luxuria*, "extravagant banquets", occurs, in the form *comesationes et luxuria* also in Deut. 21:30 (Vulgate: *filius noster ... comesationibus vacat et luxuriae atque conviviis*, Septuagint: ὁ υἱὸς ἡμῶν ... συμβολοκοπῶν οἰνοφλυγεῖ); 2 Macc. 6:4 (τὸ γὰρ ἱερὸν ἀσωτίας καὶ κώμων ... ἐπεπληροῦτο; Vulgate: *nam templum luxuria et comesationibus erat plenum*). In the list of vices in 1 Pet. 4:3, *luxuria* (ἀσέλγεια) is mentioned along with drinking wine and *comesationes, potationes* and idolatry; see further Wisd. 14:26; Eph. 5:18 (ἀσωτία); Gal. 5:19, *luxuria* (ἀσέλγεια); 2 Pet. 2:18; T. Levi 17:11; T. Judah 16:1. For *edentes et bibentes* see the commentary on 7:4.

7:9-10

The accusations which conclude the legible part of the description of the author's opponents concern impurity and, again, hypocrisy: whereas they will fear to be blemished by contact with the ritually impure, their hands as well as their minds deal with unclean things. Moreover (*super*), their mouths speak enormities, cf. Dan. 7:8 (LXX and Θ), about one of the horns of the fourth beast: στόμα λαλοῦν μεγάλα, Vulgate: *et os loquens ingentia*. Grandiloquence is a sign of hubris[1], cf. μεγαληγορία in Ps.-Phocylides 122[2]. In Isa. 65:1-4 the infidelity and impurity of Israel is exposed, the impurity of those who say (οἱ λέγοντες): Πόρρω ἀπ᾿ ἐμοῦ. μὴ ἐγγίσῃς μου, ὅτι καθαρός εἰμι (Isa. 65:5). For a similar contrast between outward purity and inward impurity, see Ps. Sol. 4:2-3 (about the man who is quick to condemn others, and ready to perpetrate all conceivable sins himself); Matt. 23:25; Mark 7:1-7. In lists of vices, impurity occurs in Jub. 21:21 (rekʷus); 23:14 *et inmunditia et fornicationes et pollutiones abominationes operum ipsorum*.

---

[1] See Bertram, "ὕβρις κτλ.", and "ὑπερηφανία κτλ.".

[2] Van der Horst, *The Sentences of Pseudo-Phocylides*, p. 198, who quotes, *inter alia*, 1 Ki. 2:3 μὴ καυχᾶσθε καὶ μὴ λαλεῖτε ὑψηλά, μὴ ἐξελθάτω μεγαλορρημοσύνη ἐκ τοῦ στόματος ὑμῶν.

8:1-5
THE FINAL PUNISHMENT

Following the all-encompassing sinfulness described in 7:3-10, the sudden appearance of the Final Enemy of the people is expected. He will execute God's definitive punishment. His actions are aimed at the destruction of Judaism. Captivity, torment, fire and sword (8:2b, 4a) are common components of descriptions of foreign rulers' actions. But also, it is expected that those who remain faithful to the Jewish tradition will be killed, and that even those who are prepared to give it up will still be tortured (8:1d-2a). They will be forced to accept paganism entirely: they must restore their prepuce (8:3), assist in pagan processions, thereby defiling themselves (8:4b), disgrace God's word and his laws by entering into the inner part of the sanctuary (pagan or Jewish, this is not clear), and by bringing unclean offerings (8:5).

In other eschatological scenarios, comparable foreign powers also occur[1]. For instance, in 1 En. 56:5-6, the Parthians and Medes fulfill a similar role, and in 1 En. 90:16 every kind of bird of prey gathers in an attempt to smash the horn of the ram; the author of Jub. 23:24 expects *peccatores gentium* to be raised against Israel. See further Dan. 7:23-25; 8:9-12, 23-25; 9:26-27; 11:30-32; 4 Ezra 13:34; Sib. Or. III 663-666. In all these instances, a foreign tyranny threatens to uproot God's people entirely, but does not succeed in its malicious design. God either intervenes to judge the nations on his own initiative (Dan. 7:25-26; 8:25; 12:1-3; 1 En. 90:17-19; Sib. Or. III 669-731), or the people repent and return to God, who will then save them (Jub. 23:26; cf. 1 En. 56:8, where the sinners are expelled from the company of the rightous ones); according to 4 Ezra 13:35-39, a son of God will be sent to reprove the nations. In any case, the Final Enemy's actions serve as the definitive purification (through the destruction of the sinners or through their conversion to God). The king of kings in As. Mos. 8 obviously has the same function.

In most of the foregoing instances, the image of the Final Enemy is simply that of a huge army which attacks God's people. This imagery may owe much to Ezekiel's description of Gog of Magog (Ezek. 38-

---

[1] See Hartman, *Prophecy Interpreted*, pp. 77-101.

39)[1]. In As. Mos. 8, however, the king is modeled on the traditional image of Antiochus IV Epiphanes, as it is known to us from the books of the Maccabees and from book XII of the *Antiquities* by Josephus. The king does not simply storm the city and murder practically all of its inhabitants (for instance out of envy, as in Sib. Or. III 657-662), but he intentionally attempts to make the Jews renegades, because of an irrational hatred of their religion[2]. This variation from the majority of eschatological scenarios in which such enemies occur is probably due to the introduction of Taxo and his sons in chapter 9. The picture of their faithfulness to the law under any circumstances, and of their willingness to die for it, is drawn from the traditions of the Maccabean uprising, which are of course inextricably connected with traditions concerning the so-called Antiochan persecution (see further below).

₁ₐ And suddenly revenge and wrath will come over them, ᵦ such as there will never have been over them since eternity until that time, ᵪ in which he will raise for them the king of the kings of the earth, and a power with great might, ᵨ who will hang on the cross those who confess circumcision, ₂ₐ but who will torture those who deny it. ᵦ And he will lead them chained into captivity, ₃ and their wives will be divided among the gentiles, and their sons will be operated on as children by physicians in order to put on them a foreskin. ₄ₐ But they will be punished by them with torments, and with fire and sword, ᵦ and they will be forced to carry publicly their idols, that are defiled, just like those who touch them. ₅ₐ And they will also be forced by those who torture them to enter into their hidden place, ᵦ and they will be forced with goads to disgracefully blaspheme the word. ᵪ Finally, after these things (*sc.* they will be forced to blaspheme) also the laws through the things they will have upon their altar.

8:1a-b

The final punishment is called *ultio* and *ira*. In the Vulgate, *ultio* usually corresponds to the Septuagint's ἐκδίκησις (see, e.g., Lev. 19:18; Num. 31:3; Deut. 32:35; Judg. 11:36; Ps. 79 [78]:10; 94[93]:1; Isa. 59:17; Jer. 11:20; Ezek. 25:12; Micha 5:14); more rarely to ἀνταπόδοσις (Isa. 34:8; 35:4; 61:2; 63:4). In the combination *ultio et ira*, the two words are near synonyms; ὀργή (the probable Greek equivalent of *ira* in

---

[1] Volz, *Die Eschatologie*, p. 150.

[2] One should of course distinguish between the eschatological enemy as an instrument of God's will and as an impious, ruthless tyrant; from the divine perspective, his actions are right, but for his own part he is, none the less, a grave sinner.

As. Mos. 8:1a) alone may mean "judicial punishment"[1] (see e.g. 1 Macc. 1:67; 3:8; Sir. 5:7; 7:16; 47:20; 1 En. 90:3; Ps. Sol. 15:4; T. Reub. 5:4; T. Levi 6:11; Sib. Or. V 76).

The punishment is said to "come suddenly". In the Latin of the Vulgate, the verb *advenire* is most often used for the arrival of a certain point in time (*tempus, dies, annus*, see e.g. Gen. 30:33; 31:10; Exod. 1:16; 14:24; 19:16[2]). The "coming" of this judgement (cf. Sir. 21:6[5]; Rev. 11:18) is the realization of the threat expressed by *adpropiabunt tempora arguendi* in 5:1. *Cita* (l. em.), the adjective determining *ultio*, is best translated as an adverb. In this context, it probably means "suddenly", not "quickly". In the Vulgate, the adverb *cito* may correspond to both: ἐξάπινα (or ἐξαίφνης), see for instance Isa. 47:11; Jer. 6:26; 15:8; but also ἐν τάχει, e.g. Bar. 4:25. In biblical and related literature, the notion of suddenness is usually related to unpleasant events, and occurs regularly in texts which speak of the coming of the judgement[3]; see especially Sir. 5:7(9), which also uses other terms that occur in As. Mos. 8:1: ἐξάπινα γὰρ ἐξελεύσεται ὀργὴ κυρίου, καὶ ἐν καιρῷ ἐκδικήσεως ἐξολῇ (Vulgate: *subito enim venit ira illius, et in tempore vindictae disperdet te*).

Finally, the punishment is said to be unprecedented: a comparable judgement has never previously occurred (cf. As. Mos. 9:2 *eminens principatum*). For the wording of this phrase, see for instance Dan. 12:1 LXX ἐκείνη ἡ ἡμέρα θλίψεως, οἵα οὐκ ἐγενήθησαν ἕως τῆς ἡμέρας ἐκείνης; cf. Matt. 24:21; Mark 13:19; Rev. 16:18; all these instances refer to the final, eschatological judgement, just as As. Mos. 8:1b does. According to K. Berger, the formula must be considered as typically apocalyptic[4].

8:1c

In the time of the final judgement, the Lord will arouse the "king of the kings of the earth, and a power with great might". For the parallelism of the concrete "king" and the abstract "power", cf. Ps. Sol. 2:30 κρίνων βασιλεῖς καὶ ἀρχάς[5]. For the use of an abstract object with the verb *suscitare*, see e.g. the Vulgate of Dan. 2:44 *suscitabit Deus caeli regnum*. The word *suscitare* ("to raise", ἐπ– or ἐξεγείρειν, cf. Isa. 13:17; Hab. 1:6; also ἀνιστάναι Deut. 18:15) stresses that the acting subject is God, and that, therefore, the terror that the king will bring is God's punishment.

Rex regum is a honorific title of the Persian (and hence, the Seleucid) kings[6]. Whereas the expression *reges terrae* is quite common, I have found no other instance

---

[1] See Sjöberg and Stählin, "ὀργή", p. 415; cf. Niermeyer, *Lexicon*, p. 1050a.

[2] In these instances, LXX simply has (ἐν +) an indication of time; cf. Numb. 36:4, where LXX has ἐὰν δὲ γένηται).

[3] Daube, *The Sudden in the Scriptures*, pp. 1-27; in the New Testament, "sudden" and "suddenly" are used in contexts of eschatology and of "supernatural, awesome occurrences", *o.c.*, pp. 28-34.

[4] Berger, *Die griechische Daniel-Diegese*, pp. 70-75 ("Exkurs I: Traditionsgeschichte der Formel 'wie es nie zuvor gewesen ist noch je sein wird'."), lists some sixty examples of the formula. In addition to eschatological contexts, the formula is also used in Exod. 9:18, 24; 10:6, in connection with the plagues of Egypt. Cf. finally 1 Macc. 9:27.

[5] Cf. the parallelism between ἀρχή or ἐξουσία and βασιλεία in Micah 4:8; Dan. 7:27.

[6] Deissmann, *Licht vom Osten*, pp. 310-311; cf. Ezra 7:12; Ezek. 26:7; Dan. 2:37; 2 Macc. 13:4; T. Judah 3:7; Jews and Christians transferred this title to their God, see 1 En. 9:4

(cont.)

of the exact words *rex regum terrae*. Comparable, however, is Rev. 1:5, where Jesus Christ is called ὁ ἄρχων τῶν βασιλέων τῆς γῆς; and Rev. 17:18, where the image of a woman is explained as Babylon, ἡ πόλις ἡ μεγάλη ἡ ἔχουσα βασιλείαν ἐπὶ τῶν βασιλέων τῆς γῆς. In As. Mos. 8:1, the words are meant to create a climax: in 8:1b, it had already been stated that the eschatological punishment was to be unprecedented. In 8:1c, use is made of the existing title *rex regum* as a contrast to the two previously prophesied foreign rulers, the king from the East (3:1), and the king from the West (6:8)—their reigns of terror will be surpassed by that of the king of the kings of the earth (who, according to the author of As. Mos., is yet to come).

The tautological expression *potestas a potentia magna*, "a power with great might" (see grammatical note nr. 66), is equally intended to provide a climactic effect. *Potestas* and *potentia* are synonyms; both occur in parallelisms with other words for "strength", such as *virtus, fortitudo*, or for "forceful rule", such as *principatus* and *imperium* (e.g. 1 Chron. 29:12; 2 Chron. 20:6; Sir. 34:16[19]; equivalent words in Greek are δύναμις, δυναστεία, ἰσχύς, in the New Testament and elsewhere ἀρχή, κράτος and ἐξουσία (e.g. Rom. 13:1-3; Col. 2:10; Jude 25; T. Reub. 5:1).

8:1d-2a

With an object in the accusative[1], or with a subordinate clause, *confiteri* can be used in forensic contexts ("to confess a crime"), and hence in persecution contexts (e.g. "to confess to be a Christian"). In the Vulgate Old Testament, the word usually agrees with the Septuagint's ἐξαγορεύειν[2]. In the New Testament, *confiteri* is a translation of ὁμολογεῖν. The opposite of ἐξαγορεύειν/ὁμολογεῖν is ἀρνεῖσθαι, Vulgate: *negare*[3] (see for the direct juxtaposition of the opposites: T. Gad 6:3-4, 6; John 1:20 *et confessus est et non negavit*; Tit. 1:5 *confitentur se nosse Deum, factis autem negant*; in a persecution context: Mart. Polyc. 9:2).

Since *confiteri* and *negare* are opposites, especially in persecution contexts, it seems that the object of *negare* must be the same as that of *confiteri* in 8:1d, namely *circumcisionem*. Since it is difficult to imagine how someone can "deny his circumcision", *circumcisio* must be taken as a metonymy for "Judaism". *Negare circumcisionem* then means "to disavow being circumcised", that is "to renounce Judaism"; cf. the Vulgate of 2 Macc. 6:6 *neque ... se quisquam Judaeum esse confitebatur* ('Ιουδαῖον ὁμολογεῖν εἶναι). The metaphoric use of *circumcisio*/περιτομή for "the status of being circumcised" is also attested by Paul, e.g. in Rom. 2:25[4].

(Syncellus); Philo, *De specialibus legibus* I 18; .*De Decalogo* 41; Rev. 17:14; 19:16; cf. Rev. 1:5; but see also Dio Chrysostom 2:75, where the title is used for Zeus.

[1] *Confiteri* may also be constructed with a dative, as in As. Mos. 10:10; then, it means "to praise (the Lord)", and it agrees in most cases with ἐξομολογεῖν + dative.

[2] Lev. 16:21; 26:40; Numb. 5:7; Neh. 1:6; 9:2, 3; Ps. 32(31):5;. In two instances, the Septuagint equivalent of *confiteri*, "to confess", is ὁμολογεῖν, Esth. 1:1 o (12:3) and Sus. 14. In Wisd. 18:13, ὁμολογεῖν/*confiteri* means "to acknowledge". Ὁμολογεῖν is used for "confessing a crime" in T. Gad 2:1.

[3] Gen. 18:15; Wisd. 12:27; 16:16.

[4] See Bauer, *Griechisch-deutsches Wörterbuch*, col. 1315. The metaphorical use of *circumcisio* can only occur if circumcision is considered to be the hallmark of Jewishness. As such it was introduced during the Maccabean revolt. The Maccabeans claimed to restore ancestral laws, although circumcision had never been a particularly important issue before. In the first century C.E., circumcision was considered (at least by some Jews) to be the charac-

(cont.)

In the religious trials which are related in martyria and similar texts, Jews or Christians are tortured in order that they may disavow their convictions, and acknowledge the persecutor's religion (e.g. 2 Macc. 6:24 μεταβαίνειν εἰς ἀλλοφυλισμόν; 4 Macc. 8:7 ἀρνεῖσθαι τὸν πάτριον... θεσμόν[1]; cf. also Josephus, *Bell. Jud.* VII 418: πάσης γὰρ ἐπ' αὐτοὺς βασάνου ... ἐπινοηθείσης ἐφ' ἕν τοῦτο μόνον, ὅπως αὐτῶν Καίσαρα δεσπότην ὁμολογήσωσιν). See further 2 Macc. 6-7, in which passage Eleazar and seven boys are tortured (αἰκίζεσθαι) in order to induce them to eat pork.

The intention of As. Mos. 8:1d-2a seems to be that the expected eschatological tyrant will be so horribly unscrupulous that those who will testify to be Jewish will be killed, but those who will renounce their being Jewish will still be tortured.[2]

The king of kings will kill those who confess their Jewishness by hanging. For the prohibition of Judaism in Antiochus Epiphanes' time, see 1 Macc. 1:48 (cf. 1 Macc. 1:60-61; 2 Macc. 6:6, 9, 10; cf. also 4 Macc. 4:25). *Suspendere in cruce* (κρεμάζειν and similar words ἐπὶ ξύλου) is possibly but not necessarily the same as "to crucify" (*crucifigere*, cf. As. Mos. 6:9; σταυροῦν). Josephus (*Ant. Jud.* XII 256) mentions crucifixions during Antiochus Epiphanes' reign (ἐμπνέοντες ἀνεσταυροῦντο), but the books of the Maccabees, on which Josephus relies, do not mention crucifixion. In the Vulgate, *crux* is used several times for ξύλον, literally "wood"[3]; see Gen. 40:19 (cf. 41:13); Esth. 5:14; 8:7; 9:25 (AO†). On other occasions, ξύλον is reflected in the Vulgate by *patibulum* ("gallows") or *stirpes*. In Josh. 8:29, *patibulum* and *crux* are used alternately. The use of *crux* as a translation for "wood" in the Vulgate is evidently a rendering by a Christian translator, influenced by Gal. 3:13. Since the Greek *Vorlage* of As. Mos. may well have used a word for "cross", it is impossible to conclude from the word *crux* that the translator was Christian.

8:2b-3

For the people's captivity as one of the punishments consistently recurring in descriptions of foreign subjugation, see the commentary on As. Mos. 3:3; 6:9. In Dan. 11:33 (both LXX and Θ) αἰχμαλωσία is mentioned together with rape, and sword and fire (see below on 8:4).

In As. Mos. 8:3, women and children especially are mentioned as victims of the eschatological enemy. They are singled out to stress his ruthlessness; cf. e.g. 2 Chron. 29:9; Jer. 14:16; 38(45):23; Judith 7:27(16); T. Judah 23:3. In the Maccabean traditions, women and children are singled out in 1 Macc. 1:32; 5:13, 23, 24; 8:10; 2 Macc. 5:13; Josephus, *Ant. Jud.* XII 251.

The difficult word *disdonare*[4] must probably be understood as a vulgar Latin variant of *didare*, "to divide" (see grammatical note nr. 36), which in its turn is a synonym

---

teristic of Jewishness *par excellence*; see further Arata Mantovani, "Circoncisi ed incirconcisi". These facts must be considered as additional evidence against a dating of As. Mos. 8 to the 2nd century B.C.E.; see further Introduction, section V, b.

[1] Cf. ἀρνεῖσθαι τὴν πίστιν 1 Tim. 5:8; Rev. 2:13, Vulgate *fidem negare*.

[2] So also Volkmar, *Mose Prophetie*, p. 44; Priest, "Testament of Moses", p. 931.

[3] Cf. *lignum* in Acts 5:30; 10:39.

[4] The manuscript reads *diisdonare*, taken by Volkmar, *Mose Prophetie*, p. 44, and many others to refer to enforced sacred prostitution (cf. 2 Macc. 6:4). However, *diis donare gentibus* ("to give to the gods among the gentiles") is not only a very awkward construction, but

(cont.)

of *dividere*, a word often used in connection with war booty. Women and children can be considered booty as well: in Judith 4:12(10), the Israelites, under the threat of being subdued by Holophernes, pray that their wives will not be divided as war booty among the enemies (μὴ δοῦναι... τὰς γυναῖκας εἰς προνομήν, Vulgate *ne darentur ... uxores eorum in divisionem*); see also Judith 9:4(3)[1]. Possibly, *disdonare* renders διαδιδόναι[2]. In Gen. 49:27 *dividere spolia* corresponds to the Septuagint's διαδιδόναι τροφήν (cf. T. Ben. 11:1; Sir. 30:32 [33:24] διαδιδόναι κληρονομίαν, *distribuere hereditatem*). In As. Mos. 8:3b the word is used pregnantly, the idea of war booty being implicit (cf. Ps. Sol. 1:4 ὁ πλοῦτος αὐτῶν διεδόθη εἰς πᾶσαν τὴν γῆν).

In 2 Macc. 5:24 Apollonius receives the order to sell, that is, to enslave the women and children of Jerusalem (the author of 2 Maccabees fails to record whether this order has been executed; cf. Josephus, *Ant. Jud.* XII 299). The author of As. Mos., however, predicts a different fate for the male children: they will be operated on in order to cover[3] their glans with a foreski (cf.1 Macc. 1:48, 60; 2 Macc. 6:10, in which passages circumcision is said to have been prohibited by the Syrians). In 1 Macc. 1:15, however, the (voluntary) undoing of circumcision is situated in an earlier stage in history, namely at the time preceding the Antiochan persecution, when the Hellenizing priests were implementing their reforms.

In 8:3b it is said that their sons will be "cut" by physicians in order to create a prepuce for them. Allusion is presumably made to the operation known as epispasm[4]. Celsus is one of the authors who describe this operation, which, according to him, was done *decoris causa: fieri potest, sed expeditius in puero quam in viro; in eo, cui id naturale est, quam in eo, qui quarundam gentium more circumcisus est*. According to Celsus, the operation *in eo, qui circumcisus est*, consisted of making an incision in the skin just below the glans, and stretching the skin released over the glans; the resulting wound would have to be carefully treated, so that its healing would produce new skin.

Whereas epispasm occurred among Jews who renounced their ancestral habits (cf. 1 Cor. 7:18 μὴ ἐπισπάσθω), it is specifically stated in As. Mos. 8:3b that their sons will be operated on when they are boys (*filii eorum pueri secabuntur*). The emphatic mention of the sons' youthfulness primarily illustrates how everything will be turned upside down: the boys will not be operated on to be circumcised, as is the normal

---

would also be a peculiar euphemism in a text which otherwise has no trouble in giving all the details.

[1] See further Deut. 21:11; Isa. 10:2; Joel 3(4):3; Nah. 3:10; for τοῖς ἔθνεσι (*gentibus*) see Ezek. 25:7; 26:5; 34:28.

[2] So Haupt, "Bemerkungen", p. 448; see further grammatical note nr. 182.

[3] *Inducere* is the medical term Celsus uses for covering a wound with skin or plaster (see *ThLL* VII, 1, p. 1235:46-51).

[4] Hall, "Epispasm", has convincingly shown that the mention of epispasm does not provide evidence of an Antiochan date for As. Mos., *pace* 1 Macc. 1:15, because the operation was practised throughout the Hellenistic-Roman period, by both Jews and pagans. Moreover, 1 Macc. 1:15 probably alludes to infibulation, rather than epispasm. Infibulation did not actually restore the prepuce, but the foreskin (or its remnants) was pierced and temporarily bound together (Celsus, *Medicina* VII, 25, 3; ed. Marx, *Corpus medicorum* I, p. 345), e.g. for the duration of an athletic event (cf. 1 Macc. 1:14, where the building of a gymnasium is mentioned).

Jewish thing to do, but instead, they will be operated on in order to provide them with a foreskin.

8:4-5a

The punishment "by torments, fire, and sword" is traditional; cf. Dan. 11:33; Jub. 23:13, 22 (which also include, among other disasters, captivity, see As. Mos. 8:2b). The combination "fire and sword" is a stock phrase, very common in Latin[1]. Less strictly bound together, the two words are found in Ezek. 23:25; Nah. 3:15; cf. Heb. 11:34.

In 8:4b, it is prophesied that the people will be forced to carry publicly images of the pagan gods. To this, one may compare the compulsion to take part in the Dionysiac procession mentioned in 2 Macc. 6:7 (where also a connection is made with tormenting: ἤγοντο δὲ μετὰ πικρᾶς ἀνάγκης κτλ. ... ἠναγκάζοντο ... πομπεύειν). For the practice of "carrying idols", see Amos 5:26; Bar. 6 (= the Epistle of Jeremiah):3, 25.

The idols are called polluted (*inquinata*), "just like" (*quomodo ... pariter*; strictly speaking, *pariter* is superfluous) those who "touch" the idols ("to touch" is the translation of an emendation, see textual commentary to line 132; on the peculiar constructions in this sentence, see grammatical notes nrs. 117 and 171). The connection between idols and pollution is made indirectly in As. Mos. 5:3-4. In the Old Testament, the idols themselves are not called unclean, although Ezekiel especially stresses that the association of Israel with the idols defiles the people (Ezek. 20:7, 18, 31; 22:4; 23:30; 36:18; 37:23; the expression used in the Vulgate is consistently *pollui in idolis*, corresponding to various expressions in the Septuagint, such as μιαίνεσθαι ἐν τοῖς ἐπιτηδεύμασιν; cf. Jos. As. 11:9, 16; 12:5).

Abditus locus means "secret place"; the obvious Greek equivalent of *abditus* would have been ἀπόκρυφος, but here *abditus* probably indicates the ἄδυτον of a temple, that is, the inner part of a sanctuary, where the image of a god is erected (cf. Deut. 27:15), the *cella*[2]. The word *abditus* may have been chosen because of its outward similarity to the Greek word (notwithstanding the fact that the word *adytum* had been adopted in the Latin language).

This "hidden place" may either be the *cella* of a pagan temple, or the Holy of Holies of the Jerusalem temple, which no one, except the high priest on the Day of Atonement, was allowed to enter; *eorum* allows for both possibilities. *Adyta* of the Jerusalem temple are mentioned in the Vulgate of 1 Chron. 28:11: *dedit autem David Salomoni filio suo descriptionem porticus et templi ... et cubiculorum in adytis* (LXX and MT have αἱ ἀποθῆκαι αἱ ἐσώτεραι and הפנימים חדריו respectively, "the inner [storage] rooms"). Josephus on several occasions designates the Holy of Holies by the term ἄδυτον (*Bell. Jud.* V 236; *Ant. Jud.* III 122, 125, 138; VII 378; VIII 71, 72, 90, 103, 104). Josephus, however, has a Hellenic audience in mind[3], and elsewhere in Old Testament and related literature, I have not found the term used in con-

---

[1] See the numerous instances in *ThLL* VI, 1, pp. 583:44-49; 586:6-12; VII, p. 291:51-52

[2] Numerous instances in *ThLL* I 902:28-56.

[3] In *Ant.* III 125 Josephus explains the Jewish terms by giving the pagan equivalents: ὁ μὲν πᾶς ναὸς ἅγιον ἐκαλεῖτο, τὸ δ' ἄβατον (= ἄδυτον) τὸ ἐντὸς τῶν τεσσάρων κιόνων τοῦ ἁγίου τὸ ἅγιον.

nection with the Jewish temple[1]. In As. Mos. 6:1 *sanctum sanctitatis* is used; in the Septuagint, רביר (the Hebrew equivalent of the *cella*) is either transliterated (δαβίρ, e.g. 1 Ki. 6:5, 16; 8:6, 18; 2 Chron. 4:20) or translated with αὐλή (1 Ki. 7:49; Ps. 29[28]:2). It may be that by using ἄδυτον, a specifically pagan term, the author of As. Mos. wished to designate the *cella* of a pagan temple[2]. In that case, a climax would be intended in 8:4b-5a: not only will the Jews be forced to carry around pagan idols, they will also be forced to enter the innermost part of the pagan sanctuary, apparently to worship the gods that are its residents. To this interpretation one may compare 2 Macc. 6:7, where it is said that the Jews were violently forced to participate in the Dionysiac cult and to bring offerings for the king's birthday.

8:5b-c
The Jews are forced with "goads" (*stimulus* is probably a translation of κέντρον; see Sir. 38:25[26]; Acts 26:14; 1 Cor. 15:55, 56; cf. Ps. Sol. 16:4, and also Eccl. 12:11 βούκεντρον) to "blaspheme the word and the laws". *Blasfemare*, a transliteration of βλασφημεῖν, means "to defame, to dishonour"; *contumeliose* is pleonastic. In the Septuagint βλασφημεῖν is rarely used; its object is usually God (2 Ki. 19:4, 6, 22; Isa. 52:5; Dan. 3:29[96] LXX). In later usage, however, concrete things, related to God, also came to be the object of βλασφημεῖν, thus "the teaching", or "the word of God" (in the New Testament, e.g. Rom. 14:16 τὸ ἀγαθόν; 1 Tim. 6:1 τὸ ὄνομα τοῦ θεοῦ καὶ ἡ διδασκαλία; 2 Pet. 2:2 ἡ ὁδὸς τῆς ἀληθείας). Most often, however, it is God's name that is blasphemed. It is possible that *verbum* should be understood as a designation for God, as in the Targumic use of מימ(י)רא[3]. On the other hand, it is equally possible that simply "word" is meant (as in Tit. 2:5 ἵνα μὴ ὁ λόγος τοῦ θεοῦ βλασφημῆται[4]); it must then be regarded as a parallel of *leges* in 8:5c (on the parallelism of *verbum* and *leges* see commentary to As. Mos. 1:9b). This meaning of "word" is well-known, although it is very rarely used absolutely, that is, without τοῦ θεοῦ, or a similar word indicating explicitly that God's word is meant (the exceptions are Deut. 30:14 ἐγγύς σου ἐστι τὸ ῥῆμα σφόδρα, and, most importantly, As. Mos. 11:16, where Moses is called *dominus verbi*[5]; cf. Par. Jer. 5:21).

The Jews are forced to blaspheme the laws through the things which they will have on their altar (on the omission of *eo* before *quod*, see grammatical note nr. 174). The words "their altar" are again ambiguous (see grammatical note nr. 57), as in the case of "their hidden place" (8:5a); they may refer to the altar in Jerusalem, but also to pagan altars. In either case, the clause may refer to the offering of pigs (see 2 Macc. 6:5 τὸ δὲ θυσιαστήριον τοῖς ἀποδιεσταλμένοις ἀπὸ τῶν νόμων ἀθεμίτοις ἐπεπλή-

---

[1] In Ps. 27(26):5 it is said that the Lord will "hide me in the secret place of his tabernacle" (ἐν ἀποκρύφῳ τῆς σκηνῆς αὐτοῦ). In this instance, reference is not made to an architectonic element of the temple, but to the function of the temple as a place of refuge for those fleeing from an enemy (cf. Ps. 31[30]:21). In 3 Macc. 5:43, the Jewish temple as a whole is called ἄβατος ἡμῖν ναός; these words, however, are put into the mouth of a gentile, who is "not allowed to enter" (the literal meaning of ἄβατος and ἄδυτος) the temple.

[2] So also Charles, *The Assumption*, p. 32

[3] So Rosenthal, *Vier apokryphische Bücher*, quoted by Clemen, *APAT* II, p. 326; cf. Jastrow, *Dictionary*, p. 775b.

[4] Cf. Augustine, *Retractationes* 2, 7, 1: *blasphemare legem et prophetas*; Gregory of Tours, *Contra Faustum* 22, 1: *blasphemare legem* (quoted in *ThLL* II 2046:12-14).

[5] So also Brandenburger, "Himmelfahrt", p. 74.

ρωτο; and Josephus, *Ant. Jud.* XII 253: οἰκοδομήσαντας δὲ ἐν ἑκάστῃ πόλει καὶ κώμῃ τεμένη αὐτῶν καὶ βωμοὺς καθιδρύσαντας θύειν ἐπ' αὐτοῖς σῦς καθ' ἡμέραν προσέταξεν; cf. 1 Macc. 1:47). In the traditions about the impious rule of Antiochus IV, the offering of pigs (or eating pork) is a constant element, cf. 2 Macc. 6:18; 7:1; 4 Macc. 5:2, 6. If the Jerusalem altar is meant, it is possible that the author of As. Mos. refers to the "abomination of desolation" (Dan. 9:27; 11:31; 12:11; 1 Macc. 1:54 [cf. 6:7]; Matt. 24:15; Mark 13:14), whatever he may have taken it to be. In any case, the laws will be blasphemed by offerings that are not legitimate according to the author of As. Mos.

THE ZEAL FOR THE LAW OF TAXO AND HIS SONS

The persecution described in As. Mos. 8 is God's final and definitive punishment of his sinful people. As an instrument of God, the king of the kings of the earth intends to uproot Judaism entirely: he will force the Jews to abandon their ancestral religion and kill the Jews who refuse to do so. Under these circumstances, one Jew, a Levite named Taxo, will admonish his seven sons to remain faithful to the commandments of the Lord, as their ancestors were. Taxo and his sons will be prepared to die for the law, knowing that the Lord is with those who are faithful to him and that he will therefore not leave unavenged the death they expect to meet presently.

The sinlessness of Taxo and his sons as well as their trust in the Lord at the eschatological hour clearly mark them as the "Remnant of Israel" (cf. Zeph. 3:12-13), that is, as the few who by their steadfastness to the covenant uphold it, thereby ensuring the continuation of God's mercy and the fulfilment of his promises to the patriarchs with regard to Israel (cf. As. Mos. 12:12). Moreover, it is Taxo's innocence and his morally impeccable descent that give his suffering the atoning effect the exaltation of "Israel" in 10:8-10 implies.

9 ₁ Then, on that day, there will be a man from the tribe of Levi, whose name will be Taxo, who, having seven sons, will speak to them, saying: ₂ 'See, my sons, behold, a second, cruel and unclean retribution is made against the people, and a punishment without mercy, and it surpasses the first one. ₃ For what nation, or what land, or what people rebellious against the Lord, having committed many crimes, has suffered woes as great as have come over us?

₄ Now then, my sons, hear me! See, then, and know that neither our parents, nor their ancestors have tempted God by transgressing his commandments. ₅ Surely you know that here lies our strength. And this we shall do: ₆ Let us fast for three days, and on the fourth day let us enter into the cave which is in the field, and let us die rather than transgress the commandments of the Lord of lords, the God of our fathers. ₇ For as we shall do this and die, our blood will be avenged before the Lord.'

9:1

Taxo is introduced by a formulaic clause which is often used in Old Testament and related literature to introduce new figures. In such clauses, it is said that "there was a man" (*erat autem homo*, or *vir*), whose tribal affiliation is specified (*de tribu N.N.*), whose name is given (*cui/cujus nomen erat N.N.*), and whose relevant family members are mentioned (*et erat ei mulier; habens uxorem* etc.); see Judg. 13:2; 1 Sam. 1:1; 9:1-2; 25:2-3; LAB 42:1; 45:1, 2; cf. Judg. 17:1; 2 Sam. 20:1; Job 1:1-2; Luke 2:25.

This is the only instance in the extant text of As. Mos., in which a figure's tribal affiliation is mentioned. Taxo's Levitical descent is of major importance: an innocent Levite, that is, a member of the priestly tribe, will make atonement for the people's sins. Atonement is a priestly task, but according to the author of As. Mos., the officiating Jerusalem priests, described in 5:4, are not qualified for this assignment because of their own moral depravation. Therefore, Taxo's innocence, and that of his ancestors, is heavily stressed in 9:4 (see further below).

For the numerous suggestions made to solve the enigmatic name *Taxo*, see the appendix to the Introduction. None of these suggestions is convincing, and I have none to add.

Taxo is said to have seven sons, which is the same number as that of the so-called Maccabean martyrs (2 Macc. 7). The number given in As. Mos. 9:1 may be a reminiscence of the tradition transmitted in 2 Macc. 7.

In the word-order *dicet ... rogans*, a metathesis seems to have taken place, since one would more readily expect *rogabit ... dicens* (= λέγων, the well-known biblical expression introducing direct speech; see grammatical note nr. 150). The context suggests that *rogare*, "to ask", should be interpreted here as "to admonish". If so, the Greek text may have used a form of παρακαλεῖν, which means both "to ask" and "to exhort" (see grammatical note nr. 182). Alternatively, *rogans* may be taken to introduce the question contained in 9:3.

9:2-3

In Taxo's first words to his sons, their situation is summarized: the divine punishment has again struck the people in an even harsher way. Taxo calls the punishment *ultio ... et traductio*. On *ultio*, see commentary to 8:1; *traductio* is the Vulgate translation of ἔλεγχος in Wisd. 2:14; 11:7(8); 18:5; in old Latin Bible translations, it also corresponds to ἐλεγμός[1]; in As. Mos. *traductio* parallels *ultio*, and must therefore mean "punishment". The opening words of Mattathias' testament are strikingly similar to Taxo's statement in As. Mos. 9:2; 1 Macc. 2:49 reads: Νῦν ἐστηρίσθη ὑπερηφανία καὶ ἐλεγμὸς καὶ καιρὸς καταστροφῆς καὶ ὀργὴ θυμοῦ (cf. *ultio et ira* As. Mos. 8:1).

Although this punishment is, as always, inflicted on behalf of God, it can nevertheless be designated as "cruel and unclean". These adjectives refer to the outward appearance of the punishment, as described in As. Mos. 8: it will be executed by a pagan tyrant, who will treat the people most cruelly in order to induce them to pollute themselves.

The punishment is referred to as an *ultio altera*, that is either "a second punishment" (as opposed to only one former punishment), or "another punishment" (as op-

---

[1] Rönsch, *Itala und Vulgata*, pp. 326-327 (cf. p. 383); *Semasiologische Beiträge* I, p. 72 (cf. III, pp. 82-83).

posed to one or more punishments). Probably, the former possibility is meant. The two clauses in As. Mos. 9:2 are clearly parallel and chiastic:

ultio facta est in plebe altera,   *crudelis, inmunda, et*

                       X

traductio sine misericordia   *et eminens principatum*

When the words are arranged in this way, it is seen that *principatum* corresponds to *altera*. It probably translates τὴν ἀρχήν, and can consequently be translated with "the beginning", designating the first punishment. The first punishment then is the ruin of Jerusalem described in As. Mos. 3:1-3[1], which to the author of As. Mos. is the paradigmatic event for the expectations concerning the final punishment, and which the second punishment is believed to surpass (*eminens*; see further the commentary on 8:1b).[2]

In the form of a rhetorical question, Taxo in 9:3 compares the suffering of the people of God to that of other peoples. Although the great woes that have come over the Lord's people are interpreted as a divine punishment (the legitimacy of which Taxo does not deny), the comparison suggests a certain disproportion: the executers of divine punishment are no less impious or malign than the people of God, yet they seem to escape judgement. The gentiles who are God's instruments are themselves sinners (see e.g. Ps. Sol. 2:1, 24; 17:5 ἐν ταῖς ἁμαρτίαις ἐπανέστησαν ἡμῖν ἁμαρτωλοί; Jub. 23:23). They should therefore be punished as well (see 10:7, and cf. Ps. Sol. 2:22-23; 2 Bar. 72:4-6; Jub. 23:24).

J. Licht interpreted 9:3 as a "plea of comparative innocence"[3]. This may be too strong an expression, but Licht is certainly right in pointing to the eschatological significance of Taxo's words. The severity of the punishment of the people of God by their complete uprooting, combined with the sinlessness of the ancestors of Taxo and his sonds, creates the conditions which ensure the effectiveness of Taxo's death. "In this situation martyrdom must be effective: truly innocent blood spilled in addition to the observed atrocities will surely fill the measure of undeserved suffering and in the event compel God to exercise His vengeance."[4] To this one may compare the suffering of the seven boys and their mother in 2 Macc. 7. Although there is no indication that the author of 2 Maccabees regards them as sinners, he makes them say that they regard the tortures inflicted on them as a punishment for their sins (see esp. 2 Macc. 7:18 and 32). Apparently, they suffer because they belong to a sinful nation, which is deservedly punished. They may therefore be seen to be suffering vicariously; because of their sinlessness, they are able to placate the Lord with their death (see 2 Macc. 7:33, 37-38).

---

[1] So also Collins, "The Date and Provenance", p. 20.

[2] Against Charles, *The Assumption*, p. 29, who contended that As. Mos. 8-9 could not be a prophecy of the final woes, because "the last woes could not be described as 'the second visitation'."

[3] Licht, "Taxo", p. 98. Licht continues: "Taxo's generation is evidently guilty, its punishment is not entirely undeserved. The punishment, however cannot be termed absolutely just; it is excessive, and cannot be fitted into the normal cycle of sin and retribution."

[4] Licht, "Taxo", p. 98.

9:4-5

Taxo reminds his sons of the innocence of their ancestors, who are thus held up as an example of righteousness; cf. Mattathias' testament in 1 Macc. 2:49-68, esp. 2:51. More importantly, the sinlessness of their ancestors[1] somehow increases the purity of Taxo and his sons (cf. Judith 8:18-20), thereby enhancing the effectiveness of their (vicarious) suffering (see Isa. 53:9 LXX; cf. Zeph. 3:13; 1 Pet. 2:22). Unlike the Levitical priests, who by their sinfulness have invalidated the normal cultic atonement, Taxo is perfectly fit to fulfill his mediatory role (cf. Heb. 7:26-27).

In the Vulgate, *tentare* (the classical form of *temptare*, see grammatical note nr. 32) is used as an equivalent of πειράζειν, "to put to the test, to tempt" (on the participle *temptantes* functioning as a finite verb, see grammatical note nr. 137). Often, it is the Lord who tries his people, in order to purify them. People who put God to the test occur much less frequently. An incident to which the Old Testament frequently refers is the trial at Massah and Meribah, where Israel, according to the Exodus version of the story, provoked the Lord, demanding that he demonstrate that he was indeed with them; see Exod. 17:2, 7; and the references to this event in Deut. 6:16-17; Ps. 78(77):18, 41; 95(94):9 (cf. Heb. 3:9); 106(105):14[2]. In As. Mos. 9:4, *temptare* is defined as *praeterire mandata illius*, and it must probably be understood as "to taunt", rather than "to try"; cf. Matt. 4:7 (par. Luke 4:12). In Ps. 78(77):56, there is a similar parallelism: καὶ ἐπείρασαν ... τὸν θεὸν τὸν ὕψιστον, καὶ τὰ μαρτύρια αὐτοῦ οὐκ ἐφυλάξαντο.

Taxo says that "this is our strength" (lit.: "these are our powers"). Possibly, *haec* refers specifically to the innocence of the ancestors (see above, and Judith 8:18-20). It is perhaps better, however, to understand *haec* as referring more generally to the law and to the strength that is gained by keeping the law (cf. 1 Macc. 2:64, where Mattathias commands his sons to "be strong in the law, for you shall be glorified in the law"; see also 1 Macc. 2:51 and the commentary to As. Mos. 10:15 and 12:3).

9:6

Taxo is said to admonish his sons to fast for three days. Fasting is a common ritual corollary to the confession of sins and expresses humility; see the commentary on As. Mos. 3:4 above. Taxo's solidarity with his people, already apparent in his willingness to suffer the punishment caused by their sins, also incites him to humiliate himself on their behalf. This characterizes his actions as vicarious (see the commentary on 9:2-3). For the same period of three days of fasting, see Tob. 3:10 (Vulgate); Esth. 4:16; 2 Macc. 13:12; T. Jos. 3:5[3].

This ritual of penance serves as a preparation for the retreat into a cave in the field, where Taxo and his sons will apparently stay in anticipation of their violent death (see

---

[1] The innocence of these ancestors is of great importance in connection with the Second Commandment, which prohibits idolatry; referring to the Lord's jealousy, it threatens that the sins of those who hate God will be avenged unto the third and fourth generation (Exod. 20:5; Deut. 5:9).

[2] Without reference to Exod. 17: Numb. 14:22; Ps. 78(77):56; Sir. 18:23(13); Isa. 7:12; Mal. 3:15; Wisd. 1:2; Matt. 4:7 = Luke 4:12; Acts 15:10. Judith 8:11 does not explicitly refer to Exod. 17, but is intentionally reminiscent of it.

[3] Other periods for fasting are seven days (1 Chron. 10:12; 4 Ezra 5:13, 20; 6:31, 35; cf. 9:23, 26); forty days (Matt. 4:2, par. Luke 4:2).

9:7). Taxo expects their death to result from their obedience to the Lord, which con-
travenes the king's ordinances: *moriamur potius quam praetereamus mandata Domini
dominorum, Dei parentum nostrorum.* Compare with these words those spoken by the
first martyr in 2 Macc. 7:2 ἕτοιμοι γὰρ ἀποθνήσκειν ἐσμὲν ἢ παραβαίνειν τοὺς
πατρίους νόμους (cf. 2 Macc. 7:29); the motif often recurs in the traditions connected
with the Maccabeans (see 1 Macc. 2:37, 50; 2 Macc. 7:29; 4 Macc. 9:1; Josephus,
Ant. Jud. XII 281-282[1]). In 1 Macc. 2:37, it is linked to the retreat into the desert (1
Macc. 2:29); in 1 Macc. 2:50-51 the example of the fathers is stressed.

The entering into the cave in the field allows Taxo and his sons to avoid transgressing the law[2]. Caves were regarded as places of refuge in times of physical dan-
ger, hidden from and practically inaccessible to one's persecutors (see Josh. 10:16-27;
1 Sam. 13:6; 22:1; 24:4-11; 2 Sam. 23:13; 1 Ki. 18:4, 13; 19:9, 13; 1 Chron. 11:15;
Ps. 57[56]:1; 142[141]:1; Isa. 2:19; Josephus, *Bell. Jud.* I 312-313; *Ant. Jud.* XIV
429; Heb. 11:38; Rev. 6:15). A retreat into the desert is also mentioned in 1 Macc.
2:29 (cf. Josephus, *Ant. Jud.* XII 271-275), and Ps. Sol. 17:17, but in these instances no caves are mentioned.

Taxo's appeal for faithfulness to the commandments in reinforced by bestowing
two titles to the law-giver, God. He is the God of their ancestors and also the omnipo-
tent God, a combination which stresses the extraordinary character of the relationship
between God and his people. The same combination is found in Deut. 10:15-17.

Parentes must here be taken as "ancestors", and not as "begetters" or "parents" in a
strict sense (γονεῖς); *parentes* corresponds to πατέρες in Prov. 19:14; Wisd. 12:21;
18:22, 24; Sir. 44:1; Heb. 11:23. The first title, "Lord of lords", points to God's
omnipotence, as in Deut. 10:17: "For the Lord is our God, he is the God of gods and
the Lord of lords, the great, strong and frightful God" (cf. also Ps. 136(135):2-3,
"God of gods and Lord of lords").

9:7

The conclusion of Taxo's speech to his sons states that his blood and that of his sons
will be avenged before (= by; see grammatical note nr. 75) the Lord in the event of
their death. Taxo's words seem to be an allusion to Deut. 32:43 ὅτι τὸ αἷμα τῶν
υἱῶν αὐτοῦ ἐκδικᾶται, but see also Ps. 79(78):10; the vindication of the blood of the
Lord's servants is not an uncommon motif in other texts (e.g. 2 Ki. 9:7; Rev. 6:10;
19:2; 6 Ezra 15:9).

It is not explicitly stated that Taxo and his sons will actually die, but Taxo clearly
expects this to happen, and the mention of "blood" also strongly suggests that the
death Taxo expects will be a violent one. Thus, two motifs traditionally associated
with zeal for the law are here brought together: violent death and a retreat into (caves
in) the desert.

---

[1] See further Kellermann, "Das Danielbuch", p. 71, item (4), and Rhoads, "The Assumption of Moses", pp. 56-57.

[2] In 2 Macc. 6:11; 10:6, caves in the desert are chosen as safe places to celebrate the Jewish
feasts.

10:1-10
THE APPEARANCE OF GOD'S KINGDOM

In the final stage of the eschatological events, the author of As. Mos. expects God to react to the death of his faithful ones, Taxo and his sons. God will manifest his kingly rule and expel the devil (10:1). The blood of Taxo and his sons will indeed be avenged (10:2, cf. 9:6), probably by Taxo himself, who, as a reward for his zeal, is exalted and consecrated as a heavenly priest. Next, the author describes nature's reaction to God rising from his throne, using traditional language to describe the theophany (10:3-6). God is said to stand up to punish the nations and to destroy their idols (10:7). The aim of his intervention, set in motion by the death of the innocent Taxo and his sons, is to redeem Israel: the entire people will mount on the eagle God will send and be exalted to heaven, where they will live among the stars and praise the Lord (10:8-10).

a. *10:1-2*

As. Mos. 10:1-2 is the introduction to the description of the theophany (10:3-7) and of Israel's exaltation (10:8-10). The eschatological and definitive intervention of God in his creation is the Lord's reaction to Taxo's faithfulness to the law in the extreme circumstances which the author of As. Mos. expects to come shortly (chapters 8-9).

1 And then his kingdom will appear in his entire creation. And then the devil will come to an end, and sadness will be carried away together with him. 2 Then the hands of the messenger, when he will be in heaven, will be filled, and he will then avenge them against their enemies.

10:1

Following the probably violent death of Taxo and his sons, God's[1] kingdom "will appear" (*parebit*; the compound *apparebit* is more common) in his entire creation. The theophany described in 10:3-7 shows that God's entire creation is involved.

For the idea that the "kingdom" of God "appears", see Sib. Or. III 47-48: τότε δὴ βασιλεία μεγίστη ἀθανάτου βασιλῆος ἐπ' ἀνθρώποισι φανεῖται, and cf. 2 Bar. 39:7. According to As. Mos. 10:3, God reigns from heaven, and according to 10:7,

---

[1] *Illius*, pregnantly referring to God (see grammatical note nr. 59).

8-10, the result of the appearance of his kingdom is the punishment of the idolatrous nations and the exaltation of Israel into heaven. Therefore, *regnum illius parebit in omnia creatura illius* is not an announcement that God will henceforth rule the earth, but rather that it will become manifest in his entire creation that God is King[1] (see further commentary on 10:3).

As a result of the coming of God's kingdom, the devil will "have an end" (the Vulgate has *finem habere* where the Greek text has τέλος ἔχειν in Mark 3:26; or συν-τελεσθῆναι [sc. sin] in Dan. 9:24; the expression is used for Solomon's death in Sir. 47:27[23]; LXX: ἀνεπαύσατο; cf. finally Heb. 7:3 *finem vitae habens* = ζωῆς τέλος ἔχων; for *zabulus* as an orthographic variant of *diabolus*, cf. grammatical notes nrs. 5 and 15). It may be that the devil in As. Mos. 10:1 is thought to be the official prosecutor, who will be removed from God's courtroom[2], so that sadness (probably λύπη, cf. e.g. Sir. 12:9; 14:1; 18:15; perhaps πένθος, e.g. Prov. 5:16; 7:4) will be dispelled with him[3] (*adducetur = abducetur*; see grammatical note nr. 28). On the other hand, the image may be less concrete; probably, the end of the devil only serves to illustrate the absoluteness of God's kingdom, in which there is no place for satanic forces[4] (cf. 1 En. 10:6; Jub. 23:29; 50:5; John 12:31; Rev. 20:10; T. Napht. 8:4; also 1 John 3:8 ἐφανερώθη ὁ υἱὸς τοῦ θεοῦ, ἵνα λύσῃ τὰ ἔργα τοῦ διαβόλου).

Similarly, the removal of sadness (which is the work of the devil) is just the obverse of the outbreak of joy (cf. As. Mos. 10:10 *gaudebis*)[5]. The appearance of God's kingdom is described as the reversal of all earthly conditions[6]: just as the mountains will be turned upside down (cf. As. Mos. 10:4-6), sadness will be turned into joy (see 4 Ezra 6:27; Jub. 23:29; 2 Bar. 73:1-4; Sib. Or. V 385; John 16:20; T. Levi 18:12-14; T. Judah 25:3-5; Apoc. Mos. 39; cf. Isa. 35:10; 51:11). For the idea that sadness will disappear at the appearance of God, see also Rev. 21:4.

10:2

With the appearance of God's kingdom, a messenger (*nuntius*) in heaven will be consecrated as priest. It has often been assumed that the *nuntius*, a translation of ἄγγελος, must be identified with the archangel Michael, the patron of Israel. At first sight, this appears to be the most natural explanation: at the revelation of God's kingdom, an angel up on high[7] (*qui est constitutus* may mean no more than "who is"[8]) will avenge Taxo and his sons. Similar concepts of patron angels are found in Dan. 10:13, 21; 12:1; 1 En. 47:2; 1QM XVII 6-7; T. Levi 3:3. More difficult to answer is the question why at this point an angel would be introduced. In Dan. 12:1, for instance, Michael is

---

[1] Cf. Volz, *Die Eschatologie*, pp. 167-169.

[2] For the devil as prosecutor, see Foerster and von Rad, "διαβάλλω κτλ.", pp. 72-78.

[3] So Camponovo, *Königtum*, p. 170.

[4] Cf. Foerster and von Rad, "διαβάλλω κτλ.", p. 77, note 43: "[Es] wird einfach konstatiert, daß es einst keinen Bösen mehr geben wird".

[5] Camponovo, *Königtum*, p. 170, tends to equate *tristitia* with the catastrophes proper that will have befallen Israel, but that is an over-interpretation.

[6] On the μεταβολὴ πάντων (Philo, *De praemiis* 169), see Volz, *Die Eschatologie*, pp. 126-127.

[7] *Summum* is used for "heaven", especially in a locative function, thus *in summo* here, and *a summo* in 10:10; cf. the Vulgate of Ps. 18(17):17 *misit de summo*, Vulgate *juxta Hebraeos*: *de alto*, and cf. *in excelsis* in e.g. Ps. 148:1.

[8] See grammatical note nr. 130.

clearly depicted as the heavenly warrior who will protect Israel. But in Daniel such angels occur more often, and they have a clear function in the heavenly counterparts of earthly struggles (Dan. 10:12-21). In As. Mos., however, there are no other angels with a comparable task[1]. G.W.E. Nickelsburg has tried to explain this problem by supposing that the angel would have been introduced in As. Mos., simply because it was traditional to have an angel judging the nations at this stage of the eschatological process[2].

On the other hand, Carlson, and Camponovo (following Kuhn)[3], have explained the angel's role as mediatory. The angel would convey Taxo's cry for vengeance (9:6) to the Lord, who would then intervene (cf. Tob. 12:12, 15; 1 En. 9:1-10; T. Levi 3:5-6). However, it is clearly said that the *nuntius* will avenge them, which is something quite different from mediating the cries of the righteous ones.

Moreover, the *nuntius* is said to be consecrated as a priest: *tunc implebuntur manus nuntii*. "Filling one's hands"[4] is a technical term for the consecration of priests, see Exod. 28:41; 29:29, 33, 35; Lev. 8:33; 16:32[5]; 21:10; Num. 3:3; Judg. 17:5, 12; 1 Ki. 13:33; 2 Chron. 13:9; T. Levi 8:10; Jos. As. 27:2. None of the proposed interpretations explains why an angel would be consecrated as a priest at this stage of the eschatological process and not earlier.

Recently, the present author has proposed identifying the *nuntius* with Taxo[6]. Whereas the ordination of an angel as priest at this stage makes no sense, Taxo's priestly ordination in 10:2, because of the specific mention of his Levitical descent (9:1), is very appropriate. If seen from the perspective of the tradition of the suffering righteous, the priestly ordination of Taxo in heaven can be naturally understood as a reward for his faithfulness to the law, for which he even died (9:6)[7].

The title *nuntius* should be explained in relation to the mediating office commonly associated with prophets and priests. These mediators may, as such, be called μεσίτης and ἄγγελος[8]. Thus, in As. Mos., Moses is called μεσίτης (*arbiter*) in 1:14, and

---

[1] *Unus qui supra eos est* 4:1 is not an angel (so Camponovo, *Königtum*, p. 170), but Ezra (see commentary on 4:1).

[2] *Resurrection*, pp. 28-31; cf. Tromp, "Taxo", pp. 203-204.

[3] Carlson, "Vengeance and Angelic Mediation", Camponovo, *Königtum*, p. 170; Kuhn, "Zur Assumptio Mosis", p. 126.

[4] The Hebrew expression has a singular "hand", but LXX has τελειοῦν τὰς χείρας, "fulfilling the hands", "making them perfect".

[5] In Exod. 29:35-36; Lev. 8:33-34 and 16:32-33, "filling the hands" is directly connected with mediation and atonement (ἐξιλάσκεσθαι, see commentary on 4:1; 11:17 and 12:6); the mediatory office of priests is also the reason why priests can be called *nuntius*, which is a term indicating mediation (see below).

[6] "Taxo, the Messenger of the Lord"; for a brief critical review of earlier suggestions, see *ibid.*, pp. 202-205.

[7] For the heavenly reward of the suffering righteous, see the instances collected by Kellermann, "Das Danielbuch", p. 75.

[8] For humans as ἄγγελοι of God see As. Mos. 11:17 (Moses); 2 Chron. 36:15-16 (cf. 3 Ezra 1:48, 49; the prophets); Eccl. 5:5 (a priest); Isa. 42:19 MT (the servant of the Lord); Hagg. 1:13 (Haggai); Mal. 2:7 (the priest); cf. Mal. 3:1 (quoted in Matt. 11:10; Mark 1:2; Luke 7:27 and applied to John the Baptist); Ps.-Hecataeus in Diod. Sic., *Bibl. Hist.* 40, 3, 5 (the high priest). Christ Jesus is emphatically described as a human mediator in 1 Tim. 2:5. See further Davies, "A Note on Josephus", pp. 138-139; Walton, "The Messenger of God".

ἄγγελος/*nuntius* in 11:17. As a mediator, his task is to establish the covenant between God and his people (1:14; 3:12); as a messenger, he is appointed to intercede for Israel (11:17; 12:6), and to defend the people against their enemies (11:17-18). This concept of Moses can be illustrated by Philo, *De vita Mosis* II 166, where it is said of Moses that, although he was shattered upon hearing on Sinai of the people's sin with the golden calf, he did not hurry towards them, but, being a mediator and reconciler (οἷα μεσίτης καὶ διαλλάκτης), he first prayed (ἱκεσίας καὶ λιτὰς ἐποιεῖτο) in order that the people's sins be forgiven. After the protector and intercessor (κηδεμὼν καὶ παραιτητής) had softened God's wrath, he returned to pronounce sentence on the offenders on behalf of the Lord (cf. Exod. 32:11-14, 28-35; Ps. 106[105]:19-23). Likewise, in *De somniis* I 141-143, Philo describes the intercessory function of the ἄγγελοι, that is, λόγοι, and cites Moses as an example of these μεσίται. Elsewhere, he constructs a similar relation between the λόγος and priests as mediators, see *De vita Mosis* II 66, 133; *De specialibus legibus* I 116; *De gigantibus* 52, 61; *De cherubim* 16-17; *Quod Deus immutabilis* 131-135. From texts like Jub. 31:14 and T. Levi 3:5; 4:2 it appears that Philo was not unique in his comparison of priests and angels; cf. Sir. 24:10, where Wisdom is described as saying ἐν σκηνῇ ἁγίᾳ ἐνώπιον αὐτοῦ ἐλειτούργησα.

Being installed as a mediator, Taxo will subsequently[1] take revenge on Israel's enemies (*vindicavit illos ab inimicis eorum*[2]), a reward which is often expected to be given to the righteous in the eschatological time (see Dan. 7:17-18; Wisd. 3:8; 4:16; 1 En. 38:5; 90:19; 91:12; 92:4; 95:3, 7; 96:1; 98:12; Matt. 19:28; cf. Ps. 49[48]:15; 149:8-9. It has been noted that the *nuntius* duplicates God's avenging actions (10:7), but such a duplication is not exceptional; see Wisd. 3:8: (Δίκαιοι) κρινοῦσιν ἔθνη καὶ κρατήσουσιν λαῶν, καὶ βασιλεύσει αὐτῶν κύριος εἰς τοὺς αἰῶνας (cf. 1 En. 91:12-14).

Taxo's ordination as a priest is said to take place *in summo*, that is: in heaven, where he will "be". The phrase *qui est constitutus* is rather vague and cannot be given an unequivocal meaning, but it seems that the considerations above recommend the translation "when he will be", or even stronger: "when he will be appointed" (see grammatical note nr. 134). *Constituere* has the latter meaning in 12:6 *Dominus me constituit pro eis*; cf. also 1:14 *invenit me qui ... praeparatus sum &c.*

There are, therefore, three elements in As. Mos. 10:2 that are closely related: (1) Taxo is rewarded in heaven for his faithfulness to the law by his ordination as a priest; (2) as such, he is called a *nuntius*, a title indicating mediation and intercession; (3) he furthermore has bestowed on him judicial power, which, being a mediator, he uses to take revenge on Israel's enemies. From As. Mos. 10:8-10 it appears that Taxo's death is indeed thought to have atoning consequences for Israel.

---

[1] *Protinus* must here be interpreted as εὐθύς/εὐθέως in many instances in the New Testament, namely as "thereupon, subsequently". See Daube, *The Sudden in the Scriptures*, pp. 46-72.

[2] For vengeance that is executed on one's "enemies", see Esther 8:13 (*de hostibus*); 9:1 (*de adversariis*); Jer. 46:10 (*de inimicis*); Wisd. 11:3 (*de inimicis*); cf. Ps. 149:7 (*in nationibus*); for vengeance executed on someone else's behalf, see Deut. 32:43 (θεὸς) ἐκδικήσει καὶ ἀνταποδώσει δίκην τοῖς ἐχθροῖς, καὶ τοῖς μισοῦσιν ἀνταποδώσει; cf. Luke 18:3, also 1 Macc. 2:67; 13:6.

b. *10:3-7*

In this passage, the author of As. Mos. describes the theophany[1]. The traditional description of a theophany is formally characterized by a division into two parts, the first peart speaking of God's coming[2], the second part describing the subsequent upsetting of the natural order.[3] This basic form is also displayed in As. Mos. 10:3-6:

(1) 10:3 The Heavenly Lord will rise from his throne and leave his holy habitation; the cause of his actions is said to be his anger on account of his servants;

(2) 10:4   a. the earth will tremble and the mountains will be made low;
    10:5   b. the heavenly bodies will be obscured and their order disrupted;
    10:6   c. the waters will be dried up.

The creation is divided into three parts: earth, heaven and the waters. In varying order, this tripartite description of the "entire creation" is found also in the theophanies Hab. 3:10-11; Sir. 16:18-19; 4 Ezra 8:23; T. Levi 3:9-4:1; 1 QH III 32-36. The earth, the heaven and the waters, in their turn are divided into three parts as well: land, mountains and valleys; sun, moon and stars, and sea, fountains and rivers, respectively.

In As. Mos. 10:7, it is restated that the Lord will rise and appear. The purpose of his advent is to punish the nations and their idols. It is clear, therefore, that in As. Mos. 10:3-7, the theophany is associated with the Day of the Lord, hence also with the manifestation of his kingship on earth[4]. There is no reference to a judgement, but this may be implicit (as for instance in Isa. 26:19-21 and Dan. 12:1-3).

3 For the Heavenly One will rise from his royal throne, and he will go out from his holy habitation with anger and wrath on account of his sons.

4 And the earth will tremble until its extremes it will be shaken, and the high mountains will be made low, and they will be shaken, and the valleys will sink. 5 The sun will not give its light, and the horns of the

---

[1] Many parallels quoted in the commentary on this passage below are derived from the great standard works on Jewish eschatology, such as Volz, *Die Eschatologie*; Mowinckel, *He That Cometh*; helpful insights were given to me by an (unpublished) essay on As. Mos. 10 by R. Oost.

[2] In As. Mos. 10:3-7, the author does not say explicitly that God will "come" (although 10:7 says that the Lord will come out in the open): he will arise from his throne and leave his dwelling-place, but it is his kingship that will appear in his creation (10:1); see commentary on 10:3.

[3] Jeremias, *Theophanie*, p. 15.

[4] Other descriptions of theophanies in Biblical and related literature are associated with the giving of the law on mount Sinai, with the crossing of the Reed Sea, with the war against the chaotic creatures, and with the Ark of the Covenant. See Jeremias, *Theophanie*, pp. 90-112, esp. pp. 97-100 about the Day of the Lord; on p. 112, Jeremias deals with the association of the theophany with the manifestation of God's kingship on earth. Cf. also the comments by A.Y. Collins, "Composition and Redaction", pp. 182-183, on As. Mos. 10:3-10 as a reflection of the "ancient mythic pattern" of the Divine Warrior Myth.

moon will turn into darkness, and they will be broken; and (*sc.* the moon) will entirely be turned into blood, and the orbit of the stars will be upset. 6 And the sea will fall back into the abyss, and the fountains of the waters will defect and the rivers will recoil.

7 For the Highest God, the sole Eternal One, will rise, and he will manifest himself in order to punish the nations, and to destroy all their idols.

10:3

Appropriately, God is here given the title the "Heavenly One". On this title, see commentary on As. Mos. 2:4 and 4:4. In heaven, the Lord is said to rise from his throne and to come out of his dwelling-place. It is not stated explicitly that he will descend upon earth (cf. 10:1, where it is said that God's kingdom will appear, not the Lord himself; in later instances of the genre, the theophany is associated with the manifestation of the kingship of the Lord[1]; see esp. Ps. 97[96]:1-2).

The Lord is expected in As. Mos. 10:3 to rise "from his royal throne" (*sedes regni sui* is a biblical style-figure, see grammatical note, nr. 191; cf. Pr. Azar. 31). This is associated with the judgement he wants to execute on account of his "sons" (see below). In the Psalms, the Lord is asked to "rise" (*exurgere*, mostly = ἀναστῆναι, sometimes = ἐξεγείρεσθαι) in order to act forcefully on behalf of those who pray to him for salvation from their enemies (cf. 10:7); see e.g. Ps. 3:7(8) ἀνάστα, κύριε, σῶσον με, ὁ θεός μου; 7:7 ἀνάστηθι, κύριε, ἐν ὀργῇ σου, ὑψώθητι ἐν τοῖς πέρασι τῶν ἐχθρῶν μου· ἐξεγέρθητι, κύριε ὁ θεός μου, ἐν προστάγματι; 68(67):2 ἀναστήτω ὁ θεός, καὶ διασκορπισθήτωσαν οἱ ἐχθροὶ αὐτοῦ (almost identical words in Num. 10:35[34]); see further e.g. Ps. 12(11):6 ; 35(34):2.

That the Lord will come to bring justice is moreover suggested by the expression *cum indignationem et iram*. *Indignatio et ira* are synonyms, frequently occurring together. They are equivalent to ὀργὴ καὶ θυμός; see e.g. Deut. 9:19; Ps. 78(77):49; 102(101):11; Isa. 10:25 (*indignatio et furor*); cf. also ὀργὴ θυμοῦ Ps. 85(84):4; Isa. 42:25; 1 Macc. 2:49. For the association of the Lord's anger with judgement, see commentary on 8:1a-b.

The Lord is said to "go out of his holy habitation" (see also 12:13). This is a common motif in theophany-descriptions[2], although the exact indication of the habitation varies: the Lord is said to go out from various mountains (Deut. 33:2; Judg. 5:4; Hab. 3:3; Ps. 50:2[49:2-3]); from "his place" (Micah 1:3; Isa. 26:21 MT); from heaven (2 Sam. 22:10; Ps. 18[17]:10; 144[143]:5; Isa. 63:19; 4 Ezra 3:18; 1 En. 1:3); "from afar" (Isa. 30:27); finally also "from his habitation": Micah 1:3; 1 En. 1:3 ἐξελεύσεται ὁ ἅγιός μου ὁ μέγας ἐκ τῆς κατοικήσεως αὐτοῦ; cf. also Sib. Or. III 308. For *habitatio sancta* cf. Isa. 63:15; Jer. 25:30; 1QS X 3; 1QM XII 1.

Finally, there are several other texts which contain the motif of the Lord rising with anger in order to pronounce verdict on his sons' enemies, e.g. Isa. 14:22; 26:20-21; 28:21; 35:4; 1 En. 1:7; 91:7; 100:4.

---

1 Jeremias, *Theophanie*, p. 112.
2 Jeremias, *Theophanie*, pp. 7-16, 115.

The word translated with "sons", *filii*, can of course be a translation of the ambiguous word παῖς; the Greek word may mean "son" as well as "servant". But the relation between the Lord and Israel is often likened to that between parents and children (see commentary on 11:13). In Deut. 32:43 MT, the Lord is said to "take revenge for the blood of his servants (עבדיו)"; in the more original text[1], represented by LXX and 4QDt 32, it is said that he will "take revenge for the blood of his sons" (αἷμα τῶν υἱ-ῶν αὐτοῦ; דם בניו).

10:4

One of the most constant elements of the theophanies is the "trembling" of the earth and the mountains; see, e.g. Judg. 5:4-5; 2 Sam. 22:8 (= Ps. 18[17]:8); 77(76):19; Isa. 24:19; 63:19; Joel 2:10; Nah. 1:5; Hab. 3:6, 10; Sir. 16:18-19; Sib. Or. III 675. Literally, earthquakes are meant, but as a metaphor, this shaking signifies the great fear which the mighty presence of the Lord causes to his creation. See esp. As. Mos. 10:6, where it is said that the rivers will be terrified.

The mountains will be shaken and "made low" (cf. Hab. 3:6; 1 En. 1:6). *Convalles cadent* may be translated as "the valleys will sink (even further)". Because of the peculiarity of this image, some scholars proposed to emend *convalles* into *colles*, so that a regular parallelism of "mountains" and "hills" would be obtained, as for instance in Isa. 40:4 πᾶν ὄρος καὶ βουνὸς ταπεινωθήσεται (cf. 1 En. 1:6). However, a corruption of *colles* into *convalles* is hard to explain.

10:5

The celestial bodies, the sun, the moon and the stars, will no longer give their light; see Isa. 13:10 (cf. Matt. 24:29; Mark 13:24); Joel 2:10; 3:15; cf. Amos 8:9; Hab. 3:11; also Ezek. 32:7-8 (darkness accompanying the downfall of the king of Egypt). More specifically, the image of the moon turning into blood seems to derive from Joel 2:31(3:4); cf. Acts 2:20; Rev. 6:12; also Isa. 24:23. To the confounding of the orbit of the stars compare 1 En. 80:6-7; 102:2; cf. also the falling of the stars in Isa. 34:4 (cf. Matt. 24:29; Mark 13:25; Rev. 6:13). The expression κύκλον ἄστρων occurs in Wisd. 13:2; cf. *cursus stellarum* in LAB 23:10. A singular image, not found in other theophany descriptions, is the breaking of the *cornua lunae*. These "horns" (κέρατα) are the extremities of the waxing and waning moon (cf. Aratus 785, 790: αἱ κεραίαι τῆς σελήνης; Or. Sib. V 517: Σεληναίης δίκερως)[2].

According to Jeremias, the defection of the celestial bodies is a secondary motif in the theophanies, which originally belonged to the concept of the "Day of the Lord". As in Hab. 3:10-11, however, both concepts, the Day of the Lord and the theophany, have been combined in As. Mos. 10:3-7[3].

---

[1] Meyer, "Die Bedeutung von Deuteronomium 32, 8 f. 43".

[2] Charles, in his reconstruction of this passage, *The Assumption*, pp. 86-87, combined the *cornua* with the sun, apparently interpreting them as "beams of light" (*via* Hebrew קרן, which has both meanings). But even then, one would like to understand how the "beams" of the sun can be broken; see Clemen, *APAT* II, p. 327.

[3] Jeremias, *Theophanie*, p. 98.

10:6

The third part of creation, the waters, are characterized as the sea, the fountains of the waters, and the rivers (see Nah. 1:4; Hab. 3:8, where the "sea" and the "rivers" are in parallel position; cf. Ps. 114[113]:3, 5).

The sea will fall down into the abyss; cf. 2 Sam. 22:16; Ps. 18(17):16; 4 Ezra 8:23. The sources of water will dry up, 4 Ezra 6:24; T. Levi 4:1; cf. Joel 1:20; Ps. Sol. 17:19; 1 En. 101:7; Rev. 16:12. The rivers will be terrified; cf. Ps. 104(103):7; 114:3, 5. For the use of *expavescere* cf. 4 Ezra 6:24 *expavescet terra* (cf. 4 Ezra 6:23). In Sib. Or. III 675-677 the entire creation, including the sea, is said to be trembling with fear.

For *ad* as an orthographical variant of *at*, see grammatical note nr. 35.

10:7

In the concluding sentence of the description of the theophany, the intention of God's coming is mentioned again. It is made explicit that the wrath of God, which is the reason he will rise from his throne, will be poured out over the gentiles, the enemies of his servants (compare 10:3 with 10:7). The Highest God, who alone is eternal, will punish the nations and destroy their idols. For the title *summus Deus*, see commentary on 6:1; for the title *aeternus solus*, see Sus. 25 LXX, 42 Θ; 2 Macc. 1:25; Rom. 16:26; 1 Tim. 1:17. The uniqueness of the eternal God is contrasted to the destruction of the pagan deities.

Palam venire ("to come out in the open, to manifest oneself") has a meaning closely related to *(ap)parere* ("to appear", cf. 10:1), but emphasizes the dynamics of the process. The expression is used in the Vulgate of Mark 4:22 and Luke 8:17, in which instances the Greek has ἔρχεσθαι εἰς φανερόν.

The motif of the destruction of the gentile idols is also found in the theophany in Micah 1:3-7; see Micah 1:7 καὶ πάντα τὰ γλυπτὰ αὐτῆς (sc. of Samaria) κατακόψουσιν καὶ πάντα τὰ μισθώματα αὐτῆς ἐμπρήσουσιν ἐν πυρί, καὶ πάντα τὰ εἴδωλα αὐτῆς θήσομαι εἰς ἀφανισμόν. See further Wisd. 14:11; 1 En. 91:9; Sib. Or. III 618.

c. *10:8-10*

In this final passage of Moses' prophecy, Israel is said to attain a blissful state in heaven. Taxo's death appears to have an atoning effect: Israel will follow him to heaven on the wings of an eagle. The close link between Taxo's death and exaltation and Israel's bliss is emphasized by the parallelism between 10:2a and 10:9-10.

8 Then you will be happy, Israel, and you will mount on the neck and the wings of an eagle, and they will be filled, 9 and God will exalt you, and make you live in the heaven of the stars, the place of his habitation. 10 And you will look down from above, and you will see your enemies on the earth, and you will recognize them. And you will rejoice, and you will thank and praise your Creator.

10:8

In As. Mos. 10:8, the eschatological fulfilment of God's promise is expected. Together with As. Mos. 3:8, this is the only occasion on which the name Israel is used; elsewhere, this name is avoided and instead *tribus* or *plebs* is used. In 3:8, the ten tribes reminded the two tribes that the distress brought by the king from the East had come over "the entire house of Israel", and according to the author of As. Mos., "the house of Israel" has not been restored since then (see commentary on 4:7-9). Only after the appearance of God's kingdom will the people regain their blissful state and be worthy of the name Israel.

The words *tunc felix eris, tu Istrahel* are practically identical to those in Deut. 33:29: μακάριος σύ, Ἰσραήλ. The connection between As. Mos. 10:8 and Deut. 33:29 is seemingly strengthened by the image of mounting on the necks of an eagle. In Deut. 33:29 LXX, it is prophesied that σὺ ἐπὶ τὸν τράχηλον[1] αὐτῶν ἐπιβήσῃ, which refers to Israel's victory over its enemies. This element from Deut. 33:29 should not also be connected with As. Mos. 10:8[2]. The eagle in As. Mos. clearly is an animal which is expected to transport Israel to heaven, and not an enemy which is to be humiliated.

The eagle (ἀετός) is a proverbially swiftly moving animal (see 2 Sam. 1:23; Job 9:26; 39:30[27]; Jer. 4:13; Lam. 4:19; Hab. 1:8; LAB 24:6), which has its nest on high (see Job 39:30[27]; Jer. 49[29]:16), even among the stars (Obad. 4, cf. As. Mos. 10:9). An eagle that carries Israel is used as an image for the Lord's leading his people out of Egypt in Exod. 19:4 and Deut. 32:11. In As. Mos. 10:8, this eagle simply carries the Lord's people out of the world into heaven, as in 1 En. 96:23[3]. The concept of an eagle transporting a new god (a dead king or emperor) to heaven also occurs in the Alexander romance (3, 33, 5)[4], but seems to derive eventually from ancient Near Eastern mythology[5].

The eagle's wings are said to be "filled". It has often been assumed that the phrase *et implebuntur* lacks a subject (e.g. *dies luctus tui*, "the days of your mourning will be ended"[6]), but the simplest explanation, peculiar though the image may be, is to understand that the number of people exalted into heaven is so large that all room on the eagle's wings is taken. The image must then be an illustration of the generosity with which God dispenses his grace.

---

[1] The Masoretic and Vulgate texts read "you will mount upon their high places"; 1QM XII 11 apparently combining both readings: תן ידכה בעורף אויביכה ורגלכה על במותי חלל (cf. 1QM XIX 3).

[2] The plural *cervices* has led scholars to assume that reference was made to the Roman, two-headed eagle. "To mount the eagle's necks" is then interpreted as referring to the victory the Lord's people will gain over the Romans ("to mount on one's neck" is a victory sign, see Josh. 10:24, esp. Deut. 33:29 LXX). However, *cervices* is here used as a *plurale tantum*; see grammatical note nr. 48.

[3] In a different way, the eagle is also associated with Israel's eschatological bliss in Isa. 40:31; T. Judah 25:5.

[4] Ed. Van Thiel, *Leben und Taten Alexanders*, p. 164.

[5] Laperrousaz, *Le Testament*, p. 129. On a broader level, the eagle is of course well-known as a divine means of transport; apart from the Ganymede-myth (e.g. Vergil, *Aeneis* V 254-255; Ovid, *Metamorphoses* X 155-161), cf. also Par. Jer. 7.

[6] So Charles, *The Assumption*, p. 88.

10:9-10

On the wings of the eagle, God will exalt Israel, and make them live in the heaven of the stars. The verb *herere* (classically spelt *haerere*, see grammatical note nr. 8) can mean "to remain, to abide in a certain place", although the verb seems to have also the negative connotation of "loitering"[1]. Hartman therefore preferred to associate *herere* with *heres* and referred to Ps. 37(36):11, where it is said that the meek ones will "inherit" the land in peace; one could further point to passages such as Wisd. 5:5; 4 Ezra 7:9, 17, 96; 1 En. 5:7, where eschatological salvation is said to be inherited by the righteous. But Hartman's suggestion to understand *herere* as a makeshift derivation from *heres* seems too far-fetched[2]. One might consider the possibility of reading *hereditare*, but the locative *caelo* then remains an obstacle.

Israel's exaltation to the stars is a traditional part of eschatological expectation. This traditional concept takes on various forms: Israel will live among the stars in heaven: Isa. 14:13; Jer. 51(28):9; Ps. Sol. 1:5; or it will be like the stars, or explicitly like angels: Dan. 12:3; 4 Ezra 7:97, 125; 2 Bar. 51:5, 10 (cf. 51:12); 1 En. 51:4; 104:2, 6; LAB 19:9; 33:5; T. Levi 14:3; 18:4[3].

Heaven is God's dwelling-place, from which he looks down on the earth and its inhabitants; cf. Deut. 26:15 κάτιδε ἐκ τοῦ οἴκου τοῦ ἁγίου σου ἐκ τοῦ οὐρανοῦ; Ps. 33(32):13-14 ἐξ οὐρανοῦ ἐπέβλεψεν ὁ κύριος, εἶδεν πάντα τοὺς υἱοὺς τῶν ἀνθρώπων· ἐξ ἑτοίμου κατοικητηρίου αὐτοῦ ἐπέβλεψεν ἐπὶ πάντας τοὺς κατοικοῦντας τὴν γῆν; similarly 1 Ki. 8:39, 43, 49; Ps. 11(10):5(4); 102(101):20; 113(112):5-6; Isa. 63:15; 66:1. Having been moved to heaven, Israel will look down on earth as well, and it will see and recognize its enemies, who stay behind, presumably to be punished (As. Mos. 10:7). In a number of comparable texts, the enemies are thrown into darkness (1 En. 108:14), or swallowed by the earth or the underworld (1 En. 56:8; 90:18, 25-27)[4].

Seeing the punishment of its enemies will be an occasion for Israel to rejoice and thank its Creator (cf. Isa. 66:14; 1 En. 62:12; Jub. 23:30). According to 1 En. 97:2, even the angels will rejoice at the punishment of the sinners.

---

[1] Lewis-Short, p. 838a.

[2] Hartman, *Prophecy Interpreted*, p. 132.

[3] Cf. Volz, *Die Eschatologie*, pp. 396-401.

[4] Apparently inspired by these parallels, Charles, *The Assumption*, p. 88, conjectured ἐν γῇ as the Greek original of *in terram*, which, in its turn would derive from בג׳, an abbreviation of בג׳ הנם, "in hell". Although this is one of Charles' most curious proposals with regard to As. Mos., it has been followed by a remarkable number of scholars.

10:11-15
CONCLUDING WORDS

Moses ends his speech by his returning to the instructions given at its beginning (1:10-18). Moreover, he gives some additional information on the chronology of the future course of history, or rather, he indicates that there is a predetermined agenda for it.

₁₁ But you, Joshua son of Nun, keep these words and this book. ₁₂ For from my death, my being taken away, until his (*sc.* God's) advent, there will be 250 times that will happen. ₁₃ And this is the course of events that will come to pass, until they will be completed. ₁₄ But I shall go to the resting-place of my fathers. ₁₅ Therefore you, Joshua son of Nun, be strong. It is you, whom God has chosen to be my successor to his covenant.

10:11-13

Having completed his prophecy, Moses is again said to command Joshua to "keep these words and this book". "These words" are the prophecy which Moses has just uttered, and which are apparently written down in a book, as is not uncommon in farewell-texts (see 11:1, and commentary to 1:16-18). The words used here probably resume those used in 1:9, 16: *Custodi* (l. em.) *verbum hoc ... percipe scribturam hanc.* Likewise, 10:14 resumes 1:15, and 10:15 resumes 1:7 (see below). So, too, the mention of the period of time which will elapse between Moses' death and the fulfilment of the prophecy as a whole fits in well here, since it has been suggested in 1:16-18 that the book containing Moses' prophecy should be preserved for a long period.

The period the book has to be preserved ("from my death until his, *sc.* God's, advent") is defined as 250 "times". The length of time meant by the word "time" cannot be determined; it may well be that it has not been the author's intention to give an exact number of years[1]. It has been suggested that the author wished to suggest a certain symmetry between the time preceding Moses' prophecy (which is located, according to As. Mos. 1:2, in the 2500th year of the creation) and the time following it without fixing a precise number of years (see commentary on 1:2). Thus, the central role of Moses in history would correspond to his chronologically central place in the history of the world. If we can assume that a "time" equals ten years, this is certainly possible. It seems, however, that the primary intention of letting Moses say how much time there will be before history comes to its completion is to ensure that there is indeed a predetermined limit to history[2], which means that the readers of As. Mos. have to re-

---

[1] Cf. the mysterious indications in Dan. 7:25 and Rev. 12:14.
[2] See Hartman, "The Function of Some So-Called Apocalyptic Timetables".

gard the time in which they live as part of the end of this world's history. But there is also a course of events that has to be completed before the end can come (cf. 4 Ezra 4:28-30, 36-37; 2 Bar. 56:2; with 250 times, compare the two and a half time in LAB 19:15 *omnia complebit tempus. Quatuor enim semis transierunt, et duo semis supersunt.*[1]). Since the author's intended readers were expected to recognize their own day and age in As. Mos. 6-7, the assurance of history being limited serves both to stress the proximity of eschatological events, and to set at ease any overpitched expectations.

Receptio is often taken to be a redactional gloss on *mors*, added after the supposed amalgamation of the Testament and the Assumption of Moses (see the Introduction, sections II and III). The argument is that the Testament of Moses originally contained no assumption of Moses, and ended, in accordance with the genre of the testament, with Moses' death and burial. *Mors* would then be the word used in the Testament. The Assumption of Moses, however, would originally have been a different document and would have replaced the original conclusion to the Testament. The redactor who wove both works together would accordingly have found it necessary to redefine *mors* in 10:12 as *receptio*, "assumption". But there is no need to assume such redactional activity[2]. For *receptio* does not necessarily mean "assumption into heaven". There are indeed instances in which *recipi* means something like "to be taken (*sc.* to heaven)"[3], but one can as well "be taken (*sc.* to [the realm of] death)"[4], a translation which recommends itself in the present context[5]. The simple translation must be: "For there will be 250 times from my death, my being taken away, until his (*sc.* God's) arrival".

Finally, the reliability of Moses' prophecy (cf. commentary to As. Mos. 1:16) is once more emphasized: these are the events[6] which will take place before the end.

10:14-15
In the concluding words to Moses' monologue, the author makes the prophet return to his introduction, again announcing his impending death (for *dormitio*, "resting-place"

---

[1] On the time that must elapse before the end can come, see further Volz, *Die Eschatologie*, pp. 138-140.

[2] One may wonder why the supposed redactor did not simply replace *mors* by *receptio*.

[3] Ovid, *Heroides* 19,135; Quintilian 3,7,5 *receptus caelo*; cf. Livy 4,15 *Romulus ab diis ortus, receptus ad deos* (instances quoted from Forcellini IV, p. 26a-b); in the Vulgate: Sir. 48:9 *(Helias) qui receptus es* (ἀναλημφθείς) *in turbine igni*; 49:16(14) *(Enoch) receptus est* (ἀνελήμφθη) *a terra*; 1 Macc. 2:58 *Helias dum zelat zelum legis receptus est* (ἀνελήμφθη) *in caelum*; 4 Ezra 6:26 *qui recepti sunt homines, qui mortem non gustaverunt a nativitate sua.*

[4] Forcellini IV, p. 26a: Plautus, *Cistellaria* 3,8: *Recipe me ad te, Mors, amicum et benevolum*; ThLL VIII, 1507:72-75 mentions Seneca, *Troades* 1156: *morte recepta.* See in the Vulgate: Tob. 3:6 *et praecipe in pace recipi* (ἀναλαβεῖν) *spiritum meum*; Wisd. 16:14 (about the man who kills) *cum exibit spiritus non revertetur, nec revocabit animam quae recepta est* (ἐξελθὸν δὲ πνεῦμα οὐκ ἀναστρέφει, οὐδὲ ἀναλύει ψυχὴν παραλημφθεῖσαν). Cf. the instances in which someone is admitted to the grave: Ennius in Cicero, *Tusculanae Disputationes* I, 44, 107; 2 Chron. 28:27.

[5] Cf. Laperrousaz' discussion of *receptio*, *Le Testament*, pp. 41-46. Laperrousaz accepts Volkmar's emendation of the text of 10:12 into *a morte et receptione mea*, and suggests that the *receptio* refers to Moses' burial (for *recipere* with subject *sepulcrum*, see preceding note).

[6] *Cursus horum*, "the course of these things", of course not "of these hours" (Priest, "Testament of Moses", p. 933; this would have to be *horarum*).

as a euphemism for death; see 1:15). Joshua is commanded to be strong, because he has been elected to be Moses' successor. The expression "be strong" (ἀνδρίζου) again refers to the farewell scene in Deuteronomy (esp. 31:6-7). See the commentary on 1:9b-10.

The genitive construction *successor testamenti* seems to imply that Joshua is to fulfill the same role with regard to the covenant as Moses; he, too, will be its mediator (cf. 1:14, where it is said that Moses has been prepared from the beginning of the world to be the *arbiter testamenti illius*). Likewise, according to 1:6-9, Joshua has been deemed worthy by the Lord to be Moses' successor on behalf of the people and of the tabernacle, so that the land will be given to the people on account of the covenant. Joshua's mediatory office is then defined as being the human leader who guides the people at God's behest.

In As. Mos. 11:1-19, Joshua is described as reacting to Moses'
prophecy in despair (11:1-4). In a long list of questions he expresses
his fear of a future without Moses. This passage forms an expansion of
the basic pattern of the testament genre. In most other examples of the
genre, the testator delivers his speech uninterruptedly and dies. A
statement concerning his death may be followed by a note on the bereaved lamenting the deceased or taking care of his funeral. The
structure is similar to Deborah's farewell-scene in LAB 33:1-6, which
is organized as follows: In verses 1-3, Deborah summons the people,
announces her death, and admonishes the people to keep the law. In
verse 4, the people answer, weeping: *Ecce nunc mater moreris, et re-*
linquens filios tuos cui commendas eos? Ora itaque pro nobis, et post
recessum tuum erit anima tua memor nostri in sempiternum. Then, in
verse 5, Deborah answers that a man can pray for himself and his sons
only as long as he lives: *Propterea nolite sperare in patres vestros. Non*
enim proderunt vobis nisi similes inveniamini eis. Finally, in verse 6,
Deborah dies and is buried; the people lament.

The questions Joshua asks can be divided into three sections. In the
first set of questions (11:5-8), the problem of Moses' burial is addressed: no human being, it is said, is worthy of burying Moses, and no
memorial matching Moses' glory can be made. This problem emerges
from the biblical passage on Moses' burial site, which is said to be unknown (Deut. 34:6), and was probably addressed in the ending of As.
Mos., which in all likelihood related the burial of Moses by angels (see
the commentary on the lost ending).

The second set of questions (11:9-15) concerns three problems: the
feeding of the people, compassion for the people, and leading them on
their way. Under Moses' leadership, these three things were taken care
of: in the desert, the people were fed by the manna that fell from
heaven after Moses had prayed for it (see commentary on 11:13);
Moses was the one who took pity on the people, when their sins threatened to estrange them from their Lord (see commentary on 11:16f-
17b); and all along Moses had been their undisputed leader. Joshua
must now succeed Moses, but is described as being doubtful of his own
ability to do the wondrous things that Moses has done. The intended

readers of As. Mos. are to understand that the doubts Joshua is made to express are without foundation, for Joshua himself is known from biblical history to have performed the exploits mentioned in 11:9-15. Under his leadership as well as that of Moses, the people were fed, and there was a leader who offered intercessory prayer.

In 11:16-19, the third section of Joshua's complaints and questions, a connection is made between Moses' military successes against the Amorites and his effective intercessory prayer. In this context, Joshua expresses his anxiety that the presence of the Holy Spirit of God among the people is dependent on Moses, nearly identifying the prophet with the spirit itself. His eulogy of Moses leads to the question "What will happen to this people?" Again, however, the readers are supposed to know their Bible, which relates that under Joshua's leadership the kings of the Amorites fled before the Israelites and their God. Apparently, the presence of God's spirit does not depend on Moses, but is guaranteed to remain among the people, and will dwell in Joshua, Moses' successor.

The author's final answer to the questions he places in Joshua's mouth is given in chapter 12. There it is set out that Joshua will be able to succeed Moses by means of God's providence, grace and long-suffering towards those who fulfill the Lord's commandments, in accordance with his covenant and oath. Only because of these gifts of God, Moses, too, has been able to fulfill his role as the superb intermediary (see further the commentary on As. Mos. 11:17 and chapter 12). It is clear that the author of As. Mos. addressed the actual needs of his intended readers by these discussions.

a. *11:1-4*

As. Mos. 11:1-4 is the introduction to Joshua's complaint over the impending death of Moses. Joshua and Moses are depicted as weeping while Moses tries to comfort his successor. In 11:4a-b, the main theme of Joshua's complaint is presented: Joshua is convinced that Moses' departure will mean complete disaster.

1 And when Joshua had heard Moses' words as they were written in his writing, everything they foretold, he rent his clothes and fell at Moses' feet. 2 And Moses comforted him and wept with him. 3 And Joshua answered him and said: 4 "Why do you terrify me, lord Moses, and how will I hide myself from what you have said with the bitter voice that came from your mouth, and which is full of tears and sighs, because you will presently go away from this people?

11:1-3

Following the prophecy which is placed in Moses' mouth the farewell-scene is continued by Joshua's complaints. Joshua is described as in mourning, dramatized by his rending his clothes, falling at Moses' feet and weeping. For similar descriptions of the despair of those left behind, see for instance Gen. 37:34-35; 50:1; 2 Sam. 13:31; Jub. 23:5-7. "To fall at someone's feet" is a gesture of self-humiliation, see for instance 1 Sam. 25:23; Esth. 8:3; Matt. 18:26; Luke 5:12. In LAB 20:2, Joshua is reproached by God for letting himself get carried away by Moses' death: *Ut quid luges et ut quid speras in vanum cogitans quod Moyses adhuc vivet? Et ideo superflue sustines, quoniam defunctus est Moyses.*

11:4

In 11:4, forms of the verb *celare* occur twice in the text. These are hard to interpret, and most scholars agree that the text is not in order. Both instances of *celare* are usually emended into forms of the verb *solari*[1]. The meaning of the sentence in 11:4 would then be: "Why do you comfort me, lord Moses, yea, how can I be comforted about the things you have said etc." There are however two serious objections to this solution.

(1) *Solari* is a deponent verb. In the proposed emendation, it is assumed that the verb is first used with an active meaning, and in the next clause with a passive meaning. While such an assumption is not impossible (cf. grammatical note nr. 91), it would seem odd for a writer to combine these two opposite usages within one sentence.

(2) From a purely technical point of view, it seems improbable that a scribe would have made the same mistake, namely writing CEL instead of SOL, twice. Since neither the appearance of the letters nor the pronunciation of these words are similar, the mistake could only be due to carelessness in its worst form. Such carelessness could hardly be expected to be so consistent.

It seems most likely, therefore, that one of the occurrences of *celare* is correct, and that the word *celare* has in the other instance been substituted for a form of some other verb. At first sight, the first occurrence, *celares*, is most likely to be the correct one, simply because it is the first. However, *celares* should then still be emended into an acceptable form of the verb. Moreover, it should be assumed that the preceding word, *me*, is a vulgarism reflecting the pronunciation of *mi(hi)*, an ethical dative. This is possible, but it must be conceded that it makes for an additional complication. On the other hand, the second occurrence, *celabor*, is a correct and sensible form of *celare*, and its construction with *de* is in perfect order (see grammatical note nr. 68). I therefore propose to accept the manuscript's reading *celabor*, and to regard the preceding form *celares* as a scribal corruption of an original reading which can only be reconstructed with a certain degree of probability. From the farewell-scenes one could think of a word like *(de)relinquere* (καταλείπειν), cf. 4 Ezra 12:41, 44; 2 Bar. 32:9; 33:9; 34:1; LAB 33:4; Par. Jer. 9:8. But *terres* seems to fit the context excellently, and is paleographically not too far removed from *celares* (see the apparatus to line 176). The answer to Joshua's expression of fear is given by Moses in 12:3 *praebe te securum*, "do not worry".

---

[1] As proposed by Schmidt and Merx, "Die Assumptio Mosis", p. 134.

The expression "bitter voice" is a figure of speech indicating that Moses' voice has conveyed a message that causes grief. 11:4b specifies Moses' voice as one that is *plena lacrimis et gemitibus* (cf. 11:2 [*Monse*] *ploravit cum eo*; on *plenus* with the ablative, see grammatical note nr. 108). *Acervus* (= *acerbus*) means "unripe, sour" (cf. "your fathers have eaten the sour grape", Jer. 31:29-30; Ezek. 18:2); as a determinant of grief it is a typically Latin metaphor. Hebrew and Greek (as well as our modern languages) prefer the metaphor "bitter".

"To hide oneself" is a way of looking for protection, against the wind (Isa. 32:2), but also against the Lord's wrath (Job 14:13; Isa. 26:20). That the latter is possible is of course usually denied (Gen. 3:8; Jer. 49:10 [30:4]; Amos 9:3), and Joshua's question implies the impossibility of concealment from the things that Moses has prophesied.

It is uncertain what *quia* in the last clause of 11:4 refers to. It may refer to Moses' sadness; if so, Moses' impending death is the reason for his own voice being full of tears and sighs. On the other hand, it may, more loosely, link up with Joshua's question about hiding himself: "How will I hide myself, because you are leaving this people?" In view of the rest of Joshua's lament, which centers on the problems Moses' absence will cause, the second possibility seems to be slightly preferable.

b. *11:5-8*

In the first set of Joshua's questions, Moses' burial is discussed (for the problems raised by the biblical accounts concerning Moses' death, see the commentary on the lost ending). The author of As. Mos. makes Joshua ask where, how and by whom Moses might be buried: it is absurd to picture humans carrying a man like Moses to a grave, attempting, perhaps, to erect an adequate monument to his memory (see esp. As. Mos. 11:8). Probably, the now lost ending of As. Mos. did give an answer to Joshua's questions, with some variant of the legends about Moses' death, burial, and possibly the assumption of his soul into heaven; see further the commentary on the lost ending.

5 What place will receive you, 6 or what will be the monument on your grave, 7 or who, being human, will dare to carry your body from one place to another? 8 a For all who die when their time has come have a grave in the earth. b But your grave extends from the East to the West, and from the North to the extreme South. c The entire world is your grave.

11:5-7

The nominal derivation of *recipere, receptio*, used in 10:12, probably refers to the being taken away into the realm of death. In 11:5, Joshua asks specifically which place should receive Moses after his death. In connection with 11:6-7, his question evidently concerns Moses' grave; cf. the Vulgate of 2 Chron. 28:27 *neque enim recepe-*

runt (LXX: εἰσήνεγκαν) *eum* (sc. *Achaz*) *in sepulchra regum Israhel.* In epitaphs, *locus* is often used as a designation for burial sites[1]. *Recipere*, however, can be said of any displacement or removal to any place to which one is transferred, especially heaven, and it is possible that the ending of As. Mos. answered Joshua's question by having Moses' soul ascend into heaven (for *recipere* and *receptio*, see further the commentary on 10:12).

Two words for "grave" are used, *sepultura* in 11:6-8 and *sepulcrum* in 11:8, with no discernible difference in meaning (see grammatical note nr. 53). In 11:6 Joshua asks what monument could be made to mark Moses' grave, and in 11:7 he asks how human hands would dare to transport his body (*corpus tuum transferre*). The latter question probably announces the account of Moses' burial by angels in the lost ending of As. Mos.

Transferre is used for the bringing of Moses' body from the place where Moses is to die (*de loco*) to the grave (*in locum*). In other words, it refers to the funeral as opposed to interment proper. For this meaning the compound *inferre* is classical usage; see also 1 Ki. 13:22; 2 Chron. 34:28; cf. *adferre* in 1 Chron. 10:12[2].

11:8

The general purport of 11:8 must be that no grave is worthy to hold Moses (*sepultura*, "grave", clearly includes the memorial on a grave, see commentary on 11:6). The major problem in 11:8 is the meaning and function of the words *secus aetatem*. If a consecutive relation between 11:8a and 11:8b-c is intended, as most scholars agree, it seems that *secus aetatem* is an adjunct to *sepulturae suae sunt*, so that one should paraphrase: "One cannot bury you, because your *aetas* is so huge, that your grave should cover the entire world." This interpretation is severely undercut by the meaning of the Latin word *aetas*, "age", because Moses' age at the time of his death (tradition holds him to have been 120 years old at the time) was not extraordinarily high[3]:

I, therefore, propose to loosen the connection between 11:8a and 11:8b-c. As. Mos. 11:8b-c is to be read primarily in connection with 11:6, and 11:8a is no more than the observation that the dead are buried. *Secus aetatem* should be constructed with *morientibus*, and *morientes secus aetatem* then simply means: "those who die in accordance with their age", that is: "when their time has come"; cf. Gen. 35:29 ἐκλιπὼν (Vulgate: *consumptusque aetate*) ἀπέθανεν (sc. Isaac) καὶ προσετέθη πρὸς τὸ γενὸς πρεσβύτερος καὶ πλήρης ἡμέρων, καὶ ἔθαψαν αὐτὸν Ἡσαῦ καὶ Ἰακὼβ οἱ υἱοὶ αὐτοῦ.

In connection with 11:6-7, one can paraphrase 11:8a-c as follows: "What will be the monument on your grave, or who will dare to carry your body there? For it is true, that everyone who at some time dies must be buried—but your grave would cover the entire world." The idea of grandeur is implicit. The author of As. Mos. describes

---

[1] Lewis-Short, p. 1075a; Blaise-Chirat, *Dictionnaire*, p. 500a. In later Latin, the plural *loca* came to mean "cemetery".

[2] In ecclesiastical Latin, *transferre* became the technical term for the transport of saintly relics to a church; see Blaise-Chirat, *Dictionnaire*, p. 824c, cf. p. 826b s.v. *translatio*.

[3] Hilgenfeld's attempt, "Die Psalmen Salomo's", p. 294, to explain the difficulty by departing from the Greek equivalent of *aetas*, ἡλικία, is unconvincing: apart from "age", ἡλικία can indeed mean "stature", as Hilgenfeld wants, but only, it seems, in a physical sense ("length"), which would make the image even more curious.

Joshua as questioning the possibility of erecting a monument worthy of Moses' glory. The burial site of Moses, if an appropriate monument could be built, would cover the entire world. Rönsch has drawn attention to a remarkable parallel to this idea in Thucydides' *Peloponnesian War* II 43. In this passage Pericles is said to praise the brave warriors who have died for their fatherland: they have gained by their sacrifice a most glorious grave (τάφος ἐπισημότατος), not so much the one in which they lie buried, but rather the one in which their fame remains an everlasting memory—"for the entire world is the grave of excellent men" (ἀνδρῶν γὰρ ἐπιφανῶν πᾶσα γῆ τάφος), since their memory lives on throughout the world[1].

c. *11:9-15*

In As. Mos. 11:9a, the basis of Joshua's anxiety is stated: "Lord, you are leaving". 11:9b-15 contains the second set of questions placed in Joshua's mouth. In 11:9b-11 he asks who will care for the people when Moses has gone away. Joshua is described as regarding the protection that Moses offered during his leadership as indispensable for his own (Joshua's) success. In 11:12-15 questions similar to the ones in 11:9b-11 are asked, but they are now related to Joshua himself ("how will I be able" etc.).

₉ Lord, you are leaving. And who will feed this people, ₁₀ or who will be there to take mercy on them, and who will be their leader on the way, ₁₁ or who will pray for them, not omitting one single day, so that I can lead them into the land of the Amorites?

₁₂ ₐHow will I be able to <guard> this people, ᵦ like a father his only son, ᵤ or like a woman her daughter (a virgin who is being prepared to be given to a man), ₔ and who is anxious to protect her (*sc.* daughter's) body from the sun and her feet from going unshod over the ground? ₁₃ And whence will I procure for them the food and drink they urgently need? ₁₄ For their <number> was a hundred thousand, but now they have grown into this multitude here, only because of your prayers, lord Moses. ₁₅ And what wisdom or understanding have I to administer justice or pronounce a verdict in accordance with the words of the Lord?

11:9-11

On *abhis* as a form of *abire*, see grammatical notes nrs. 18 and 96.

The questions with regard to Joshua's competence to succeed Moses are answered by the history told in the Bible. Under Moses' leadership the Lord provided the people with manna from heaven (see Exod. 16:35; Deut. 8:16; Ps. 78[77]:29; Hos. 11:4; Wisd. 16:20). Under Joshua's leadership, the people were fed, no longer by the manna from heaven, but by the fruits of the land the people then entered (Josh. 5:11-

---

[1] Rönsch, "Miscellen", pp. 103-104.

12; LAB 20:8: *Et postquam defunctus est Moyses, desiit manna descendere filiis Is-rael, et tunc ceperunt manducare de fructibus terre*). Likewise, Joshua succeeded Moses as Israel's leader on its way (*dux in via*), see Deut. 3:28; Judg. 1:1; 1 Macc. 2:55; for *dux in via*, cf. the Vulgate's *dux itineris* Exod. 13:21; Ps. 80:9(79:10) (Vulgate *juxta LXX*); *praecedere in via* Deut. 1:33. In fact, there has always been one, and only one, leader: God; see the Vulgate of Exod. 14:13 *dux fuisti in misericordia tua populo quem redemisti*; see further Exod. 13:21; 15:13; Deut. 1:30; 4:37; 31:8; 32:12[1].

The mention of Moses' unremitting prayer for the people, so that they might enter into the land, notwithstanding their sinfulness, may be compared to Deut. 9:19, 25, 28 and 10:10-11. In these passages, Moses is said to have prayed for forty days in order to persuade the Lord not to destroy his people, but to allow them to enter and to possess the land; cf. also Exod. 32:11-14, 28-35; Ps. 106(105):19-23. In As. Mos. 11:11 Moses is said not to have missed a single day[2]; cf. LAB 19:3 *Quis dabit nobis pastorem unum sicut Moyses aut judicem talem filiis Israel, qui in omni tempore oret pro peccatis nostris et exaudiatur pro iniquitatibus nostris?* For Joshua's own interces-sory prayer, see Josh. 7:6-9; Sir. 46:5, 7(9); 4 Ezra 7:107. Whether Moses or Joshua prays for the people, it is the Lord who has mercy on them (see again Exod. 14:13 and Deut. 8:16); therefore, intercessory prayer will always be possible, with or with-out Moses (see esp. As. Mos. 4:1).

11:12

This sentence has a complicated construction; this may have caused some of the cor-ruptions. The general meaning is clear: Joshua is said to question his own ability to care for the people. In 11:12b-d this care is compared to that of a father towards his only son, and to that of a mother towards her marriageable daughter. Apparently, Joshua compares himself to Moses, and doubts that he will be able to care for the people as well as Moses has. However, just as in 11:9-10, the point is that the one who has effectively shown this great love is the Lord.

The auxiliary verb *posse* has no complement infinitive in 11:12a (contrast 4:8; 7:7; 12:12). Such an infinitive has probably been lost. Rönsch has attempted to avoid the need for emendation by citing some instances in which *posse* is used as a substantive verb[3]. *Posse* in this usage can be equated with *potens esse* ("to be powerful", "to have control over"). However, in these instances the complement of *posse* can either be easily supplemented from the context, or it means "to be more powerful than some-one, and therefore able to defeat him"; see 1 Macc. 5:40 *potens poterit adversum nos*

---

[1] In Exod. 14:19; 23:20, 23; 32:34 it is said that the angel of God lead the way through the desert. Is it possible that the author of As. Mos. was thinking of this passage when he called Moses a *nuntius* in 11:17?

[2] The sentence is abundantly negated; see grammatical note nr. 169. *Pati* is probably a mis-translation of a Greek word meaning both "to allow" and "to let pass"; see grammatical note nr. 182.

[3] "Sprachliche Parallelen", p. 105; "Weitere Illustrationen", pp. 226-228. The instances Rönsch cites are Ps. 139(138):6; Jer. 3:5 and 1 Cor. 3:2. To these may be added 1 Sam. 26:25; Jer. 5:22; 1 Macc. 5:40, 41; T. Reub. 6:5 and the instances quoted by Hollander and De Jonge, *The Testaments of the Twelve Patriarchs*, p. 106 (they translate: "to overcome").

(LXX: δυνάμενος δυνήσεται πρὸς ἡμᾶς; cf. 1 Macc. 5:41; Ps. 129[128]:2). The notion of hostility implied in the latter usage cannot have been intended in As. Mos. 11:12[1]. It seems necessary, therefore, to supply some infinitive meaning "to take care of" or "to guard" (e.g. *servare*). 11:12a should be paraphrased as: "How shall I be able to guard this people, like a father his only son?"

The relation between the Lord and Israel has often been likened to the relation between parents and children; see for instance Deut. 14:1; Ps. 103(102):13; Isa. 1:2; Hos. 2:1; 11:1-4; Jub. 1:24-25, 28; cf. 1QH IX 35. For Israel as God's only son, see Exod. 4:22; Jer. 31(38):9; Sir. 36:11(14); 4 Ezra 6:58; 3 Macc. 7:6; Jub. 19:29. In this connection, it is worthwhile quoting Num. 11:12, where Moses is reported to pose a question to God with words similar to the ones ascribed to Joshua in As. Mos.:

> Did I conceive all this people? Did I bring them forth, that thou shouldst say to me, "Carry them in your bosom, as a nurse carries the sucking child, to the land which thou didst swear to give their fathers?" (trans. RSV)

See also below on 11:13.

The love of a father towards his only son (11:12b) is self-evident[2] (see for instance Gen. 22:2, 12, 16; Amos 8:10; Zach. 12:10; cf. Prov. 4:3; Jer. 6:26). In 11:12c, *domina* must, in view of the parallelism, indicate a mother (on the chiastic construction of these clauses, see grammatical note nr. 168). In the Vulgate, *domina* in most cases corresponds to κυρία (see e.g. Gen. 16:4; 2 Ki. 5:3; Isa. 24:2). The word can indicate the wife[3] as the head of a household (see e.g. Ps. 123[122]:2); in 1 Ki. 17:17, κυρία τοῦ οἴκου corresponds to *mater familias*[4]. For the image of a loving mother, one may compare 1QH IX 35-36, in which passage God's love for the "sons of his truth" is likened to that of a mother (מרחמת) towards her child. In Sir. 7:24-25(26-27), advice is given on the special care that has to be given to a daughter with regard to her marriage:

> θυγατέρες σοί εἰσιν; πρόσεχε τῷ σώματι αὐτῶν
> καὶ μὴ ἱλαρώσῃς πρὸς αὐτὰς τὸ πρόσωπόν σου[5].
> ἔκδου[6] θυγατέρα, καὶ ἔσῃ τετελεκὼς ἔργον μέγα,
> καὶ ἀνδρὶ συνετῷ δώρησαι αὐτήν.

> If you have daughters, take care of their bodies,
> and let your face not be merry in their presence[7];

---

[1] Rönsch's examples from Martial, in which *posse* is used substantively and constructed with an accusative, have hostile meanings as well ("to overpower").

[2] Büchsel, "μονογενής".

[3] Cf. Gen. 39:7, where ἡ γύνη τοῦ κυρίου αὐτοῦ corresponds to the Vulgate's *domina*; in the enumeration of the exiles in Jer. 29(36):2, one finds King Jeconiah and the βασιλίσσα, *domina* in the Vulgate).

[4] In 1 Tim. 5:14, *mater familias esse* is a translation of οἰκοδεσποτεῖν.

[5] This line is probably a warning against allowing offensive behaviour, cf. Sir. 26:14 Vulgate.

[6] The Vulgate reads for this word *trade*, cf. the emendation *tradi* for *tali* in the manuscript's text of As. Mos.

[7] That is, be serious in dealing with your daughters; see Ryssel, "Die Sprüche Jesus'", p. 281.

give your daughter in marriage, and you will have perfected a great work,
and give her away to a sensible man.

Since the image is clearly meant to illustrate parental love, *quae timebat* in 11:12d probably refers to the mother who is anxious on behalf of her daughter. Grammatically, *quae timebat* can also refer to the daughter, but the daughter's fear (of being given to a man) would not particularly clarify the point the author wishes to make. *Timere* must therefore be understood as "to be afraid", referring to the mother's fear that something may happen to her daughter which could reduce her chances of a good marriage. In As. Mos. 11:12d, this special care is defined as protecting the daughter's skin from the sun. A fair skin was thought to be an indication of wealth, since it suggested that the daughter had not been obliged to do hard work[1].

Similarly, it was considered as particularly refined (even if not practical) to always wear something on one's feet[2]; cf. the curse in Deut. 28:56 on the "effeminate and spoilt woman who has never dared to set the sole of her feet on the ground".

The syntax of 11:12b-c seems somewhat disrupted. Apart from the position of *custodiens* (on which see grammatical note nr. 101), one misses a verbal form such as *sint* in the second half of 11:12c: *custodiens ... ne scalciati* <u>*sint*</u> *pedes ejus*, "taking care that her feet are not unshod" (*scalciatus = descalceatus*, "unshod", see grammatical notes nrs. 4 and 14). Moreover, *custodire* is used in two different meanings and constructed in two different ways: *a sole* ("to protect from the sun"), and *ne scalciati sint* ("to take care they are not unshod"); see further grammatical note nr. 173. The syntax of 11:12b-c can be visualized as follows:

custodiens   1) *corpus ejus a sole et*
             2) *ne scalciati* (sc. *sint*) *pedes ejus ad currendum supra terram*[3].

11:13

The sentence in 11:13 appears to have given the translator or the scribes a good deal of trouble. The general sense must be: "How could I supply for them drink and food according to their wish?" *Praestare voluntatem* means "to fulfil a need"[4]; *ciborum* and *potui* must be taken as dependent on *voluntas* as objective genitives (for *potui* as a genitive of *potus*, see grammatical note nr. 81). A complete sentence is formed by the words *unde voluntatem eorum praestabo illis ciborum et potui*, meaning "whence will I fulfil their need of food and drink?" Yet a limping phrase, which does not seem to give any new information, is added: *secus voluntatem voluntatis eorum*. Possibly, these words are an explanatory gloss, made by a scribe who objected to the concrete meaning of *voluntas*, and who preferred to construct the sentence as *unde praestabo illis cibos et potus secus voluntatem eorum*.

---

[1] See Cant. 1:5-6, cf. 5:10; Lam. 4:7.

[2] See Dalman, *Arbeit und Sitte*, V, p. 356, cf. pp. 287-288, 295-296.

[3] Another possibility, requiring however a change of the text, would be to read *descalciatos* instead of *ne scalciati*. Then, *ad currendum* would have to be understood as *ab currendo* (on *ad* instead of *ab*, see grammatical note nr. 67). The meaning of the clause would be about the same: "protecting her body from the sun and her feet from going unshod over the ground" (lit.: "and her unshod feet from going &c."); but the syntax would be considerably simpler: *custodiens* (1) *corpus ejus a sole et* (2) *descalciatos pedes ejus ad currendum supra terram*.

[4] Cf. Ps. 78(77):29 καὶ τὴν ἐπιθυμίαν αὐτῶν ἤνεγκεν αὐτοῖς.

For the use of *unde* (which is a conjectural supplement of an illegible part of the manuscript) in connection with the procuring of food, see for instance Num. 11:13 πόθεν μοι κρέα δοῦναι παντὶ τῷ λαῷ τούτῳ; John 6:5 πόθεν ἀγοράσωμεν ἄρτους ἵνα φάγωσιν οὗτοι;

11:14
The manuscript is defective: at the beginning of 11:14 at least one word is illegible. Schmidt and Merx proposed to supplement *numerus*, which at least matches the plural *erant* and which can be modified by *illorum*.

The manuscript's *C milia* is often emended into *DC milia* on account of various passages in the Old Testament[1]. Of these, Num. 11:21 is of special interest: Ἑξακόσιαι χιλιάδες πεζῶν ὁ λαός, ἐν οἷς εἰμι ἐν αὐτοῖς, καὶ σὺ εἶπας Κρέα δώσω αὐτοῖς φαγεῖν, καὶ φάγονται μῆνα ἡμέρων; The emendation into six hundred thousand is unnecessary, but it once again attracts the attention to Num. 11:4-35, a passage already quoted in connection with As. Mos. 11:12. Indeed, As. Mos. 11:14 may intentionally refer to Num. 11:21. In any case, Joshua's question to Moses must be understood in the same way as that posed by Moses in Numbers.

The increase in the number of people is seen as a result of Moses' prayers. Reference is probably made to the occasions on which Moses is said to have prevented the Lord from uprooting his people: only because of Moses' intercession, the people were able to multiply instead of being destroyed (see the commentary on 11:9-11).

11:15a-b
In 11:15, Joshua complains that he does not have the wisdom and understanding needed to administer justice. "Wisdom" and "understanding" are a word-pair, possibly reflecting σοφία and ἐπιστήμη or σύνεσις. In Sir. 45:26(31), too, wisdom is explicitly required of a judge. Incidentally, the word is constructed, just like in As. Mos. 11:15, with a simple final infinitive (see grammatical note nr. 127): δῴη ὑμῖν σοφίαν ἐν καρδίᾳ ὑμῶν κρίνειν τὸν λαὸν αὐτοῦ ἐν δικαιοσύνῃ.

It may be conjectured that Joshua's question is intended to anticipate the bestowal of wisdom on Joshua instead of Moses; see Deut. 34:9 καὶ Ἰησοῦς υἱὸς Ναύη ἐνεπλήσθη πνεύματος συνέσεως (Vulgate: *spiritu sapientiae*), ἐπέθηκεν γὰρ Μωυσῆς τὰς χεῖρας αὐτοῦ ἐπ' αὐτόν. In the scene in LAB 20:2 (cf. 20:3), relating the installation of Joshua as Moses' successor, God commands Joshua not to lament Moses, but to put on the latter's garments of wisdom: *Accipe vestimenta sapientiae ejus et indue te, et zona scientiae ipsius precinge lumbos tuos.*

The text of 11:15b is not in good order. In 11:15, the manuscript reads: *Et quae est mihi sapientia aut intellectus in domo verbis aut judicare aut respondere?* The word *domo* raises the question which house may have been meant, and the instrumental *verbis* is a hard pleonasm with *aut judicare aut respondere*. In order to solve the first problem, Schmidt and Merx added to the text *Domini* on the basis of Ceriani's indication of a lacuna of about three letters (*Domini* can be abbreviated as DNI, see the apparatus on lines 39 and 41). A close inspection of the photographs of the manuscript shows, however, that there is some room left on the line which ends with DOMO, but that there are no apparent traces of letters in this space. Moreover, the blank space al-

---

[1] Exod. 12:37; Num. 11:21; Sir. 16:10(11); 46:8(10); cf. Num. 1:46; 2:32; 26:51.

lows for one large or two small letters, but certainly not for DNI, unless the scribe went beyond the right hand margin. It seems, however, that the scribe has chosen to begin the next syllable (UER) on the next line, because he saw it would certainly not fit between DOMO and the right hand margin. Therefore, the addition *dni* to *domo* is unwarranted.

If, however, *domo* is emended into *domi*, that is, an abbreviation of *Domini* (cf. the textual commentary on line 140), Joshua's question becomes much clearer, and its sense is: "I have not the wisdom that is required to lawfully administer justice." *Verba Domini* is a designation for the law (see commentary on 8:5); "to administer justice by the law" is constructed with *in* in Sir. 46:14(17): ἐν νόμῳ (Vulgate: *in lege*). In Ezek. 7:3(5), 8(7), the criteria used in judgement are also indicated by the preposition ἐν: κρινῶ/ἐκδικήσω σε ... ἐν ταῖς ὁδοῖς σου, Vulgate: *juxta vias tuas*, whereas in Ezek. 7:27 κατὰ τὰς ὁδοὺς αὐτῶν (*juxta vias suas*) is used[1]; in Acts 23:3 the expressions are κατὰ τὸν νόμον and *secundum legem*.

Respondere is a Latin judicial term, meaning "to give a decision". A *responsum* can be used for a judicial order (cf. Cicero, *De Oratore* I, 56, 239; *pro Murena* 13, 29: *res judicatae, decreta, responsa*)[2].

d. *11:16-19*

In this passage, the author presents Joshua as closely associating the presence of the Holy Spirit with the presence of Moses. The implicit answer to the questions Joshua has asked up till now is that Joshua himself will fulfil the role he ascribes to Moses alone. Analogously, the point the author wants to make in 11:16-19 seems to be that the spirit of God has indeed been present in Moses, but that the spirit will not leave the people when Moses will have died; instead, it will be transferred to Joshua himself (see commentary on As. Mos. 11:15).

The association of Moses with the Holy Spirit in 11:16 is so strong, that one could speak of near-identity. The way in which Joshua is made to praise Moses as the embodiment of God's spirit can be schematically visualized as follows.

b. *sanctum*	*et sacrum*	*spiritum*	*dignum Domino*
c. *multiplicem*	*et inconpraehensibilem*	*dominum verbi*	*fidelem in omnia*
d. *divinum*	*per orbem terrarum*	*profetem*	
e. *consummatum*	*in saeculo*	*doctorem*	

Philo, speaking as a philosopher, occasionally shows a similar strong association between Moses and the divine λόγος, e.g. in *Quis rerum divinarum* 206. The adjectives *multiplex* and *incomprehensibilis* are divine epithets, belonging to the Holy Spirit, but applied by "Joshua" to Moses himself. To this, one may compare Philo's characterization of Moses as the λόγος ἔμψυχος in *De vita Mosis* I 162. To the titles "perfect teacher" and "divine prophet" one may compare *De Decalogo* 175, where

---

[1] See further Ezek. 18:30; 24:13; 33:20.
[2] The relevant Greek equivalent is ἀπόκριμα; ἀποκρίνεσθαι in this meaning seems to have been rare, but it did exist. See Büchsel and Herntrich, "κρίνω κτλ.", p. 947.

Moses is called ὁ τελειότατος τῶν προφητῶν[1], whom God has filled with divine
spirit (ἐνθέον πνεῦμα); in *De gigantibus* 54 Moses is called μύστης, ἱεροφάντης ὁρ-
γίων καὶ διδάσκαλος θείων; cf. *Questiones in Exodum* II 54: "the divine and holy
Moses". Indeed, in his youth, many of those who observed him wondered with regard to Moses' mind πότερον ἀνθρώπειος ἢ θεῖος ἢ μικτὸς ἐξ ἀμφοῖν (*De vita Mosis* I 27)[2]. In fact, according to Philo, someone perfect is neither man, nor God (*De
somniis* II 234), and only when Moses was about to die, God decided to transform
his mixed character into a "monad", consisting entirely of νοῦς (*De vita Mosis* II
288)[3].

Of course, Philo has a special interest in presenting Moses as the paradigm of man
united with God in mystical communion. No such interest is apparent from
"Joshua's" words in Ass. Mos, but there is an important *trait d'union* between the two
concepts of Moses: in both cases Moses owes his outstanding position to the spirit of
God (whether that is called wisdom, *spiritus*, λόγος or whatever). In the view of
Philo, Moses achieved unity with the spirit and with God through perfection (*De
sacrificiis* 8); according to the author of As. Mos., Moses was made perfect through
the bestowal of the spirit on him by God's sovereign will. Therefore, the laudations of
Moses in 11:16 are in reality a description of the spirit of God, which dwelled in
Moses during his lifetime, but did not become dependent on him.

16 a Furthermore, the kings of the Amorites, after they have heard—
whilst believing that they can defeat us—, that b the holy and sacred
spirit, the worthy one before the Lord, c the versatile and inscrutable
lord of the word, the trusted one in everything, d the divine prophet for
this world, e the perfect teacher for this earth, f is no longer with them,
will say: 'Let us go at them. 17 a If the enemies will sin against their
Lord once more, there is no longer an advocate for them, b who will
supplicate to the Lord for them, as Moses was, the great messenger, c
who bent his knees on earth every hour of the day and of the night,
praying; d and who could look at him who rules the entire world with
mercy and justice, e reminding him of the covenant with the fathers,
and placating the Lord with his oath'; 18 surely they will say: 'He is no
longer with them. Let us go, then, and let us wipe them from the face
of the earth.' 19 What then will happen to this people, lord Moses?"

---

[1] Cf. *De vita Mosis* I 1: ἀνήρ ... μέγιστος καὶ τελειότατος.

[2] According to Artapanus, the priests of Egypt no longer wondered, see Eusebius,
Praeparatio IX 27, 6: [τὸν Μώυσον] ὑπὸ τῶν ἱερέων ἰσοθέου τιμῆς καταξιωθέντα
προσαγορευθῆναι Ἑρμῆν διὰ τὴν τῶν ἱερῶν γραμμάτων ἑρμηνείαν.

[3] Goodenough, *By Light, Light*, pp. 223-234, has defended the view that Philo took care
not to call Moses a god explicitly, but that he did tend to regard him as a divine being; more
carefully Meeks, *The Prophet-King*, pp. 103-107; and Tiede, *The Charismatic Figure*, pp.
123-127.

11:16a

In As. Mos. 11:16 Joshua reminds Moses of the kings of the Amorites. The defeat of the Amorites was one of Moses' military exploits according to Num. 21:21-30. In Deut. 1:23-46; 2:24-36 there is a presentation of the same war, which differs considerably from that in Num. 21:21-30. In Numbers, Israel is described as simply capturing the entire land of the Amorite king Sihon of Hesbon when the latter did not want the people to pass through his land in peace. In the version of Deuteronomy, it is told that the Amorites initially destroyed Israel after it had murmured against the Lord (Deut. 2:27). The defeat was followed by a long sojourn of Israel in Kadesh (Deut. 2:46) after which the battle against Sihon was successfully fought (Deut. 2:32-33). The author of As. Mos. may have had this second version in mind, in which the people's sins nearly prevented them from entering the land. Although the account in Deut. 2 does not mention that Moses acted as an intercessor, Joshua in As. Mos. clearly connects the eventual victory with Moses' intervention (see commentary on 11:17a-b). Therefore, Joshua fears that once Moses is gone, he himself will not be able to lead the people into "the land of the Amorites" (see As. Mos. 11:11, of which 11:16-18 is an elaboration). It seems probable that the Amorites (and not, for instance, Amalek) are mentioned in As. Mos. 11:16 because Joshua will later win a victory over them (see commentary on 11:18). In this way, the author of As. Mos. has Joshua's fears implicitly falsified. Cf. Deut. 31:4: the Lord will deal with the inhabitants of the land they will enter "as he has done to Sihon and Og, the kings of the Amorites".

The verb of the main clause in which "the kings of the Amorites" are the subject (*dicent*), is separated from the subject by two accusative with infinitive constructions, one of which must be constructed with *audierint*. One can read (1) *cum audierint expugnare nos*, "when the kings of the Amorites will have heard that we will wage war"[1]; or (2) *cum audierint ... jam non esse sanctum et sacrum spiritum*, "when they will have heard that the holy and sacred spirit is no longer". In the second interpretation, *expugnare nos credentes* is an adjunct with the kings of the Amorites, who "believe that they can defeat us". This interpretation, proposed by Schmidt and Merx, seems to me to match the context of Joshua's complaint better: Moses' successor assumes that the Amorites will attack Israel as soon as it is seen to offend the Lord, and that they will achieve their aim because Moses, the Holy Spirit, will no longer be there to appease the Lord's wrath. Similarly, in LAB 64:2, the Philistines are reported to say to one another:

> Ecce Samuel propheta mortuus est, et quis orat pro Israel? Et David, qui pugnavit pro eis, inimicus est Saul et non est cum eis. Et nunc exsurgentes eamus et pugnantes expugnemus eos, et vindicemus sanguinem patrum nostrorum[2].

---

[1] Thus Volkmar, *Mose Prophetie*, p. 49.

[2] Schmidt and Merx, "Die Assumptio Mosis", p. 151, quoted the following parallel from the Samaritan Chronicle IV, 8 (= the Book of Joshua), quoted by Haacker, "Nachbiblische Traditionen", p. 159, in Juynboll's translation: *nam laetatae erant (sc. Gentes) quam maxime, postquam Prophetae mors iis innotuerat, et Israelitis bellum inferre volebant* (Juynboll, *Chronicon Samaritanum*, p. 140).

11:16b-c

In 11:16b, Joshua is said to believe that when Moses has died the "holy and[1] sacred spirit, worthy of the Lord" will no longer be with the people. For the Holy Spirit dwelling in Moses, see Isa. 63:11-12. In this passage the people are said to remember the days of Moses, and ask: ποῦ ἐστιν ὁ θεὶς ἐν αὐτοῖς τὸ πνεῦμα τὸ ἅγιον; ὁ ἀγαγὼν τῇ δεξιᾷ Μωυσῆν, ὁ βραχίων τῆς δόξης αὐτοῦ; Similarly, in Wisd. 10:8 it is said that Wisdom (the spirit of God) led the people through the desert, and that Wisdom εἰσῆλθεν εἰς ψυχὴν θεράποντος κυρίου, that is, Moses (Wisd. 10:16); cf. also Neh. 9:20; Hagg. 2:6. According to Deut. 34:9 and LAB 20:2-3, Joshua, as Moses' successor, was equally filled with the spirit of wisdom (see the commentary on 11:15a-b).

For the expression "Holy Spirit" (πνεῦμα ἅγιον), see Ps. 51(50):13(11); Isa. 63:10, 11; Dan. 4:5 Θ, 6 Θ, 15 Θ; 5:12 LXX; 6:4 LXX; Wisd. 1:5; 9:17; Ps. Sol. 17:37; 4 Ezra 14:22; T. Levi 18:11 reads πνεῦμα ἁγιωσύνης; *spiritus sanctus* LAB 28:6 (18:11; 32:14: *sancti spiritus*)[2]. I have not found the adjective *sacer* (ἱερός) applied to the spirit of God elsewhere. However, ἱερὸς καὶ ὅσιος or ἅγιος are used as a word-pair by Philo, *Legum allegoriae* III 126; *Quod deterius* 133; *De confusione linguarum* 27.

Moses is called *dignus Domino*, "worthy before the Lord"; compare the title given to Joshua in 1:6 *homo probatus Domino ut sit successor*, and see further the commentary on the parallel expression *fidelis in omnia* below[3].

As far as I know, a parallel for the concept that someone is lord (or master) of the word (*dominus verbi*, As. Mos. 11:16c) is lacking. The god Hermes was known as ἡγεμὼν τῶν λόγων, the "spokesman" of the gods[4]. In Acts 14:12(11), the people of Lystra are said to mistake Barnabas and Paul for gods, because of the apostles' divine speech; Paul is taken to be Hermes, because he is the one who acts as the spokesman (ὁ ἡγούμενος τοῦ λόγου, Vulgate: *dux verbi*). Perhaps one may consider the possibility that the reading *dominus verbi* is the result of a kind of metathesis which occurs elsewhere in As. Mos. (see esp. *scenae testimonium* in 2:4, and grammatical note nr.

---

[1] The manuscript reads *jam non esse* SEMET *sacrum spiritum*, which makes no sense. My conjecture rests on the slight alteration of SEMET into SCM ET, in which SCM is understood as an abbreviation of *sanctum*, see further the textual commentary to line 196.

[2] In Jub. 1:21, 23, *manfasa qᵉdus* ("holy spirit") occurs as a future characteristic of Israel purified by God; similarly, Daniel's spirit is called "holy" in Sus. 45 Θ.

[3] In view of the unique connection between Moses and the Holy Spirit supposed here, one may perhaps compare Philo, *De vita Mosis* I 158, who says that Moses' communion with God was so intimate that he was deemed worthy (ἀξιωθείς) to be called by the same name: ὠνομάσθη γὰρ ὅλου τοῦ ἔθνους θεὸς καὶ βασιλεύς, cf. Exod. 4:16; 7:1. See also Artapanus (in Eusebius, *Praeparatio* IX 27, 6): (τὸν Μώϋσον) ὑπὸ τῶν ἱερέων ἰσοθέου τιμῆς καταξιωθέντα.

[4] Cf. Jamblichus, *De mysteriis*, 1, 1 θεὸς ὁ τῶν λόγων ἡγεμὼν ὁ Ἑρμῆς; also Aelianus, *De natura animalium* 10, 24 τῷ Ἑρμῇ ... τῷ πατρὶ τῶν λόγων (quoted by Wettstein, II, pp. 542-543, on Acts 14:12); see further Eitrem, "Hermes", pp. 781-782. However, Haacker, "Nachbiblische Traditionen", p. 158, is wrong in asserting that "'Herr des Wortes' ist ein traditioneller Titel des Hermes", because ἡγεμὼν τῶν λόγων here simply means "spokesman" ("Wortführer"), and has nothing to do with some sort of dominion.

82), and that the originally intended reading was *Domini verbum*, "the word of the Lord". The parallel in 11:16b *sanctus et sacer spiritus* may support this suggestion.

Multiplex, literally "manifold", here probably means "many-sided, versatile". It may refer to the mind or character of human beings (both *in bonam* and *in malam partem*, "versatile" and "changeable, fickle"). In this meaning, it may be a rendering of ποικίλος. In Wisd. 7:22, *multiplex* is applied to Wisdom (LXX: πολυμερής); it is juxtaposed to *unicus*/μονογενής[1].

Inconpraehensibilis is a characteristic connected with deities and spirits. This word means "intangible", in a concrete and in a metaphorical way (the two usages may overlap[2]). If "intangible" or "invisible" is meant, this is an appropriate adjective with *Domini verbum* (λόγος), and one may compare Wisd. 7:22, where the spirit of God is called λεπτός, "thin, fine"[3]. In its metaphorical meaning, "inscrutable", the word *incomprehensibilis* was particularly popular with ecclesiastical writers as an epithet of God or of demons[4]. In the Vulgate of the Old Testament, the word *incomprehensibilis* is used in Job 9:10(7) and Jer. 32:19, meaning "inscrutable" (LXX: ἀνεξιχνίαστος[5]); the concept of the inscrutability of God's ways is not uncommon (see Ps. 77[76]:20; Wisd. 9:13; Tob. 3:20; Job 36:23).

Fidelis in omnia, parallel to *dignum Domino*, refers to the trust the Lord has vested in Moses; see for instance Num. 12:7, where the Lord says of Moses, ἐν ὅλῳ τῷ οἴκῳ μου πιστός (Vulgate: *fidelissimus*) ἐστιν (cf. the Vulgate of Heb. 3:5, where Num. 12:7 is quoted: *et Moses quidem fidelis erat in tota domo ejus*[6]). *Fidelis* should therefore be understood as "confidant", "one whom the Lord trusts", rather than in its usual active sense, "faithful"[7].

---

[1] Grimm, *Weisheit*, p. 153: "obwohl *e i n z i g*, einartig, ihrem *Wesen* nach, ist sie doch *v i e l f a c h*, mannigfaltig in ihren *Aeusserungen, Wirkungen* und *Gaben*. Analog ist, was Paulus 1 Kor. 12,4 u. 11 vom h. Geiste sagt."

[2] See also the enumeration in Ps.-Callisthenes C, 28:14 θεὸν ἀληθινὸν ἀνεκήρυξεν ἀκατανόητον ἀθεώρητον ἀνεξιχνίαστον ἐπὶ τῶν Σεραφὶμ ἐποχούμενον.

[3] Grimm, *Weisheit*, pp. 153-154: "*dünn, fein*, höchst wahrsheinlich s. v. a. *immateriell*, ohne welche Eigenschaft der Weisheitsgeist das Geisterreich und das Weltall nicht durchdringen könnte, vgl. [Wisd. 7:]23, 24b".

[4] See *ThLL* VII, 1, cols. 995:47-996:42, esp. cols. 995:64-996:42. Haacker, "Nachbiblische Traditionen", p. 158, regards the identification of Moses with the Holy Spirit as an analogy to the identification of Jesus with the Logos in the Gospel according to John, and compares *incomprehensibilis* with Ign., *Magn.* 15 ἀδιάκριτον πνεῦμα, ὅς ἐστιν Ἰησοῦς Χριστός.

[5] Cf. Rom. 11:33 ὡς ἀνεξεραύνητα (Vulgate: *quam inconprehensibilia*) τὰ κρίματα αὐτοῦ καὶ ἀνεξιχνίαστοι (*investigabiles* = *ininvestigabiles*) αἱ ὁδοὶ αὐτοῦ; Eph. 3:8 τὸ ἀνεξιχνίαστον πλοῦτος τοῦ Χριστοῦ καὶ ... ἡ οἰκονομία τοῦ μυστηρίου τοῦ ἀποκεκρυμμένου. Ἀνεξιχνίαστος is only known from biblical and related literature according to Peterson, "ἀνεξιχνίαστος", p. 359.

[6] Incidentally, in Heb. 3:3 *dignus* is used in the same sentence as *fidelis*, as in As. Mos. 11:16b-c.

[7] Cf. 1 Pet. 5:12, which passage can be translated as: "I have written briefly through Silvanus, a trustworthy brother (πιστὸς ἀδέλφος), I am convinced"; see Sevenster, *Do You Know Greek?*, p. 3.

11:16d-e

Moses is called "divine prophet" and "perfect teacher". The former title indicates of course one of Moses' best-known qualities: Moses was the prophet *par excellence* (see especially Num. 12:6-8; Deut. 34:10)[1]. In Wisd. 11:1, Moses is called προφήτης ἅγιος, in whom Wisdom, the spirit of God, dwelled (Wisd. 10:16). Compare also Jeremiah, who in the Lives of the Prophets is called ὅσιος προφήτης; and Jesus, who is called a προφήτης ὑψηλός in T. Levi 8:15, and μονογενὴς προφήτης in T. Ben. 9:2. For *divinus* see Josephus, *Ant. Jud.* III 170, who calls Moses a θεῖος ἀνήρ; for *consummatus* see the instances in Philo quoted in the introduction to this section.

Per orbem terrarum and *in saeculo* are parallel expressions, "for the entire world" and "for all time". The universal validity of Moses' offices expressed by these phrases is probably merely superlative, and it is not intended to assert that Moses' teachings are, or should be, acknowledged as authoritative by the gentiles. In Dan. 9:6 LXX, it is said of the prophets that they have spoken to "all nations in the world" (MT: "the entire population of the land").

The other term, *doctor*, is less usual. However, προφῆται and διδάσκαλοι are also juxtaposed in Acts 13:1; 1 Cor. 12:28, 29; Eph. 4:11 and Did. 15:1-2 (sometimes listed together with other functions). In these instances, "teacher" is a no less divinely inspired function than "prophet" (cf. 1 Cor. 14:26). In *De gigantibus* 54 Moses is called μύστης, ἱεροφάντης ὀργίων καὶ διδάσκαλος θείων. *Docere* is a verb which is especially used with regard to the law, see for instance Lev. 10:11; Deut. 4:1, 5, esp. Deut. 6:1 καὶ αὗται αἱ ἐντολαί ... ὅσα ἐνετείλατο κύριος ὁ θεὸς ἡμῶν διδάξαι ὑμᾶς. The title may therefore indicate his quality as a lawgiver (see also commentary on 5:5).

11:16f-17

To Joshua, the imminent absence of Moses from his people implies the absence of Moses' effective intercessory prayer (described in 11:17c-e). Without him as *defensor*, Joshua is said to fear that the Lord will not allow the sinful people to overcome the powerful kings of the Amorites. On the contrary, the Amorites will seize the opportunity to destroy the people when they have sinned once more. Joshua's fears are of course baseless (see commentary on 11:18-19).

Semel adhuc probably renders ἔτι ἅπαξ, "once more", referring to a single and final iteration of an act. In the Vulgate the word-order is always the other way around: *adhuc semel* (see Gen. 18:32; Judg. 6:39; 16:18 [cf. 16:28 LXX]; 2 Macc. 3:37; Heb. 12:26, 27).

In the Vulgate, the noun *defensor* occurs in Judith 6:13, Sir. 30:6, and in 2 Macc. 4:2. Of these occurrences, only 2 Macc. 4:2 has a Greek counterpart in the Septuagint, κηδεμών[2]. To this, one may compare Philo, *De vita Mosis* II 166, where Moses is described as the perfect high priest, praying for remission of the people's sins (ἱκεσίας

---

[1] Tiede views Moses' qualities as mediator, intercessor and suffering one as various aspects of his role as prophet ("The Figure of Moses", pp. 87-90); this, however, is a one-sided reduction.

[2] In Sir. 30:6, one may compare the Septuagint's ἔκδικον; ἐκδικεῖν corresponds to the Vulgate's *defendere* in Rom. 12:19, and ἐκδίκησις to *defensio* in Sir. 48:7. Judith 6:13 (*Deus caeli defensor eorum est*) refers to Judith 6:2, where the Greek version has ὁ θεὸς αὐτῶν ὑπερασπιεῖ αὐτῶν; ὑπερασπίζειν is a usual Greek equivalent of *protegere*.

καὶ λιτὰς ἐποιεῖτο συγγνῶναι τῶν ἡμαρτημένων δεόμενος), and in that role is called κηδεμὼν καὶ παραιτητής; this usage matches perfectly with that in As. Mos. 11:17, where Moses is called *defensor qui ferat pro eis praeces*. In this context of intermediation between God and his people, Moses is also called *magnus nuntius*, the great messenger, that is, of God. *Nuntius* undoubtedly translates ἄγγελος, a word that may refer to human messengers of God as well as angels (see further commentary on 10:2). In Orphic literature, Hermes, in his role as a mediator between the gods and men, is called an ἄγγελος as well. According to Philo, priests, Moses, and λόγος, all have the role of mediator in common[1], compare *De somniis* I 142 with *De vita Mosis* II 166, and see further *De gigantibus* 52; *De specialibus legibus* I 116; *Quod Deus immutabilis* 131-135; for mediators, priests and Moses having the same status as angels, whom Philo often calls λόγοι, see *De fuga* 5; *De somniis* I 142[2].

The Latin expression for "to supplicate" is *preces ferre*. It is not used in the Vulgate, except for a compound in Heb. 5:7, where *preces supplicationesque ... offerens* is a translation of δεήσεις τε καὶ ἱκετηρίας ... προσενέγκας; *preces* and *precari* are commonly used as equivalents of the Septuagint's δέησις and δέεσθαι.

The periphrastic construction *genua infixa habere* is used to express the durative aspect of Moses' praying ("every single hour of the day and the night", see grammatical note nr. 93). For Moses' intercessory prayer, see the commentary on 1:11. For *genua infigere in terra*, a common Latin expression for "to kneel", see the Vulgate of 1 Ki. 8:54 *genu in terram fixerat*, LXX: ὀκλακὼς ἐπὶ τὰ γόνατα αὐτοῦ. In 1 Ki. 19:18, the verb ὀκλάζειν corresponds to the Vulgate's *incurvare*. The latter verb is most often used in the Vulgate for "to kneel".

Moses is said to "look at the Almighty ruler of the entire world" (for *Omnipotens* l. em., constructed with an accusative, see grammatical note nr. 107). In the Vulgate of Acts, *intueri* is used as a translation of ἀτενίζειν, "to watch" (e.g. Acts 1:10; 3:4; 6:15; 10:4; so also Luke 22:56). Most other occurrences of the word in the Vulgate correspond to a Greek compound of βλέπειν with for instance ἐπι– or ἐν– (e.g. Gen. 19:28; 1 Sam. 16:7; Isa. 8:22; Jer. 4:25; 42:2; Lam. 5:1; Mark 10:21, 27; John 1:42), meaning not simply "to see", but "to look at, to observe intently" (in Luke 4:20 and 2 Cor. 3:7, 13, ἀτενίζειν is translated with *intendere*). Therefore, if it is said in As. Mos. 11:17d that Moses "saw" God, one should probably not think of the famous passage according to which Moses received a glimpse of the Lord's back (Exod. 33:12-32), but rather of those passages in which it is stated that God spoke to Moses face to face, "as a man is used to speak to his friend" (Exod. 33:11; cf. Num. 12:8; Deut. 5:4; 34:10)[3]. Such amical conversation with God is a rare privilege for a human

---

[1] Goodenough *By Light, Light*, pp. 115-116, warns that, although the high priest and the λόγος are equated by Philo, they are not identical: the priest is the "Logos o n l y as it presented itself in relation with the elements".

[2] At this point, too, Moses, the interpreter (ἑρμηνεύς) of God's word, is identified with Hermes (see Goodenough, *By Light, Light*, p. 291), who, just like Moses, is called ἑρμηνεύς, προφήτης and ἄγγελος, cf. Quandt, *Orphei Hymni*, p. 23, Hymn 28:1, 4, 6; Kern, *Orphicorum Fragmenta*, p. 309, fragment 297a.

[3] Contra Tiede, "The Figure of Moses", p. 91.

being, and it characterizes Moses as a most outstanding intercessor[1]; cf. Philo, *Quis rerum divinarum* 21.

God's rule over the entire world is described as "merciful and just". In the Vulgate, the word-pair *justitia et misericordia* occurs at least once, in Prov. 21:21 (LXX: δικαιοσύνη καὶ ἐλεημοσύνη); more common is *misericordia et judicium* (ἐλεημοσύνη or ἔλεος and κρίσις or κρίμα, see Ps. 33[32]:5; 101[100]:1; Hos. 12:6; Micah 6:8; cf. Ps. 112[111]:4; 116[115]:5). For God's merciful rule, see 3 Macc. 6:2 ὕψιστε παντοκράτωρ θεὲ τὴν πᾶσαν διακυβερνῶν ἐν οἰκτιρμοῖς κτίσιν; cf. Ps. Sol. 17:3.

With his prayers, Moses has been able to "placate" the Lord. *Placare Deum* means "to appease God, to soothe his anger"; in the Vulgate, it most often corresponds to the Septuagint's ἐξιλάσκεσθαι. One may placate the Lord with offerings, or, as in As. Mos. 11:17, with prayers (e.g. Gen. 32:20; Exod. 30:10; Lev. 14:29; Prov. 16:14; Ezek. 16:63; Dan. 9:19 ϴ). In As. Mos. 11:17, *placando* stands in synthetical parallelism with *reminiscens* (on the gerund *placando* functioning as a participle, see grammatical note nr. 129): by reminding God of the covenant which he made with the fathers[2], and which he confirmed with an oath, Moses has been able to placate the Lord. As in 11:17c, the author of As. Mos. may refer in particular to Moses' forty days' fast and prayers as described in Deut. 9:25-29 (with an implicit appeal to the oath in Deut. 9:27, μνήσθητι Ἀβραάμ κτλ.); cf. Deut. 10:10-11[3]. However, the efficacy of Moses' prayer and appeal to the oath is most elaborately described in Num. 14:13-20, where Moses' intercessory prayer is answered by the Lord: Ἵλεως αὐτοῖς εἰμι κατὰ τὸ ῥῆμά σου.

11:18-19

The sentence begun in 11:16, but twice interrupted by the passages with elaborate praise of Moses, is here resumed. According to Joshua, the expected absence of Moses will incite the Amorites to seize the opportunity to destroy[4] the people when they have sinned once more (see 11:16f-17a). In As. Mos. 12:7-8 Moses puts his own importance into proper perspective, giving all credit to God's grace. He gives a similar interpretation to the sinfulness of the people: *non enim propter pietatem plebis hujus exterminabis gentes* (see further commentary on 12:7-8).

As. Mos. does not further inform us about Joshua's battle with the Amorites, but the book of Joshua relates an outcome which is quite contrary to Joshua's fears as expressed in As. Mos. 11:16-18; cf. Josh. 5:1

> When all the kings of the Amorites that were beyond the Jordan to the west, and all the Canaanites that were by the sea, heard that the Lord had dried up the waters of the

---

1 Cf. Oepke, "μεσίτης, μεσιτεύω", p. 616.

2 For the role of the covenant and the oath in prayers for mercy, see the commentary on 3:8-9. On *parentes* for "fathers", see the commentary on As. Mos. 9:4.

3 So also Tiede, "The Figure of Moses", p. 88.

4 *Confundere*, "to confuse", came to mean "to destroy utterly", see grammatical note nr. 50.

Jordan for the people of Israel until they had crossed over, their heart melted, and
there was no longer any spirit in them, because of the people of Israel (trans. RSV)[1].

From this passage, it clearly appears that Joshua is Moses' perfect successor: both
under Moses' and under Joshua's leadership, God dries up the waters and the Amorites are defeated. Cf. in general Sir. 46:1-9 and commentary to 11:9-11.

---

[1] Cf. LAB 20:9 *Populus autem et Ihesus pugnabant contra Amorreos, et, invalescente
pugna super inimicos suos per omnes dies Ihesu, consumpti sunt triginta et novem reges qui
habitabant terram.*

12:1-13
MOSES' ANSWER TO JOSHUA'S COMPLAINT

In chapter 12, Moses responds to Joshua's questions in chapter 11. In this response, the author of As. Mos. returns to the things said in the introduction of the book (1:12-15) concerning God's intentions for his creation and for his people. Possibly, as has been suggested by Von Nordheim[1], little of Moses' speech has been lost. See the commentary on the lost ending for the way in which As. Mos. might have ended.

The response to Joshua's questions is a theological discourse, intended to comfort him and others (including the intended readers of As. Mos.) who are left behind. In this passage, the predetermined course of history and the people's own responsibility are artfully combined. God is presented as the one who has created all, and therefore knows and commands all (12:4-5a). Moses' role is seen from this perspective; rather than having gained influence on the Lord because of of his virtue or strength, his role as mediator and intercessor is all part of God's plan (12:6-7; cf. 1:14). Joshua's fears, therefore, that the people's sinfulness will prevent their entrance into the land under his leadership (cf. esp. 11:16-18), are unfounded, because entry into the land does not depend on the people's piety (or impiety), but is likewise part of God's plan (12:8-9). Because of his omniscience, God has always recognized that some of his people will disobey his commandments. They will be removed, but the faithful will prosper and unto them the promises of the covenant will be fulfilled (12:10-13).

a. *12:1-3*

The scene pictured in 11:1-4 is recapitulated. Moses is described as comforting Joshua.

1 And after Joshua finished speaking, he again fell at Moses' feet. 2 But Moses took his hand and raised him up into the seat before him. And he answered and said to him: 3 "Joshua, do not think too lightly of yourself, but show yourself free from care. And give heed to my words."

---

[1] *Die Lehre der Alten* I, p. 204; see also the Introduction, section IV, e.

The author begins Moses' answer to Joshua's desperate questions by making the prophet grasp his successor's hand and raise him up from his self-humiliation. As Volkmar noted[1], this action is reminiscent of similar gestures made by angels who have revealed some heavenly truth to a human being, who is consequently bewildered and afraid. Occasionally, encouraging words such as those of Moses to Joshua in As. Mos. 12:3, are also spoken. See especially Dan. 8:18; 10:8-10; 4 Ezra 5:14-15; 10:29-31; cf. Rev. 1:17.

But Moses' gesture seems to be more than just encouragement: Moses makes Joshua sit in the seat before him. Possibly, this represents Joshua's investiture as Moses' successor, and the chair on which he is made to sit may accordingly be the καθέδρα Μωυσέως, on which the scribes and Pharisees (Moses' successors as interpreters of the law[2]) are sitting according to Matt. 23:2[3].

Next, Moses is reported to tell Joshua "not to despise himself"[4], or in the more modest expression used in the translation above: "Do not think too lightly of yourself". One could translate *contemnere* in this way in 1 Tim. 4:11-12 *praecipe haec et doce—nemo adulescentiam tuam contemnat*, "let no one think little (καταφρονείτω) of your teaching because you are young"; cf. the Vulgate of Ps. 119(118):141 *adulescentulus sum ego et contemptus* (Jerome *juxta Hebraeos: parvulus ego sum et contemptibilis*). In Rom. 2:4, too, the Vulgate has *contemnere* for Paul's καταφρονεῖν.

Furthermore, Moses is seen to encourage his successor by saying "do not worry". The expression *se praebere* with an adjective in the accusative is a common Latin idiom, meaning "to show or to conduct oneself in a certain quality". On a few occasions, it occurs in the Vulgate: Tob. 3:17: *neque cum his qui in levitate ambulant participem me praebui*[5]. The idiom has no exact counterpart in Greek, as appears from two comparable New Testament instances, Acts 1:3 *praebuit se ipsum vivum*, in Greek παρέστησεν ἑαυτὸν ζῶντα, and Tit. 2:7 *te ipsum praebe exemplum*, in Greek σεαυτὸν παρεχόμενος τύπον. *Securus* as a state of mind occurs in e.g. Judg. 8:11 (LXX A and B: πεποιθυῖα); 2 Chron. 20:20 (LXX: ἐμπιστεύεσθαι pass.); Matt. 28:14 (ἀμέριμνος). *Securus* means "safe", and, subjectively, "free of care". The reasons why Joshua should not worry are extensively set out in the next passage.

---

[1] *Mose Prophetie*, p. 51.

[2] Cf. Jeremias, "Μωυσῆς", pp. 857, 868-869; Strack-Billerbeck, *Kommentar*, II, pp. 654-655.

[3] See Renov, "The Seat of Moses", p. 262 (233): "the 'Seat of Moses' ... was a symbol of Jewish legal authority conferred upon teachers of Jewish law. It expressed itself in the form of special seats for them in a conspicuous place at the head of the congregation in the synagogue"; see further Vermes *et alii*, *The History of the Jewish People* II, p. 442; further literature in Schrage, "συναγωγή", p. 819, n. 134.

[4] Instead of *te ne contemnas*, the reading adopted here, the manuscript reads *et ne contemnas*, without an object.

[5] There is no corresponding clause in the extant Greek versions.

b. *12:4-5a*

This section seems somewhat repetitive, expressing a single thought three times, with only slight variations in wording. These variations clearly serve to build a climax, which makes the comprehensiveness of divine prescience stand out. In 12:4a, God's lordship over all nations and over the entire history is stated; in 12:4b, Moses stresses that not the slightest detail (*pusillum*) has been overlooked by God. Thus, in the statement of 12:5a that God has known beforehand all things that were to happen in this world, *omnia* is set in the right perspective: "all things" means "really every-thing". In Judith 9:5-6, God's foreknowledge is treated with a similar abundance:

> For you have made the things that were before these things, and these things, and those that will be hereafter, and the present and the future you devised, and the things that you devised came into being, and the things that you wanted came about, and they said: "Behold, we are here", for all your ways have been prepared, and your judgement is with foreknowledge[1].

₄ God has created all nations on earth, and he foresaw us, them as well as us, from the beginning of the creation of the earth until the end of the world. And nothing has been overlooked by him, not even the smallest detail, but he has seen and known everything beforehand. When he made them, ₅ ₐ the Lord saw beforehand all things that were to happen in this world.

In his explanation of divine providence, Moses begins by stating that God has created all the nations on earth. As the Creator, God is naturally able to oversee the work of his hands. He is the author, as it were, of a drama whose plot, including its denoue-ment, he has known from the beginning[2]. With emphasis, God's elected people are included among the nations that God has created; for the author refers to these *gentes* with the pronoun *nos*, clarifying this *nos* with the appositional phrase *illos et nos*: "God has created all nations and he has foreseen our entire history, that is, their his-tory as well as ours". God's authority, the author apparently wishes to stress, extends over nations other than his own. If, therefore, the nations subdue God's people, this must not be considered a failure of God's efforts, but as an integral part of his prede-termined plan.

The divine prescience, preceding even creation itself, is a common topic in Jewish literature[3]; see, for instance, Sir. 23:20(29): πρὶν ἢ κτισθῆναι τὰ πάντα ἔγνωσται αὐτῷ, οὕτως καὶ μετὰ τὸ συντελεσθῆναι. See further Judith 9:5-6 (quoted above);

---

[1] Cf. also 4 Ezra 6:1-6.

[2] In speaking of divine prescience, Philo, *Quod Deus immutabilis* 30-31, compares God to parents who naturally know their children, or to an artist who knows his work. Likewise, since God is the maker of time as well as of all things, he knows this work as well, even the future that, to humans, is obscure.

[3] For an extensive treatment of this so-called determinism in apocalyptic literature, see von Rad, *Weisheit*, pp. 337-363.

Wisd. 8:8; 1 En. 9:11; 39:11; Jub. 1:29; 1QS III 15-16; CD II 7-10; Philo, *Quod Deus immutabilis* 29; Aristeas 132, and some instances cited below. The word used for "to see beforehand" is *praevidere*[1]; so also in 12:4b, where it stands parallel to *pronoscere*, "to know beforehand". In the Greek fragment of As. Mos. 1:14, προθεᾶσθαι is used (the Latin reads *excogitavit et invenit*, see the commentary there).

As Hilgenfeld recognized[2], *usque ad pusillum* is the second half of the expression "from the greatest to the smallest"; see ἀπὸ μεγάλου ἕως μικροῦ (1 Chron. 34:30; Jonah 3:5), cf. ἀπὸ μικροῦ (καὶ) ἕως μεγάλου (e.g. 1 Sam. 5:9; 30:2, 19; 2 Ki. 23:2; 25:26). It parallels the expression in 12:4a, *ab initio ... usque ad exitum*. However, by using only the second part of the expression, emphasis is placed on God's attention for the seemingly insignificant: he has foreseen and foreknown everything, and he has not neglected (*neglegere* probably renders ἀμελεῖν[3]) anything (*nihil*), not even the pettiest detail. In Wisd. 6:7(8), it is said that God has created both great and small, and that therefore he takes care for both in equal manner: ὅτι μικρὸν (Vulgate: *pusillum*) καὶ μέγαν αὐτὸς ἐποίησεν, ὁμοίως τε προνοεῖ περὶ πάντων. For the idea in general, cf. Matt. 10:30 (par. Luke 12:7).

Solemn combination of near-synonyms (see grammatical note nr. 170) is found again in *praevidit et pronovit*, "he has seen and known beforehand". It should be noted that *pronovit* is a conjectural emendation (the manuscript reads *provovit*, which makes no sense), and that, moreover, the verb *pronoscere* does not seem to occur elsewhere in Latin. Yet the emendation can be defended: the prefixes *prae-* and *pro-* are frequently confused in Latin manuscripts (because of their similarity and overlap in meaning, but also because of their nearly identical graphic appearance[4]). In this instance, the prefix *pro-* may also have been used for reasons of variation. Finally, a form of προγινώσκειν in the Greek original may have influenced the translator (see the grammatical notes nrs. 46 and 167). *Praenoscens* occurs in the Vulgate of Gen. 15:13; elsewhere, *praescire* and *praescientia* are used, see esp. Wisd. 19:1 (LXX: προῄδει γὰρ αὐτῶν καὶ τὰ μέλλοντα); cf. 2 Ki. 19:27; Acts 2:23; 26:5; Rom. 8:29; 11:2; 1 Pet. 1:2, 20; 2 Pet. 3:17. For προγινώσκειν see further e.g. Wisd. 8:8; in Josephus, *Ant. Jud.* VIII 234, mention is made of the θεία πρόγνωσις; and in *Ant. Jud.* XV 373, an Essene Menahem is introduced, πρόγνωσιν ἐκ θεοῦ τῶν μελλόντων ἔχων[5].

The clause *omnia praevidit et pronovit* is followed in the manuscript by CUM and an uncertain reading: EISDNS. The last three letters can easily be recognized as the subject of the following sentence, "the Lord", but it is difficult to fit *cum eis* into either the preceding or the following sentence[6]. *Cum* should, therefore, be taken as the

---

[1] In 12:5a, *providere* is used, see the commentary on that passage.

[2] "Die Psalmen Salomo's", p. 297.

[3] Cf. Wisd. 3:10; 2 Macc. 4:14; Matt. 22:5; 1 Tim. 4:14; Heb. 2:3; 8:9; cf. also πλημμελεῖν Num. 5:6; Sir. 26:11(14).

[4] *Per, pro* and *prae* are commonly abbreviated by the letter P, distinguished only by the position of a stroke through, under or above the letter, see Reynolds and Wilson, *Scribes and Scholars*[3], p. 224.

[5] Cf. Jos., *Bell.* I 69; *Ant. Jud.* X 142; also Judith 9:6, quoted in the introduction to this section.

[6] Volkmar, *Mose Prophetie*, p. 52, proposed to retranslate *cum eis* into τὰ μετ' αὐτῶν, "das, was sie begleitet, ihr Schicksal". *Cum eis*, however, would be a rather awkward translation of such a phrase (cf. 12:5, where *omnia quae futura essent* may well be a translation of

(cont.)

conjunction, complementing a verb meaning "to create"; to stay as close to EIS as possible, one might conjecture *fecit*, which might translate ἐποίησεν, "he created"[1]. The clause can then best be connected with 12:5a, which otherwise lacks a link with what precedes. Moreover, it provides that sentence with the past tense perspective which the form *futura essent* requires: "When God created (it), he foresaw everything that was to happen in this world". Cf. 12:4 *nos praevidit ... ab initio creaturae orbis terrarum* and the parallels quoted above; these parallels also suggest that *omnia quae futura essent* renders πάντα τὰ μέλλοντα.

Instead of *praevidere*, which is the classically correct form used in 12:4 and 12:13, *providere* is used in 12:5 (*providere* usually means "to take care", but see also Gal. 3:8 προϊδοῦσα δὲ ἡ γραφή, Vulgate: *providens autem scriptura*).

c. *12:5b-9*

This passage is the specific answer to the anxious questions placed in Joshua's mouth in 11:9-11. In 11:9-11, Joshua complained that, without the intercessory prayers of Moses, he could not lead the sinful people into the land. Here, Moses answers that Joshua will indeed lead the people into the land, even without Moses' intercessory prayers. It is not the prayers of Moses which have allowed the people to journey thus far, nor will their sinfulness hinder their entrance into the land.

₅ ᵦ And behold, ... will be taken away. ₆ The Lord has appointed me for them and for their sins, that I should pray and supplicate for them; ₇ yet not on account of my virtue or strength, but out of long-suffering his mercy and his patience have befallen me. ₈ Therefore, I say to you, Joshua, not on account of the piety of this people will you defeat the nations. ₉ ₐ All the firmaments of heaven and earth are made as approved of by God, ᵦ and they are under the ring of his right hand.

12:5b

In the manuscript, the phrase *et ecce aufertur* is followed by an illegible section of some length[2], which makes it uncertain whether this phrase should be connected to the preceding or to the following, no longer extant, sentence. Most scholars have connected *et ecce aufertur* to the preceding sentence, reading: "the Lord has foreseen everything that was to happen in this world, and, behold, it will happen accordingly". *Aufertur* is then interpreted as *affertur*[3]. However, if one supposes that *aufertur* was

---

πάντα τὰ μέλλοντα). Moreover, one would expect such an attributive adjunct immediately after the noun it determines (*omnia* at the beginning of the clause).

[1] The conjecture was suggested to me by H.J. de Jonge.

[2] As noted in the apparatus on line 217, there is a considerable difference between Ceriani's and Clemen's report on the length of the illegible section.

[3] Hilgenfeld, *Novum Testamentum*, p. 108, proposed to emend the text accordingly; Volkmar, *Mose Prophetie*, p. 52, maintained that *aufertur* (*avfertur*) is a Vulgar variant of *affertur*, just like *adducetur* is a variant of *abducetur* in 3:5 and 10:1 (see grammatical note nr.

(cont.)

part of the following sentence, one may complement a subject like *corpus, anima* or *animus* with a possessive pronoun. "And, behold, my body (or soul, or spirit) will be taken away". If the text had been something like this, there would be a clear transition from 4-5a to 6-7, which would fit perfectly. *Ecce* in that case more clearly stands out as the introduction of a new thought. In this way, 12:5b-6 could be the answer to Joshua's question put in 11:9a, 11: "Lord, you will be leaving ... but who will pray for them?". See further the commentary on 12:6.

12:6
The remaining legible letters in 12:6 make it possible to suggest a plausible supplementation. The subject of *me constituit* can only be the Lord (*Dominus* or *Deus*); *constituere* is logically continued by an *ut*-clause, and *pro eis* at the end of 12:6 is best explained if the verb to which the prepositional phrase belonged was something like "to pray", so that the sense of 12:6 must be "the Lord has appointed me on their behalf so that I might pray for them." *<Ut orarem> et in<pr>ecare<r>* fills the gaps in the second half of 12:6 perfectly.

It seems likely, therefore, that Moses is made to say in As. Mos. 12:6 that he has been appointed to pray for the people and for their sins. This theme is elaborately treated in chapter 11, and Moses' role as intercessor needs no further comment. The supposed formulation of 12:6, however, raises the question whether Moses will be an intercessor after his death, as W.A. Meeks has strongly argued[1].

Meeks views 12:6 as the answer to Joshua's question, put in 11:17. There, Joshua complained that, after Moses' death, there would no longer be an advocate to atone for Israel's sins by prayer, allowing the Amorites to defeat the people. According to Meeks, Moses' answer in 12:6 counsels Joshua not to worry, because he (Moses) will continue to serve as an intercessor, apparently (if read in connection with 11:17 alone) after his death[2]. This is not, however, a necessary interpretation. In 12:6, Moses does not unambiguously say that he will be an intercessor after his death, only that he has been appointed as one, which may refer to his office during his lifetime as well as to a future task[3]. Because of the emphasis placed by the author of As. Mos. on Joshua being Moses' successor (see 1:7; 2:1-3; 10:15; 12:2), one would be more likely to expect that Moses' intercessory role ends with his death, and that his leadership is transferred to Joshua (on Joshua as an intercessor, see the commentary on 11:9-11).

This interpretation is corroborated when 12:6 is read in connection with 12:7-9. Moses was not appointed intercessor because of his strength. Likewise, the people's piety, or lack of it, will not determine whether Joshua will defeat the nations (compare the fear expressed by "Joshua" in 11:16-18). God, in his mercy and long-suffering,

---

28). In those instances, however, as well as in the case of *accedere* in 2:7, *ab-* is fully assimilated, so that it comes to look like *ad-*. There are no instances in which *ad-* is partly assimilated to *au-* (or even *av-*), so that it could be confused with *ab-*.

[1] *The Prophet-King*, pp. 160-161. The concept that someone may after his death pray for those he has left behind is known from other sources, see 2 Macc. 15:13-16; Josephus, *Ant. Jud.* I 231; Philo, *De praemiis* 166; negatively in 4 Ezra 7:102-112; 2 Bar. 85:12; LAB 33:4. The concept is of course well-known in Christian texts, see e.g. 1 John 2:1-2, also Matt. 10:33 par.; Rom. 8:34; Heb. 7:25.
[2] Meeks, *The Prophet-King*, p. 125, n. 3.
[3] So also Haacker, "Nachbiblische Traditionen", p. 160.

answered Moses' prayers; he will also enable Joshua to lead the people into the land. The success of Moses and Joshua does not depend upon their virtues or the piety of others, but is a result of God's grace.

12:7

As. Mos. 12:7 gives the basis forh Moses' role as an intercessor (and its effectiveness): "Not on my own account, but on account of the Lord's mercy" (see Deut. 7:7-8; cf. Acts 3:12; Rom. 9:16; 1 Cor. 15:10; also Isa. 48:5). Literally, Moses is made to say: "not on account of my virtue (*virtus*) or strength (*firmitas*)"[1]. *Firmitas* (a word the Vulgate rarely uses[2]) means "strength", or, metaphorically, "steadfastness". It is debatable whether *virtus* means "strength" in this instance, or is to be understood as "virtue" (ἀρετή). In Philo, *De specialibus legibus* I 209; *De vita contemplativa* 26 δύναμις and ἀρετή are used as a word-pair.

A problem is posed by the adverb *temperantius*[3], "rather moderately". It can only be constructed with the verb *contegerunt*, notwithstanding the relatively long distance between the two words. It is inconceivable, however, that Moses should be supposed to have said that God's grace has befallen him "in a rather moderate measure" (contrast e.g. Isa. 63:15 τὸ πλῆθος τοῦ ἐλέους σου καὶ οἰκτιρμῶν σου). Perhaps one may take the word to mean here "forbearingly". The verb *temperare* sometimes means "to abstain, refrain from", or pregnantly, "to forbear, tolerate"[4]. A Greek equivalent is ἀνέχεσθαι; the derivate ἀνοχή means "forbearance" in Rom. 2:4, where three characteristics of God are listed: χρηστότης, ἀνοχή (Vulgate: *patientia*), and μακροθυμία. See further Rom. 3:25-26; 1 Clem. 49:5; Ign., *Pol.* 1:2; ad Diogn. 9:1-2. The last instance also may serve to illustrate the divergent construction of one of three near identical concepts: οὐκ ἐμίσησεν ἡμᾶς ... ἀλλὰ ἐμακροθύμησεν, ἠνέσχετο ἐλεῶν.

Misericordiae must be explained as a plural inspired by biblical language, probably οἰκτιρμοί (which, in the Septuagint, is usually in the plural); see, for instance, Ps. 119(118):77 ἐλθέτωσάν μοι οἱ οἰκτιρμοί σου.

12:8

In order to comfort and encourage Joshua, Moses in 12:6-7 reappraises his own merits, which Joshua had so highly praised in chapter 11. The Lord heeded Moses' prayers, not because Moses was virtuous or strong, but because the Lord is merciful and patient. Answering Joshua's concern, expressed in 11:16-18, Moses assures

---

[1] This is the manuscript's reading. Often, *in* is taken as a prefix, and *virtus* and *infirmitas* are seen as polar concepts, expressing inclusiveness (alternatively, this prefix is simply deleted). However, Schmidt and Merx, "Die Assumptio Mosis", p. 136, rightly recognized *in* as a preposition, in this case synonymous with *propter* (an instance of variation, see grammatical note nr. 167); they also regarded the final *-m* of *firmitatem* as an abbreviation, and dissolved it into *mea*. This is certainly possible, but in view of the confusion of cases after prepositions, *in firmitatem* may be the original reading.

[2] Gen. 41:32; Prov. 22:21; 2 Macc. 10:34; 2 Pet. 3:17; in all these instances, *firmitas* is used metaphorically.

[3] The word is often emended into the substantive *temperantia* and is sometimes translated with "mildness". Hilgenfeld, "Die Psalmen Salomo's", p. 298, translated *temperantia* back as ἐπιείκια; *temperantia*, however, is neither "mildness", nor ἐπιείκια.

[4] Lewis-Short, p. 1849c.

Joshua that the Amorites (and the other hostile nations) will be defeated under his leadership, notwithstanding the people's sins. To this, one may compare Deut. 9:5-6 (cf. CD VIII 14-15):

> Not because of your (*sc.* the people's) righteousness or the uprightness of your heart are you going in to possess the land; but because of the wickedness of these nations the Lord your God is driving them out from before you, and that he may confirm the word which the Lord swore to your fathers, to Abraham, to Isaac, and to Jacob. Know therefore, that the Lord your God is not giving you this good land because of your righteousness; for you are a stubborn people (trans. RSV).

12:9

In 12:8, the view that the people would themselves be able to defeat their adversaries, is rejected. If the victory were to depend on the people's piety, the conquest of the land would certainly fail. In contrast to this view it is said , in 12:9, that it is the divine Creator who governs all things. The foundations of heaven and earth were made as he saw fit[1], and he controls everything that is in them.

In biblical literature, the "firmament" (στερέωμα) is primarily associated with the heavens[2]; the earth is more readily seen as having "foundations" (θεμέλια). In connection with the peculiar word-order and the asyndetic construction in 12:9a, it is natural to assume that the text has suffered damage in the process of transmission[3]. An addition such as *caeli firmamenta <et fundamenta> orbis* recommends itself[4]. However, *firmamentum*/στερέωμα does simply mean "foundation", and if one wants to keep the manuscript's text as it stands, *caeli firmamenta orbis* can be regarded as an ellipse, and one could translate: "the foundations of heaven and earth". In this way, the plural *firmamenta*, too, would be explained, but the lack of a copulative, e.g. *et*, remains somewhat problematic.

Textual problems also arise in the second half of 12:9. The manuscript's text has *et sub nullo dexterae illius sunt*. Von Gutschmid and Weiss proposed to read *anullo* instead of *nullo* (*anullus* = *anulus*, "ring"); the gemination of *-l-* is a regular phenomenon in manuscripts and in Vulgar Latin, see grammatical note nr. 23), and the conjecture is generally accepted. In support, one can point to Jer. 22:24; Hagg. 2:23, and Sir. 49:11. In these verses Jeconiah (Jeremiah) and Zerubbabel (Haggai and Sira) are "made as God's right-hand signet ring", that is, his authorized agents. The author of As. Mos., however, does not wish to speak of authorization, but of God's authority itself. If the conjecture is nevertheless accepted (and there seems to be no alternative), it must be concluded that the author of As. Mos. contaminated the expression "to be under someone's hand" (ὑπὸ χείρα), that is, "to be in someone's power", with the

---

[1] *Provatum* (= *probatum*, see grammatical note nr. 21), "approved", cf. Gen. 1, esp. 1:31 καὶ εἶδεν ὁ θεὸς τὰ πάντα, ὅσα ἐποίησεν, καὶ ἰδοὺ καλὰ λίαν.

[2] Bertram, "στερεός κτλ.", pp. 609-610.

[3] The impression that words have been lost is strengthened by the absence of a finite form of *esse* with *facta*, now to be sylleptically constructed with *sub anullo dexterae illius sunt* (see grammatical note nr. 172); and by the use of *orbis* only, without *terrarum*, which is the normal expression in As. Mos. (it occurs eleven times; cf. *orbis terrae* 1:2; *orbis stellarum* 10:5); finally, by the corruption in 12:9b.

[4] The conjecture was suggested by Fritzsche, see the textual commentary to line 222.

expression "to be as a signet ring", that is, "to have full power". The meaning of this contaminated idiom must then be that God has full power over his creation.

d. *12:10-13*

The last extant lines of As. Mos. give the impression of being the conclusion to Moses' and Joshua's dialogue. Moses makes a short theological statement, summarizing the dual aspect of "Deuteronomistic" covenantal theology: God's judicial righteousness, punishing the sinners, and his gracious righteousness, maintaining the covenant and his oath[1].

10 If they therefore do the commandments of God perfectly, they will grow and prosper. 11 But the sinners and those who neglect the commandments <must> miss the goods that have been foretold, and they will be punished by the nations with many torments. 12 But it cannot happen that he will exterminate and leave them entirely. 13 For God, who sees everything beforehand in eternity, will go out, and his covenant stands firm. And through the oath which ...

12:10-12

Having elaborated on the predetermined plan underlying creation, which ensures the safety of the people, the author of As. Mos. makes plain that the Lord's protection is no licence to neglect his commandments. Only if the people will fulfil his commandments (*facientes ... et consummantes mandata*) they will grow[2] and prosper. Those, however, who will sin and neglect the commandments (*peccantibus et neglegentibus mandata*), must do without the Lord's blessing and be punished and tortured by the pagans[3].

This distinction within the people of God between the righteous and the sinful is the theological formulation of the divisions that were already expressed in historical terms in 4:7-9, where the "two tribes" were contrasted with "some parts of the tribes" and the "ten tribes". In 12:12, the concept of a faithful remnant is made explicit: although the nations will deal severely with the people (because of the sins committed), it is impossible that the Lord will abandon his people entirely (*in totum* probably renders εἰς τέλος; on the omission of *ut* after *non potest*, see grammatical note nr. 157). This belief is found in various strands of Jewish piety; see 2 Chron. 12:12; Ju-

---

[1] Cf. Münchow, *Ethik*, p. 73-74, on the tension between predeterminism and ethical responsibility, solved by the notion of the covenant. Breaking the covenant must within history lead to punishment, but at the same time the covenant itself warrants (eschatological) salvation.

[2] It is possible to consider this as another reassessment of the importance of Moses' intercessory role, which Joshua linked to the people's multiplication in 11:14, but which is now made dependent on the people's own obedience to the Lord.

[3] Cf. Jaubert, *La notion d'alliance*, p. 260: the Gentiles "servent à punir les Israélites infidèles (12:11), mais eux-mêmes seront châtiés (10:7)".

dith 7:30; Ps. 103(102):9; Isa. 65:8; Amos 9:8 LXX; Dan. 3:34; cf. Rom. 11:5; T. Levi 5:6. More specifically, however, it has been expressed in Deut. 4:31, in which ideas corresponding to the two verbs *exterminare* and *relinquere* can be recognized. There, too, the connection with the covenant is made (cf. As. Mos. 12:13):

ὅτι θεὸς οἰκτίρμων κύριος ὁ θεός σου, οὐκ ἐγκαταλείψει σε οὐδὲ μὴ ἐκ–
τρίψει σε (Vulgate: *nec omnino delebit*), οὐκ ἐπιλήσεται τὴν διαθήκην τῶν
πατέρων σου, ἥν ὤμοσεν αὐτοῖς.

For "doing the law", a usual double expression is *custodire et facere* (φυλάσσεσθαι καὶ ποιεῖν), whereas As. Mos. 12:10 reads *facientes itaque et consummantes mandata Dei*. *Consummare* does not occur elsewhere in connection with the commandments. It should probably be taken as a specification of *facere*: "doing the commandments, doing them perfectly" (cf. As. Mos. 1:10) See also the Vulgate of Josh. 22:5 *ita dumtaxat ut custodiatis adtente et opere conpleatis mandatum et legem* (LXX: ἀλλὰ φυλάξασθε ποιεῖν σφόδρα τὰς ἐντολὰς καὶ τὸν νόμον). With regard to the words *bonam viam exigunt* (12:10), literally, "to reach the good way", one cannot but agree with Hilgenfeld's proposal that this peculiar phrase must be an analytical translation of εὐοδοῦν, "to prosper". A verb must be supplemented to account both for the ablative or (rather) dative forms *peccantibus* and *neglegentibus* and for the infinitive *carere* (12:11). *Est* or *necesse est* are obvious possibilities.

12:13

The impossibility of the perishing of the people as a whole is explained with reference to God's intervention; for this pregnant use of *exire* see commentary on 10:3. With this intervention, the author probably means God's final, eschatological intervention, not his continuous protection throughout Israel's history[1]. Although God has acted to save his people before (according to As. Mos. 4:5-6), that action was not characterized as a "going out". Moreover, the primary interest of the author of As. Mos. here is to reassure his readers of the impending salvation, which is the eschatological one.

The last extant passage in the manuscript reiterates the motif of the divine prescience. Connected with the covenant, the meaning of the motif now becomes entirely clear: the people's sins are not unforeseen disruptions of God's plan, but part of it. God has always known such things would happen (*praevidit omnia in saecula*). Apparently, he has intended the world's history as a way of distilling the perfect people of the covenant. The Gentiles were to be disgraced (cf. 1:13), and the people were to be purified; for them, the world was created (1:12) and the covenant established (cf. 1:14). For their sake, too, the promises of the covenant will be fulfilled.

---

[1] So Laperrousaz, *Le Testament de Moïse*, p. 137.

THE LOST ENDING OF AS. MOS.

The Latin text of the only surviving manuscript of As. Mos. is incomplete. Especially at the end, a portion of the text of some length is missing. Several scholars—including Charles, James, Loewenstamm and Bauckham[1]—have attempted to reconstruct the lost ending of the work. All these scholars recognize the speculative character of such reconstructions, but this view does not prevent them from giving detailed reconstructions of the lost ending. Bauckham even reconstructs two conclusions, attributing one to the Testament of Moses, and the other to the Assumption of Moses. In this chapter, however, it will be shown that reliable traces of As. Mos. in ecclesiastical literature are few, and that they allow only very modest conclusions with regard to the ending of this work[2].

The little that can safely be said can be summarized as follows.

(1) The extant text of As. Mos. displays all the characteristics of the testament form. Therefore, the sequel to the dialogue between Joshua and Moses (chapters 11-12) must have contained some account of the way in which Moses ended his earthly life.

(2) As. Mos. 1:15 and 10:14 state that Moses himself expected his imminent death. These passages also suggest that As. Mos. included an account of Moses' death. Perhaps *et palam omnem plebem* in 1:15 is meant to stress that many people witnessed Moses' death, and that, therefore, there can be no doubt about that event.

(3) In As. Mos. 11:7, Joshua asks how a human being would dare to bury Moses' body. This may be an allusion to the well-established tradition of Moses' burial by God or by angels. In the fragments of the lost conclusion, Moses' body ($\sigma\tilde{\omega}\mu\alpha$) is mentioned as the object of a dispute between Michael and the devil (see below, section b). Conse-

---

[1] Charles, *The Assumption*, pp. xlix-l; James, *The Lost Apocrypha*, pp. 48-49; Loewenstamm, "The Death of Moses", pp. 208-211; Bauckham, *Jude*, pp. 73-76. See further Denis, *Fragmenta*, pp. 63-67. In chapter 5 of his recent monograph, *Jude and the Relatives of Jesus*, pp. 235-280, Bauckham again treated this subject. In the following pages I will refer, however, to Bauckham's more concise exposition in his commentary on Jude.

[2] Laperrousaz, *Le Testament*, pp. 50-79, has extensively discussed the most important passages that have been said to contain traces of As. Mos. (Jude 16; 2 Pet. 2:3, 13; Acts 7:36; Matt. 24:21, 29 and parallels; 2 Bar. 84:3-5). Laperrousaz only accepts Acts 7:36 as a quotation from As. Mos. (3:11); the other passages he rightly rejects as such. But even Acts 7:36 is probably no quotation of As. Mos.; the similarities are far too superficial.

quently, the presence of Michael probably means that the archangel was sent in order to bury Moses' body.

(4) It is not at all improbable, however, that Michael also came in his function as psychopomp, that is, as someone who was to transport Moses' soul to heaven[1]. The extant fragments do not strictly support this possibility, but they do not exclude it either. Moreover, the tradition that Moses was given a heavenly existence after his death is well documented in Jewish literature of the period.

a. *The Greek fragments*

Later Greek authors who quote, or allude to, As. Mos. shed light on the contents of the lost ending. Students of As. Mos. have detailed many such passages from ecclesiastical literature, and these have been conveniently arranged by A.-M. Denis in his *Fragmenta Pseudepigraphorum Graecorum* of 1970. As will be shown below, however, there are only four passages that derive with certainty from As. Mos., three of which occur in Gelasius' *Ecclesiastical History*, one in the Epistle of Jude.

Gelasius Cyzicenus († ca. 476), whose quotation from As. Mos. 1:14 ensures the identification of our text as the Ἀνάληψις Μωσέως (see the Introduction, section V, a), includes two more quotations referring to a dispute between the archangel Michael and the devil which come from what must have been the end of As. Mos. Since a comparison of Gelasius' abundant quotations from biblical books with the Septuagint text shows that they conform to the latter with great accuracy, we can also assume that these two quotations from the Assumption of Moses are trustworthy. They refer to a dispute between the archangel Michael and the devil. Since Jude 9 contains a passage which corresponds almost word for word to Gelasius' quotation concerning the quarrel between Michael and the devil, it can safely be assumed that Jude 9, too, goes back to the lost ending of As. Mos. The quotation from As. Mos. in the Epistle of Jude enables us to deduce that the dispute concerned Moses' body.

Hence we may be reasonably certain that the following sentences were taken from As. Mos.

---

[1] On Michael as psychopomp, see Lueken, *Michael*, pp. 43-49, 120-127.

(1) Μωσῆς προσκαλεσάμενος Ἰησοῦν υἱὸν Ναυῆ καὶ διαλεγόμενος πρὸς αὐτὸν ἔφη· ... καὶ προεθεάσατό με ὁ θεὸς πρὸ καταβολῆς κόσμου εἶναί με τῆς διαθήκης αὐτοῦ μεσίτην.
(2) ἀπὸ γὰρ πνεύματος ἁγίου αὐτοῦ πάντες ἐκτίσθημεν.
(3) ἀπὸ προσώπου τοῦ θεοῦ ἐξῆλθε τὸ πνεῦμα αὐτοῦ, καὶ ὁ κόσμος ἐγένετο.
(4) ἐπιτιμήσαι σοι κύριος.

We shall now proceed to discuss them in detail.

Quotation (1) is treated in the commentary on 1:14 above.

Quotations (2) and (3) occur in a single passage in Gelasius' *Ecclesiastical History*:

> ἐν βίβλῳ δὲ ἀναλήψεως Μωσέως Μιχαὴλ ὁ ἀρχάγγελος διαλεγόμενος τῷ διαβόλῳ λέγει· ᾽ἀπὸ γὰρ πνεύματος ἁγίου αὐτοῦ πάντες ἐκτίσθημεν᾿, καὶ πάλιν λέγει· ᾽ἀπὸ προσώπου τοῦ θεοῦ ἐξῆλθε τὸ πνεῦμα αὐτοῦ, καὶ ὁ κόσμος ἐγένετο᾿.[1]

In the book of the Assumption of Moses, the archangel Michael, in a discussion with the devil, says: "For by his Holy Spirit, all of us have been created", and further he says: "God's spirit went forth from his face, and the world came into being."

Quotation (4) is found in Jude 9, where a dispute between Michael and the devil is also mentioned.

> Ὁ δὲ Μιχαὴλ ὁ ἀρχάγγελος ὅτε τῷ διαβόλῳ διακρινόμενος διελέγετο περὶ τοῦ Μωϋσέως σώματος οὐκ ἐτόλμησεν κρίσιν ἐπενεγκεῖν βλασφημίας, ἀλλὰ εἶπεν· ᾽ἐπιτιμήσαι σοι κύριος᾿.

And the archangel Michael, when he was in a dispute with the devil over Moses' body, did not dare to declare him guilty of slander, but said: "May the Lord rebuke you."

The way in which the dispute between Michael and the devil is described is almost verbally identical in quotations (3) and (4). Therefore, it is likely that both Gelasius and the author of Jude used the ending of As. Mos. It may be concluded from Jude 9 that the discussion between Michael and the devil was in fact about Moses' body.

---

[1] *Ecclesiastical History* II, 21, 7, ed. Loeschcke & Heinemann, *GCS* 28, p. 86. In Gelasius' *Ecclesiastical History*, a quotation is found from a βίβλος λόγων μυστικῶν Μωσέως (see Denis, *Fragmenta*, pp. 64-65), but there is no relation to As. Mos. Likewise, Clement of Alexandria twice refers to opinions of the μύσται (Denis, *Fragmenta*, p. 64), but in these cases it is not even sure whether Clement refers to a book.

The archangel's words quoted in Jude 9 are also found in Zech. 3:2, again in the context of a discussion between Michael and the devil. In a vision, the prophet sees the high priest Joshua standing before the angel of the Lord and Satan standing at his right hand to oppose him (τοῦ ἀντικεῖσθαι αὐτῷ 3:1). A mitre is set upon the high priest's head, and he is clothed in radiant garments. He is furthermore ordered to walk in the Lord's ways. Because Satan apparently objects to this, probably accusing Joshua of sinful behaviour, the angel of the Lord[1] says to him: Ἐπιτιμήσαι κύριος ἐν σοί, διάβολε. I suspect that this scene from Zechariah's visions has taken on a life of its own, and re-emerged, with a different application, in As. Mos.[2] In short, a tradition concerning someone called Joshua has been applied to Moses, a comprehensible development in view of the common association of another Joshua with Moses in the Old Testament. Jude 9 may then be accepted as a quotation of As. Mos., not of Zech. 3:2.

There is, however, only one external confirmation of this supposition, namely in Origen's *Principles* (see below). Passages in other ecclesiastical writers have been used as evidence that Jude 9 derives from As. Mos., but wrongly so.

It has been inferred from an annotation by Clement of Alexandria (†before 215) that Jude 9 corresponds to a passage in As. Mos.[3] Clement writes: "'Quando Michael archangelus cum diabolo disputans altercabatur de corpore Moysi' [= Jude 9]—Hic confirmat assumptionem Moysi". It is unlikely, however, that Clement's comment refers to a book called the "Assumption of Moses"[4]. The most natural translation of his annotation is: "Here he confirms that Moses was taken up". Clement was indeed of the opinion that Moses was taken up (see below), and in the Epistle of Jude, which he considered an authoritative book, he saw his view confirmed. Therefore, this passage is not evi-

---

[1] The text literally says that the Lord himself said these words. But in Zech. 3, the angel of the Lord is constantly present, and he and the Lord act as one. Of course, if the angel speaks, he speaks on behalf of the Lord.

[2] Slightly differently Grotius *ad* Matt. 27:9 (*CS* VI, *ad Matt.* col. 949): "Zacharias illud, *Increpet te Deus, ô Satan!* sumsit ex antiqua traditione, quae deinde perscripta est in libro ἀποκρύφῳ [*abscondito*] cui titulus Ἀνάληψις Μωσέως [*Assumptio Mosis*]." Milik, "4Q Visions de 'Amram", p. 95, supposes that As. Mos. depends on 4QAmram^b 1-3.

[3] *Adumbrationes in ep. Jud.*, ed. Stählin-Früchtel, *GCS* 17[2], p. 207.

[4] Even if it does, his words should still be translated as: "Here he agrees with the Assumption of Moses", words which can hardly be taken as meaning to indicate that Jude derived this clause from a book bearing that title. As to the Latin form of Clement's comment, see Altaner-Stuiber, *Patrologie*, p. 194: "die Erklärungen zu 1 Petr., Jud. und 1 und 2 Joh. sind in lateinischer, auf Cassiodor (um 540) zurückgehender Übersetzung überliefert".

dence that Clement knew As. Mos., nor that Jude 9 is a quotation from As. Mos.

In Rufinus' translation of the *Principles* by Origen († ca. 254), a reference is found to the *Ascensio Mosis*, which can be equated with the Ἀνάληψις Μωσέως quoted by Gelasius. Origen apparently wants to refer to As. Mos. to give an example of the way in which adverse forces or the devil himself try to incite human kind to sin:

> Et primo quidem in Genesi serpens Evam seduxisse perscribitur: de quo serpente in Ascensione Moysi, cujus libelli meminit in epistola sua apostolus Judas, Michahel archangelus cum diabolo disputans de corpore Moysi ait a diabolo inspiratum serpentem causam extitisse praevaricationis Adae et Evae[1].

According to this passage, the Assumption of Moses must have contained a passage in which Michael told the devil that Adam's and Eve's sin was caused by the devil, who had inspired the serpent. That As. Mos. ever contained such a passage, however, is unlikely. The mention of Adam and Eve, of the serpent and of original sin is probably based on the *Vita Adae et Evae* (VAE), known in the Greek tradition as the *Apocalypse* of Moses. Apparently, Origen knew As. Mos., and also that Jude 9 derives from it. Therefore, the passage *in Ascensione Moysi, cujus libelli meminit in epistola sua apostolus Judas, Michahel archangelus cum diabolo disputans de corpore Moysi* may be taken to confirm the provenance of Jude 9 from As. Mos.

The information Origen provides on the contents of this dispute, however, must derive from the Apocalypse of Moses (whatever form it may have had when Origen knew it). According to Apoc. Mos. 11, Eve and her son Seth meet a serpent on their way to pray for Adam. This animal reminds Eve of her misdeed, that is, her eating the forbidden fruit. Apoc. Mos. 12:1 continues:

> Λέγει δὲ ὁ Σὴθ πρὸς τὸ θηρίον· κλεῖσαί σου τὸ στόμα καὶ σίγα, καὶ ἀπόστηθι ἀπὸ τῆς εἰκόνος τοῦ θεοῦ ἕως ἡμέρας τῆς κρίσεως.

The words ascribed to Michael in Origen's *Principles* as deriving from As. Mos. are more likely to be situated in this context. It may be noted that in Apoc. Mos./VAE Seth is often an intermediary between the

---

[1] *De principiis* III, 2, 1, ed. Crouzel-Simonetti, *SC* 268, p. 152. The subject of this section is "quomodo contrariae virtutes vel ipse diabolus reluctantur humano generi, provocantes et instigantes ad peccatum" (*ibid.*). Cf. Rönsch, "Weitere Illustrationen", p. 214. To this passage, one may compare Severus on Jude 9, see Cramer, *Catenae,* VIII, pp. 162-163; James, *The Lost Apocrypha*, p. 46.

archangel Michael and Eve. Indeed, the Latin text of VAE 39 includes the very words Michael is said to speak in Jude 9:

> *Tunc dixit Seth ad bestiam: "Increpet te Dominus Deus. Stupe, obmutesce: claude os tuum, maledicte inimice veritatis confusio perditionis; recede de imagine Dei usque in diem, quando Dominus Deus jusserit in comprobationem te adduci".*

In conclusion: the passage quoted from Origen's *Principles* confirms that Jude 9 is a quotation from As. Mos. But the additional information the passage provides, does not derive from As. Mos., but from the Apocalypse of Moses[1].

b. *The Struggle Between Michael and the Devil*

We know from the extant fragments that the lost ending of As. Mos. included an account of a struggle between Michael and the devil. There is, however, no indication of the exact nature of the dispute. Moses' body was involved, and the devil is said to have "slandered". But the content of his βλασφημία is not mentioned in the passages discussed above, and Michael's arguments shed little light on the charges to which he is responding.

It has often been maintained, on the basis of Christian comments on Deut. 34:6 and Jude 9, that the subject of the dispute was the soul of Moses (despite the mention of his σῶμα in Jude 9). As K. Berger has shown[2], the struggle between good and bad angels is a traditional motif, and can be found, for example, in 4QAmram[b] I 10-11:

בחזוי חזוה די חלמא והא תרין דאנין עלי ואמרין [...]
ואחדין עלי תגר רב

---

[1] There is a passage in Didymus (313-398) which also deals with the nature of the devil, cf. *Didymi Alexandrini in epistolam beati Judae apostoli enarratio,* ed. Migne, *PG* 39, col. 1815. It seems evident, however, that the testimony of Didymus, who was well acquainted with the works of Origen (Altaner, *Patrologie,* p. 280), must be dependent on the latter's *Principles.* To Origen and Didymus, Denis, *Introduction,* p. 129 adds as a testimony Photius, "Ad Amphilochium Quaestio CLI" (ed. Migne, *PG* 101, p. 813B): Ἰούδας μὲν οὖν ὁ ἀπό–στολος ἐν τῇ αὑτοῦ Ἐπιστολῇ ἐκ τῶν λεγομένων ἀποκρύφων Μωϋσέως ταύτην τὴν χρείαν κτλ. However, the other examples of quotations of apocryphal sources in the New Testament given by Photius allow us to conclude only that he recognised that the quotation in Jude 9 came from an apocryphal source, probably without knowing which one.

[2] Berger, "Der Streit um die Seele".

[I saw] in a vision, a vision in a dream, that two of them were speaking about me, and they said ... and they had a great fight over me[1].

Berger refers to a large number of other texts, which are Christian and late, and cannot, therefore, serve as independent testimonies of such a tradition, since we must assume that their authors knew at least Jude 9. 4QAmram, however, shows that the motif was known in the first century C.E. It is important to note that the quarrel between the angels does not take place at Amram's death, but is seen in a vision. The choice the visionary must make between Darkness and Light (4QAmram[b] I 12) may well concern his earthly life[2]. This point is all the more important, because the first occurrence of a scene in which angels quarrel before God over a human being is not in 4QAmram, but in Zech. 3:1-2, as was pointed out above (in section a). Whether or not the vision in Zech. 3 is the basis of the traditional motif of the struggle between Michael and the devil in As. Mos.[3], it does show, together with 4QAmram, that such a dispute does not necessarily concern the destination of a dead man's soul.

A considerable number of Christian texts, most of them found in the *Catenae*, attempt to fill in the details of the dispute mentioned in Jude 9, mainly by providing the arguments which the devil might have adduced. The *Catena* edited by Cramer includes several versions of such speculative supplements.

According to one comment on Jude 10, the devil's blasphemy to which Jude 9 alludes, is equivalent to an accusation of murder against Moses. Having killed the Egyptian, Moses should be regarded as a murderer:

> Τελευτήσαντος ἐν τῷ ὄρει Μωϋσέως, ὁ Μιχαὴλ ἀποστέλλεται μεταθήσων τὸ σῶμα, εἶτα τοῦ διαβόλου κατὰ τοῦ Μωϋσέως βλασφημοῦντος, καὶ φονέα ἀναγορεύοντος διὰ τὸ πατάξαι τὸν Αἰγύπτιον, οὐκ ἐνεγκὼν τὴν κατ' αὐτοῦ βλασφημίαν ὁ Ἄγγελος, ᾽ἐπιτιμήσαι σοι ὁ θεός᾽ πρὸς τὸν διά–βολον ἔφη.

Moses having died on the Mount, Michael is sent to transfer the body to heaven. The devil subsequently slandered Moses, and accused him of being a

---

[1] Milik, "4Q Visions de ῾Amram", p. 79.

[2] So also Bauckham, *Jude*, p. 66.

[3] Bauckham, *Jude*, pp. 65-66 points to various stories in which good and bad angels appear as (legal) opponents who in heaven interfere before God with earthly matters. Satan is often depicted in this connection as a tempter of pious humans; cf. Origen's *De Principiis*, quoted above, on the question "how the devil attempts to instigate human kind to sin."

murderer, because he had slain the Egyptian. But the Angel did not bear his slander, but said to the devil: "May God rebuke you."[1]

In this passage, the devil is presented in his traditional role as accuser[2]. Pointing at one of Moses' sins (Exod. 2:12; cf. Acts 7:24[3]), he apparently tries to prevent him from being taken up to heaven. Μετατιθέναι is the term used for the assumptions of Enoch and Elijah into heaven, see Gen. 5:24; Wisd. 4:10; Sir. 44:16; 49:14 (A; BS have a form of ἀναλαμβάνεσθαι). In these instances, no mention is made of a "body" being taken up (although a bodily assumption is implied), and the explicit mention of σῶμα in the *Catena*-comment is probably inspired by Jude 9[4]. The *Catena* uses other traditions on Moses to try to elucidate the passage in Jude 9. The presentation of the devil as an accuser probably agrees with the story in the original ending of As. Mos., because another role for the devil in this context cannot be conceived. But the remaining details provided by this comment (the exact contents of Michael's mission, the nature of the devil's accusation) cannot be used to reconstruct the lost conclusion of As. Mos. These details are probably no more than rationalizations or elucidations of the biblical text of Jude 9.

In the same *Catena*, another explanation is given, according to which the devil claimed Moses' body, trying to seduce Michael into accepting that the devil was the "Master of matter" (ὁ γὰρ διάβολος ἀντεῖχε θέλων ἀπατῆσαι, ὅτι ἐμὸν τὸ σῶμα ὡς τῆς ὕλης δεσπόζοντι)[5]. It is true, as Bauckham notes, that such a claim is appropriately answered by Michael's words on creation quoted above: "For through his Holy Spirit, all of us have been created", and: "God's spirit went forth from his face, and the world came into being." Although the devil's claim on

---

[1] Cramer, *Catenae*, VIII, p. 163; Denis, *Fragmenta*, pp. 66-67. The same point is raised in the commentary on Jude by Ps.-Oecumenius of Tricca (10th century?); see Denis, *Fragmenta*, p. 67.

[2] See Foerster and von Rad, "διαβάλλω κτλ.", pp. 74-76. Cf. especially 1 En. 40:7; Jub. 48:15-18.

[3] On Moses' sins, see further Loewenstamm, "The Death of Moses", section A., "Explanations for Moses' Death Outside the Land", pp. 186-193.

[4] Compare the exegesis preferred by Severus, quoted below, according to which Michael came to fetch Moses' soul.

[5] Cramer, *Catenae*, VIII, p. 160:30. In an eleventh-century manuscript of these *Catenae*, the two versions have been merged, see Denis, *Fragmenta*, p. 67; cf. Rönsch, "Weitere Illustrationen", p. 219; in a scholion quoted by Rönsch, "Weitere Illustrationen", pp. 219-220, and James, *The Lost Apocrypha*, p. 46, both versions are placed side by side.

authority over matter could have been answered by the appeal to the divine and spiritual origin of matter, the angel's words in the ending of As. Mos. do not necessarily presuppose "the debate with gnostic dualism"[1]; see for instance Ps. 104(103):30, and cf. Job 33:4; Isa. 57:16; 2 Macc. 7:28; Col. 1:16; Heb. 11:3; Rev. 4:11. Bauckham, who rightly regards another comment in the *Catenae* as a speculative, Christian interpretation of Jude 9[2], does accept this passage as part of Jude's source[3]. In no way, however, do the *Catenae* suggest that they derive their explanations from sources other than (Christian) exegetical tradition.

An extensive commentary by Severus († ca. 539) on Jude 9 is also found in the *Catenae*. Severus lists the following interpretations:

(1) When someone dies and the spirit is separated from the body, the good angels and a mass of demons fight with each other over the nature of the things deceased has done when alive. Thus, says Severus, it is decided whether one will be led into eternal life or into everlasting fire. The story of the dispute over Moses' body is intended to teach us that there is a struggle over our spirits after their departure from the body, and it makes clear that we should, through good works, prepare ourselves in order to have the (good) angels as our allies[4]. Severus himself prefers this explanation[5].

(2) Some say that "Moses' body" is Jude's designation of the law itself[6], and that the devil attempted to prevent the law from being given to the people; he would have argued that they were not worthy of receiving it.

(3) Others say that by "Moses' body" the Hebrew people is meant; the devil would have tried to prevent the people from leaving Egypt, because they were not worthy of freedom.

---

[1] Bauckham, *Jude*, p. 75, cf. Loewenstamm, "The Death of Moses", pp. 210-211.

[2] Bauckham, *Jude*, p. 72.

[3] Bauckham, *Jude*, p. 74, correctly designates these comments on Jude 9 as "traditions", but on p. 75, he suddenly calls them "texts" and "sources".

[4] Cf. the anonymous comment preceding that of Severus in the *Catenae*, Cramer, *Catenae*, VIII, p. 161.

[5] Καὶ ταύτην μὲν τὴν ἐξήγησιν τὸ προκείμενον ἔχειν δοκεῖ καὶ οὕτως αὐτὸ νενοήκαμεν: "And this interpretation seems to be the most obvious one, and this is the way we understand it."

[6] So Origen, *In Jesu Nave* I, 3, ed. Jaubert, *SC* 71, p. 100; cf. ed. Baehrens, *GCS* 30, p. 290; Baehrens, *ibid.*, quotes a similar statement by Procopius († 538).

The second and third explanations are clearly guesses. This casts some doubt on the value of the first explanation as well, since Severus indicates no source for it. It is unlikely that he knew As. Mos., because he presents this "exegesis" as the most obvious one—that is to say, he prefers this explanation on grounds of probability—, and because he does not appeal to any source as his authority. Severus' first explanation, too, must therefore be regarded as no more than a speculative reconstruction of the story underlying Jude 9, and not as a reference to As. Mos. The same explanation is found in Severus' comment on Deut. 34:6, where he adds: ταῦτα δὲ ἐν ἀποκρύφῳ βιβλίῳ λέγεται κεῖσθαι, λεπτοτέραν ἔχοντι τῆς Γενέσεως, ἤτοι τῆς κτίσεως, τὴν ἀφήγησιν[1]. Rönsch and James identified this apocryphal λεπτοτέρα ἀφήγησις as *Leptogenesis* or Jubilees[2]. Apparently, Severus himself had not seen this apocryphon, since Jubilees does not contain such an account[3].

In these Christian comments on Jude 9 Bauckham believes to find two versions of a story about the dispute between Michael and the devil over Moses. In one version, the devil would appear as the traditional accuser, trying to prove Moses' guilt; in the other, represented by Gelasius' quotations, the devil would appear as a kind of gnostic demiurge, claiming Moses' body as a piece of matter. Bauckham regards both versions as mutually exclusive, and explains their existence by ascribing the second version to As. Mos. as a *"revised version* of the earlier *T. Mos.".* Bauckham notes: "It is hard to believe that a Palestinian work of the early first century A.D. would have included the kind of refutation of dualism which the texts quote from the *As. Mos.* It is much more plausible to attribute the *As. Mos.'* version of the dispute over Moses' body to the concerns of Christian anti-gnostic argument in the second century A.D."[4] But if he is right, it is much more probable to assume that such Christian anti-gnostic arguments were not included in any version, revised or not, of As. Mos., especially since none of Bauckham's sources refers to As. Mos. as the authority for their exegesis.

In the *Palaea* (10th century?[5]), it is said that Samuel (= Samael, an angel of death) tried to bring Moses' body to the people, so that they

---

[1] Νικήφορος, Σεῖρα, col. 1673 Δ.
[2] Rönsch, *Das Buch der Jubiläen*, pp. 271-273; James, *The Lost Apocrypha*, pp. 45-46.
[3] See James, *The Lost Apocrypha*, p. 50, and cf. section V,a of the Introduction.
[4] Bauckham, *Jude*, pp. 75-76.
[5] So *Tusculum-Lexikon*, p. 593.

might make him a god[1]. It is unlikely that the *Palaea* in this case represents an old, independent tradition, "based ultimately on the Assumption proper"[2]. It is full of specifically Christian terms (e.g. σκύνωμα =
σκήνωμα for "body"; ὁ ἀρχιστρατήγος for Michael[3] and ὁ ἀντικεί–
μενος for "the devil"; Θεὸς ὁ Χριστὸς ἡμῶν), and the entire story can
be explained as an amalgam of traditions about Moses' death[4], such as
reflected in Jude 9 (on the struggle between good and bad angels), and
Josephus, *Ant. Jud.* IV 326 (on the risk of Moses being deified[5]; on this
passage see further below). A similar tradition is found in the midrash
Deuteronomy Rabba 11 (207c)[6].

The dispute between Michael and the devil which must have formed
part of the conclusion of As. Mos. was about Moses' body. It can be assumed that Michael was sent to take the body, but met with the devil,
who claimed the body to be his. Probably, the devil appeared in his
traditional role as accuser, contesting Michael's rights to the body on
account of Moses' sins. The use of the word σῶμα/*corpus* strongly suggests that Moses' body was inanimate at the time of the dispute. Perhaps, Michael was sent to bury Moses' body, as in Philo, *De vita Mosis*
II 291; Targum Jonathan Deut. 34:6[7]; Epiphanius (315-403), *Adversus
haereses* 9, 4, 13[8]; 64, 69, 6[9]; Ps.-Oecumenius[10]; cf. LAB 19:16, where
God himself is said to have buried Moses.

---

[1] Greek text in Charles, *The Assumption*, pp. xlix-l, quoted from Vassiliev, *Anecdota graeco-byzantina*, pp. 257-258.

[2] So Charles, *The Assumption*, p. l.

[3] Rohland, *Der Erzengel Michael*, p. 24: "Als 'Archistrategos' ... war Michael in vorchrist-licher Zeit noch nicht bekannt."

[4] Berger, "Der Streit um die Seele", pp. 13-14, 18, has not proven his claim that the ac-count in the *Palaea* is "im ganzen ursprünglicher" than the version reflected by Jude 9.

[5] Cf. Leqah Tov, quoted by Loewenstamm, "The Death of Moses", p. 204, and Origen on Deut. 34:6, see Migne (ed.),"Ex Origene selecta in Deuteronomium", *PG* 12, col. 808B: Μωϋσῆς, μὴ δοξάσας τὸν Θεὸν ἐπὶ τοῦ λαοῦ, ἐκωλύθη παρελθεῖν μετ' αὐτῶν, ἵνα μὴ ὃν ἐτίμων ζῶντα, ἐν θεῶν θεραπείαις τιμήσωσιν ἀπέλθοντα. Διὸ δὴ καὶ ἀποθανόντος ἀφανῆ τὸν τάφον ἐποίησεν. Practically the same words are found in Migne (ed.),"Origenis selecta in Numeros", *PG* 12, col. 577B. Cf. Palmer, "The Literary Back-ground", p. 434: "The polytheistic Graeco-Roman tradition was free to take the further step of making assumption the means of deification of a new divinity."

[6] Zeitlin, "The Assumption of Moses", pp. 42-43 (Hebrew text); cf. Wettstein, *Novum Testamentum*, II, p. 735; Strack and Billerbeck, *Kommentar*, III, pp. 786-787; Loewen-stamm, "The Death of Moses", pp. 205-206.

[7] Wettstein, *Novum Testamentum graecum*, II, p. 735.

[8] Ed. Holl, *GCS* 25, I, p. 202; cf. Wettstein, *Novum Testamentum graecum*, II, p. 735; Denis, *Fragmenta*, p. 66.

[9] Ed. Holl-Dummer, *GCS s.num.*, II, p. 514.

As appears from Gelasius' quotations from As. Mos., the dispute occasioned Michael to expound some *theologoumena* on the creative activity of God. How they relate to the dispute over Moses' body cannot be established.

c. The "Assumption" of Moses

Finally, some attention must be paid to the question of how Moses departed from earthly life, that is, how As. Mos. conceived his "assumption". From the title of our text, 'Ανάληψις Μωσέως or *Assumptio Mosis* (in the Latin translation of Origen it is called *Ascensio Moysi*, see above), it has been concluded that the ending of As. Mos. must have described the (bodily) ascension of Moses into heaven while he was still alive, comparable to that of Elijah (2 Ki. 2:11) or, in a way, to that of Jesus (Acts 1:9). There exist Christian traditions according to which Moses did not die[1]. Thus, Ambrose († 397) writes: "nemo scit sepulturam ejus usque in hodiernum diem; ut translationem magis, quam interitum intelligas ... quis enim in terrenis reliquias ejus potuit deprehendere, quem secum esse Dei filius in Evangelio demonstravit?"[2] (Ambrose refers here to the story of Jesus' Transfiguration on the Mount). The problem this conclusion poses, is the fact that it contradicts the information given in the extant text of As. Mos. Moses clearly speaks of his own death (1:15; 10:14). This apparent contradiction has led to the hypothesis of the merging of the *Assumption* and the *Testament* of Moses (see the Introduction, section II).

It is now clear, however, especially due to the excellent investigation by G. Lohfink[3], that the words ἀνάληψις and *assumptio*, meaning "being taken away", do not necessarily refer to the assumption into heaven of someone who is alive. Enoch and Elijah remain, in this respect, rare exceptions in pre-Christian Jewish literature. The normal usage of

---

[10] Cramer, *Catenae,*VIII, p. 161; Denis, *Fragmenta*, p. 67.

[1] Assumption accounts occur in both Jewish and pagan literature, see Palmer, "The Literary Background", pp. 432-434, and Tabor, "'Returning to the Divinity'", p. 225n. (bibliographical references), pp. 230-236.

[2] *De Cain et Abel* I, 2, 8, ed. Migne, *PL* 14, col. 337C, quoted by Sixtus Senensis, *Bibliotheca sancta* (1566), pp. 436-437. Sixtus mentions as those who agree with Ambrose Hilary of Poitiers (who adds as proof that Moses has not died his appearing as one of the witnesses in Rev. 11), and "temporibus nostris" Ambrose of Compsa and John Arboreus, see also *Bibliotheca sancta*, pp. 585-586

[3] *Die Himmelfahrt Jesu*, pp. 61-69. See also Van Stempvoort, "The Ascension", p. 32.

ἀνάληψις and *assumptio* refers to somebody's soul being taken away, which is tantamount to his death[1]. For this perfectly normal concept, see also Ps.-Phocylides 107-108:

> For we have a body out of earth, and when afterwards we are resolved, again into earth we are but dust; but the air has received our spirit.[2]

In VAE 43 Seth is ordered by Michael to tell his father that the time of his life is fulfilled, *et cum exierit anima ejus de corpore videbis mirabilia magna in celo &c.*[3] (cf. Apoc. Mos. 13:6 ἐξερχομένης δὲ τῆς ψυχῆς αὐτοῦ μέλλεις θεάσασθαι τὴν ἄνοδον αὐτῆς φοβεράν).

A large number of texts reflect the concept of death as the departure of the soul from the body. In these instances, the bereaved may lament the deceased one and bury his body, whereas his soul ascends into heaven. In a number of cases, the ascent is elaborately described, for instance in T. Abr. A 20:10-14[4] and T. Job 52:8-12. In other instances the ascent of the soul is treated as a natural thing, not needing any particular explanation, see 4 Ezra 14:9, 49 (Syr); 2 Bar. 46:7 (cf. 76:2); esp. Apoc. Mos. 32:4

> ἰδοὺ γὰρ ὁ Ἀδὰμ ὁ ἀνήρ σου ἐξῆλθεν ἀπὸ τοῦ σώματος αὐτοῦ. Ἀνάστα καὶ ἴδε τὸ πνεῦμα αὐτοῦ ἀναφερόμενον εἰς τὸν ποιήσαντα αὐτὸν τοῦ ἀ-παντῆσαι αὐτῷ.

> For, behold, your husband Adam has left his body. Rise and see his spirit being carried up to meet his Maker.

In LAB, the dichotomy of soul and body with regard to death is perfectly normal. See, apart from the passage on Enoch (LAB 1:16), the allusions to Moses' ascension in 32:9 (esp. in connection with the silence on this subject in the account of Moses' death in chapter 19), and to that of Deborah in 34:4. One may further compare the story of the apparition of Samuel to Saul in LAB 64:6-7. In this account, Samuel rebukes Saul, saying: *Propterea post redditionem anime mee conturbata sunt ossa mea, ut dicerem tibi mortuus quae audirem vivens.* Samuel's

---

[1] Cf. Lohfink, *Die Himmelfahrt Jesu*, p. 67: "Man sollte vielleicht den Titel 'Himmelfahrt des Moses', weil er falsche Assoziationen weckt, vermeiden und ihn lieber mit 'Tod des Moses' oder 'Aufnahme der Seele des Moses' wiedergeben."

[2] Translation in Van der Horst, *The Sentences*, p. 191; text and commentary *ibid*. The concept is well-known in paganism, cf. Tabor, "'Returning to the Divinity'", pp. 230-231.

[3] Cavallin, *Life after Death*, p. 73, sees here a reference to *post mortem* life, but perhaps this passage simply refers to the seven days of mourning in heaven after Adam's death: *cum hoc dixisset emisit spiritum. Et obscuratus est sol et luna et stelle per dies septem* (VAE 46:1).

[4] Cf. the short recension, B 14:6-7.

soul had been given back to God, but is sent back to stir up his bones, so that the dead one may speak.

In all these instances, the ascension of the soul to heaven is the same thing as dying[1]. One may contrast Phineas, who, according to LAB 48:1, did not die when his time had come, but did not go to heaven either. After he had reached the age of 120, he was ordered to live quietly on Mt. Danaben, being taken care of by an eagle of the Lord, until the time the Lord saw fit to send him back to the people[2]—*et postea elevaberis in locum ubi elevati sunt priores tui, et eris ibi quousque memorabor seculi. Et tunc adducam vos, et gustabitis quod est mortis.*

It may be concluded that whenever Moses was said to have died, the idea of his death was not incompatible with the idea of the assumption of his soul into heaven. Philo, too, speaks of Moses' death in terms of his soul departing from his body. In *De vita Mosis* II 288-291, Philo relates how Moses' body and soul were transformed into a "monad" shortly before he was to go to heaven, being called by the Father to leave the mortal life in order to become immortal (τὸν θνητὸν ἀπολιπὼν βίον ἀπαθανατίζεσθαι, § 288). He was then possessed by the spirit and uttered prophecies to each tribe separately. His greatest achievement, however, was to prophesy his own death and burial by the angels at the very moment he was being taken up (ἀναλαμβανόμενος, § 291; cf. *De virtutibus* 75-76; *De sacrificiis* 8-10).

Clement of Alexandria speaks of a "double Moses", preferring not to use the terms "body" and "soul" or "spirit". The concept, however, is quite the same, and the use of the word διττόν is inspired by the subject matter Clement is treating in this passage, namely the "double" meaning of Scripture.

> τὸν Μωυσέα ἀναλαμβανόμενον διττὸν εἶδεν Ἰησοῦς ὁ τοῦ Ναυῆ, καὶ τὸν μὲν μετ' ἀγγέλων, τὸν δὲ ἐπὶ τὰ ὄρη περὶ τὰς φάραγγας κηδείας ἀξιού-μενον[3].

Joshua, the son of Nun, saw a double Moses being taken away, one who (went) with the angels, and the other who was deigned worthy to be buried in the ravines.

---

[1] Cf. the story of the rich man and Lazarus, Luke 16:19-31, see esp. vs. 22: ἐγένετο δὲ ἀποθανεῖν τὸν πτωχὸν καὶ ἀπενεχθῆναι αὐτὸν ὑπὸ τῶν ἀγγέλων εἰς τὸν κόλπον Ἀβραάμ. This passage does not mention a separation of body and soul or spirit, but it illustrates that the concept could occur in a rather naive way.

[2] The point which LAB seems to make, is that Phineas is no other than Elijah. See Cavallin, *Life After Death*, p. 77; cf. Perrot, *Les Antiquités* II, pp. 209-210.

[3] *Stromateis* VI 132, 2, ed. Stählin-Früchtel, *GCS* 52 (15), p. 498; cf. Denis, *Fragmenta*, p. 65.

To Philo and Clement, one may compare Origen in his second sermon on the book of Joshua:

> *in libello quodam, in quo, licet in canone non habeatur, mysterii tamen hujus figura describitur, refertur quia duo Moyses videbantur: unus vivus in spiritu et alius mortuus in corpore[1].*

> in a certain small book (which, to be sure, is absent from the canon), an image of this mystery is described; it is said that two Moseses were visible: one alive in the spirit, and the other dead in the body.

A similar concept of a twofold Moses can be found in a letter by Bishop Evodius of Uzala (ca. 360-after 426) to Augustine. Evodius mentions an apocryphal book (it is unclear whether he regards *Apocrypha et secreta Moysis* as the book's title):

> *in apocryphis et secretis ipsius Moysi, quae scriptura caret auctoritate, tunc cum ascenderet in montem ut moreretur, vi corporis efficitur ut aliud esset, quod terrae mandaretur, aliud quod angelo comitanti sociaretur[2].*

> in the apocrypha and secrets of this Moses, a writing which lacks authority, (it is said, that) in the time when he went up the mountain to die, corporeal force caused that what had to be committed to the earth was something different from what had to go along with an angel as companion.

A different picture of the end of Moses' terrestrial life is given by Josephus. In *Ant. Jud.* IV 326, he uses words which do suggest that Moses was taken up to heaven without having died: he was saying goodbye to Joshua and Eleazar, when suddenly a cloud made him disappear—ἀφανίζειν, a word which in itself strongly suggests assumption[3]. But Josephus adds that Moses was taken into "some ravine" (κατά τινος φάραγγος), and that Moses himself had taken the precaution to lay down in the holy writs that he had died, lest one would say that he had been taken up to God (§ 330). This passage shows that Josephus was aware of a tradition according to which Moses had been bodily taken away from earth and transferred to heaven, a view which Josephus himself rejected[4] (cf. *Ant. Jud.* III 96).

---

[1] *In Jesu Nave* II,1, ed. Jaubert, *SC* 71, p. 118; cf. Rönsch, "Weitere Illustrationen", p. 217; Denis, *Fragmenta*, pp. 65-66. Like Clement, Origen treats Moses' death in connection with the law. He comments (*ibid.*) that the law, when read in its literal sense, is dead, but that the *lex spiritalis* is very much alive.

[2] Evodius, *In Augustinum Epistulae* 158, 6, ed. Goldbacher, *CSEL* 44, p. 492. Cf. Denis, *Fragmenta*, p. 65, and Rönsch, "Weitere Illustrationen", pp. 217-218.

[3] Lohfink, *Die Himmelfahrt Jesu*, p. 38; Palmer, "The Literary Background", p. 432

[4] For an extensive treatment of this and similar passages in Josephus, see Lohfink, *Die Himmelfahrt Jesu*, pp. 61-64; and Tabor, "'Returning to the Divinity'", pp. 226-230. Loe-

(cont.)

In view of the material surveyed above it is reasonable to conclude that As. Mos. considered Moses to have been taken up to heaven. But since the author of As. Mos. makes Moses allude to his own death (1:15; 10:14), an assumption must not in this case be conceived as a bodily assumption (which would imply that Moses did not die at all). If indeed Moses was thought to have been taken up, it is likely that the author of As. Mos. had only the assumption of a spiritual component of Moses' person (something like an ethereal, glorified, spiritual body, or perhaps his spirit or soul) in mind. An assumption of such a spiritual part of someone's person into heaven does not exclude death.

All in all, then, As. Mos. is likely to have narrated the end of Moses' terrestrial life as a death followed by the burial of his body by Michael and the ascent of a spiritual part of his person to heaven, possibly accompanied or transferred there by the archangel.

---

wenstamm, "The Death of Moses", pp. 197-198, draws attention to a similar description, including both his disappearance and his being buried, in Memar Marqah V 3.

BIBLIOGRAPHY AND INDICES

Editions and Abbreviations

a. *Biblical Books (Including Apocrypha)*

The Hebrew Bible is quoted according to Elliger and Rudolph (eds.), *Biblia Hebraica Stuttgartensia* (1967-1977).

The Septuagint is quoted according to Rahlfs (ed.), *Septuaginta* (1935).

The Vulgate is quoted according to Weber and Fischer (eds.), *Biblia sacra* (1969).

The Greek New Testament is quoted according to Aland *et alii* (eds.), *Novum Testamentum graece* ([26]1979).

In cases in which the chapter and/or verse number(s) of a Septuagint passage differ(s) from that/those of the corresponding Hebrew passage, the reference to the Hebrew text is followed by a bracketed reference to the Greek text.

In cases in which the chapter and/or verse number(s) of a passage of the Latin Vulgate differ(s) from those of the corresponding passage in the Septuagint, and a corresponding Hebrew text is not extant, the reference to the Greek text is followed by a bracketed reference to the Vulgate.

The following abbreviations are used.

Bar.	Baruch	Hos.	Hosea
1, 2 Chron.	1, 2 Chronicles	Isa.	Isaiah
Col.	Colossians	Jer.	Jeremiah
1, 2 Cor.	1, 2 Corinthians	Josh.	Joshua
Dan.	Daniel	Judg.	Judges
Deut.	Deuteronomy	1, 2 Ki.	1, 2 Kings
Eccl.	Ecclesiastes	Lam.	Lamentations
Eph.	Ephesians	Lev.	Leviticus
Esth.	Esther	1, 2, 3, 4 Macc.	1, 2, 3, 4
Exod.	Exodus		Maccabees
Ezek.	Ezekiel	Mal.	Malachi
Gal.	Galatians	Matt.	Matthew
Gen.	Genesis	Mic.	Micah
Hab.	Habakkuk	Nah.	Nahum
Hagg.	Haggai	Neh.	Nehemiah
Heb.	Hebrews	Num.	Numbers

Obad.	Obadiah	1, 2 Sam.	1, 2 Samuel
1, 2 Pet.	1, 2 Peter	Sir.	Jesus Sira
Phil.	Philippians	1, 2 Thess.	1, 2 Thessalonians
Pr. Azar.	Prayer of Azariah	1, 2 Tim.	1, 2 Timothy
Pr. Man.	Prayer of Manasseh	Tit.	Titus
Prov.	Proverbs	Tob.	Tobit
Ps.	Psalms	Wisd.	Wisdom of
Ps. Sol.	Psalms of Solomon		Solomon
Rev.	Revelation	Zech.	Zechariah
Rom.	Romans	Zeph.	Zephaniah

b. *Anonymous and Pseudepigraphic Jewish and Christian Works Closely Related to the Olde Testament*

Apoc. Mos.	Apocalypse of Moses (= VAE in Greek), ed. Nagel, "Vie grecque"
2 Bar.	2 Baruch, ed. Dedering, "Apocalypse of Baruch"
1 En.	1 Enoch, ed. Knibb, *The Ethiopic Book of Enoch* I; ed. Black, *Apocalypsis Henochi graece*
Jos. As.	Joseph and Aseneth, ed. Philonenko, *Joseph et Aseneth*
Jub.	Jubilees, ed. VanderKam, *The Book of Jubilees* I
LAB	Ps.-Philo, *Liber Antiquitatum Biblicarum*, ed. Harrington, *Les Antiquités bibliques* I
Par. Jer.	*Paraleipomena Jeremiou*, eds. Kraft and Purintun, *Paraleipomena Jeremiou*
Sib. Or.	Sibylline Oracles, ed. Geffcken, *Die Oracula Sibyllina*
T. Abr.	Testament of Abraham, ed. Schmidt, *Le Testament grec d'Abraham*
T. Job	Testament of Job, ed. Brock, *Testamentum Jobi*
T.(12 Patr.)	Testaments of the Twelve Patriarchs, eds. De Jonge *et alii*, *The Testaments of the Twelve Patriarchs*
—T. Ben.	Testament of Benjamin
—T. Iss.	of Issachar
—T. Jos.	of Joseph
—T. Napht.	of Naphtali
—T. Reub.	of Reuben
—T. Sim.	of Simeon
—T. Zeb.	of Zebulun
VAE	*Vita Adae et Evae*, ed. Meyer, "Vita Adae et Evae"

c. *Qumran Writings*

1QS	Community Rule, ed. Lohse, *Die Texte aus Qumran*
1QSa	The Rule of the Congregation, ed. Lohse, *Die Texte aus Qumran*
1QSb	The Blessings, ed. Lohse, *Die Texte aus Qumran*
1QH	Thanksgiving Hymns, ed. Lohse, *Die Texte aus Qumran*
1QM	War Scroll, ed. Lohse, *Die Texte aus Qumran*
1QpHab	Habakkuk Commentary, ed. Lohse, *Die Texte aus Qumran*
4Q390	Pseudo-Prophecy of Moses, ed. Dimant (not yet published)
4QpNah	Nahum Commentary, ed. Lohse, *Die Texte aus Qumran*
4QAmram	Visions of Amram, ed. Milik, "4Q Visions de 'Amram"
4QTest	Testimonia, ed. Lohse, *Die Texte aus Qumran*

| 11QT | Temple Scroll, ed. Yadin, *The Temple Scroll* |
| CD | Damascus Scroll, ed. Lohse, *Die Texte aus Qumran* |

d. *Other Ancient Writings, Jewish and Christian*

Josephus, *Ant. Jud.*   Flavius Josephus, *Antiquitates Judaicae*, ed. Thackeray, Marcus, Wik-
                        gren and Feldman, *Josephus*
Josephus, *Bell. Jud.* Flavius Josephus, *De Bello Judaico*, ed. Thackeray, Marcus, Wikgren
                        and Feldman, *Josephus*
Philo   ed. Cohn and Wendland, *Philonis Alexandrini opera omnia.*
   —De fuga   *De fuga et inventione*
   —De praemiis   *De praemiis et poenis*
   —De sacrificiis   *De sacrificiis Abelis et Caini*
   —Quis rerum divinarum *Quis rerum divinarum heres sit*
   —Quod deterius   *Quod deterius potiori insidiari soleat*
   —Quod Deus immutabilis *Quod Deus immutabilis sit*

Aristeas	Epistle of Aristeas, ed. Pelletier, *Lettre d'Aristée*
Barn.	Epistle of Barnabas, ed. Funk and Bihlmeyer, *Die apostolischen Väter* I
1 Clem.	First Epistle of Clement, ed. Funk and Bihlmeyer, *Die apostolischen Väter* I
Did.	Didache, ed. Funk and Bihlmeyer, *Die apostolischen Väter* I
ad Diogn.	Epistle to Diognetus, ed. Funk and Bihlmeyer, *Die apostolischen Väter* I
Hermas, *Vis.,*	
Mand., Sim.	Hermas, *Visiones, Mandata, Similitudines*, ed. Whittaker, *Die apostolischen Väter* I
Ign.	Epistles of Ignatius, ed. Funk and Bihlmeyer, *Die apostolischen Väter* I
—Magn.	to the Magnesians
—Pol.	to Polycarp
Mart. Polyc.	Martyrdom of Polycarp, ed. Funk and Bihlmeyer, *Die apostolischen Väter* I

e. *Bibliographical Abbreviations*

AAT	Apócrifos del Antiguo Testamento
AGJU	Arbeiten zur Geschichte des antiken Judentums und des Urchristentums
ALGHJ	Arbeiten zur Literatur und Geschichte des Hellenistischen Judentums
APAT I-II	Kautzsch, *Apokryphen und Pseudepigraphen des Alten Testaments* I-II
APOT I-II	Charles, *Apocrypha and Pseudepigrapha of the Old Testament* I-II
Blaß-Debrunner	Blaß, Debrunner and Rehkopf, *Grammatik*
BWANT	Beiträge zur Wissenschaft vom Alten und Neuen Testament
BZNW	Beihefte zur *ZNW*
CB NTS	Coniectanea biblica. New Testament Series
CBQ	*Catholic Biblical Quarterly*
CS	Pearson *et alii, Critici sacri*

CSEL   Corpus scriptorum ecclesiasticorum latinorum
Ernout-Thomas   Ernout and Thomas, *Syntaxe latine*
Forcellini   Forcellini *et alii*, *Lexicon totius latinitatis*
FRLANT   Forschungen zur Religion und Literatur des Alten und Neuen Testaments
GCS   Die Griechischen christlichen Schriftsteller der ersten drei Jahrhunderte
GGA   *Göttingische gelehrte Anzeigen*
HAW   Handbuch der Altertumswissenschaft
Hen   *Henoch*
Hofmann-Szantyr II   Hofmann and Szantyr, *Lateinische Grammatik* II. *Lateinische Syntax und Stilistik*
HTR   *Harvard Theological Review*
IEJ   *Israel Exploration Journal*
JBL   *Journal of Biblical Literature*
JJS   *Journal of Jewish Studies*
JQR   *Jewish Quarterly Review*
JSJ   *Journal for the Study of Judaism in the Persian, Hellenistic and Roman Period*
JSP   *Journal for the Study of the Pseudepigrapha*
JThS   *Journal of Theological Studies*
Leumann I   Leumann, *Lateinische Grammatik* I. *Lateinische Laut- und Formenlehre*
Lewis and Short   Lewis and Short, *A Latin Dictionary*
Liddell and Scott   Liddell, Scott *et alii*, *A Greek-English Lexicon*
MS   Monograph Series
NT   *Novum Testamentum*
NTS   *New Testament Studies*
OTP I-II   Charlesworth, *Old Testament Pseudepigrapha* I-II
PG   Patrologiae cursus completus. Series graeca
PL   Patrologiae cursus completus. Series latina
PVTG   Pseudepigrapha Veteris Testamenti graece
RB   *Revue Biblique*
RCAW   Real-Encyclopädie der classischen Alterthumswissenschaft
SBL   Society of Biblical Literature
SBS   Stuttgarter Bibelstudien
SC   Sources chrétiennes
SCS   Septuagint and Cognate Studies
SNTS   Society for New Testament Studies
SPB   Studia Post-Biblica
STDJ   Studies on the Texts of the Desert of Judah
Supp   Supplement

SVTP	Studia in Veteris Testamenti Pseudepigrapha
ThGL	*Thesaurus graecae linguae*
ThLL	*Thesaurus linguae latinae*
ThLZ	*Theologische Literatur-Zeitung*
ThZ	*Theologische Zeitschrift*
TU	Texte und Untersuchungen zur Geschichte der altchristlichen Literatur
TWNT	*Theologisches Wörterbuch zum Neuen Testament*
Väänänen	Väänänen, *Introduction au latin vulgaire*
VT	*Vetus Testamentum*
WMANT	Wissenschaftliche Monographien zum Alten und Neuen Testament
WUNT	Wissenschaftliche Untersuchungen zum Neuen Testament
ZAW	*Zeitschrift für die Alttestamentliche Wissenschaft*
ZDMG	*Zeitschrift der Deutschen Morgenländischen Gesellschaft*
ZNW	*Zeitschrift für die Neutestamentliche Wissenschaft*
ZThK	*Zeitschrift für Theologie und Kirche*
ZWT	*Zeitschrift für wissenschaftliche Theologie*

BIBLIOGRAPHY

Abel, F.-M., *Les Livres des Maccabées*, Paris 1949

Adams, J.N., *The Vulgar Latin of the Letters of Claudius Terentianus (P. Mich. VIII, 467-72)*, Manchester 1977

Aland, K.; Black, M.; Martini, C.M.; Metzger, B.M.; Wikgren, A. (eds.), *Novum Testamentum graece*, Stuttgart [26]1979

Altaner, B.; Stuiber, A., *Patrologie. Leben, Schriften und Lehre der Kirchenväter*, Freiburg &c. [8]1978

Arata Mantovani, P., "Circoncisi ed incirconcisi", *Hen* 10 (1988), pp. 51-67

Attridge, H.W. "The Ascension of Moses and the Heavenly Jerusalem", in: Nickelsburg (ed.), *Studies on the Testament of Moses*, pp. 122-125

Bacher, W., (ed.), *Die exegetische Terminologie der jüdischen Traditionsliteratur* I-II, Leipzig 1899-1905

Baehrens, W., (ed.), *Origenes Werke* VII, 2 (GCS 30), Leipzig 1921

Baldensperger, W., *Die messianisch-apokalyptischen Hoffnungen des Judentums*, Strassburg [3]1903

Balforeus, R., (ed.), *Γελασίου τοῦ Κυζικηνοῦ Σύνταγμα τῶν κατὰ τὴν ἐν Νικαίᾳ ἁγίαν σύνοδον πραχθέντων. Gelasii Cyziceni commentarius Actorum Nicaeni Concilii cum corollario Theodori Presbyteri, de Incarnatione Domini, nunc primum Graece prodeunt, ex optimis Bibliothecis*, Paris 1599, Heidelberg [2]1604

Bauckham, R.J., *Jude. 2 Peter* (Word Biblical Commentary 50), Waco (Texas) 1983

—— *Jude and the Relatives of Jesus in the Early Church*, Edinburgh 1990

Bauer, W.; Aland, K.; Aland, B., *Griechisch-deutsches Wörterbuch zu den Schriften des Neuen Testaments und der frühchristlichen Literatur*, Berlin/New York [6]1988

Beek, M.A., *Inleiding in de joodse apocalyptiek van Oud- en Nieuw-Testamentisch tijdvak* (Theologia 6), Haarlem 1950

Berger, K., *Die griechische Daniel-Diegese. Eine altkirchliche Apokalypse* (SPB 27), Leiden 1976

—— "Die Streit des guten und des bösen Engels um die Seele. Beobachtungen zu 4Q Amr[b] und Judas 9", *JSJ* 4 (1973), pp. 1-18

—— "Hellenistische Gattungen im Neuen Testament", in: W. Haase, *Aufstieg und Niedergang des Römischen Weltreiches* II 25.2, Berlin/New York 1984, pp. 1031-1432

Bergren, Th.A., *Fifth Ezra. The Text, Origin and Early History* (SCS 25), Atlanta 1990

Bernard, E., (ed.)., *Flavii Josephi Antiquitatum Judaicarum libri quatuor priores, et pars magna quinti*, Oxford 1700

Bertram, G., "στερεός κτλ.", *TWNT* VII (1964), pp. 609-614

—— "ὑπερήφανος, ὑπερηφανία", *TWNT* VIII (1969), pp. 526-530

—— "ὕβρις κτλ.", *TWNT* VIII (1969), pp. 295-307

Beyer, K., "Woran erkennt man, daß ein griechischer Text aus dem Hebräischen oder Aramäischen übersetzt ist?", in: M. Macuch (ed.), *Studia semitici necnon iranica Rudolpho Macuch septuagenario ab amicis et discipulis dedicata*, pp. 21-31.

Black, M., *The Book of Enoch or I Enoch. A New English Edition with Commentary and Textual Notes* (SVTP 7), Leiden 1985

—— (ed.), *Apocalypsis Henochi graece* (PVTG 3), Leiden 1970

Blaise, A.; Chirat, H., *Dictionnaire Latin-Français des auteurs chrétiens*, Paris 1954

Blaise, A., *Manuel du latin chrétien*, Strasbourg 1955

Blaß, F.; Debrunner, A.; Rehkopf, F., *Grammatik des neutestamentlichen Griechisch*, Göttingen [14]1975

Boecker, H.J., *Redeformen des Rechtslebens im Alten Testament* (WMANT 14), Neukirchen-Vluyn 1964

Bonsirven, J., *Exégèse rabbinique et exégèse paulinienne*, Paris 1939

Bousset, W., *Die Religion des Judentums im neutestamentlichen Zeitalter*, Berlin 1903, ²1906

Boyarin, D., "Penitential Liturgy in 4 Ezra", *JSJ* 3 (1972), pp. 30-34

Boyce, B., *The Language of the Freedmen in Petronius' Cena Trimalchionis* (Mnemosyne Supplements 117), Leiden 1991

Brandenburger, E., "Himmelfahrt Moses", *Jüdische Schriften aus hellenistisch-römischer Zeit* V/2, Gütersloh 1976, pp. 57-84

Brock, S.P., (ed.), *Testamentum Jobi* (PVTG 2), Leiden 1967

Büchsel, F., "μονογενής", *TWNT* IV (1942), pp. 745-750

Büchsel, F.; Herntrich, V., "κρίνω κτλ.", *TWNT* III (1938), pp. 920-955

Buchwald, W.; Hohlweg, A.; Prinz, O., *Tusculum-Lexikon griechischer und lateinischer Autoren des Altertums und des Mittelalters*, München &c. ³1982

Bultmann, R., "καυχάομαι κτλ.", *TWNT* III (1938), pp. 646-654

Burchard, C., "Ein vorläufiger griechischer Text von Joseph und Aseneth", *Dielheimer Blätter zum Alten Testament* 14 (1979), pp. 2-53

—— "Verbesserungen zum vorläufigen Text von Joseph und Aseneth", *Dielheimer Blätter zum Alten Testament* 16 (1982), pp. 37-39

Burkitt, F.C., "Moses, Assumption of", in: J. Hastings (ed.), *A Dictionary of the Bible, Dealing with its Language, Literature, and Contents, Including the Biblical Theology* III, Edinburgh 1900, pp. 448-450

Calmet, A., "Dissertation sur la mort, et la sépulture de Moyse", in: idem, *Commentaire littéral sur tous les Livres de l'Ancien et du Nouveau Testament* VIII, Paris 1726, pp. 753-755; repr. of the Latin translation in Migne (ed.), *Scripturae sacrae cursus completus* 7

Camponovo, O., *Königtum, Königsherrschaft und Reich Gottes in den frühjüdischen Schriften* (Orbis biblicus et orientalis 58), Freiburg/Göttingen 1984

Cappelli, A., *Dizionario di abbreviature latine ed italiane usate nelle carte e codici specialmente del Medio-Evo*, Milano ⁶1929

Carlson, D.C., "Vengeance and Angelic Mediation in Testament of Moses 9 and 10", *JBL* 101 (1982), pp. 85-98

Carrière, A., "Note sur le *Taxo* de l'*Assomption de Moïse*", *Revue de Théologie* 6 (1868), pp. 94-96

Cavallin, H.C.C., *Life After Death. Paul's Argument for the Resurrection of the Dead in 1 Cor 15. Part I. An Enquiry into the Jewish Background* (CB NTS 7:1), Lund 1974

Ceriani, A.M., *Monumenta sacra et profana ex codicibus praesertim Bibliothecae Ambrosianae* I and V, Milano 1861, 1868

Charles, R.H., *The Assumption of Moses. Translated from the Latin Sixth Century MS., the Unemended Text of Which is Published Herewith, Together with the Text in its Restored and Critically Emended Form*, London 1897

—— (ed.), *The Apocrypha and Pseudepigrapha of the Old Testament in English. With Introductions and Explanatory Notes to the Several Books* I-II, Oxford 1913

—— "The Assumption of Moses", in: idem, *APOT* II, pp. 407-424

Charlesworth, J.H., (ed.), *The Old Testament Pseudepigrapha* I-II, London 1983-1985

—— *The Old Testament Pseudepigrapha and the New Testament. Prolegomena for the Study of Christian Origins* (SNT MS 54), Cambridge etc. 1985

Clark, K.W., "Worship in the Jerusalem Temple after A.D. 70", *NTS* 6 (1969/1960), pp. 269-280

Clemen, C., "Die Himmelfahrt Moses", in: Kautzsch (ed.), *APAT* II, pp. 311-331

——*Die Himmelfahrt des Mose* (Kleine Texte für theologische Vorlesungen und Übungen 10), Bonn 1904

—— "Die Entstehungszeit der Himmelfahrt des Mose", in: *Hundert Jahre A. Marcus und E. Webers Verlag 1818-1918*, Bonn 1919

Clericus, J., (ed.), *Desiderii Erasmi Roterodami opera omnia* VI, Leiden 1705

Cocus, R., *Censura quorundam scriptorum, quae sub nominibus sanctorum & veterum auctorum citari solent &c.*, Helmstedt, [2]1655

Cohn, L.; Wendland, P.; Reiter, S., (eds.), *Philonis Alexandrini opera quae supersunt* I-VI, Berlin 1896-1915

Colani, T., "L'Assomption de Moïse", *Revue de Théologie* 6 (1868), pp. 65-94

Collins, A.Y., "Composition and Redaction of the Testament of Moses 10", *HTR* 69 (1976), pp. 179-186

Collins, J.J., "The Date and Provenance of the Testament of Moses", in: Nickelsburg (ed.), *Studies on the Testament of Moses*, pp. 15-32

—— "Some Remaining Traditio-Historical Problems in the Testament of Moses", in: Nickelsburg (ed.), *Studies on the Testament of Moses*, pp. 38-43

—— *Apocalypse. The Morphology of a Genre* (Semeia 14), s.l. 1979

—— "The Testament (Assumption) of Moses", in: M. de Jonge (ed.), *Outside the Old Testament* (Cambridge Commentaries on Writings of the Jewish and Christian World 200 BC to AD 200, 4), Cambridge 1985, pp. 145-158

Collura, P. *Studi paleografici. La precarolina e la carolina a Bobbio* (Fontes Ambrosiani 22), Milano 1943

Cortès, E., *Los discursos de adiós des Gn 49 a Jn 13-17. Pistas para la historia de un género literario en la antigua judía*, Barcelone, 1976

Cramer, J.A., (ed.), *Catenae Graecorum Patrum in Novum Testamentum. VIII. In Epistolas catholicas et apocalypsin*, Oxford 1844

Crouzel, H.; Simonetti, M., (eds.), *Origène. Traité des Principes* III (SC 268), Paris 1980

Dalman, G., *Arbeit und Sitte in Palästina* V. *Webstoff, Spinnen, Weben, Kleidung* (Schriften des deutschen Palästina-Instituts 8), Gütersloh 1937

Daube, D., *The Sudden in the Scriptures*, Leiden 1964

Davies, W.D., "A Note on Josephus, Antiquities 15:136", *HTR* 47 (1954), pp. 135-140

Dedering, S., (ed.), "Apocalypse of Baruch" (*The Old Testament in Syriac According to the Peshitta Version* IV, 3), Leiden 1973, pp. i-50

Deissmann, A., *Licht vom Osten. Das Neue Testament und die neuentdeckte Texte der hellenistisch-römischen Welt*, Tübingen [4]1923

Delcor, M., "Contribution à l'étude de la législation des sectaires de Damas et de Qumrân (suite)", *RB* 62 (1955), pp. 60-75

—— *Le Testament d'Abraham. Introduction, traduction du texte grec et commentaire de la recension grecque longue, suivi de la traduction des Testaments d'Abraham, d'Isaac et de Jacob d'après les versions orientales* (SVTP 2), Leiden 1973

Denis, A.-M.; Janssens, Y., *Concordance latine du Liber Jubilaeorum sive Parva Genesis* (Informatique et étude de textes 4), Louvain 1973

—— *Concordance grecque des Pseudépigraphes d'Ancien Testament*, Louvain-la-Neuve 1987

Denis, A.-M., *Fragmenta pseudepigraphorum quae supersunt graeca una cum historicorum et auctorum Judaeorum hellenistarum fragmentis* (PVTG 3), Leiden 1970

—— *Introduction aux pseudépigraphes grecs d'Ancien Testament* (SVTP 1), Leiden 1970

Díez Macho, A., *Introducción general a los Apócrifos del Antiguo Testamento* (AAT I), Madrid 1984

Díez Macho, A.; Navarro, M.A.; Fuenta, A. de la; Piñero, A., *Apócrifos del Antiguo Testamento* I-V. Madrid 1984-1987

Dobschütz, E. von, *Das Decretum Gelasianum de libris recipiendis et non recipiendis* (TU 38, 4), Leipzig 1912

Doran, R., "*T. Mos.* 4:8 and the Second Temple", *JBL* 106 (1987), pp. 491-492

Drummond, J., *The Jewish Messiah. A Critical History of the Messianic Idea Among the Jews from the Rise of the Maccabees to the Closing of the Talmud*, London 1877

Drusius, J., *Annotationes in totum Jesu Christi Testamentum*, in: Pearson *et alii* (eds.), *CS* [3]1698

Dupont-Sommer, A., *Aperçus préliminaires sur les manuscrits de la Mer Morte* (l'Orient ancien illustré 4), Paris 1950

Dutripon, F.P., *Vulgatae editionis bibliorum sacrorum concordantiae*, Paris 1838

Eitrem, "Hermes", *RCAW* VIII (1913), cols. 738-792

Elliger, K., *Studien zum Habakuk-Kommentar vom Toten Meer* (Beiträge zur historischen Theologie 15), Tübingen 1953

Elliger, K.; Rudolph, W., (eds.), וכתובים נביאים תורה. *Biblia Hebraica Stuttgartensia*, Stuttgart 1967-1977

Erasmus, D., *In Novum Testamentum annotationes*, in: idem (ed.), *Novum Testamentum*, Basel 1516

Ernout, A., and Thomas, F., *Syntaxe latine*, Paris [2]1953

Ewald, H., *Geschichte des Volkes Israel* I-V, [3]1867

E[wald], H., Review of Ceriani, *Monumenta sacra et profana I,1*, *GGA* 1862, pp. 1-9

—— Review of Langen, *Das Judenthum in Palästina*, and Hilgenfeld, *Novum testamentum*, *GGA* 1867, pp. 100-118

Fabricius, J.A., *Codex pseudepigraphus Veteris Testamenti collectus, castigatus, testimoniisque, censuris et animadversionibus illustratus* I-II, Hamburg [2]1722-1723

Faye, E. de, *Les apocalypses juives. Essai de critique littéraire et théologique*, Paris 1892

Ferrar, W.J., *The Assumption of Moses* (Translations of Early Documents I), London/New York [2]1918

Fischer, B., *Novae concordantiae bibliorum sacrorum iuxta Vulgatam versionem critice editam* I-V, Stuttgart/Bad Cannstadt 1977

—— "Limitations of Latin in Representing Greek", in: B.M. Metzger, *The Early Versions of the New Testament. Their Origin, Transmission, and Limitations*, Oxford 1977

Fitzmyer, J.A., "The Use of Explicit Old Testament Quotations in Qumran Literature and in the New Testament", *NTS* 7 (1960/1961), pp. 297-333

——*The Gospel According to Luke (I-IX). Introduction, Translation and Notes* (Anchor Bible 28), Garden City (N.Y.) 1981

Foerster W.; Rad, G. von, "διαβάλλω κτλ.", *TWNT* II (1935), pp. 69-80

Foerster, W., "ἄσωτος, ἀσωτία", *TWNT* I (1933), pp. 504-505

—— "Der Ursprung des Pharisäismus", *ZNW* 34 (1935), pp. 35-51

—— "σέβομαι κτλ.", *TWNT* VII (1964), pp. 168-195

Forcellini, E.; Furlanetto, G.; Corradini, F.; Perin, G., *Lexicon totius Latinitatis* I-VI, Padua [4]1864-1926

Freyburger, G., *Fides. Etude sémantique et religieuse depuis les origines jusqu'à l'époque augustéenne*, Paris 1986

Friedländer, L., *Petronii Cena Trimalchionis mit deutscher Übersetzung und erklärenden Anmerkungen*, Leipzig [2]1906

Fritzsche, O.F., (ed.), *Libri apocryphi Veteris Testamenti Graece. Accedunt libri Veteris Testamenti pseudepigraphi selecti*, Leipzig 1871

Funk, F.X.; Bihlmeyer, L., (eds.), *Die apostolischen Väter* I: *Didache, Barnabas, Klemens I und II, Ignatius, Polykarp, Papias, Quadratus, Diognetbrief* (Sammlung ausgewählter Kirchen- und Dogmengeschichtlicher Quellenschriften II, 1, 1), Tübingen [2]1956, [3]1970

Furrer, K., "Das Wort Taxo in der Himmelfahrt Moses", *Jahrbücher für protestantische Theologie* 1 (1875), p. 368

Gaulmyn, G., *De vita et morte Mosis libri tres*, Paris 1628-1629

Geffcken, J., (ed.), *Die Oracula Sibyllina* (GCS 8), Berlin 1902

Geiger, A., "Apokryphische Apokalypsen und Essäer", *Jüdische Zeitschrift für Wissenschaft und Leben* 6 (1868), pp. 41-47

Giraudo, C., *La struttura letteraria della preghiera eucaristica. Saggio sulla genesi letteraria di una forma. Tôdâ veterotestamentaria, bᵉraka giudaica, anafora cristiana* (Analecta Biblica 92), Rome 1981

Goetz, G., *Corpus Glossariorum latinorum* I-VII, Leipzig/Berlin 1888-1923

Goldbacher, A., (ed.), *S. Aureli Augustini Hipponiensis episcopi Epistulae* III (CSEL 44), Vienna/Leipzig 1904

Goldstein, J.A., "The Testament of Moses: Its Content, its Origin, and its Attestation in Josephus", in: Nickelsburg (ed.), *Studies on the Testament of Moses*, pp. 44-52

Goodenough, E.W., *By Light, Light. The Mystic Gospel of Hellenistic Judaism*, New Haven 1935

Grandgent, C.H.; Moll, F. de B., *Introducción al latín vulgar*, Madrid 1928

Grausem, J.-P., "Pisanus, Alphonse", *Dictionnaire de Théologie Catholique* XII, Paris 1933, cols. 2127-2128

Grimm, C.L.W., *Das Buch der Weisheit* (Kurzgefasstes exegetisches Handbuch zu den Apokryphen des Alten Testaments VI), Leipzig 1860

Grotius, H., *Annotationes in Novum Testamentum* (1641-1650), in: Pearson *et alii* (eds.), *CS³*, VI

Grundmann, W., "ἀγαθός κτλ.", *TWNT* I (1933), pp. 10-18

Haacker, K., "Assumptio Mosis — eine samaritanische Schrift?", *ThZ* 25 (1969), pp. 385-405

Haacker, K.; Schäfer, P., "Nachbiblische Traditionen vom Tod des Mose", in: O. Betz; K. Haacker; M. Hengel, (eds.), *Josephus-Studien. Untersuchungen zu Josephus, dem antiken Judentum und dem Neuen Testament, Otto Michel zum 70. Geburtstag gewidmet*, Göttingen 1974, pp. 147-174

Haase, F., (ed.), *L. Annaei Senecae opera quae supersunt* III, Leipzig 1878, pp. 474-479

Hafemann, S.J., "Moses in the Apocrypha and Pseudepigrapha: A Survey", *JSP* 7 (1990), pp. 79-104

Hahn, F., *Christologische Hoheitstitel. Ihre Geschichte im frühen Christentum* (FRLANT 83), Göttingen 1963, ³1966

Hall, R.G., "Epispasm and the Dating of Ancient Jewish Writings", *JSP* 2 (1988), pp. 71-86

Harrington, D.J.; Cazeaux, J.; Perrot, C.; Bogaert, P.-M., *Pseudo-Philon. Les Antiquités bibliques*. I. *Introduction et texte critiques*. II. *Introduction littéraire, commentaire et index* (SC 229-230), Paris 1976

Harrington, D.J., "Interpreting Israel's History: The Testament of Moses as a Rewriting of Deut 31-34, in: Nickelsburg (ed.), *Studies on the Testament of Moses*, pp. 59-68

—— "Summary: Günther Reese, 'Die Geschichtsdarstellung der sog. Assumptio Mosis (AssMos 2-10)'", in: Nickelsburg (ed.), *Studies on the Testament of Moses*, pp. 69-70

Hartman, L., *Prophecy Interpreted. The Formation of Some Jewish Apocalyptic Texts and of the Eschatological Discourse Mark 13 Par.*, Uppsala 1966

—— "The Function of Some So-Called Apocalyptic Timetables", *NTS* 22 (1976), pp. 1-14

Harvey, J., *Le plaidoyer prophétique contre Israël après la rupture de l'alliance. Etude d'une formule littéraire de l'Ancien Testament*, Bruges/Paris/Montreal 1967

Hatch, E.; Redpath, H.A., *A Concordance to the Septuagint and the Other Greek Versions of the Old Testament (Including the Apocryphal Books)* I-II, Supplement, Oxford 1897-1906

Hauck, F.; Schulz, "πόρνη κτλ.", *TWNT* VI (1959), pp. 579-595

Haupt, "Bemerkungen zu der editio princeps der Himmelfahrt des Moses", *ZWT* 10 (1867), p. 448

Hausrath, A., *Neutestamentliche Zeitgeschichte* IV, Heidelberg ²1877

Haussleiter, J., "Die lateinische Apokalypse der alten afrikanischen Kirche", in: Haussleiter, J., and Zahn, Th., *Forschungen zur Geschichte des neutestamentlichen Kanons und der altkirchlichen Literatur* IV, Erlangen/Leipzig 1891, pp. 1-224

Heater, H., *A Septuagint Translation Technique in the Book of Job* (CBQ MS 11), Washington 1982

Heidenheim, M., "Beiträge zum bessern Verständniss der 'Ascensio Moysis'", *Vierteljahrschrift für deutsch- und englisch-theologische Forschung und Kritik* 4 (1871), pp. 63-102

Hengel, M., *Die Zeloten. Untersuchungen zur jüdischen Freiheitsbewegung in der Zeit von Herodes I. bis 70 n. Chr.* (AGJU 1), Leiden 1976

—— *Juden, Griechen und Barbaren. Aspekte der Hellenisierung des Judentums in vorchristlicher Zeit* (SBS 76), Stuttgart 1976

—— *The "Hellenization" of Judaea in the First Century after Christ*, London/Philadelphia 1989 (trans. from the German by J. Bowden)

Henten, J.W. van, (ed.), *Die Entstehung der jüdischen Martyrologie* (SPB 38), Leiden 1989

Henten, J.W. van, "Traditie en interpretatie in TestMos 9:1-10:10", *Summa. Blad van de Theologische Faculteit van de Universiteit van Amsterdam* 19 (1987), pp. 18-29

Herrmann, J.; Foerster, W.,"κλῆρος κτλ.", *TWNT* III (1938), pp. 757-786

Hilgenfeld, A., "Mosis Assumptionis quae supersunt primum edita et illustrata", in: id., *Novum Testamentum extra canonem receptum. Clementis Romani Epistulae*, Leipzig 1866, pp. 93-115; [2]1884, pp. 107-135

—— "Die Psalmen Salomo's und die Himmelfahrt des Moses, griechisch hergestellt und erklärt. B. Die Himmelfahrt des Moses", *ZWT* 11 (1868), pp. 273-309

—— *Messias Judaeorum, libris eorum paulo ante et paulo post Christum natum conscriptis illustratus*, Leipzig 1869, pp. 435-468

—— "Moses, Ezra und Tobit unter den Apokryphen und Pseudepigraphen des Alten Testaments", *ZWT* 29 (1886), pp. 129-152

—— "Die Himmelfahrt des Moses und der Ezra-Prophet", *ZWT* 41 (1898), pp. 616-619

Hilhorst, A., *Sémitismes et latinismes dans le Pasteur d'Hermas*, Nijmegen 1976

Hofmann, J.B.; Szantyr, A., *Lateinische Grammatik II. Lateinische Syntax und Stilistik* (HAW II, 2, 2), München 1965

Holl, K., (ed.), *Epiphanius*, I (GCS 25), Leipzig 1915

Holl, K.; Dummer, J., (eds.), *Epiphanius*, II (GCS sine num.), Berlin [2]1980

Hollander, H.W., *Joseph as an Ethical Model in the Testaments of the Twelve Patriarchs* (SVTP 6), 1981

Hollander, H.W.; Jonge, M. de, *The Testaments of the Twelve Patriarchs. A Commentary* (SVTP 8), Leiden 1985

Hölscher, G., "Über die Entstehungszeit der 'Himmelfahrt Moses'", *ZNW* 17 (1916), pp. 108-127, 149-158

Hoogterp, P.W., *Etude sur le latin du codex bobiensis (k) des Evangiles*, Wageningen 1930

Horsley, G.H.R., "The Fiction of 'Jewish Greek'", in: idem, *New Documents Illustrating Early Christianity 5. Linguistic Essays*, North Ryde 1989, pp. 5-40

Horst, P.W. van der, *The Sentences of Pseudo-Phocylides. With Introduction and Commentary* (SVTP 4), Leiden 1978

Isenberg, S.I., "On the Non-Relationship of the Testament of Moses to the Targumim", in: Nickelsburg (ed.), *Studies on the Testament of Moses*, pp. 79-85

James, M.R., *The Lost Apocrypha of the Old Testament. Their Titles and Fragments*, London 1920

Janssen, E., *Das Gottesvolk und seine Geschichte. Geschichtsbild und Selbstverständnis im palästinensischen Schrifttum von Jesus Sirach bis Jehuda ha-Nasi*, Neukirchen-Vluyn 1971

Jastrow, M., *A Dictionary of the Targumim, the Talmud Babli and Yerushalmi, and the Midrashic Literature* I-II, New York 1886-1903

Jaubert, A., *La notion d'alliance dans le judaïsme aux abords de l'ère chrétienne* (Patristica Sorbonensia 6), Paris 1963

Jaubert, A., (ed.), *Origène. Homélies sur Josué* (SC 71), Paris 1970

Jeremias, J., "Μωυσῆς", *TWNT* IV (1942), pp. 852-878

—— "Ἡ(ε)λίας", *TWNT* II (1935), pp. 934-935

Jeremias, J., *Theophanie. Die Geschichte einer alttestamentlichen Gattung* (WMANT 10), Neukirchen-Vluyn 1965

Jöcher, C.G., *Allgemeines Gelehrten-Lexicon* I-IV, Leipzig 1750-1751

Johnson, N.B., *Prayer in the Apocrypha and Pseudepigrapha. A Study of the Jewish Concept of God* (JBL MS 2), Philadelphia 1948

Jonge, M. de; with Hollander, H.W.; Jonge, H.J. de; Korteweg, Th, (eds.), *The Testaments of the Twelve Patriarchs* (PVTG 1, 2), Leiden 1978

Juynboll, T.G.J., (ed.), *Chronicon Samaritanum, arabice conscriptum, cui titulus est Liber Josuae*, Leiden 1848

Kamlah, E., *Die Form der katalogischen Paränese im Neuen Testament* (WUNT 7), Tübingen 1964

Kautzsch, E., (ed.), *Die Apokryphen und Pseudepigraphen des Alten Testaments* I-II, Leipzig 1900

Kellermann, U., "Das Danielbuch und die Märtyrertheologie der Auferstehung", in: Van Henten (ed.), *Die Entstehung*, pp. 50-75

Kern, O. *Orphicorum Fragmenta*, Berlin 1922

Kittel, G.; Friedrich, G., *Theologisches Wörterbuch zum Neuen Testament* I-X, Stuttgart 1933-1979

Klausner, J., *Jesus of Nazareth. His Life, Times, and Teaching* (trans. from the Hebrew by H. Danby), London 1928

—— *The Messianic Idea in Israel. From its Beginning to the Completion of the Mishnah* (trans. from the Hebrew by W.F. Stinespring), New York, 1955

Klein, R.W., "The Text of Deuteronomy Employed in the Testament of Moses", in: Nickelsburg (ed.), *Studies on the Testament of Moses*, p. 78

Kleinknecht, H. *et alii*, "ὀργή κτλ.", *TWNT* V (1954), pp. 382-448

Knibb, M.A., (in consultation with Ullendorff, E.), *The Ethiopic Book of Enoch. A New Edition in the Light of the Aramaic Dead Sea Fragments* I-II, Oxford 1978

Knöll, P., (ed.), *Sancti Aureli Augustini Confessionum libri tredecim* (CSEL 33, I, 1), Vienna 1896

Knowles, M.P., "Moses, the Law, and the Unity of 4 Ezra", *NT* 31 (1989), pp. 257-274

Koester, C.R., *The Dwelling of God. The Tabernacle in the Old Testament, Intertestamental Jewish Literature, and the New Testament* (CBQ MS 22), Washington 1989

Koffmahn, E., *Die Doppelurkunden aus der Wüste Juda. Recht und Praxis der jüdischen Papyri des 1. und 2. Jahrhunderts n. Chr. samt Übertragung der Texte und deutscher Übersetzung* (STDJ 5), Leiden 1968

Kolenkow, A.B., "The Assumption of Moses as a Testament", in: Nickelsburg (ed.), *Studies on the Testament of Moses*, pp. 71-77

—— "The Genre Testament and Forecasts of the Future in the Hellenistic Jewish Milieu", *JSJ* 6 (1975), pp. 57-71

Kraft, R.A.; Purintun, A.-E., (eds.), *Paraleipomena Jeremiou* (Texts and Translations 1; Pseudepigrapha Series 1), Missoula (Mont.) 1972

Kuhn, G., "Zur Assumptio Mosis", *ZAW* 43 (1925), pp. 124-129

Lagrange, M.-J., "Notes sur le Messianisme au temps de Jésus", *RB* 14 (N.S. 2; 1905), pp. 481-514

Lampe, G.W.H., *A Patristic Greek Lexicon*, Oxford 1961

Langen, J., *Das Judenthum in Palästina zur Zeit Christi. Ein Beitrag zur Offenbarungs- und Religions-Geschichte als Einleitung in die Theologie des N.T.*, Freiburg im Breisgau 1866

Laperrousaz, E.-M., "Le Testament de Moïse (généralement appelé 'Assomption de Moïse'). Traduction avec introduction et notes", *Semitica* 19 (1970)

—— "Testament de Moïse", in: A. Dupont-Sommer; M. Philonenko (eds.), *La Bible. Ecrits Intertestamentaires* (Bibliothèque de la Pléiade), Paris 1987, pp. 993-1016

Lapide, C.C. a, *In Pentateuchum Mosis Commentaria (editio ultima, aucta & recognita)*, Paris 1626; also in A. Crampon (ed.), *Commentaria in Scripturam Sacram R.P. Cornelii a Lapide ... editio nova* II, Paris 1877

—— *In Epistulam S. Judae Commentarium*, repr. in Migne (ed.), *Scripturae sacrae cursus completus* 25, Paris 1840

Lattey, C.C., "The Messianic Expectation in 'The Assumption of Moses'", *CBQ* 4 (1942), pp. 9-21

—— "Vicarious Solidarity in the Old Testament", *VT* 1 (1951), pp. 267-274

Lebram, J.C.H., review of Von Nordheim, *Die Lehre der Alten* I, in: *Bibliotheca Orientalis* 38 (1981), cols. 413-416

Lechner-Schmidt, W., *Wortindex der lateinisch erhaltenen Pseudepigraphen zum Alten Testament* (Texte und Arbeiten zum neutestamentlichen Zeitalter 3), Tübingen 1990

Leumann, M., *Lateinische Grammatik I. Lateinische Laut- und Formenlehre* (HAW II, 2, 1), München 1977

Lewis, C.T.; Short, C., *A Latin Dictionary*, Oxford 1879

Licht, J., "Taxo, or the Apocalyptic Doctrine of Vengeance", *JJS* 12 (1961), pp. 95-103

Liddell, H.G.; Scott, R.; Stuart Jones, H.; McKenzie, R., *A Greek-English Lexicon*, Oxford ^{9}1940

Lipiński, E., *La liturgie pénitentielle dans la bible* (Lectio divina 52), Paris 1969

Loeschcke, G.; Heinemann, M., (eds.), *Gelasius. Kirchengeschichte* (GCS 28), Berlin 1918

Loewenstamm, S.E., "The Death of Moses", in: G.W.E. Nickelsburg, *Studies in the Testament of Abraham*, pp. 185-217 (rev. trans. of the author's article in *Tarbiz* 27 [1958], pp. 142-157)

—— "The Testament of Abraham and the Texts Concerning Moses' Death", in: Nickelsburg (ed.), *Studies in the Testament of Abraham*, pp. 219-225

Löfstedt, E., *Philologischer Kommentar zur Peregrinatio Aetheriae. Untersuchungen zur Geschichte der lateinischen Sprache*, Uppsala 1911

—— *Syntactica. Studien und Beiträge zur historischen Syntax des Lateins* I^2-II, Lund 1933-1942

Lohfink, G., *Die Himmelfahrt Jesu. Untersuchungen zu den Himmelsfahrts- und Erhöhungstexten bei Lukas* (Studien zum Alten und Neuen Testament 26), München 1971

Lohse, E., *Die Texte aus Qumran Hebräisch und Deutsch. Mit masoretischer Punktuation, Übersetzung, Einführung und Anmerkungen*, Darmstadt ^{2}1971

Loman, A.D., "Quaestiones Paulinae. 3e Stuk. Vervolg van het eerste hoofdstuk, behelzende: De uitwendige bewijzen voor en tegen de echtheid van den Brief aan de Galatiërs", *Theologisch Tijdschrift* 16 (1882), pp. 452-487

Lowe, E.A., *Codices latini antiquiores. A Paleographical Guide to Latin Manuscripts Prior to the Ninth Century* III, Oxford 1938

—— *Palaeographical Papers 1907-1967* I-II (ed. L. Bieler), Oxford 1972

Lucius, P.E., *Der Essenismus in seinem Verhältniss zum Judenthum*, Strasbourg 1881

Lueken, W., *Michael. Eine Darstellung und Vergleichung der jüdischen und der morgenländisch-christlichen Tradition vom Erzengel Michael*, Göttingen 1898

Madvig, J.N., *Adversaria critica ad scriptores latinos* II, Copenhagen 1873

Malherbe, A.J., *Moral Exhortation. A Greco-Roman Sourcebook* (Library of Early Christianity 4), Philadelphia 1986

Manson, T.W., "Miscellanea apocalyptica", *JThS* 46 (1945), pp. 41-45

Marcus, R., *Questions and Answers on Exodus Translated from the Ancient Armenian Version of the Original Greek* (Philo in Ten Volumes and Two Supplement Volumes, Supp. II), London/Cambridge (Mass.) 1953

Marx, F., *Corpus medicorum latinorum* I. *A. Cornelii Celsi quae supersunt*, Leipzig 1915

Mauersberger, A., *Polybius-Lexikon* I, Lief. 1-4, Berlin 1956-1975

Meeks, W.A., *The Prophet-King. Moses Traditions and the Johannine Christology* (SuppNT 14), Leiden 1967

Meyer, R., "Die Bedeutung von Deuteronomium 32, 8 f. 43 (4 Q) für die Auslegung des Moseliedes, in: A. Kuschke (ed.), *Verbannung und Heimkehr. Wilhelm Rudolph zum. 70. Geburtstag*, Tübingen 1961, pp. 197-209

Meyer, W., "Vita Adae et Evae. Herausgegeben und erklärt," in: *Abh. der phil.-philol. Classe der königl. bayer. Akademie der Wissensch.* XIV, 3, München 1878, pp. 185-250

Migne, J.-P., (ed.), Ὠριγένους τὰ εὑρισκόμενα πάντα. *Origenis opera omnia* II (PG 12), Paris 1862

—— Τοῦ ἐν ἁγίοις πατρὸς ἡμῶν Ἀθανασίου ἀρχιεπισκόπου Ἀλεξανδρείας τὰ εὑρισκόμενα πάντα. *S.P.N. Athanasii archiepisopi Alexandrini opera omnia quae exstant vel quae ejus nomine circumferuntur* IV (PG 28), Paris 1887

—— Διδύμου τοῦ Ἀλεξανδρέως τὰ σωζόμενα πάντα. *Didymi Alexandrini opera omnia* (PG 39), Paris 1863

—— Φωτίου, πατριάρχου Κωνσταντινουπόλεως, τὰ εὑρισκόμενα πάντα. *Photii, Constantinopolitani patriarchae, opera omnia* I (PG 101), Paris 1900

—— *Sancti Ambrosii, Mediolanensis episcopi, opera omnia* I,1 (PL 14), Paris 1882

M[igne], J.-P., (ed.), *Scripturae sacrae cursus completus* 25, Paris 1840

M[igne], J.-P.; M[igne], V.-S., (eds.), *Scripturae sacrae cursus completus* 7, Paris 1838

Milik, J.T., "4Q Visions de 'Amram et une citation d'Origène", *RB* 79 (1972), pp. 77-97

—— "*Milkî-ṣedeq* et *Milkî-reša'* dans les anciens écrits juifs et chrétiens", *JJS* 23 (1972), pp. 95-144

Mohrmann, C., *Etudes sur le latin des chrétiens* I-IV, Rome 1961-1977

Mowinckel, S., *He That Cometh* (trans. from the Norwegian by G.W. Anderson), Oxford 1956

—— "The Hebrew Equivalent of Taxo in Ass. Mos. ix", in: *Congress Volume Copenhagen 1953* (Supp. VT I), Leiden 1953, pp. 88-96

Müller, U.B., "Die Parakletenvorstellung im Johannesevangelium", *ZThK* 71 (1974), pp. 31-77

Münchow, C., *Ethik und Eschatologie. Ein Beitrag zum Verständnis der frühjüdischen Apokalyptik mit einem Ausblick auf das Neue Testament*, Göttingen 1981 (pp. 65-75 esp. on As. Mos.)

Mussies, G., "Greek in Palestine and the Diaspora", in S. Safrai, M. Stern (eds.), *The Jewish People in the First Century* (Compendia Rerum Iudaicarum ad Novum Testamentum I, 2), Assen/Amsterdam 1976, pp. 1040-1064

Nagel, M., (ed.), "Vie grecque d'Adam et Eve", in: Denis and Janssens, *Concordance grecque*, pp. 815-818

Nickelsburg, G.W.E., (ed.), *Studies in the Testament of Abraham* (SCS 6), Missoula 1972

—— *Studies on the Testament of Moses. Seminar Papers* (SCS 4), Cambridge (Mass.) 1973

Nickelsburg, G.W.E., *Resurrection, Immortality, and Eternal Life in Intertestamental Judaism* (Harvard Theological Studies 26), Cambridge (Mass.) 1972

—— "Introduction", in: Nickelsburg (ed.), *Studies on the Testament of Moses*, pp. 5-14

—— "An Antiochan Date for the Testament of Moses", in: Nickelsburg (ed.), *Studies on the Testament of Moses*, pp. 33-37

Niebuhr, K.-W., *Gesetz und Paränese. Katechismusartige Weisungsreihen in der frühjüdischen Literatur* (WUNT 2:28), Tübingen 1987

Niermeyer, J.F., *Mediae Latinitatis lexicon minus*, Leiden 1976

Νικηφόρος ἱερομόναχος τοῦ Θεοτόκου, *Σεῖρα ἑνὸς καὶ πεντήκοντα ὑπομνηματιστῶν εἰς τὴν Ὀκτάτευχον καὶ τὰ τῶν βασιλέων* I, Leipzig 1772

Nordheim, E. von, *Die Lehre der Alten* I. *Das Testament als Literaturgattung im Judentum der hellenistisch-römischen Zeit* (ALGHJ 13), Leiden 1980

Oepke, A., "μεσίτης, μεσιτεύω", *TWNT* IV (1942), pp. 602-629

Oost, R., *"Tunc Implebuntur Manus Nuntii"*. *Een onderzoek naar Assumptio Mosis, speciaal caput 10* (unpublished M.A.-thesis), Groningen 1969

Orbán, Á.P., *Les dénominations du monde chez les premiers auteurs chrétiens* (Graecitas Christianorum Primaeva 4), Nijmegen 1970

Palmer, D.W., "The Literary Background of Acts 1:1-14", *NTS* 33 (1987), pp. 427-438

Paredi, A., *Inventario Ceruti dei manoscritti della Biblioteca Ambrosiana* (Fontes Ambrosiani 50), Trezzano 1973

Pearson, J., *et alii* (eds.), *Critici sacri*, Amsterdam/Utrecht ^{3}1698

Pelletier, A., (ed.), *Lettre d'Aristée à Philocrate*. *Introduction, texte critique, traduction et notes, index complet des mots grecs* (SC 89), Paris 1962

Peterson, E., "ἀνεξιχνίαστος", *TWNT* I (1933), pp. 359-360

Peyron, A., (ed.), *M. Tulli Ciceronis Orationum pro Scauro, pro Tullio, et in Clodium fragmenta inedita; pro Cluentio, pro Caelio, pro Caecina etc. variantes lectiones; Orationem pro T.A. Milone a lacunis restitutam. Ex membranis palimpsestis Bibliothecae R. Taurinensis Athenaei edidit et cum Ambrosianis parium orationum fragmentis composuit...*, Stuttgart and Tübingen 1824

Philonenko, M., *Joseph et Aseneth. Introduction, texte critique, traduction et notes* (SPB 13), Leiden 1968

Priest, J., "Testament of Moses (First Century A.D.). A New Translation and Introduction", in: Charlesworth (ed.), *OTP* I (1983), pp. 919-934

Purvis, J.D., "Samaritan Traditions on the Death of Moses", in: Nickelsburg (ed.), *Studies on the Testament of Moses*, pp. 93-117

Quandt, G., (ed.), *Orphei Hymni*, Berlin 1962

Quell, G.; Kittel, G.; Bultmann, R., "ἀλήθεια κτλ.", *TWNT* I (1933), pp. 233-251.

Rad, G. von, *Das 5. Buch Mose. Deuteronomium* (Das Alte Testament Deutsch 8), Göttingen 1964

—— *Weisheit in Israel*, Neukirchen ^{2}1980

Rahlfs, A., *Septuaginta, id est Vetus Testamentum graece iuxta LXX interpretes*, Stuttgart 1935

Rainoldus, J., *Censura librorum apocryphorum Veteris Testamenti adversum Pontificios &c.*, Oxford 1611

Rajak, T., *Josephus. The Historian and His Society*, London 1983

Reese, G., *Die Geschichte Israels in der Auffassung des frühen Judentums. Eine Untersuchung der Tiervision und der Zehnwochenapokalypse des äthiopischen Henochbuches, der Geschichtsdarstellung der Assumptio Mosis und der des 4 Esrabuches* (unpublished doctoral thesis), Heidelberg 1967

Renov, I., "The Seat of Moses", *IEJ* 5 (1955), pp. 262-267; repr. in J. Gutmann (ed.), *The Synagogue*, New York 1975, pp. 233-239

Reuss, E.[W.E.], *Die Geschichte der Heiligen Schriften des Alten Testaments*, Braunschweig 1881 (^{2}1890)

Reventlow, H. Graf, *Gebet im Alten Testament*, Stuttgart 1986

Reynolds, L.D.; Wilson, N.G., *Scribes and Scholars. A Guide to the Transmission of Greek and Latin Literature*, Oxford ^{3}1991

Rhoads, D.M., "The Assumption of Moses and Jewish History: 4 B.C.-A.D. 48, in: Nickelsburg (ed.), *Studies on the Testament of Moses*, pp. 53-58

Riessler, P., *Altjüdisches Schrifttum ausserhalb der Bibel*, Tübingen 1928

Rohland, J.P., *Der Erzengel Michael, Arzt und Feldherr. Zwei Aspekte des vor- und frühbyzantinischen Michaelskultes* (Beihefte der Zeitschrift für Religions- und Geistesgeschichte 9), Leiden 1977

Rönsch, H., "Sprachliche Parallelen aus dem Bereiche der Itala und Vorschläge zu Mosis Prophetia et Assumptio", *ZWT* 11 (1868), pp. 76-108

—— "Weitere Illustrationen zur Assumptio Mosis", *ZWT* 12 (1869), pp. 213-228

—— *Itala und Vulgata. Das Sprachidiom der urchristlichen Itala und der katholischen Vulgata, unter Berücksichtigung der römischen Volkssprache durch Beispiele erläutert*, Marbug/Leipzig 1869

—— "Die Leptogenesis und das Ambrosianische altlateinische Fragment derselben", *ZWT* 14 (1871), pp. 60-98

—— "Xeniola theologica. Zweite Serie. 3. Chronologisches und Kritisches zur Assumptio Mosis", *ZWT* 17 (1874), pp. 542-562

—— *Das Buch der Jubiläen oder die Kleine Genesis. Unter Beifügung des revidierten Textes der in der Ambrosiana aufgefundenen lateinischen Fragmente sowie einer von Dr. August Dillmann aus zwei äthiopischen Handschriften gefertigten lateinischen Übertragung erläutert, untersucht und mit Unterstützung der königl. Gesellschaft der Wissenschaften zu Göttingen herausgegeben*, Leipzig 1874

—— "Xeniola theologica (Fortsetzung)", *ZWT* 23 (1880), pp. 441-448

—— "Itala-Studien", *ZWT* 24 (1881), pp. 198-204

—— "Die Doppelübersetzungen im lateinischen Texte des cod. Boernerianus der Paulinischen Briefe", *ZWT* 25 (1882), pp. 488-509; *ZWT* 26 (1883), pp. 73-99; 309-344

—— "Worauf beruht die Italaform Istrahel?", *ZWT* 26 (1883), pp. 497-499

—— "Miscellen", *ZWT* 28 (1885), pp. 102-104

—— *Semasiologische Beiträge zum lateinischen Wörterbuch* I-III, Leipzig 1887-1889

Rowley, H.H., "The Figure of 'Taxo' in *The Assumption of Moses*", *JBL* 64 (1945), pp. 141-143

—— *The Relevance of Apocalyptic. A Study of Jewish and Christian Apocalypses from Daniel to the Revelation*, London ³1963 (¹1944)

Russell, D.S., *The Method and Message of Jewish Apocalyptic. 200 BC-AD 100*, London 1964

Ryssel, V., "Die Sprüche Jesus', des Sohnes Sirachs", in: Kautzsch (ed.), *APAT* I, pp. 230-475

Schäfer, P., "Tempel und Schöpfung. Zur Interpretation einiger Heiligtumstraditionen in der rabbinischen Literatur", *Kairos* 16 (1974), pp. 122-133; repr. in idem, *Studien zur Geschichte und Theologie des rabbinischen Judentums* (AGJU 15), Leiden 1978, pp. 122-133

Schalit, A., *Untersuchungen zur Assumptio Mosis* (ALGHJ 17), Leiden 1989

Schlier, H.,"θλίβω κτλ.", *TWNT* III (1938), pp. 139-148

Schmidt, F., *Le Testament grec d'Abraham. Introduction, édition critique des deux recensions grecques, traduction* (Texte und Studien zum antiken Judentum 11), Tübingen 1986

Schmidt, K.L., "ἀσφάλεια κτλ.", *TWNT* I (1933), p. 503

Schmidt, M., and Merx, A., "Die Assumptio Mosis mit Einleitung und erklärenden Anmerkungen", *Archiv für wissenschaftliche Erforschung des Alten Testaments* I, 2, Halle 1869, pp. 111-152

Schniewind, J., "ἀγγελία κτλ." *TWNT* I (1933), pp. 56-71

Scholten, J.H., *Historisch-critische bijdragen naar aanleiding van de nieuwste hypothese aangaande Jezus en den Paulus der vier hoofdbrieven*, Leiden 1882

Schrage, W., "συναγωγή κτλ.", *TWNT* VII (1964), pp. 798-850

Schrenk, G., "ἱερός κτλ.", *TWNT* III (1938), pp. 221-284

Schrenk, G.; Quell, G., "πατήρ κτλ.", *TWNT* V (1954), pp. 946-1024

Schuchardt, H., *Der Vokalismus des Vulgärlateins* I-III, Leipzig 1866-1868

Schürer, E., *Geschichte des jüdischen Volkes im Zeitalter Jesu Christi* I-IV, Leipzig, ³-⁴1901-1911 (see also Vermes *et alii*)

Schwartz, D.R., "The Tribes of *As. Mos.* 4:7-9", *JBL* 99 (1980), pp. 217-223

Schwyzer, E., *Griechische Grammatik* (HAW II, 1, 1-4), München 1939-1971

Sevenster, J.N., *Do You Know Greek? How Much Greek Could the First Jewish Christians Have Known?* (SuppNT 19), Leiden 1968

Sixtus Senensis, *Bibliotheca sancta*, Venice 1566 (Cologne 1626)

Sjöberg, E., *Gott und die Sünder im palästinischen Judentum* (BWANT 27), Stuttgart 1938

Smallwood, E.M., *The Jews under Roman Rule from Pompey to Diocletian. A Study in Political Relations* (Studies in Judaism in Late Antiquity 20), Leiden 1976 ([2]1981)

Soisalon-Soininen, I, *Die Infinitive in der Septuaginta* (Annales Academiae Scientiarum Fennicae B 132, 1), Helsinki 1965

—— "Der Gebrauch des Verbs EXEIN in der Septuaginta", *VT* 28 (1978), pp. 92-99; repr. in: id., *Studien zur Septuaginta-Syntax*, Helsinki 1987, pp. 181-188

Souter, A., *A Glossary of Later Latin to 600 A.D.*, Oxford 1949

Stählin, G., "χήρα", *TWNT* IX (1973), pp. 428-454

Stählin, O; Früchtel, L., (eds.), *Clemens Alexandrinus* II (GCS 52[15]), Berlin [3]1960

—— *Clemens Alexandrinus* III (GCS 17[2]), Berlin 1970

Staples, P., "Rev. xvi 4-6 and its Vindication Formula", *NT* 14 (1972), pp. 280-293

Stauffer, E., "Probleme der Priestertradition", *ThLZ* 81 (1956), cols. 135-150

Steck, O.H., *Israel und das gewaltsame Geschick der Propheten. Untersuchungen zur Überlieferung des deuteronomistischen Geschichtsbildes im Alten Testament, Spätjudentum und Urchristentum* (WMANT 23), Neukirchen-Vluyn 1967

Stempvoort, P. van, "The Interpretation of the Ascension in Luke and Acts", *NTS* 5 (1958-1959), pp. 30-42

Stephanus, H.; Hase, C.B. *et alii*, Θησαυρὸς τῆς Ἑλληνικῆς Γλώσσης. *Thesaurus graecae linguae* I-VIII, Paris [3]1831-1865

Stone, M.E., "Three Armenian Accounts of the Death of Moses", in: Nickelsburg (ed.), *Studies on the Testament of Moses*, pp. 118-121; repr. in: Stone, *Selected Studies*, pp. 54-57

—— "Lists of Revealed Things in the Apocalyptic Literature", in: W. Lemke; P.D. Miller; F.M. Cross (eds.), *Magnalia Dei = The Mighty Acts of God. Essays on the Bible and Archaeology in Memory of G. Ernest Wright*, Garden City (N.Y.) 1976, pp. 414-452; repr. in: Stone, *Selected Studies*, pp. 379-414

—— *Fourth Ezra. A Commentary on the Book of Fourth Ezra* (Hermeneia), Minneapolis 1990

—— *Selected Studies in Pseudepigrapha and Apocrypha. With Special Reference to the Armenian Tradition* (SVTP 9), Leiden 1991

Stone, R.C., *The Language of the Latin Text of Codex Bezae. With an Index Verborum*, Urbana (Ill.), 1946

Strack, H.L.; Billerbeck, P., *Kommentar zum Neuen Testament aus Talmud und Midrasch* I-VI, München 1922-1928

Strack, H.L.; Stemberger, G., *Einleitung in Talmud und Midrasch*, München [7]1982

Sweet, J.P.M., "The Assumption of Moses", in: H.F.D. Sparks (ed.), *The Apocryphal Old Testament*, Oxford 1984, pp. 601-616

Tabor, J.D., "'Returning to the Divinity': Josephus's Portrayal of the Disappearances of Enoch, Elijah, and Moses", *JBL* 108 (1989), pp. 225-238

Thackeray, H.St.J.; Marcus, R.; Wikgren, A.; Feldman, L.H., *Josephus* I-IX, London/Cambridge (Mass.), 1926-1965

Thesaurus linguae latinae I-X (*partim*), Leipzig 1900-1991

Thiel, H. van, *Leben und Taten Alexanders von Makedonien. Der griechische Alexanderroman nach der Handschrift L* (Texte zur Forschung 13), Darmstadt 1974

Tiede, D., "The Figure of Moses in the Testament of Moses", in: Nickelsburg (ed.), *Studies on the Testament of Moses*, pp. 86-92

—— *The Charismatic Figure as Miracle Worker* (SBL Dissertation Series 1), Missoula 1972

Tischendorf, C., *Apocalypses apocryphae Masis, Esdrae, Pauli, Iohannis, item Mariae Dormitio, additis Evangeliorum et Actuum apocryphorum supplementis*, Leipzig 1866

Torrey, C.C., "'Taxo' in the Assumption of Moses", *JBL* 62 (1943), pp. 1-7

—— "'Taxo' Once More", *JBL* 64 (1945), pp. 395-397

Tromp, J., "Taxo, the Messenger of the Lord", *JSJ* 21 (1990), pp. 200-209

Väänänen, V., *Introduction au latin vulgaire* (Bibliothèque française et romane Série A, 6), Paris ³1981

VanderKam, J.C., (ed.), *The Book of Jubilees* I-II. *A Critical Text. Translation* (Corpus scriptorum christianorum orienalium 510-511), Leuven 1989

Vegas Montaner, L., "Testamento de Moisés", in: A. Díez Macho *et alii* (eds.), *Testamentos o discursos de adiós* (AAT V), Madrid 1987, pp. 217-275

Vermes, G.; Millar, F.; Black, M.; Vermes, P., revision and edition of: Emil Schürer, *The History of the Jewish People in the Age of Jesus Christ* I-III, Edinburgh 1973-1987

Vernes, M. *Histoire des idées messianiques depuis Alexandre jusqu' à l'Empereur Hadrien*, Paris 1874

Vögtle, A., *Die Tugend- und Lasterkataloge im Neuen Testament exegetisch, religions- und formgeschichtlich untersucht* (Neutestamentliche Abhandlungen 16:4/5), Münster 1936

Volkmar, G., *Mose Prophetie und Himmelfahrt. Eine Quelle für das Neue Testament zum ersten Male deutsch herausgegeben, im Zusammenhang der Apokrypha und der Christologie überhaupt* (Handbuch der Apocryphen 3), Leipzig 1867

Volz, P., *Die Eschatologie der jüdischen Gemeinde im neutestamentlichen Zeitalter*, Tübingen 1934

Wallace, D.H., "The Semitic Origin of the Assumption of Moses", *ThZ* 11 (1955), pp. 321-328

Weber, R.; Fischer, B., (eds.), *Biblia Sacra iuxta Vulgatam versionem*, Stuttgart ³1983

Westermann, C., *Grundformen prophetischer Rede* (Beiträge zur evangelischen Theologie 31), München ⁵1978

Wettstein, J.J., Ἡ Καίνη Διαθήκη. *Novum Testamentum graecum editionis receptae cum lectionibus variantibus ... nec non commentario pleniore* I-II, Amsterdam 1751-1752

Whittaker, M., (ed.), *Die Apostolischen Väter* I. *Der Hirt des Hermas* (GCS 48²), Berlin ²1967

Wibbing, S., *Die Tugend- und Lasterkataloge im Neuen Testament und ihre Traditionsgeschichte unter besonderer Berücksichtigung der Qumran-Texte* (BZNW 25), Berlin 1959

Wieseler, K., "Die jüngst aufgefundene Aufnahme Moses nach Ursprung und Inhalt untersucht", *Jahrbücher für deutsche Theologie* 13 (1868), pp. 622-648

—— "Beiträge zur jüdisch-apokalyptischen Litteratur", *ZDMG* 36 (1882), pp. 185-194: "II. Θασσί und Taxo", pp. 193-194

Wiesenberg, E., "The Jubilee of Jubilees", *RQ* 3 (1961), pp. 3-40

Wintermute, O.S., "Jubilees (Second Century B.C.). A New Translation and Introduction", in: Charlesworth (ed.), *The Old Testament Pseudepigrapha*, pp. 35-142

Woodcock, E.C., *A New Latin Syntax*, London 1959

Woude, A.S. van der, *Die messianischen Vorstellungen der Gemeinde von Qumrân*, Groningen 1957

Yadin, Y., מגלת־המקדש II. הנוסח ופירושו (*The Temple Scroll* II. *Text and Commentary*), Jerusalem 5737 (1977)

Zahn, Th., *Geschichte des neutestamentlichen Kanons* I-II, Erlangen/Leipzig 1888-1890

Zeitlin, S., "The Assumption of Moses and the Revolt of Bar Kokba. Studies in the Apocalyptic Literature", *JQR* 38 (1947/1948), pp. 1-45

Ziegler, J., *Randnoten aus der Vetus Latina des Buches Iob in spanischen Vulgatabibeln* (Bayerische Akademie der Wissenschaften, Phil.-Hist. Kl.; Sitzungsberichte 1980, Heft 2), München 1980

Zwaan, J. de, "The Use of the Greek Language in Acts", in: F.J. Foakes Jackson and K. Lake (eds.), *The Beginnings of Christianity Part I. The Acts of the Apostles*, vol. II, London 1922, pp. 30-65

INDEX OF PASSAGES

b. *Anonymous and Pseudepigraphic Jewish and Christian Works Closely Related to the Old Testament*

g. *Other Ancient Writings*

Jewish

INDEX TO THE GRAMMATICAL NOTES

The figures in italics refer to the numbers *in margine* of the grammatical notes (pp. 26-78).

INDEX OF THE WORDS OCCURRING IN THE CRITICAL EDITION

This index includes only those words that occur in the emended text of As. Mos. as edited in the present volume. Neither the original readings of the manuscript, nor words marked by daggers (that is, incomprehensible words or words in an incomprehensible context) are included. Conjectures are not marked. The orthography of the words is normalized in this list.

a, ab 1:2, 5, 13, 14, 17; 2:3; 3:1, 9; 5:6; 6:1; 7:7; 8:1(2x), 3, 5; 10:2, 3, 10, 12; 11:8(2x), 12, 18; 12:4(2x), 9, 11
abditus 8:5
abire 11:9
Abraham 3:9
abrumpere 2:3
abyssus 10:6
accedere 2:7; 5:3
acceptio 5:5
accipere 5:5
acerbus 6:5; 11:4
acrobystia 8:3
ad 1:6, 9, 16; 2:7; 3:10; 5:2, 3; 7:7; 8:1; 9:1, 10:4; 6, 12, 14; 11:1, 8(2x), 12, 16; 12:1, 4(2x)
adducere 3:5; 10:1
adhuc 11:17
advenire 3:7, 13; 8:1
adventus 10:12
aedis 3:2; 6:9
Aegyptius 6:6
Aegyptus 3:11
aetas 11:8
aeternus 10:7
afferre 2:6
affirmatio 3:13
ager 9:6
agere 10:10
ala 10:8
alienus 2:8; 4:3; 5:3
aliqui 4:7
aliquis 6:9
allophylus 4:3
altare 10:9
altarium 5:4; 8:5

alter 9:2
altus 4:2; 10:4
amare 7:4
Amman 1:4
Amorraeus 11:11, 16
anima 4:6
animal 2:9
animus 7:4
annus 1:2, 15; 2:3(3x), 6; 3:11, 14; 6:6
ante 12:2
anulus 12:9
appropiare 5:1
apud 4:9
aqua 10:6
aquila 10:8
aquilo 11:8
arbiter 1:14; 3:12
arguere 1:13(2x); 5:1
ascendere 4:7; 10:8
at 12:6
attendere 12:3
audere 11:7
audire 3:6; 9:4; 11:1, 16
auferre 12:5
auster 11:8
aut 9:3(2x); 11:6, 7, 10, 11, 12, 13, 15(3x); 12:7
autem 1:16; 2:3; 4:8; 10:14
bajulare 8:4
benedicere 2:2
bibere 7:8
bis 1:2
blasfemare 8:5
bonus 7:6; 12:10, 11
brevis 6:7
cadere 10:4

XL 3:11
XVIII 2:3
XVIIII 2:3
XX 2:6

XXX et IIII 6:6
LXXVII 3:14
CCL 10:12
C milia 11:4

STUDIA IN VETERIS TESTAMENTI PSEUDEPIGRAPHA

EDITED BY A.-M. DENIS AND M. DE JONGE

2. DELCOR, M. (ed.). *Le Testament d'Abraham*. Introduction, traduction du texte grec et commentaire de la recension grecque longue. Suivi de la traduction des Testaments d'Abraham, d'Isaac et de Jacob d'après les versions orientales. 1973. ISBN 90 04 03641 5

3. JONGE, M. de (ed.). *Studies on the Testaments of the Twelve Patriarchs*. Text and interpretation. 1975. ISBN 90 04 04379 9

4. HORST, P. W. van der (ed.). *The sentences of Pseudo-Phocylides*. With introduction and commentary. 1978. ISBN 90 04 05707 2

5. TURDEANU, É. *Apocryphes slaves et roumains de l'Ancien Testament*. 1981. ISBN 90 04 06341 2

6. HOLLANDER, H. W. *Joseph as an ethical model in the Testaments of the Twelve Patriarchs*. 1981. ISBN 90 04 06387 0

7. BLACK, M. (ed.). *The Book of Enoch or I Enoch*. A new English edition with commentary and textual notes. In consultation with J. C. Vanderkam. With an appendix on the 'astronomical' chapters by O. Neugebauer. 1985. ISBN 90 04 07100 8

8. HOLLANDER, H. W. and M. DE JONGE (eds.). *The Testaments of the Twelve Patriarchs*. A commentary. 1985. ISBN 90 04 07560 7

9. STONE, M. E. *Selected studies in Pseudepigrapha and Apocrypha*. With special reference to the Armenian tradition. 1991. ISBN 90 04 09343 5

10. TROMP, J. (ed.). *The Assumption of Moses*. A critical edition with commentary. 1993. ISBN 90 04 09779 1